Vincent van Gogh,
Dr Gachet

Camille Corot,
Ville d'Avray

Anton Mengs,
Portrait of Winkelmann

Sir John Everett Millais, *Death of Ophelia*

Edgar Degas,
Girl Drying Herself

Georges Seurat,
Les Poseuses

Ernst Ludwig Kirchner,
Berlin Street Scene

intellectual function of their art. Each subject was shown from whatever angle would make it most clearly identifiable, and according to a rank-based scale, large or small dependent on social hierarchy. This resulted in a highly patterned, schematic, and almost diagrammatic appearance. This over-riding concern with clarity and "thorough" representation applied to all subject matter: hence, the human head is always shown in profile, yet the eyes are always drawn from the front. For this reason, there is no perspective in Egyptian paintings – everything appears two-dimensional.

STYLE AND COMPOSITION

Most Egyptian wall paintings, as in this example, a *Fowling Scene (5)* from a nobleman's tomb in Thebes, were created with the *fresco secco* technique. In this method, tempera (see glossary, p.390) is applied to plaster that has been allowed to dry first, unlike the true *buon fresco* technique in which the

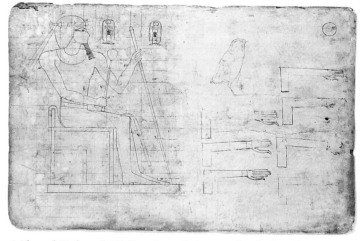

6 Pharaoh Tuthmosis III, *Egyptian painting on a drawing board, c. 1450 BC, 37 cm (14½ in) high*

5 Fowling Scene *from the tomb of Nebamun, Thebes, Egypt, c. 1400 BC, 81 cm (31 in) high*

painting is made on wet plaster (see p.46). The wildlife of the papyrus marshes and Nebamun's retriever cat are shown in great detail, yet the scene is idealized. The nobleman stands in his boat, holding three birds he has just caught in his right hand, and his throwing-stick in his left. He is accompanied by his wife, who appears in an elaborate costume with a perfumed cone on her head, holding a bouquet. Between Nebamun's legs squats the small figure of his daughter, picking a lotus flower from the water (this is an example of how, as mentioned above, it was conventional for figures to be shown large or small according to their status). Originally this painting was only one part of a larger work, which also included a fishing scene.

EGYPTIAN RULES OF REPRESENTATION

In Egyptian art, representation of the full-length human figure was organized within the so-called "rule of proportion", a strict, geometric grid system that ensured the accurate repetition of the Egyptian ideal form on any scale and in any position. It was a foolproof system, regulating the exact distances between parts of the body, which was divided into 18 equal-sized units and placed in relation to fixed points on the grid. It even specified the exact width of the stride in walking figures, and the distance between the feet (which were both shown from the inside view) in standing figures. Before beginning a figure, artists would first draw a grid of the required size onto the surface, and then fit the figure within it. A surviving 18th-dynasty wooden drawing board shows the Pharaoh Tuthmosis III drawn within such a grid (6).

It was not only tombs that the Egyptians decorated: they also painted sculpture. This beautiful painted limestone sculpture, of the *Head of Nefertiti (7)*, who was wife of the Pharaoh Akhenaten, is thought to have been a workshop model, because it was found in the ruins of a sculptor's studio. It is as poignant as a Botticelli head (see p.94), with the same touching and exquisite wistfulness. It also demonstrates a loosening of the rigid conven-tions that governed earlier (and later) Egyptian art, because Akhenaten broke with the traditional style. During his reign, the paintings, carvings, and sculptures that were produced were refreshingly graceful and original.

7 Head of Nefertiti, *c. 1360 BC*

AEGEAN CULTURES OF THE BRONZE AGE

The Bronze Age Minoan civilization (3000–1100 BC), named after the mythical King Minos, was the earliest to develop in Europe. Its home was the small island of Crete, in the Aegean Sea between Greece and Turkey, and its society developed roughly in parallel to that of its African neighbour, Egypt. Despite their proximity and certain shared influences, Egyptian and Minoan cultures remained very separate, though the latter was to have enormous influence on the art of ancient Greece. Crete formed the centre, both culturally and geographically, of the Aegean world. Also in parallel with Minoan civilization was that of the Cyclades, an Aegean island group. Idols have been recovered from this society (8), objects whose ancient, quasi-neolithic forms are reduced to the barest abstraction, but still retain the magical power of the fetish. Here we have a weird forerunner of the abstract art of our own century in which the human body is seen in geometrical terms with an immense raw power, contained and controlled by linear force. Originally the idols had painted eyes, mouths, and other features.

8 Female idol from Amorgos, an island in the Cyclades Archipelago (now part of Greece), c. 2000 BC

MINOAN AND MYCENAEAN ART

Minoan art is largely represented by its carvings and painted pottery, and it is not until 1500 BC, during the great "Palace period", that we see paintings at all; and generally these have only survived in fragments. Although a certain degree of Egyptian stylization is apparent in the schematic repetition of human figures, for instance, Minoan representation reveals a naturalism and suppleness largely absent in Egyptian art. The Minoans took inspiration from nature and their art exhibits an astonishing degree of realism. They were a seafaring civilization and their paintings reflected their knowledge of the oceans and of sea creatures, such as dolphins.

9 Fresco with dolphins, from the Palace of Knossos, Crete, c. 1500–1450 BC

10 "Toreador Fresco" from the royal palace at Knossos, Crete (restored detail), c. 1500 BC, 80 cm (31½ in) high including borders

This lively example (9) is from the Palace of Knossos, which was excavated in the first two decades of the 20th century. Another recurrent Minoan theme is bull jumping, a ritual thought to be connected with Minoan religion. A second work from the royal palace of Knossos, the *"Toreador Fresco"* (10), is one of the best-preserved Minoan paintings, although fragmentary. The fragments have been pieced together to reveal three acrobats, two girls (they are fair-skinned), and a darker-skinned man somersaulting over a magnificent bull. The usual interpretation of this picture is as a "time-lapse" sequence. The girl on the left is taking hold of the bull's horns in preparation to leap; the man is in mid-vault; the girl on the right has landed and steadies herself with arms outstretched, like a modern gymnast.

27 Mummy case and portrait, from Faiyum, Egypt, 2nd century AD

28 Bearded Youth, 2nd century AD, 43 x 22 cm (17 x 8½ in)

is carved into the likeness of a scroll that twists in a spiral up the column. The "scroll" is more than 180 m (600 ft) in length and contains over 2,500 human figures. It shows a series of scenes from Trajan's triumphant campaigns in Dacia (the present-day Romania). The examples shown on this page depict soldiers and builders at work constructing the walls of a fortification (29). The reliefs are shallow and have a painterly feel to them. They make up a continuous and clearly intelligible narrative, leading the "reader" through 150 episodes in succession.

During the 16th century the carvings on this column were an important inspiration and influence for the artists of the Renaissance (see p.80), who regarded the column's dense carvings as an idealized, three-dimensional demonstration of what two-dimensional art was really about.

ROMAN SCULPTURE

Long after the ancient Roman civilization had disappeared, examples of its sculpture have continued to be visible in all parts of the empire. In Rome itself, the great narrative reliefs on Trajan's Column and the Arch of Titus in the Forum were on display to visitors and inhabitants of the city. Trajan's Column is as tall as a ten-storey building and stands on a pedestal two stories high. It was built in AD 113 to honour the Emperor Trajan, a gilded statue of whom (replaced in the 16th century by a statue of St Peter) was placed at the top. The marble outer surface of the column

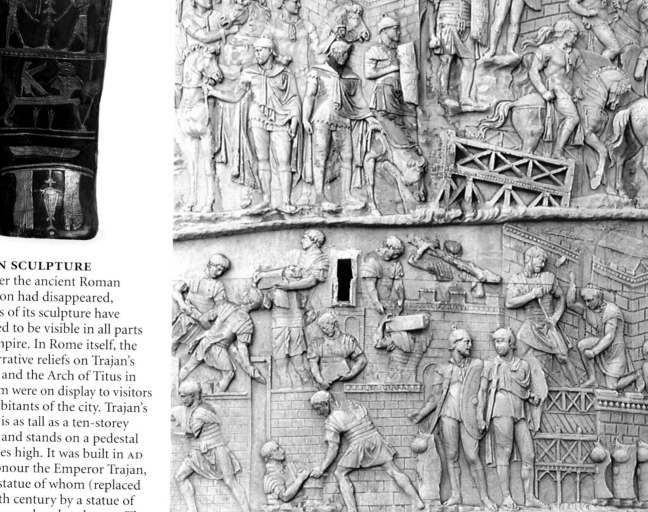

29 Detail from Trajan's Column, AD 113

EARLY CHRISTIAN AND MEDIEVAL ART

The great Roman empire was in decline by the early 2nd century AD, and by the 3rd century its political life had degenerated into chaos. When the Emperor Diocletian divided the empire in half, splitting East from West, the final collapse of the Western section

was set in motion. In the 5th century, the Western empire succumbed to the Germanic barbarians. In the East, at Byzantium, a new, Christian-based empire slowly emerged, destined to endure for a thousand years, and with it a new art form, born out of Christianity.

In Rome, in the network of ancient burial chambers known as the catacombs, there is a series of wall paintings dating from the time when the Christians were persecuted in the 3rd and 4th centuries AD. In style, these paintings bear the marks of the continuing Greco-Roman tradition. Unimpressive as art, this figure *(30)* is nonetheless deeply moving as an image of faith. It carries a secret charge of conviction that compensates for any technical incompetence.

THE FIRST GOLDEN AGE OF BYZANTINE ART

In 313, after 300 years of Christian persecution, the Emperor Constantine recognized the Christian church as the official religion of the Roman Empire. Early Christian art differed from the Greco-Roman tradition in subject matter more than style. Later, in the east, it evolved into Byzantine art, as artists turned away from Greco-Roman style to develop an entirely new style. The importance of Byzantine art is seen

30 Wall painting from catacombs of Rome, 3rd century, 40 x 27 cm (16 x 10½ in)

in its profound influence on Gothic art (see pp.36–77). It was the first part of a tradition that was to remain predominantly Christian, and was to run right through the Middle Ages to the time of the Renaissance.

The emotional yet straight-faced intensity of the "Faiyum" paintings of 2nd-century Egypt (see p.22) lingers on into the early Christian mosaics created between 526 and 547 in the church of San Vitale, Ravenna, capital of the area liberated from the Goths by Byzantium). These mosaics achieved a maturity of stylistic convention – restrained elegance,

emotional austerity, and a "frozen", authoritative solemnity – that would form the basis for all Byzantine art. The artist who created the image of *Justinian and His Attendants (31)* gave us a great and lordly image of a mid 6th-century Byzantine emperor. Slender, imperious, remote, and exalted, Justinian is shown with his bishop, clergy, and a representative section of his army: an image of the united forces of church and state, and an echo of the deification of kings practised during the Roman Empire. All Justinian's princely qualities are also seen, in due proportion, in his

31 Justinian and His Attendants, *from the Great Cycle of mosaics at the church of San Vitale, Ravenna, c. 526–547*

attendant lords. They gleam far above us, both materially and spiritually, aloft on the Basilica walls. There is an equally glittering companion mosaic on the other side of the altar, depicting Justinian's wife, the Empress Theodora.

That same century, we can find both the emotional intensity of Faiyum and the priestly remoteness of Ravenna, in an icon from the Monastery of St Catherine on Mount Sinai. Icons, a great tradition within the life of the Eastern church, were religious images, usually of Christ, the Madonna, or the saints. They were painted on small and often portable panels for devotional purposes, and each detail of the image could be charged with a special religious significance. The *Virgin and Child Enthroned Between St Theodore and St George (32)* has

32 **Virgin and Child Enthroned Between St Theodore and St George,** *icon from Mount Sinai, c. 6th century AD, 68 x 48 cm (27 x 19 in)*

all the sacred beauty that gives icons their unique power. Mary has wide eyes, which are intended to suggest her purity of heart: she is a woman of vision, one who sees God. She does not look at the small King on her lap: as her Lord, the Child can, as it were, fend for Himself, and it is on us that the Virgin bends her sternly maternal look. The two accompanying saints are dear to the Eastern church tradition – George, the holy warrior and dragon killer (though here his sword is sheathed), and Theodore, less well known to us today, another

33 **Christ as Ruler of the Universe, the Virgin and Child, and Saints,** *c. 1190*

warrior. Both saints wear the uniforms of the Imperial Guard, but as weapons each now holds a Cross. The angels behind the throne look upwards, alerting us to the hand of God that beckons and announces the Child. The Child holds in His hand a symbolic scroll. God is silent, only the angels see Him, though the eyes of the saintly figures seem to suggest that they sense the divine presence. The four halos of the Madonna, Child, and saints form a Cross and alert us to the message that the closed scroll must contain. It is a strange, mystical work, and this kind of painting continues to this day in Eastern churches.

THE SECOND GOLDEN AGE OF BYZANTINE ART

In the 8th and 9th centuries, the Byzantine world was torn with bitter controversy over the use of pictures or carvings in religious life. Any human image that was at all realistic could be seen as a violation of the commandment not to worship any "graven image". In 730, Emperor Leo III decreed any image of Christ, the Virgin, or any saint or angel, in human form, to be illegal. The decree gave power to religious militants known as iconoclasts (image breakers) who saw to it that, for over a century, religious art was restricted to non-human imagery such as leaves or abstract patterns. There was a steady migration of Byzantine artists to the West.

When the law was abolished in 843, and human images were tolerated again, resumption of contact with the artists of the West led to a renewed influence of classical form and illusionistic qualities.

This mosaic, from the apse (a domed recess behind the altar) of the Cathedral of Monreale, Sicily (33), is a large-scale, quintessentially Byzantine work in which the figure of Christ is huge and authoritative. He looms out at us from the sanctuary, a great, luminous image of power; not the gentle Jesus, but the "Judge". Beneath Him the enthroned Madonna with Child, and the standing figures of archangels and saints, are all seen, rightfully, as small. They are beautiful, but relatively unimportant. The golden background of the mosaic is one of the most distinctive features of Byzantine art and continued into the Gothic era (see p.40).

INTIMATE ICON

Not all Byzantine art was on such a grand scale. One of the most beautiful small icons from the period is the so-called "Vladimir Madonna" (34). This was probably painted in Constantinople in the 12th century and later taken to Russia. The position of the Virgin and Child, their faces touching tenderly, introduces a new note in sacred art. Previously the two figures had appeared as symbols of the Christian faith – Christ and His Mother not sharing any emotional closeness. Here they appear in their intimate, human relationship.

34 "Vladimir Madonna", c. 1125, 75 x 53 cm (30 x 21 in)

RUSSIAN ART

Russia was converted to Christianity in the 10th century, and eventually took over the Byzantine tradition, making it very much its own. The most exquisite example of this meeting of two very dissimilar cultures, at the highest point in the development of Russian Byzantine art, is surely this vivid *Trinity (35)*, painted by Andrei Rublev (c. 1360–1430). Rublev is the most famous of Russian icon painters. The figures represent the three angels that appeared to Abraham in the Old Testament. This is grace made visible, and it is this Byzantine heritage that gives special poignancy to the mysterious works of El Greco (see p.146) 300 years later.

36 **David and Goliath**, *fresco at Tahull, Spain, c. 1123*

35 *Andrei Rublev*, Trinity, *c. 1422–27, 140 x 112 cm (55 x 44 in)*

THE "DARK AGES" IN WESTERN EUROPE

The phrase "Dark Ages" is sometimes used to refer to the early Middle Ages in European civilization, up to the beginning of the High Middle Ages around 1100. The thousand-year period from 400 to 1400 was a time of gradual mingling of influences from the Greco-Roman tradition, Christianity, and Byzantine art, as well as the growing Celtic and Germanic cultures of the North. Despite its pejorative implication, this was far from being an artistically barren or regressive period filling the empty space between the Roman empire and the Renaissance, as was believed for centuries, it was a period of development and metamorphosis within the stronghold of Christianity. The "Dark Ages" held the seeds of future scientific and technical innovation and prepared the way for such things as the coming invention of printing.

The art of the Western church was less mystical and more human than that of the Byzantine empire, and throughout the Middle Ages, painting was the preferred manner of popular religious instruction, at a time when a large majority of people were illiterate. Even the poorest church buildings covered their walls with brightly coloured biblical stories, often to spectacular effect. In the tiny Catalan church of Santa Maria, at Tahull, Spain, the 12th-century frescoes have only four main colours: white, black, ochre, and vermilion, with touches of blue and orange. This passionate simplicity is repeated in the forms as David sways forward to decapitate an inert Goliath *(36)*. David, in adolescent garb, is slight, dreamy, and defenceless, while Goliath, immense in his huge armour, is the consummate worldling whom the children of God, even poor shepherds such as the young David, defeat.

ILLUMINATED MANUSCRIPTS

The art of the nomadic barbarian peoples who had conquered the West was mostly object-based, small scale, and portable. After conversion to Christianity it was logical that this highly decorative art form should be translated into a religious art that is also small scale and portable: the illuminated manuscript. This most accessible and perhaps even most lovely of early medieval artefacts has been discussed by some critics as being the work of craftsmen, but where do we draw the line? The original meaning of the Latin word *ars* was "craftsmanship", the exact equivalent of the Old High German word *kunst,* which originally meant knowledge or wisdom, and by extension came to mean a craft or skill. The discipline of a trained eye and a trained hand was essential to create an object either for delight or for function or – the continual desire of the creator – for both. The distinction between aristocratic art and plebeian craft is only a modern one. It dwindles away into insignificance when we look at the work of the great "craftsmen" of the Middle Ages.

THE CAROLINGIAN EMPIRE

The single most powerful political figure in Europe in the early middle ages was Charlemagne. His contemporary name translates as "Charles the Great", and Charlemagne is a version of the Latin for this. The adjective relating to his time is *Carolingian.*

Charlemagne's armies took control of extensive territories in northern Europe from 768 to 814. With his military might, he was responsible for the enforcement of Christianity in the North, and for a revival of the art of antiquity that had flourished before the collapse of the Roman Empire in the West 300 years earlier.

When Charlemagne was crowned emperor of what is now France and Germany in 800, he became a great patron of the arts. He was fluent in Latin and could understand Greek, though he could hardly write at all. He wanted his artists to reflect both the Christian message and the magnificence and importance of his own empire. For his court at Aachen, he recruited the greatest scholar known in Europe at that time, Alcuin of York, an Englishman from Northumbria.

Charlemagne commissioned several glorious sets of illuminated Latin Gospels. Some of the work that these contain has an almost classical majesty, a magnificent serenity. The emperor sent artists to Ravenna (see p.25), where they could study the early Christian and Byzantine murals and mosaics, whose style offered itself as more appropriate to the religious development of the new empire than did the pagan art of Greece and Rome. He may have employed Greek artists to work on some of the illuminated Gospels. The Byzantine influence, together with elements from early Christian,

37 St Matthew *from the* Harley Golden Gospels, *c. 800, 37 x 25 cm (14½ x 10 in)*

Anglo-Saxon, and Germanic art, are seen in these illuminated manuscripts. These traditions combined to produce the Carolingian style, embodied in this painting *(37)* from the *Harley Golden Gospels.* This book was produced under Charlemagne and takes its present name from a collector, Lord Harley, who once owned it. St Matthew writes his Gospel in a setting that displays a rather lopsided perspective, but is eminently balanced emotionally. He leans forward to listen to the Holy Spirit, calmly collected, half smiling. His emblem, an angel, hovers above him with equal poise, and expressing the same quiet happiness.

38 Symbols of the Evangelists, from the Book of Kells, *c. 800,*
33 x 24 cm (13 x 9½ in)

CELTIC ILLUMINATION

The missionary zeal of the Christian church, which spread
its influence across Europe, is seen at its most intense in the
relatively tiny Christian stronghold of Celtic Ireland, which
had converted to Christianity in the 5th century. Advanced
Celtic monastic communities were also established in Britain
and northern Europe. The intricate art that was created in
all these communities reveals a blend of Celtic and Germanic
styles. In their convoluted manner, the Celtic manuscripts
appeal to us across the centuries with a remarkable intensity.

There can be few works of art more exquisite in every
sense than the *Book of Durrow*, the *Lindisfarne Gospels*,
or the *Book of Kells*. This last, created by Irish monks
on the island of Iona in the 8th and early 9th centuries,
and later taken to the monastery of Kells in Ireland, is
possibly the greatest work of manuscript illumination
ever created. The figurative images have an iconic
strength, as we see in the page that shows the symbols
of the four evangelists: Matthew's angel, Mark's lion,
Luke's ox, and John's eagle *(38)*.

ILLUMINATED INITIALS

But the true glory of the *Book of Kells* is in the illuminated
initials. Here intricacy becomes so integrated, so wild yet
so controlled – a marvellous paradox – that it is impossible
even to imagine how such lace-like perfection could have
been drawn by the unaided human hand. One of the most

wonderful initial pages presents the words *Christi autem
generatio* ("the birth of Christ") from St Matthew's Gospel.
The word *Christi*, shortened to *"XPI"*, fills most of the
page; *autem* is abbreviated as *h*, while *generatio* is spelt out *(40)*.

The shortened form of the name of Christ is made out of
the two characters XP, the Greek letters *chi* and *rho*. This is
the symbolic abbreviation known as the *Chi-Rho*. The entire
ornate pattern is based upon the material form and spiritual
meaning of these two characters.

The whole page is densely covered with a network of lines,
faces, shapes, and animals (human figures are not often the
main focus of Irish illuminations). There are three figures of
men (or angels), three being the mystic trinitarian number;
there are butterflies, cats playing with mice (or are they
kittens?), and a fine otter, upside down and clutching a fish
in its mouth. But we have to search these creatures out,
disguised as they are by a glorious swirl of geometric patterning.
The floating human faces, glimpsed here and there amid the
tracery, make clear to us that the central and all-encompassing
reality in life is Christ. His very name, even in its abbreviated
form, simply subsumes all else.

The ambitious approach of this page is more easily
appreciated if we compare it with its equivalent in the
Lindisfarne Gospels (39). This manuscript was produced in
Northumberland, in northern England, shortly before 698,
by the monk Eadfrith. Here too the illumination is magnificent,
but it is much less complicated in its layout and scope.

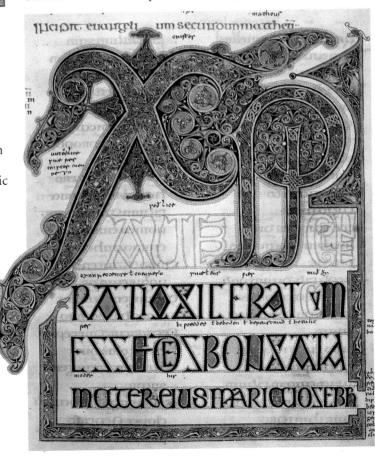

39 Chi-Rho *page from the* Lindisfarne Gospels, *c. 690,*
34 x 25 cm (13½ x 10 in)

40 Chi-Rho page from the Book of Kells, *c. 800, 33 x 24 cm (13 x 9½ in)*

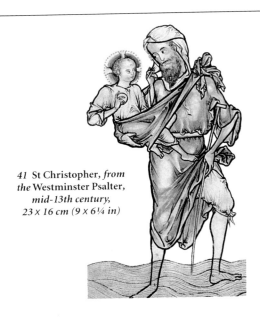

41 St Christopher, *from the* Westminster Psalter, *mid-13th century, 23 x 16 cm (9 x 6¼ in)*

43 Christ and the 24 Elders, *from the* Apocalypse of Beatus, *c. 1028–72, 37 x 55 cm (14½ x 22 in)*

42 St Peter, from the Oscott Psalter, *c. 1270, 30 x 19 cm (12 x 7½ in)*

SPANISH ILLUMINATION

The very smallness of manuscript art gives it an intimacy that can prove tremendous. The most dramatic of medieval illuminations tend to be Spanish. The book of Revelation, the final and apocalyptic book of the Bible, provided a never-failing source of blazingly powerful images. The monk Beatus, who lived in the 8th century at Liebana in Spain, wrote a commentary on the Apocalypse (as Revelation is also known) that entranced the visual imaginations of a whole series of painters for centuries to come. Here is how another monk (probably Spanish or Spanish-trained), who worked at the monastery of Saint-Sever in Gascony, envisioned *Christ and the 24 Elders* in an 11th-century copy of Beatus *(43)*. Around the outer edge of a great circle containing Christ and His blessed are the souls of the saints, pure and free as birds. There is a wonderful exhilaration in the image of the elders, including the four evangelists, waving their goblets to toast the triumphant Lord, while the winged saints stretch out longing hands towards the celestial glory.

ENGLISH ILLUMINATION

Like the Irish monks, the British also produced manuscripts of great beauty, this being one of the very few periods in which the least visual of national groups, the English speakers, attained international fame as artists. Matthew Paris, who died in 1259, was a monk at the flourishing Abbey of St Albans, just outside London, and his 42 years in the cloister were mainly distinguished by a series of books that he not only wrote, but illustrated, giving them the benefit of his remarkable draughtsmanship. In this example from the *Westminster Psalter*, the patron saint of travellers, *St Christopher (41)*, is shown carrying the Christ Child across the river.

Another outstanding work from St Albans, known as the *Oscott Psalter (42)*, illustrated by an artist who is not named, shows the same nervous delicacy of line, with an elegance and psychological subtlety that enchant the viewer. St Peter, identifiable by the keys he holds and the fact that he stands on a rock, is one of ten saints depicted in the psalter.

44 The Death of Harold's Brothers, *from the* Bayeux Tapestry, *c. 1066–77 (detail)*

45 *Page from the* St Denis Missal, *c. 1350, 23 × 16 cm (9 × 6¼ in)*

ENGLISH EMBROIDERY

The so-called *Bayeux Tapestry* is not really a tapestry, but a woollen embroidery supported by cloth. For a long time it was thought to have been made in Normandy for Queen Matilda, wife of William the Conqueror, by her "court ladies". However, it has recently been proved to have been commissioned by Bishop Odo, William's half-brother, and made in England. It displays the same jerky animation that we find in English manuscripts. A sort of Anglo-Saxon glorified comic strip, it tells its exciting story of the Norman Conquest of England with economy and charm. It takes the form of a long cloth frieze, with upper and lower borders that provide a commentary on the action in the main panel. In this particular scene *(44)*, the brothers of the English King Harold are slain by Norman soldiers. The top border is given over to decorative, almost emblematic animals, while the bottom one is filled with images of dead soldiers and an assortment of their abandoned weapons and armour.

FRENCH ILLUMINATION

A lovely missal (a book of texts for church services through the year) survives from the 14th century at the abbey of St Denis in Paris. It is by a follower of Jean Pucelle, an illuminator with a workshop in Paris. One page shows liturgical text for the feast day of St Denis *(45)*, with a magnificent pictorial "O" and two other miniatures telling of the saint's relationships with the royal family. Even if we do not know the legends about the stag that hid in a church when pursued by Prince Dagobert, and how the prince and his father King Clotaire are eventually reconciled through a dream appearance of St Denis, we can still enjoy the pale and meticulous figurines, living out their holy adventures in the missal.

ROMANESQUE PAINTING

In an illustration in a mid 13th-century French *Bible moralisée* (biblical text with moralizing commentary), God the Father is seen as an architect *(46)*. This work shows the increasing return to the natural-looking style of Roman art (see p.20) – especially visible in the relaxed drapery and the suggestion of volume beneath – a style that would reach unprecedented heights of realism in Gothic painting. Although, as was typical of medieval paintings, the artist did not leave us his name, the picture has an almost Giottoesque power (see p.46). Almost 600 years later, William Blake would also show God bending over a compass in an illustration in his book *The Ancient of Days (47)*. But Blake's God is narrowed by geometry, and this artist is rebelling against the rule of cold law, and glorying in the majesty of a strong, free deity. God strides through space, barely contained by the brilliant blue and scarlet borders of the human imagination. The great swirls of His royal robes recall the sculptural pleats on the figures in Reims Cathedral. God is utterly intent upon his creative work, putting forth every effort of his mighty will to control and discipline the wild waters, stars, planets, and earths of His world. He will soon, we feel, send it spinning into space, but first, He orders it. He labours with barefoot concentration, the perfect integrator of art and skill.

When the Florentine artist Giotto (see p.46) started producing frescoes in the early 14th century, his genius was so massive that he changed the course of European painting. However, the illuminators' art did not come to an immediate end. Contemporary with Giotto and past his time, influenced but yet distinct, the manuscript artists continued with their intricate craft, reaching greater heights precisely because Giotto had set them free from any imaginative limitation.

47 William Blake, illustration from The Ancient of Days, *1794*

CLASSICAL INFLUENCES

Other works that can be seen to prefigure Giotto's naturalism include the paintings and mosaics of the Italian artist Pietro Cavallini (active 1273–1308). He worked mainly in Rome, and Giotto would have seen examples of his art there early in his career. Cavallini's style was strongly influenced by classical Roman art. Unfortunately, his work has been preserved for us, for the most part, only in fragments.

This example is a detail from his best surviving fresco, in the church of Santa Cecilia in Trastevere, Rome *(48)*. The three seated Apostles shown here form part of a larger group surrounding the figure of Christ in the Last Judgment. In the unidentified but youthful Apostle in the centre, we see a sweetness and a gravity that has great human appeal as well as a supernatural power. He is an accessible saint, yet still incontrovertibly a "saint".

46 God the Father as Architect, illustration in a French Bible moralisée *from the mid-13th century, 34 x 25 cm (13½ x 10 in)*

48 Pietro Cavallini,
The Last Judgment,
c. 1295 (detail)

Gothic Painting

The Gothic style began with the architecture of the 12th century, at the height of the Middle Ages, when Europe was putting the memory of the "Dark Ages" behind it and moving into a radiant new era of prosperity and confidence. At the same time, Christianity was entering a new and triumphant phase of its history, and so the age of chivalry was also the time of the building of the magnificent Gothic cathedrals, such as those in the northern French towns of Chartres, Reims, and Amiens. In the realm of painting, the change to the new style became visible around a century after the first of these cathedrals rose. In contrast to the Romanesque and Byzantine styles, the most noticeable feature of the art of the Gothic period is its increased naturalism. This quality, which first appeared in the work of Italian artists in the late 13th century, became the dominant painting style throughout Europe until the end of the 15th century.

Ambrogio Lorenzetti, **Allegory of Good Government: Effects of Good Government in the City and in the Country,** *1338–39 (detail)*

GOTHIC TIMELINE

The Gothic era in painting spanned more than 200 years, starting in Italy and spreading to the rest of Europe. Towards the end of this period there were some artists in parts of the North who resisted Renaissance influences and kept to the Gothic tradition. As a result, the end of the Gothic timeline overlaps with both the Italian and the Northern Renaissance timelines (see pp.80–81, 150–51).

CIMABUE, MAESTA, 1280–85
Although this painting shows strong Byzantine influences, Cimabue's work marked a departure from that tradition in the more three-dimensional rendering of space and the apparent humanity of his Madonna. In addition, the drapery is much softer than that in Byzantine art (p.42).

GIOTTO, DEPOSITION OF CHRIST, C. 1304–13
Giotto's art heralded an entirely new tradition of painting, and his art even belongs in some ways to the Renaissance. This fresco from the Arena Chapel, Padua, is a good example of his characteristic psychological intensity, spatial clarity, and solidity of form (p.47).

WILTON DIPTYCH, C. 1395
Although little is known about the origin of this work, it is a perfect example of the courtly International Gothic style that swept Europe at the end of the 14th century. The rich blue and the crowded composition of the panel showing the Virgin surrounded by angels contrasts with the simplicity of the left-hand panel, with its gold background (p.54).

1290	1310	1330	1350	1370	1390

DUCCIO, THE HOLY WOMEN AT THE SEPULCHRE, 1308–11
Duccio's most celebrated work is his wonderful Maestà altarpiece. It still impresses, even though now dismembered and partially dispersed, with its huge Virgin in Majesty. It was free-standing, and the back showed scenes from the life of Christ (p.45).

SIMONE MARTINI, THE ANGEL AND THE ANNUNCIATION, 1333
The Sienese artist Simone Martini painted several versions of the Annunciation. In this glittering example, the fluid lines of the draperies of the Virgin and the angel clearly reveal the solid forms beneath them – a characteristic feature of Gothic painting (p.50). The similarly-named Angel of the Annunciation, a diptych panel showing the angel without Mary, is another display of Martini's consummate skill in the portrayal of drapery (p.51).

ROGIER VAN DER WEYDEN, DEPOSITION, C. 1435
In the hands of this great Flemish artist, the removal of Christ's body from the Cross is a moment of intense emotional drama. Everyone in the scene is overwhelmed by grief, though each expresses it differently (p.67).

HIERONYMUS BOSCH, TEMPTATION OF ST ANTHONY, 1505
Bosch stands out among his peers for the bizarre and fantastic images that appear in many of his paintings (p.72).

ROBERT CAMPIN, PORTRAIT OF A WOMAN, C. 1420–30
Northern artists began to show individual personalities in their head-and-shoulders portraits of wealthy townsfolk (p.61).

MASTER OF AVIGNON PIETA, PIETA, C. 1470
Depictions of the Pietà, the Virgin Mary viewing or holding the dead body of her Son, abound in Gothic art. This poignant 15th-century version was created by an anonymous artist in France (p.66).

| 1410 | 1430 | 1450 | 1470 | 1490 | 1510 |

JAN VAN EYCK, THE ARNOLFINI MARRIAGE, 1434
Van Eyck was one of the first artists to exploit the new medium of oil paint. In this double portrait, one of his most famous paintings, he uses it to great effect in the realistic rendering of light and shadows. The unifying result of this treatment was extremely original in its time. The interior domestic setting is found in many of the paintings of contemporary Netherlandish artists (p.65).

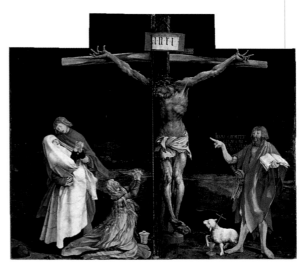

MATTHIAS GRÜNEWALD, CRUCIFIXION, C. 1510–15
The German artist Grünewald typifies the emphasis on horrific suffering of some late Gothic art. His Crucifixion scene has a harrowing intensity (p.76).

EARLY GOTHIC ART

In the early Gothic period, art was produced chiefly for religious purposes. Many paintings were teaching aids, to make Christianity "visible" to an illiterate population; others were displayed, like icons (see p.27), to enhance contemplation and prayer. The early Gothic masters created images of great spiritual purity and intensity, and, in doing so, preserved the memory of the Byzantine tradition. But there was much that was new as well: strikingly persuasive figures, perspective, and a wonderful elegance of line.

AMIENS CATHEDRAL
This cathedral, with its pointed arches and ornate stonework, is typical of the High Gothic architecture of 13th-century France. Building work commenced in 1220.

THE MIDDLE AGES
Gothic art belongs chiefly to the last three centuries of the Middle Ages. The Middle Ages extended from the fall of Rome in 410 until the start of the Renaissance in the 15th century.

STAINED GLASS
The Gothic cathedral at Chartres attracted the most accomplished makers of stained glass. It has three rose windows, a popular Gothic feature. In the windows under the north rose (above), completed c. 1230, are the figures of St Anne holding the Virgin Mary as a child, and four Old Testament figures, including David and Solomon.

The term "Gothic" denotes a period of time rather than describing a set of identifiable features. Although there are certain recognizable characteristics of Gothic style, Gothic art's numerous manifestations are easier to make sense of if we bear in mind that the period spanned over 200 years, and that its influence spread throughout Europe. The Italians were the first to use the term "Gothic", and they used it as a derogatory word for art that was produced during the late Renaissance (see p.139), but that was of a medieval appearance. The word was a reference to the "barbaric past" – in particular to the Goths, a Northern, Germanic people of ancient times whose armies had invaded Italy and sacked Rome in the year 410. Eventually the word Gothic lost its derogatory overtones and was adopted as a broad term describing the new style of architecture and art that emerged after the Romanesque period (see p.34) and before the Renaissance.

THE INFLUENCE OF GOTHIC ARCHITECTURE
The innovation that separates the churches of the Gothic period from the Romanesque architecture was a new type of ceiling construction, the ribbed vault. With this strengthening structure, the supporting walls no longer needed to be so massive. In addition, flying buttresses were employed as load-bearing devices on the outside of the building, so that not all the weight of the roof needed to be supported by the columns and walls. Thus the walls could be thinner and large parts could be given over to glass, allowing in more light.

A common misconception about Gothic architecture is that the pointed arch was one of its innovations. In fact, such arches were not new, but enjoyed much greater popularity in Gothic designs than at any earlier time. More variable in shape than semicircular arches, they offered architects greater freedom of choice.

The first churches to be built in the Gothic style were in France, notably at Notre Dame in Paris, St Denis in Paris, and at Chartres. A less elaborate, but similar, style appeared in England, for instance at Salisbury; and Gothic churches were also built in Germany, Italy, Spain, and the Netherlands. In all of them there was a startling

49 Jean Fouquet, The Building of a Cathedral, *from a 15th-century manuscript copy of the writings of the 1st-century Jewish historian Josephus*

and revolutionary use of stained glass. Coloured light now flooded the interior, creating a new and unearthly atmosphere. Whereas before each coloured panel had to be held in place by stonework, Gothic craftsmen learned to make a mesh of lead tracery to hold the glass in place. The art of making stained glass windows reached its greatest height in the church of Sainte Chapelle in Paris *(50)*, where windows make up three-quarters of the wall area.

EMERGENCE OF GOTHIC PAINTING

Gothic painting has its beginnings in Italy. Painting in 13th-century Italy was still dominated by Byzantine art, which was known in Italy as "the Greek manner". Painting was much slower to assimilate the Gothic influence than architecture and sculpture. It was not until the end of the 13th century that the Gothic style appeared in painting, in the brilliant panel paintings of Florence and Siena. Early Gothic painting displayed a greater realism than had been found in Romanesque and Byzantine art. There is an obvious fascination with the effects of perspective and in creating an illusion of real-looking space.

50 *Interior of the church of Sainte Chapelle, Paris, 1243–48*

RIBBED VAULTS
The ribbed vaulting and delicate, pointed arches of the Lady Chapel in Wells Cathedral, England are typical of the Gothic style. So too is the light that streams into the chapel through the large windows. This part of the cathedral was completed in 1326.

SCULPTURE
This figure of Simeon holding Christ is from the exterior of the north transept of Chartres Cathedral. It illustrates the shift from the rigid Romanesque style of sculpture towards more personalized and elegant figures, typified by the folds in the drapery. This was echoed in Gothic painting.

**ST FRANCIS
OF ASSISI**

St Francis (christened Giovanni di Bernadone, 1182–1226) had a profound influence on the Gothic era, and was a popular subject in Gothic paintings. His love of nature (as illustrated above) is reflected in many works of art. He founded the Franciscan Order in 1210; the first order of friars. Instead of staying in their country abbeys, the Franciscans took Christianity to the people of the towns. The Basilica at Assisi was built shortly after the saint's death, in memory of him. Many important Italian painters decorated its interior, including Cimabue.

*51 Cimabue, Maestà, 1280–85, 386 x 225 cm
(12 ft 8 in x 7 ft 5 in)*

Many of the pictures show a sinuous elegance and delicacy. Other characteristics of the Early Gothic style are an interest in pictorial story-telling, and a heightened, often passionate, expression of spirituality.

TURNING AWAY FROM BYZANTINE ART

The most prominent artist working in Florence at the end of the 13th century was Cimabue (Cenni di Peppi, c.1240–c.1302), who is traditionally held to be Giotto's teacher. So many works have been attributed to him that his name has almost come to represent a group of like-minded artists rather than an individual, though we know he existed.

Although Cimabue remained a painter in the Byzantine style, he went a long way towards liberating himself from the flatness of traditional icon-painting, and in doing this he took the first steps in the quest for realism that has played such a fundamental role in Western painting.

We know that in 1272 Cimabue travelled to Rome, which was then the main centre in Italy for muralists. The mural painters and mosaic makers of that time were particularly interested in creating a greater naturalism in their work,

**OTHER WORKS BY
CIMABUE**

Crucifix
(Church of San Domenico, Arezzo)

Virgin and Child Enthroned
(Church of Santa Maria dei Servi, Bologna)

St Luke
(Upper Church, Basilica of San Francesco, Assisi)

St John
(Pisa Cathedral, Pisa)

Virgin and Child With Six Angels
(Louvre, Paris)

The Gualino Madonna
(Galleria Sabauda, Turin)

52 Duccio, Maestà, main front panel, 1308–11, 213 x 396 cm (7 x 13 ft)

and Cimabue may well have shared their concern. Cimabue is best known for his *Maestà (51)*, originally on the altar of the church of Santa Trinità in Florence. The word *maestà* means "majesty", and was used to refer to a painting of the Madonna and Child in which the figure of Mary sits on a throne and is surrounded by angels. Cimabue's *Maestà* has a great sweetness and dignity, surpassing in emotional content the rigid, stylized figures of the Byzantine icon. The handling of the soft texture of the drapery, together with the "open", three-dimensional space created by the inlaid throne on which the Madonna and Child sit; all this is new and exciting.

DUCCIO AND THE SIENESE SCHOOL

Regardless of all the developments he initiated, Cimabue's work still has a certain flatness if we compare it with the works of the great, and almost contemporary, Sienese painter Duccio (Duccio di Buoninsegna, active 1278–1318/19).

During the 13th and 14th centuries the city of Siena vied with Florence in the splendour of its arts. If Giotto (see p.46) revolutionized Florentine art, then Duccio and his followers were responsible for their own smaller, but very significant, revolution to the south. Duccio is a painter of tremendous power. His greatest work was his *Maestà*, commissioned for Siena Cathedral in 1308 and installed there in 1311 with great ceremony. A chronicler recorded the

53 *Duccio,* The Holy Women at the Sepulchre
(*from the* Maestà*), 1308–11, 102 x 53 cm (40 x 21 in)*

festivities: "The Sienese took [the *Maestà*] to the cathedral on the 9th June, with great devotions and processions ... ringing all the bells for joy, and this day the shops stayed closed for devotions". It is extraordinary that this great work was in later times cut up and sold, at least in part because it was no longer appreciated. The beneficial result of this cultural folly is that museums all around the world now have panels from the *Maestà*.

Duccio's *Maestà* was painted on both sides; the front was in three parts. The main panel *(52)* showed the Mother and Child enthroned, surrounded by angels and saints. At the base of the main panel ran a predella (a pictorial strip along the bottom), decorated with scenes from Christ's childhood. A corresponding strip at the top displayed scenes from the last years of the life of the Virgin. Both these strips are now lost. The reverse was painted with scenes from the life of Christ (26 are known).

Among the scenes from the back of the *Maestà* that remain in Siena is *The Holy Women at the Sepulchre (53)*. It is the moment in the Passion when the three Marys discover Christ's empty tomb, and are told by the Angel Gabriel that He has risen. This painting is a work of such powerful austerity and grace that we become conscious of the urgency of its Christian message.

It is not the psychology of the women that interests Duccio (as it would Giotto), but the wonder of the sacred interaction between them, at this all-important point in the story of the Passion. The figures in the painting sway towards one another, yet there is never actual contact. We are being shown a world of inwardness that none of us can understand, not even the artist himself. The wonderful self-containedness and detachment of Duccio's work is one of his most distinctive qualities.

RECONSTRUCTING THE MAESTA

Duccio's masterpiece was dismantled in 1771, and individual panels can now be seen in a variety of cities, including Washington, New York, and London, as well as Siena.

Art historians have made a visual reconstruction of the work by matching the grain of the wood and worm holes. However, because some sections have disappeared we still cannot envisage the exact arrangement of the whole work.

KINGDOM OF ITALY

Pisa • • Florence
• Siena

• Rome

PAPAL STATES

KINGDOM OF THE TWO SICILIES

ITALY

During the Gothic period the independent states of the Italian peninsula were generous and competitive patrons of the arts. The political map of Italy changed many times – this one dates from 1450. In earlier times, the Papal States had occupied a larger area in the north, and the southern mainland was part of the Kingdom of Naples, which was taken over by Sicily in 1443. The Papal States and the north of Italy were both parts of the Holy Roman Empire.

CONTEMPORARY ARTS

1264
Italian philosopher and theologian Thomas Aquinas begins writing his *Summa Theologica*

1290s
Cavallini (see p.34) creates a series of mosaics in Santa Maria in Trastevere, Rome, and some frescoes in Santa Cecilia in Trastevere, Rome

1296
Building work commences on Florence Cathedral

1307
Dante (see p.47) begins writing his epic poem *The Divine Comedy*

MARCO POLO

In 1271 Marco Polo, a Venetian merchant, travelled to China with his father and uncle. This French miniature shows the Polos receiving their safe-conduct documents from Kublai Khan, the emperor of the Mongol empire in China. Whilst acting as an ambassador for Kublai Khan, Marco Polo saw lapis-lazuli stone being extracted from quarries in Afghanistan. This was to become an important pigment in Italian painting. When Polo returned to Italy in 1295, accounts of his travels provoked a fashion for all things oriental.

He seems to paint from a distance, whereas Giotto (see p.46) wholly identifies with his stories, creating real dramas, and involving us as he tells them. Although the stiffly formal composition of the front of the *Maestà* reveals strong ties with the Byzantine tradition, the influence of Northern Europe (which Duccio received second-hand through the sculpture of Nicola and Giovanni Pisano, see p.46) can be seen in the graceful, undulating forms of the figures – an early example of the refined charm that characterizes the whole period of Gothic art.

With Duccio, we see a real change of style, and his influence was greater than Cimabue's. His figures seem to have volume, and their robes relax into fluid, sinuous lines, which also describe the forms beneath. Though the panels on the reverse of the *Maestà* are small, they are painted with an epic sense of scale, and a bold simplicity new to Italian painting. The *Maestà* is the only extant work we know to be by Duccio, although not all of it is by his hand. As far as we know, he always worked on a small scale.

JESUS CALLING THE APOSTLES

Another small panel from the predella on the reverse of Duccio's masterpiece, *The Calling of the Apostles Peter and Andrew (54)* is a luminous and bare image of tremendous power.

Duccio divides the world into three: a great golden heaven, a greeny-gold sea, and a rocky shore, where Jesus stands at the picture's edge. At the centre are the two brothers Andrew and Peter, stunned by the incursion of the miraculous into their workaday existence. They have fished all night in vain; Jesus shouts to them to cast their net to one side, and they humour the stranger by obeying Him. The net comes up laden with fish, but they hardly seem to look at it. Peter turns questioningly to Jesus while Andrew stands motionless, looking out at us.

The clothes of the two disciples are pale in hue, whereas Jesus, in token of His spiritual profundity, wears blood-crimson to symbolize His Passion, and purple to indicate His royal status; and the gold edging of His robe outlines His figure, dividing it from the golden background.

54 Duccio, The Calling of the Apostles Peter and Andrew *(from the* Maestà*), 1308/11, 43 x 46 cm (17 x 18 in)*

THE CALLING OF THE APOSTLES PETER AND ANDREW

In this panel from his *Maestà*, Duccio portrays the scene from Christ's life when He summons the two Galilean fishermen, Peter and his brother Andrew, to be His disciples. He is calling them to become "fishers of men" and bring new followers to Christ.

THE APOSTLE ANDREW
Andrew is shown in the moment of the revelation of his faith. Whereas his brother Peter (who, according to the Scriptures, was always the active one) confronts Jesus, Andrew appears to be listening to another, unseen calling. As he pauses in his task of hauling in the nets laden with fish, he stands transfixed, with an expression of slow comprehension dawning on his face.

JESUS' CARVED HALO
The halo as a symbol of divinity was originally attributed to the sun gods Apollo, Mithras and Helios, and signified the sun's radiance and power. It first appeared in Christian art in the 4th century. Here, Christ's halo is carved into a wooden panel – a feature of Gothic panel painting, which would also often incorporate precious stones. The patterned surface of the halo attracts and reflects light, thereby intensifying its radiance, and distinguishing it from the background.

CHRIST CALLING
Duccio portrays Jesus as a regal, authoritative figure. With His hand outstretched towards the two fishermen Peter and Andrew, He does not exactly invite, but gently commands. He stands barefoot on the rock, a symbol for the Church, and communes with Peter, whose name, meaning "the rock", was chosen by Jesus.

THE FISHING NET
The net comes up full, and this suggests that the apostolic mission will be richly rewarding. Although clearly suspended in the water, the net is superimposed over the transparent green sea (enlivened by the layer of warm gold beneath). Duccio shows little concern with three-dimensional space – the boat is a kind of wooden "envelope" slicing into the water with just enough depth to accommodate the two fishermen.

55 Giotto, Madonna and Child, probably c. 1320/30, 85 x 62 cm (34 x 24½ in)

time, and before his time. His dates, however, place him firmly in the time we call Gothic, with its climate of spiritual grace, and a springtime delight in the freshness of colour and the beauty of the visible world. What the Gothic artists had achieved was to depict a solidity of form, where earlier painters had shown an essentially linear world, lacking in bulk, thin in substance despite its spiritual forcefulness.

INFLUENCES ON GIOTTO

We know that Giotto went to Rome in 1300 and painted a fresco in the Lateran Palace. He understood the innovations of Pietro Cavallini (see p.34), the Roman artist whose strong, beautiful frescoes and mosaics show an amazing grasp of naturalism. Giotto's frescoes did not assimilate the Roman influence from within the Byzantine style, as Cimabue's panel paintings did; they went further, and transcended it. The real world was primary for Giotto. He had a true feeling for natural form, a wonderful sculptural solidity, and an unaffected humanity, that changed the course of art.

Equal with Giotto in stature and innovation, and massively important to the way Giotto visualized his world, were Italy's greatest sculptors of the period, Nicola Pisano (d. 1278) and his son Giovanni (c. 1250 until after 1314).

Nicola Pisano came to live in Tuscany, Giotto's native province, in 1250. He was devoted to studying the sculptures of classical Rome, but more importantly he brought with him a new and vital influence; his special inspiration was the Gothic art of Northern Europe. The French court of Anjou, which had established itself in Naples in c. 1260, had brought a new influence to Italian sculpture (see column, p.41). Pisano's art showed a convincing solidity of form and human individuality (see column, right), far removed from the rather wooden, stylized nature of all other sculpture in Tuscany in his time (see column, left).

If we look at Giotto's paintings in direct relation to Pisano's sculpture, Giotto's pictorial "leap" is partly explained: sculptural form and space have entered the flat space of painting, and the paintings breathe, released once and for all from the rigid and stylized Byzantine tradition.

Giotto's panel paintings are necessarily physically smaller than his frescoes, but in them he seems to transcend size. Even a small *Madonna and Child (55)* has a weight of human significance that makes it seem large. Mary looks out on us with tender dignity, and the Child, kingly in person, sits on her arm as on a throne. Yet we are not kept at a distance: we approach with reverence, but we do not stay shyly away.

EARLY SCULPTURE
Guido da Como (active 1240–60) was a contemporary of the sculptors, Nicola and Giovanni Pisano. However, his work belongs to the earlier, rigidly stylistic tradition. His figures, such as these riders and their horses, lack physical vitality.

GIOTTO, FATHER OF WESTERN PAINTING

Whereas Duccio was a reinterpreter of Byzantine art, his great Florentine contemporary, Giotto (Giotto di Bondone, c. 1267–1337) transformed it. His revolutionary approach to form, and his way of depicting realistic "architectural" space (so that his figures are in scale in relation to his buildings and the surrounding landscape), mark a great leap forward in the story of painting. Gothic painting is widely regarded as reaching its height in Giotto, who so splendidly subsumed and reinvigorated all that had gone before. For the first time, we have in European painting what the historian Michael Levey calls "a great creative personality". The true age of the "personalities", however, was the Renaissance, and it is not without cause that writers on the Renaissance always begin it with Giotto. Giantlike, he straddles the two periods, being of his

GIOTTO'S FRESCOES

The Arena Chapel in Padua is decorated with Giotto's greatest surviving work, a cycle of frescoes painted about 1305–06 showing scenes from the life of the Virgin and from the Passion. The frescoes run all the way round the chapel.

Giotto's *Deposition of Christ* (56), which is one of the frescoes on the north wall of the Arena Chapel, is the end of the same adventure we see starting in Duccio's *Calling of the Apostles* (see p.44). Giotto has called all his forces into play in this visualization of one of the great episodes in the story of Christ. In contrast to the towering, remote heights of Duccio's and Cimabue's enthroned Madonnas, Giotto brings the action down to our human eye-level, creating a startling truthfulness, and transforming the familiar event into a humanly real, intensely moving drama. The great square is vibrant with activity, with saintly mourners, each clearly distinct and intent in a specific action. His Mother, a woman of almost masculine determination (Giotto always

depicts her as tall and stately), clasps the dead body to herself, controlled and tragic. Mary Magdalene humbly holds His feet, contemplating through her tears the marks of the nails. St John makes a wild gesture of despairing grief, flinging back his arms, offering his breast to the terrible reality. The older men, Nicodemus and Joseph of Arimathea, stand to the side, reticent, mournful, while Mary's companions, who supported her at the foot of the cross, wail and lament and shed the tears that she does not. Such a bloodstained earth is no place for the angels, but they swoop and somersault with the roarings of their sorrow.

One lone and leafless tree on the arid hillside behind hints at the horror of the death, yet the darkened blue of the sky has a secret luminosity. Giotto and his contemporaries knew, even if the wildly passionate angels do not, that Christ would rise again. The strange self-possession of the Virgin may spring from this prophetic inner certainty, and it is a measure of Giotto's

DANTE

Dante Alighieri (1265–1321) is one of Italy's greatest poets. His most famous work, the *Divine Comedy*, was considered innovatory because it was written in Tuscan (the language of the common people) rather than Latin. The allegorical poem was divided into three parts and told the story of the poet's journey through Hell, Purgatory, and Paradise. It is filled with detailed descriptions of real people as well as legendary ones. Giotto, for example, appears in the *Purgatorio* section. Here, Dante is shown reading from the *Divine Comedy*.

56 *Giotto*, Deposition of Christ, *c. 1304–13, 230 x 200 cm (7 ft 7 in x 6 ft 7 in)*

PISANO'S SCULPTURES

Nicola Pisano's *Allegory of Strength* is one of the supporting column figures from the Baptistery pulpit at Pisa, Italy. Completed in 1260, the pulpit is acknowledged as Pisano's masterpiece. Many of Pisano's sculptures had a strong influence on Giotto.

GIOTTO'S CAMPANILE

Although we now think of Giotto primarily as a painter, he was also a skilled architect and sculptor. In 1334 he was appointed architect of Florence's city walls and fortifications. He also designed a *campanile* (bell tower) for the cathedral, although when it was built (above) only the lower sections were completed to Giotto's original specifications.

57 Giotto, The Kiss of Judas, c. 1305–06, 200 x 185 cm (6 ft 7 in x 6 ft 1 in)

ARENA CHAPEL

The Arena Chapel in Padua was founded by Enrico Scrovegni in 1303 to atone for the sins of his father, a notorious usurer. The chapel contains many of Giotto's finest frescoes, including *The Kiss of Judas*.

narrative conviction that we should ponder these possibilities. The very colour and forms, so clear, solid, and whole, so forthright, reassert this mystic certainty, without any concession to the apparent hopelessness. Six centuries afterwards, the great French artist Henri Matisse (see p.336) was to say that we need not know the Gospel story to catch the meaning of a Giotto painting: it carries its own truth within.

MOMENT OF BETRAYAL

Giotto has a startling power to organize the excitement of a scene around a central image. *The Kiss of Judas (57)*, another fresco from the Arena Chapel, sways and surges, every actor alive and functioning, either for or against Christ. Torches blaze and weapons whirl.

But at the heart there is only a tragic stillness, as Jesus looks into the mock-friendly eyes of His disciple Judas, and truth confronts falsehood with sorrowful love. The betrayer and the betrayed form the solid centre, with the jaundiced yellow of Judas' cloak billowing over the figure of Christ as if to swallow Him up. As in all Giotto's work, the heads are of the utmost importance, the natural focal point of the human dramas.

Time and again in the cycle, it is the facial expression, the direction of the eyes, sheer body language, that expresses the emotion. Artists working in the Byzantine style had a formula for the head: they painted a three-quarter view, and so the characters looked sideways. The effect of this was to exclude any personal involvement with the viewer or among themselves. But, for Giotto, art was all about involvement.

THE KISS OF JUDAS

Judas Iscariot was the Apostle who betrayed
Jesus to the authorities, and then, unable
to live with the consequences of his action,
hanged himself. Giotto's painting depicts
the moment when Judas identifies Jesus to
the high priests and soldiers, with a kiss.

A FROZEN MOMENT
*Christ and Judas provide the only still part in this
impassioned scene. Christ is an image of constancy, His
calm brow and steady eye contrasting with Judas' already
troubled, frowning face. Giotto has suspended time,
and Jesus' searching gaze silently communicates
both foreknowledge that He is being betrayed,
and understanding of Judas' heart.*

PETER DEFENDS JESUS
*All action draws our attention to the main figures of Christ and Judas. The swords
and torches fan out from them, almost as an extended halo, or sway towards them.
The gesticulating priest on the right is counterbalanced by the Apostle Peter on the
left, who, in his anger, has cut off a soldier's ear.*

THE ARREST
*In the dense, organic mass of soldiers, Giotto creates
an unstoppable, tidal force. They advance in one
movement towards Christ, who is already engulfed
in Judas' cloak. Many are indistinguishable, non-
persons, their ranks merely punctuated
by the repeated diagonals
of their weapons.*

COMBINING GOTHIC ELEMENTS

The most quintessential Gothic artist is Simone Martini (c. 1285–1344). Of the Sienese painters, he is the only one who can be said to have rivalled his teacher, the great Duccio. As Simone was, artistically, a direct descendant of Duccio, his art still held links with the Byzantine tradition of remote spirituality. It also acknowledged Giotto's spatial innovations and the elegant Gothic style of Northern Europe (represented by France), which was by then popular in Siena. As early as 1260, the French monarch, Robert of Anjou, brought his court to Naples, and before 1317, Simone was called to the court to paint a commission for the king. Simone was greatly influenced by the art of the Angevin court,

with its characteristic elegance and courtly refinement that distinguished the French Gothic tradition from the early Italian developments. The influence of Northern Gothic style (see p.60) on Italian art is strongest in Simone's work: his concern with graceful form, and with uninterrupted, free-flowing line and pattern; the mannerisms and delicate gestures of his figures; and the "precious" quality and craftsmanship of his paintings reveal him as the definitive artist of the "Gothic-Italian" genre, and an early exponent of the International Gothic style (see p.54).

GOTHIC GRACE

Simone's figures have an extraordinary physical fluidity: whether angelic or human, they sway and sweep across the scene, dazzlingly beautiful, like some magical inhabitants both of our

*58 Simone Martini, **The Angel and the Annunciation**, 1333, 265 x 305 cm (8 ft 8 in x 10 ft)*

event, is considered to have been a diptych, the right panel of which is now lost. It contained the Virgin, to whom the angel extends an arm, holding an olive branch. The absence of the Virgin is almost a *felix culpa* (happy mischance) since we are each forced to take her place, entering into the silent drama.

FAMILY CONFLICT

Simone's graciousness and love of beautiful clothes is not superficial and he can combine it with an electric sense of conflict. *Christ Discovered in the Temple (60)* is an extraordinary evocation of the generation gap, as the Child Jesus and His Mother oppose each other with dismaying incomprehension, and St Joseph tries ineffectually to bridge the gap between them. This is the chilling moment when Jesus reaches that crucial stage in growing up, when we come to realize that even those we love and trust do not understand and cannot be expected to. We are each alone and each singular, and this applies even to the best of families.

9 *Simone Martini*, The Angel of the Annunciation, c. 1333,
0.5 x 22 cm (12 x 8½ in)

world and of Heaven; feet are firmly on the earth, yet the whole being breathes the enchantments of another reality. There is no artist quite like Simone, both in the great daring of his colour combinations and in the persuasive force with which he invites us to enter the world of his singular imagination. This applies equally to his later, more intensely passionate works. His sense of drama is poignantly clear in *The Angel and the Annunciation (58)* in the Uffizi Gallery, Florence. In it we see Mary shrinking, almost aghast at the solemnity of being asked to bear God's Son.

But even at this moment of profound spiritual bewilderment, Mary sways with the Gothic grace that is so characteristic of Simone's art. She is all in blue, usually understood to symbolize the heavens. The angel is a dazzle of golden colour. The observer is aware of a sacred encounter in which heaven and earth become one. Mary and the angel lock eyes, each affecting the other. *The Angel of the Annunciation (59)*, another version of the same

60 *Simone Martini*, Christ Discovered in the Temple, 1342,
50 x 35 cm (20 x 14 in)

61 *Pietro Lorenzetti,* St Sabinus before the Governor, *c. 1342,*
37.5 X 33 cm (14¾ X 13 in)

THE LORENZETTI BROTHERS

If Simone is a worthy disciple of Duccio, then his contemporaries, the two Lorenzetti brothers, Pietro (active 1320–48) and Ambrogio (active 1319–48), are stamped with the mark of Giotto, though both are Sienese. They represent Giotto "Duccioed", painting great columnar forms that yet have a tender grace. Their paintings reveal a stronger affinity with Giotto's unique psychological vitality than with the conscious elegance and refined craftsmanship of their own most illustrious contemporary, Simone Martini. Both brothers died suddenly in 1348, probably victims of that great European epidemic, the Black Death (see p.58).

There is near monumentality as well as a great gentleness in Pietro Lorenzetti's panel painting of *St Sabinus before the Governor (61)*. Sabinus, one of the four patron saints of Siena, refuses to offer sacrifice to the strange little idol as directed by the Roman Governor of Tuscany. The white-clad figure of the saint, who exudes an air of calm stillness and resolution, commands our attention, whilst the seated figure of the governor is depicted with his back to the observer. We are aware of spaciousness, both literally and of the mind.

Ambrogio, the younger brother, combines the weighty and the perceptive in his small painting *The Charity of St Nicholas of Bari (63)*. It depicts the moment in the legend when the saint throws the three golden balls into the bedroom of the daughters of an impoverished aristocrat.

62 *Ambrogio Lorenzetti,* Allegory of Good Government: Effects of Good Government in the City and the Country *, 1338–39, 2.4 X 14m (8 X 46 ft)*

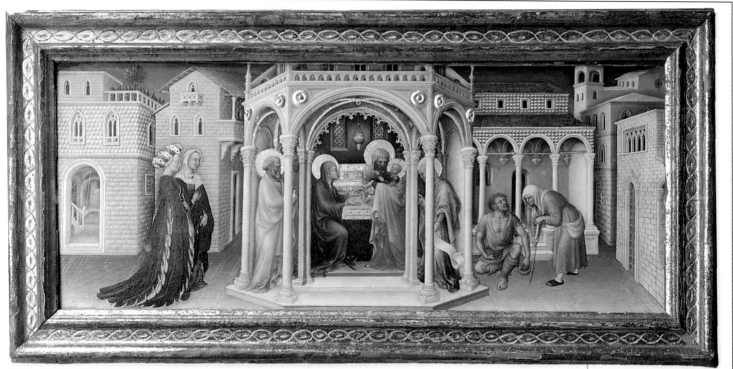

68 *Gentile da Fabriano,* **The Presentation of the Child in the Temple,** *1423, 25 x 65 cm (10 x 26 in)*

The strong anecdotal feeling in Gentile da Fabriano's work is also clear in *The Presentation of the Child in the Temple (68).* The sacred event is the central feature of the painting, but on either side life goes on, with two stately women gossiping, and beggars seeking alms.

PAINTER AND MEDALLIST
This same lucidity of Gentile's is also seen in his fellow Italian artist Antonio Pisanello (c. 1395–1455/6). For decades it was thought that almost all of his frescoes had perished. Happily, a number have recently been uncovered in Mantua.

His panel painting *The Virgin and Child with St George and St Anthony Abbot (69)* shows an extraordinary confrontation. The almost savage rusticity of St Anthony the Hermit, in his rust-coloured cloak, is contrasted with the urban sophistication of St George, attired with the utmost modishness from large, white hat to elaborately spurred bootlets. (St George has no halo, but this is more than compensated for by his hat.)

Yet, despite the bizarre fascination of these two saintly figures, never for a single moment does Pisanello let us forget the importance of the Virgin and Child. They hang in the air, enclosed in what seems to be the circle of the sun, and it is they who integrate and give meaning to the scene.

69 *Antonio Pisanello,* **The Virgin and Child with St George and St Anthony Abbot,** *mid-15th century, 47 x 29 cm (18½ x 11½ in)*

" Michelangelo ...in speaking of Gentile [da Fabriano], used to say that his hand in painting corresponded to his name. "

Giorgio Vasari,
Lives of the Painters,
1568

PISANELLO MEDAL
Pisanello was as famous for his portrait medals as he was for his paintings. The medals carried a likeness of the patron on one side and an allegory or landscape on the reverse. This example, produced c. 1445, shows the Duke of Rimini.

Although the identity
of the creator of the
Rohan Hours (active
1410–25) is unknown,
he is thought to have
been responsible
for a number of
French miniatures
and panel paintings.
The majority of the
manuscripts illustrated
in his workshop were
Books of Hours.
The *Rohan Hours*
was so called because
it belonged to the
Rohan family during
the 15th century.

THE BLACK DEATH
In 1347, the plague, known
as the Black Death, spread
down the trade routes from
China and by 1348, it had
taken hold in most of
Europe. The key symptoms
were glandular swellings
and black boils, leading to
a swift but painful death.
In some towns, the
population was reduced
by 40 per cent and whole
villages were wiped out.
The severity of the
epidemic led to heightened religious
fervour and an obsession
with death. This illustration
shows the Angel of Death
indiscriminately destroying
all classes of people, as
did the Black Death.

70 *The Master of the Rohan Hours,* The Dead Man before
His Judge, *c. 1418–25, 27 x 19 cm (10½ x 7½ in)*

THE BLACK DEATH AND THE ARTS

Some Gothic art clearly shows the impact of
the great medieval disaster, the Black Death.
This epidemic, now probably of bubonic and
pneumonic plague, devastated Europe from
1347 to 1351, claiming almost a third of the
population. Many contemporaries viewed the
Black Death as a judgment from God on the
corruption of His people. This provoked a wave
of popular enthusiasm, not, unfortunately, for
religion itself, but for the "comfort religion"
that excessive penances, like flagellation,
provide. Artists, such as the Master of the Rohan
Hours, reflected their interest in death and
judgment in their work. The terrible realism of
the miniature illumination *The Dead Man before
His Judge (70)*, for example, presents a striking
contrast with the Limbourgs' miniatures
(see p.55). Here, the unknown artist shows his
unflinching consciousness of the meaning and
inevitability of death. The painting, with its
archaic perspective and spatial ambiguities,

seems to be all the more impressive
for these qualities. The horror of
such death is intensified by the way
the pock-marked and rotting corpse
fills the page, seeming near to us,
and striking even the casual viewer
with holy dread.

The dead man's last prayer is
written in Latin on a white scroll:
"Into Thy hands I commend my
spirit; thou hast redeemed me,
O Lord, the God of truth."

God holds a globe and a sword
as symbols of His power and as the
Supreme Judge. In response to the
dead man's prayers, He replies in
French: "For your sins you shall do
penance. On judgment day you
shall be with Me."

The small figures at the top left
of the miniature depict St Michael,
aided by his army of inconspicuous
angels, attacking a devil who is
attempting to take possession of
the dead man's soul, represented
by an adolescent nude.

SIENESE ASSURANCE

Other examples of contemporary
art in the International Gothic style
seem to be unaffected by the terror
of the Black Death. Indeed, in our
confused and divided times, there
seems to be a happy inner security
in many of the Gothic painters that is infinitely
poignant. It may have a touch of the fairy tale
about it, as it does in the delightful Sienese
master, Sassetta (Stefano di Giovanni, 1392–
1450), whose panel painting *The Meeting of St
Anthony and St Paul (71)* shows the
enduring influence of French illuminated
manuscripts. The two hermits meet in a "Red
Riding Hood" sort of woods, and embrace as
simply as children, affirming love in the desert.

The panel is one of a series telling the story
of St Anthony Abbot, said to be the founder of
monasticism. At the top we see St Anthony, who
at the age of 90 abandoned his hermit life after
having a vision, setting out to visit St Paul the
Hermit, who was by then 113. On his journey he
encounters a centaur (half man and half horse),
a symbol of paganism. St Anthony blesses him
and converts him to Christianity.

The foreground shows the story's conclusion
as the two saints greet each other fondly, their
staffs lying on the ground beside them (St
Anthony's staff is always shown as a T-shaped
crutch) as they lean in to one another.

For almost all of Sassetta's life, the Sienese people lived peacefully (apart from a short period in the 1430s) under a republican government. This meant that they could enjoy a fertile relationship with their rival, the bigger and more powerful neighbouring city of Florence.

Sassetta was the most important Sienese artist of the 15th century. His art was steeped in the Sienese Gothic tradition, but he happily absorbed influences from the great, innovative Florentine artists of the day, such as Masaccio (see p.82) and the sculptor Donatello (see p.83).

CHAUCER

By 1500, the language of the English court had changed from French to English. The change to the use of English is seen much earlier in the writings of Geoffrey Chaucer. Born in 1343 to a wealthy London family, he became one of King Edward III's attendants, a position that enabled him to travel and earn enough money to write. His most famous work, *The Canterbury Tales*, describes a wonderful cross-section of 14th-century society, while for the first time using a poetic language that could be understood by everybody in the country.

71 Sassetta, **The Meeting of St Anthony and St Paul,** *c. 1440, 48 x 35 cm (19 x 14 in)*

OTHER WORKS BY SASSETTA

St Thomas Aquinas before a Crucifix (Vatican Museum, Rome)

St Francis Renounces his Earthly Father (National Gallery, London)

The Mystic Marriage of St Francis (Musée Condé, Chantilly)

The Journey of the Magi (Metropolitan Museum of Art, New York)

The Burning of Jan Geus (National Gallery of Victoria, Melbourne)

The Betrayal of Christ (Detroit Institute of Arts)

INNOVATION IN THE NORTH

In the 15th century the International Gothic style developed in two directions: both could be called revolutions. One was in the South, in Florence, and was the birth of the Italian Renaissance (see p.82). The other took place in the North, in the Low Countries, where painting went through an independent but equally radical transformation: this was the beginning of the Northern Renaissance movement (see p.148).

THE NETHERLANDS
In the 15th century the area shown above (with modern boundaries) was known either as the Low Countries or as the Netherlands. Flanders (shaded) was the centre of artistic activity. Netherlandish and Flemish were used interchangeably, although the latter refers to the smaller area of Flanders.

The new form of painting that appeared in the Netherlands at the beginning of the 15th century was distinguished by a depth of pictorial reality that had not been seen before. It rejected the seductive elegance and overtly decorative elements of the International Gothic style, and whereas before, in the sacred painting of the 14th century, there was a sense of the viewer being offered glimpses of Heaven – of putting an insignificant foot in the door, so to speak – the Flemish painters brought the sacred down to our real world. Instead of depicting a form of high drama for which the world served as a kind of grand stage, artists chose to portray real-life domestic interiors – living rooms and bedrooms that revealed the commonplace belongings of everyday human existence. We find a growing peace with the world and one's place in it in the work of the Northern painters. Robert Campin (active 1406–44), one of the earliest great Northern innovators and the teacher of van der Weyden (see p.67), is now believed to be the artist known as the Master of Flémalle. (This name is derived from a group of panel paintings that were thought to have originated in an abbey at Flémalle-lez-Liège.) In fact, Campin lived and worked in Tournai (both these places were in Flanders).

THE SACRED IN THE EVERYDAY
In his *Nativity (72)*, Campin presents an intense abundance, a world crowded with individuals and the unromantic realities of being alive. He portrays a puny newborn Christ, a sullen midwife, coarse shepherds, and a cow in its rickety stable, yet everything is solid, lovely, true, and despite its realism, all is pervaded by a deep, though unself-conscious faith.

Even more striking is Campin's *Virgin and Child Before a Firescreen (73)*, where simple domesticity is emphasized by the wickerwork firescreen that provides the Virgin's halo. By tradition, International Gothic style indicated holiness with a golden circle.

The painting's upper left-hand corner contains a view of a town seen through the open window. Little landscapes like this were

72 Robert Campin, Nativity, c. 1425, 85 x 71 cm (34 x 28 in)

GLIMPSE OF A TOWNSCAPE
This detail from Virgin and Child Before a Firescreen *shows a miniature landscape glimpsed through the open window. Campin depicts a busy town dominated by a Gothic-style church. The gabled buildings are typical of contemporary Netherlandish architecture.*

73 *Robert Campin,* **The Virgin and Child Before a Firescreeen,** *c. 1430 , 63 x 49 cm (25 x 19½ in)*

often seen in Netherlandish painting, and the idea of encapsulating the world through a window was later attractive to Italian artists.

Spirituality and reality are now brought together, and the setting is Campin's own world: the bourgeois interior. Once we have an alliance of the sacred and the commonplace, it becomes possible for representational painting in all its specificity to express the sacred. The close attention given to ordinary objects – each awarded absolute clarity – invested them with a quality of silent, mystical significance. There is an aura of mystery here, and the seemingly ordinary can be startling and powerfully present, and this is fully applicable to portraiture.

Up to this time, portraiture as we understand it today had not existed since antiquity. Paintings that resembled "portraits" had served specific functions, such as recording an event. Robert Campin was the first to look at people with a new artistic eye, bringing out the psychological individuality of the subject. His *Portrait of a Woman (74)*, with its animated face peering out from a plain white headdress, shows his mastery of light effects. His focus is sharp, forcing us to look at what he paints. The

74 *Robert Campin,* **Portrait of a Woman,** *c. 1420–30, 40 x 28 cm (16 x 11 in)*

CHIVALRY
Many medieval paintings illustrated chivalry, which was part of the contemporary concept of knighthood. Gradually the basic forms of chivalry, with an emphasis on valour, honour, courtesy, loyalty, and chastity, gave way to the courtly love inspired by Arthurian romances. This was a movement towards the idea of unfulfilled desire – love as a religion in itself. On this painted Flemish shield, a lady stands before a kneeling knight who vows to honour her or die.

75 *Follower of Robert Campin,* **Madonna and Child with Saints in an Enclosed Garden,** *c. 1440/60,* *120 x 148cm (47 x 58½ in)*

portrait is a good example of the new style of painting in the Netherlands. Portraits began to reveal less of a family look and more of the individuality of the sitter. Campin introduced a new facial type that continued in van der Weyden (see p.67).

In *Madonna and Child with Saints in an Enclosed Garden (75)*, a follower of Campin attains the same comforting assurance that

Campin showed in his *Nativity* (see p.60). The enclosed garden in which Mother and Child are shown with a group of saints is the Garden of Paradise – a "managed" Paradise. A walled or fenced garden is a traditional symbol of the virginity of Mary.

A NEW REALISM

This inner certainty reaches its peak in Jan van Eyck (1385–1441), a contemporary of Campin and one of the enduring influences on his century. He had an eye almost miraculously responsive to every detail of his world, not just in that he saw it, but that he understood its value. Van Eyck's natural habitat was one of luminous clarity; he saw the most ordinary things with a wonderful sharpness and a great sense of their awesome beauty. We know little about him personally, but he is the most overwhelming of painters in the convictions he enables us to share.

Like the 17th-century Dutch painter Vermeer (see p.208), van Eyck takes us into the light, and makes us feel that we, too, belong there. Van Eyck's meticulously detailed *Adoration of the Lamb (76)* is part of a huge altarpiece; painted

76 *Jan van Eyck,* **Adoration of the Lamb** *(detail), completed 1432, 135 x 235 cm (53 x 93 in)*

77 Jan van Eyck, Annunciation, c. 1434/36,
92 x 37 cm (36½ x 14½ in)

on both sides, it is the largest and most complex altarpiece produced in the Netherlands in the 15th century. This monumental work still hangs in its original setting, the Cathedral of St Bavo in Ghent, drawing the worshipper deeper and deeper into the sacred world it makes visible. There has been much debate over the parts the two van Eyck brothers, Jan and Hubert, played in the creation of the *Ghent Altarpiece*: whether

Jan, about whom we have the most information, was mostly responsible, or whether it was Hubert, about whom we know almost nothing. For what it is worth, Hubert is given precedence in the inscription. It reads: "The painter Hubrecht Eyck, than whom none was greater, began this work, which his brother Jan, who was second to him in art, completed at the behest of Jodoc Vijdt..."

This panel shows the sacrificial Lamb on the high altar, its sacred blood pouring into a chalice. Angels surround the altar, carrying reminders of the Crucifixion and in the foreground gushes the Fountain of Life. Coming from the four corners of the earth are the worshippers, a diverse collection that includes prophets, martyrs, popes, virgins, pilgrims, knights, and hermits. It is likely, as with many great religious works of the time, that van Eyck would have been advised by a theologian, and these figures seem to represent the hierarchy of the Church. Set in a beautiful, lush landscape, the holy city gleams on the horizon, its outline very much that of a Dutch city; the church on the right is probably Utrecht Cathedral. This is a detail from the vast altarpiece, but its very perfection and accuracy, its convincingness, explain why this mystic vision has laid such a hold on the affections of those who see it. The *Ghent Altarpiece* envelops the viewer in a mood of contemplation, but any more rigorous analysis becomes a massive intellectual effort. We can move more easily into a smaller painting, such as his long, slender *Annunciation (77)*.

SYMBOLIC LIGHT IN VAN EYCK

As we look at the *Annunciation*, we become warmly conscious of the gentle radiance of the light, illuminating everything it embraces, from the dim upper roofing to the glancing gleam of the angel's jewels. The clarity would be too intense were it not also soft, an integrating, enveloping presence. This diffused presence, impartial in its luminescence, is also a spiritual light, surrogate of God Himself, who loves all that He has made.

The symbolism goes even deeper: the upper church is dark, and the solitary window depicts God the Father. Below though, wholly translucent, are three bright windows that remind us of the Trinity, and of how Christ is the light of the world. This holy light comes in all directions, most obviously streaming down towards the Virgin as the Holy Spirit comes to overshadow her: from this sacred shadow will arise divine brightness. Her robes swell out as if in anticipation, and she answers the angelic salutation "*Ave Gratia Plena*" ("Hail, full of

COPIED ELEMENTS
In this book illustration (attributed to a later Flemish painter), elements derived from *"The Arnolfini Marriage"* include the inscription, mirror, beads, and brush.

grace") with a humble *"Ecce Ancilla Domini"* ("Behold the handmaid of the Lord"). But with charming literalness, van Eyck writes her words reversed and inverted, so that the Holy Spirit can read them. The angel is all joy, all smiles, all brightness: the Virgin is pensive, amazed, unbejewelled. She knows, as the angel apparently does not, what will be the cost of her surrender to God. Her heart will be pierced with grief when her Child is crucified, and we notice that she holds up her hands in the symbolic gesture of devotion, but also as if in unconscious anticipation of a piercing.

The angel advances over the tiles of a church, where we can make out David slaying Goliath. (Goliath represents the power – ultimately fruitless – of the Devil.) The message the angel gives Mary sets her forth on her own road to the giant-slaying that is her motherhood and holiness.

OIL: A NEW PAINTING MEDIUM

The van Eycks started their careers as manuscript illuminators. The often miniature detail and exquisite rendering found in van Eyck paintings, such as The *Annunciation*, reveal a strong affinity with this art form. However, the single factor that most distinguishes the van Eycks from the art of manuscript illumination was the medium they used.

For many years Jan van Eyck was wrongly credited with the "discovery of painting in oil". In fact, oil painting was already in existence, used to paint sculptures and to glaze over tempera paintings. The van Eycks' real achievement was the development – after much experimentation – of a stable varnish that would dry at a consistent rate. This was created with linseed and nut oils, and mixed with resins.

The breakthrough came when Jan or Hubert mixed the oil into the actual paints they were using, instead of the egg medium that constituted tempera paint. The result was brilliance, translucence, and intensity of colour as the pigment was suspended in a layer of oil that also trapped light. The flat, dull surface of tempera was transformed into a jewel-like medium, at once perfectly suited to the representation of precious metals and gems and, more significantly, to the vivid, convincing depiction of natural light.

Van Eyck's inspired observations of light and its effects, executed with technical virtuosity through this new, transparent medium, enabled him to create a brilliant and lucid kind of reality. The invention of this technique transformed the appearance of painting.

A MARRIAGE PORTRAIT

"The Arnolfini Marriage" (78) is a name that has been given to this untitled double portrait by Jan van Eyck, now in the National Gallery, London. It is one of the greatest celebrations of human mutuality. Like Rembrandt's *"Jewish Bride"* (see p.204, another picture that had no known title of its maker's giving), this painting reveals to us the inner meaning of a true marriage.

The bed, the single burning candle, the solemn moment of joining as the young groom is about to place his raised hand in his betrothed's, the fruit, the faithful little dog, the rosary, the unshod feet (since this is the ground of a holy union), and even the respectful space between Giovanni Arnolfini and his wife, Giovanna Cenami, are all united in the mirror's reflection. All these details exalt us and at the same time make us aware of the human potential for goodness and fulfilment.

78 Jan van Eyck, "The Arnolfini Marriage", 1434, 82 x 60 cm (32¼ x 23½ in)

"THE ARNOLFINI MARRIAGE"

This title has traditionally been given to this painting because it was thought to be a form of "wedding certificate" for Giovanni Arnolfini and Giovanna Cenami, who married in Bruges in 1434. He was an Italian merchant, she the daughter of an Italian merchant. Their grave, youthful faces both have a lovely responsibility that is typical of van Eyck.

CONVEX MIRROR
The mirror is painted with almost miraculous skill. Its carved frame is inset with ten miniature medallions depicting scenes from the life of Christ. Yet more remarkable is the mirror's reflection, which includes van Eyck's own tiny self-portrait, accompanied by another man who may have been the official witness to the ceremony.

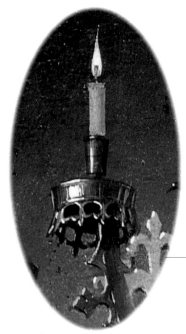

SYMBOLIC CANDLE
The solitary flame burning in bright daylight can be interpreted as the bridal candle, or God's all-seeing eye, or simply as a devotional candle. Another symbol is St Margaret (the patron saint of women in childbirth), whose image is carved on the high chairback.

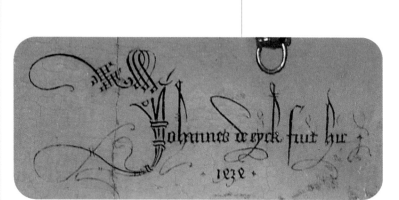

AN ELABORATE SIGNATURE
As today, marriages in 15th-century Flanders could take place privately rather than in church. Van Eyck's Latin signature, in the Gothic calligraphy used for legal documents, reads: "Jan van Eyck was present", and has been interpreted by some as an indication that the artist himself served as a witness.

SYMBOL OF FAITHFULNESS
Almost every detail can be interpreted as a symbol. The companion dog is seen as a symbol of faithfulness and love. The fruits on the window ledge probably stand for fertility and our fall from Paradise. Even the discarded shoes are not thought to be incidental, but to signify the sanctity of marriage.

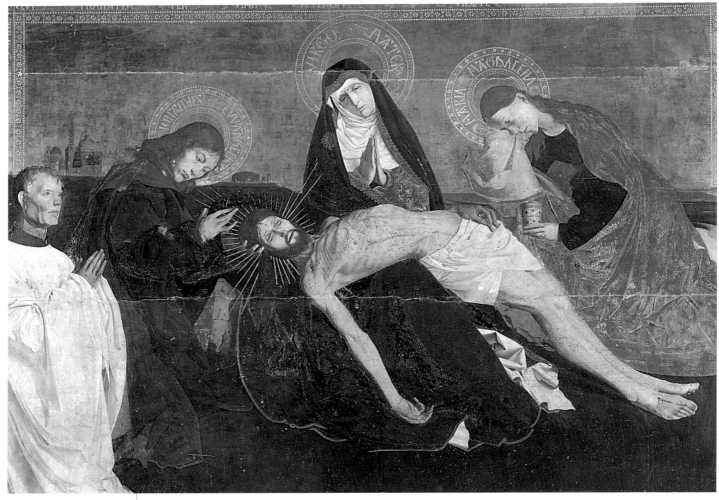

79 Master of the Avignon Pietà, Pietà, c. 1470, 160 x 215 cm (5 ft 3 in x 7 ft 1 in)

THE SPREAD OF NATURALISM

The new realism of the Netherlands had begun to spread in the first quarter of the 15th century, and by the 1450s its influence was widespread throughout northern Europe and as far as Spain and the Baltic. The *Pietà (79)*, painted by an unknown artist in Avignon, France, retains the flat golden background of early Gothic and Byzantine painting, but we hardly notice. Our attention is completely absorbed by this passionate meditation on the death of Christ. It takes place in no earthly location, only in the heart of the praying and kneeling donor on the left. For sheer impact, this wonderful and terrible painting is unsurpassed until we meet the Passion scenes of Bosch (see p.72). We can see that the Gothic era was a freely emotional period, one that accepted tears as a natural expression of our frail vulnerability.

The strangely named Petrus Christus (1410–72/3) is another Fleming with a mysterious sense of emotional truth. He was a follower of van Eyck (who was possibly his teacher) and many of his works reveal his debt to the older Fleming. To

TAPESTRIES

During the 15th century Arras and Tournai, in Flanders, were important centres for the profitable tapestry industry. The Devonshire Hunting Tapestries were woven on the looms of Tournai between 1425 and 1430. Their subject matter appears to be related to the marriage of Henry VI of England to Margaret, the daughter of King René of Anjou.

80 Petrus Christus, The Man of Sorrows, c. 1444–72/3, 11.5 x 8.5 cm (4½ x 3⅜ in)

van Eyck's influence was added that of Antonello da Messina (see p.111), whose art Petrus Christus certainly knew. This led Christus to somewhat "Italianize" van Eyck's style. The tiny picture *Man of Sorrows (80)* in Birmingham, England, shows the crucified Jesus wearing His crown of thorns and displaying three of His wounds. He is flanked by two angels, one of whom holds a lily and the other a sword, symbolizing innocence and guilt. This is the Last Judgment, at which every man must face his judge: it captures the attention of the viewer, making it impossible to avoid the reality of the Passion and ultimately its significance for us.

THE INFLUENTIAL VAN DER WEYDEN

Rogier van der Weyden (1399/1400–64) is another giant of the Northern tradition. He was a pupil of van Eyck and Campin, and became the most influential Northern artist of the first half of the 15th century. Though he began his career relatively late (in his late twenties), he was very successful and had a large workshop with many assistants. The success of his art at the court of Philip the Good, Duke of Burgundy (see right), ensured and prolonged the popularity of his style. His paintings were exported to other parts of Europe, reaching Castille, Spain, in 1445 and Ferrara, Italy, in 1449, and his fame became widespread.

Van der Weyden was a master of expressing human emotion; he moves us in a way that van Eyck cannot. Perhaps the best example of this is his *Deposition (81)*. It is of its nature an emotional subject; the handling of any dead body is a disturbing experience, let alone that of a young man executed in the full flower of his beauty, and this young man is, of course, Christ. But no artist has ever imbued this scene with more majestic pathos than van der Weyden. Like a great sculptured frieze, the holy mourners spread across the surface of the painting. Christ and His Mother echo the same position: He falls from the Cross physically dead; she falls to the ground emotionally dead.

Van der Weyden explores all the degrees and kinds of grief, from the controlled and grave anguish of St John on the left, prominent in pink, to the anguished abandon of Mary Magdalene on the right, a striking colour composition of red, palest yellow, and purple.

The extravagance of the emotion never escapes the artist's control. All remains firmly believable and we are swept into an experience that is at once beautiful and terrible.

PHILIP THE GOOD
The Duke of Burgundy, Philip the Good (1396–1467), was a brother of the Duc de Berry (see p. 55) and another great patron of the arts. As Duke of Burgundy he was also the Count of Flanders. In 1425 he employed van Eyck as his official court painter and equerry. Later van der Weyden, too, received the patronage of the Duke's court. Philip is said to have prided himself on his appearance – here he wears the high fashion of the period.

81 Rogier van der Weyden, Deposition (The Descent from the Cross), *c. 1435, 220 x 260 cm (7 ft 3 in x 8 ft 6 in)*

GUILDS

In medieval Europe most tradespeople and artisans, including painters, belonged to a guild. These men (above) would have been members of the glassblowers' guild. Guilds served to keep a particular craft profitable, protect standards, and provide social benefits. They were a vital part of city life and members were often represented on town councils. Some of the large guilds representing several crafts were split into confraternities, each with a patron saint.

POWERFUL PORTRAITURE

The compositional structure of the *Deposition*, with its shallow space and cropped shape, deliberately excludes any distracting background, thereby concentrating all attention on the dramatic scene. A similar effect is achieved in another van der Weyden painting, his *Portrait of a Lady (82)*. Here, the stark background focuses all our attention on the sitter. The subject has a haunting quality, a sense of almost painful reserve, as if she was willing to give the artist only her exterior. Yet he has circumvented her resistance and brought us into contact with the lady in her actuality. Her unadorned

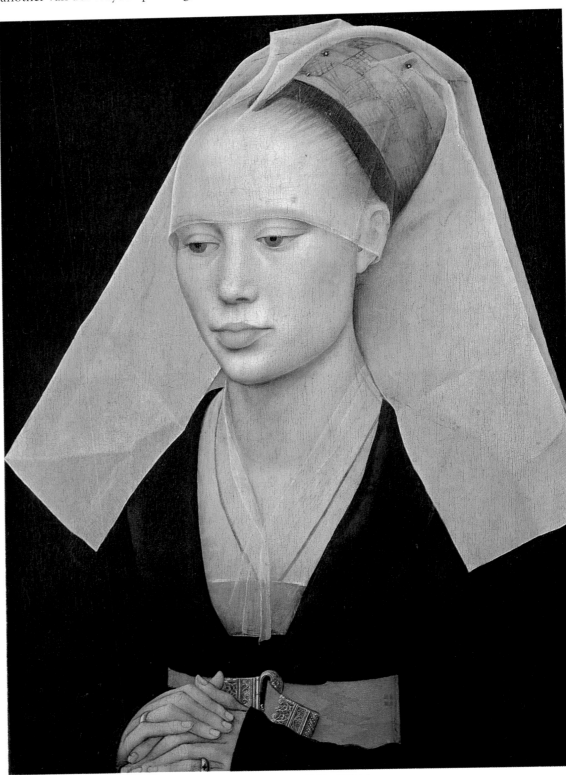

82 Rogier van der Weyden, Portrait of a Lady, *c. 1460, 37 x 27.5 cm (14½ x 10¾ in)*

83 Hugo van der Goes, **The Portinari Altarpiece,** *c. 1476, 254 x 140 cm (100 x 55 in) each wing, 254 x 305 cm (8 ft 4 in x 10 ft) central panel*

clothing and downcast gaze suggest modesty. To the modern observer she has an exceptionally high forehead; in fact, this was the fashion, achieved by plucking the hairline.

It has been suggested that the woman is Marie de Valengin, the daughter of Philip the Good, Duke of Burgundy (see p.67), but this identification is somewhat doubtful.

A GRAND SCALE

Hugo van der Goes (c. 1436–82) is an extraordinary painter, and produced paintings on a surprisingly large scale, both literally and in the unprecedented monumentality of the figures. His most famous work, *The Portinari Altarpiece (83),* now in the Uffizi, Florence, was to prove very influential in Italy, where it decorated the church of the Hospital of Santa Maria Nuova in Florence. It was commissioned by a Florentine banker, Tommaso Portinari, who lived in Bruges and acted as the Flanders agent for the powerful Italian de' Medici family (see pp.93, 97). The dimensions of the painting, which when open measures over 2.5 m (8 ft) long, were dictated by a Florentine precedent.

Van der Goes is said to have died of religious melancholia, and knowing this, we may persuade ourselves that we see a barely controlled passion in his work. But without this biographic information, it may simply strike us as immensely dignified. Like the wings, the central panel, *The Adoration of the Shepherds,* shows two different scales in use, with the angels strangely small in comparison to the rest of the scene. This was a common device in medieval painting; it makes it easy to spot the important characters.

SAINTS AND THE DONOR'S FAMILY

The two large figures of St Margaret and St Mary Magdalene, who appear in the right panel of The Portinari Altarpiece, *are presenting Portinari's wife, Maria, and their daughter. St Margaret (patron saint of childbirth) can be identified by the fact that she is standing on a dragon. According to legend, she was swallowed by a monster, but burst out of it. Mary Magdalene carries the jar of ointment with which she anointed Christ's feet.*

SHRINE BY MEMLING
One of Memlings' most famous works is the Shrine of St Ursula. The carved wooden casket is in the shape of a Gothic chapel with six painted panels. Each panel tells the myth of St Ursula's pilgrimage to Rome with 11,000 virgins from England. On their return they were massacred by pagans from Cologne. The shrine is now the centrepiece of the Memling Museum in Bruges, Belgium.

MEMLING'S PLACIDITY

Van der Goes' vision is immensely powerful, and his paintings combine the gravity of van Eyck and the emotional intensity of van der Weyden. Certainly the power in his work is absent in that of the other Flemings, such as Gerard David (see p.71) and Hans Memling. Memling (also known as Memlinc; c. 1430/35–94) was possibly trained in the workshop of van der Weyden (see p.67), but also contains influences from Dieric Bouts (see below), a follower of van Eyck. Although a German by birth, Memling settled in Bruges, Flanders, and it was there that he lived and worked. In fact, he worked so successfully that he became one of Bruges' wealthiest citizens.

Memling is a gentle artist, unobtrusively regarding the world about him and sharing his response with us. His *Portrait of a Man with an Arrow (84)* is immediately likeable. Various possibilities have been suggested as to the meaning of the arrow: something about his kindly and mild countenance seems to rule out

84 **Hans Memling, Portrait of a Man with an Arrow,** *c. 1470/5, 32.5 x 26 cm (12¾ x 10¼ in)*

the possibility that he is a soldier. We are shown a very human gentleman, but one with firm and sensual lips. This small masterpiece grows on us the longer we contemplate it.

There could not be a greater contrast than between this and the work of Memling's contemporary, Bosch (see p.72), in whose work we often find a face that appears mean with suppressed hatreds.

A VAN DER WEYDEN FOLLOWER

Of all the Northern painters, the greatest influence on the Dutch-born painter Dieric Bouts (c. 1415–75) was van der Weyden (see p.67), who was possibly his teacher. Bouts did most of his work in Louvain, Flanders, where he was appointed the official city painter in 1468. His paintings are recognizable for their solemn dignity and deeply religious feeling. The spare composition and simple rendering of the drapery folds in Bouts' sensitively painted and elegant *Portrait of a Man (85)* are typical. He was an accomplished landscape painter, and here we get a glimpse of a landscape through the open window.

85 **Dieric Bouts, Portrait of a Man,** *1462, 32 x 20 cm (12½ x 8 in)*

LATE GOTHIC PAINTING

Gerard David, Hieronymus Bosch, and Matthias Grünewald were all early 16th-century artists and contemporaries of the other Northern artists Albrecht Dürer, Lucas Cranach, and Hans Holbein (see pp.148–162). However, the paintings of the former artists maintain connections with the Gothic tradition, while the latter were strongly influenced by the Italian Renaissance (see p.79). Thus the two strands of Gothic and Renaissance art coexisted in Northern Europe in the first half of the 16th century.

Gerard David (c. 1460–1523) was Memling's natural successor in Bruges at the end of the 15th century, and was a highly successful artist with a busy workshop. He is a wholly delightful painter, whose childlike Madonna makes an immediate and unforced emotional appeal. In *The Rest on the Flight into Egypt (86)*, she holds grapes for her baby, a symbol of the wine of His adult Passion, yet her quiet and abstracted expression is not one of foreboding. She seems enwrapped with her baby Jesus in a timeless reverie, while all the burden is borne by the active St Joseph in the background, and the watchful ass.

The distinct early 15th-century style of the Low Countries, which we see in the paintings of Campin and van Eyck (see pp.60–65), comes to its peak in David's paintings. We find in him the

THE HANSA
The Hanseatic League was formed in the 14th century as an association of German towns to protect its merchants in foreign parts and to extend trade. It grew to encompass 200 cities in Germany, the Low Countries, and England. Hansa merchants exported wool, cloth, metals, and furs to the East, and imported pigments, raw materials, silk, spices, and a variety of other oriental goods into Europe.

86 *Gerard David,* **The Rest on the Flight into Egypt,** *c. 1510, 44 x 45 cm (17½ x 17¾ in)*

BRUGES
Until the late 15th century Bruges was the hub of international commerce in northern Europe. Bruges was a self-governing commune and the city was also the headquarters of the Hanseatic League. Although self-governing, the city was, like the rest of Flanders, under the overlordship of the Dukes of Burgundy until 1477. Bruges lost its trading dominance after the River Zwijn became unnavigable and Antwerp assumed its position of influence.

87 Hieronymus Bosch, **The Temptation of St Anthony** *(central panel), c. 1505, 132 x 120 cm (52 x 47 in)*

ST ANTHONY
This early Christian hermit (c. 251–356) appears in a number of Bosch paintings. He is regarded as the founder of Christian monasticism and lived for most of his life in seclusion in Egypt.

monumental qualities of the Northern tradition, vitalized by a new pictorial vision, that would influence Quentin Massys and Jan Gossaert (see p.163). In these two, the divergent traditions of North and South come together again, though this happened later, when Italian Renaissance art was exerting an enormous and compelling influence. Northern art kept its sharp veracity, but with Italian modulations.

THE UNIQUE VISION OF BOSCH
The extraordinary painter Hieronymus Bosch (c. 1450–1516) stands apart from the prevailing Flemish traditions in painting. His style was unique, strikingly free, and his symbolism, unforgettably vivid, remains unparalleled to this day. Marvellous and terrifying, he expresses an intense pessimism and reflects the anxieties of his time, one of social and political upheaval.

Very little is known about Bosch, which somehow seems fitting since his work is so enigmatic. We know that he adopted the name of the Dutch town of s'Hertogenbosch (near Antwerp) as his own, that he belonged to an ultra-orthodox religious community called the Brotherhood of Mary, and that in his own day he was famous. Many of his paintings are devotional, and there are several on the theme of the Passion. He is specially famous for his fantastic, demon-filled works, one of which is *The Temptation of St Anthony (87)*.

The central panel of this triptych illustrates the kneeling figure of St Anthony being tormented by devils. These include a man with a thistle for a head, and a fish that is half gondola. Bizarre and singular as such images seem to us, many would have been familiar to Bosch's contemporaries because they relate to Flemish proverbs and religious terminology. What is so extraordinary is that these imaginary creatures are painted with utter conviction, as though

88 *Hieronymus Bosch*, **The Path of Life**, *c. 1500–02, 135 × 90 cm (53 × 35½ in)*

they truly existed. He has invested each bizarre or outlandish creation with the same obvious realism as the naturalistic animal and human elements. His nightmarish images seem to possess an inexplicable surrealistic power.

Even a more naturalistic painting like *The Path of Life (88)* contains sinister elements. Apart from the dog snarling at the poverty-stricken old man, and the animal bones and skull in the foreground, robbers attack a traveller in the background, and a gallows is visible on the skyline above the old man's head. *The Path of Life* is on the outer face of the wings of a triptych. The three inside panels display Bosch's tragic view of human existence, dwelling upon the triumph of sin. Man's exile from Paradise is shown on the left, the infinite variation of human vice in the centre, and its consequence – exile to Hell – on the right.

ILLUSTRATED ALLEGORIES

In *The Ship of Fools (89)* Bosch is imagining that the whole of mankind is voyaging through the seas of time on a ship, a small ship, that is representative of humanity. Sadly, every one of the representatives is a fool. This is how we live, says Bosch – we eat, drink, flirt, cheat, play silly games, pursue unattainable objectives. Meanwhile our ship drifts aimlessly and we never reach the harbour. The fools are not the

89 *Hieronymus Bosch*, **The Ship of Fools**, *c. 1490–1500, 58 × 33 cm (23 × 13 in)*

❝ *The master of the monstrous… the discoverer of the unconscious.* **❞**

Carl Gustav Jung, on Hieronymus Bosch

DRAMA

Mummers like these, who appear in a 14th-century French illumination, were a common sight in the Middle Ages in the towns of northern Europe. They were masked players who travelled around in groups and put on entertainments and mystery plays in the streets and private houses. The religious community that Bosch belonged to is also known to have performed mystery plays.

DEATH AND THE MISER

This moralistic panel from Bosch's middle phase is an example of the 15th-century Flemish insistence on exposing the folly and vices of humanity. Religious sects proliferated in the Low Countries at that time, and Bosch belonged to one with strongly orthodox beliefs.

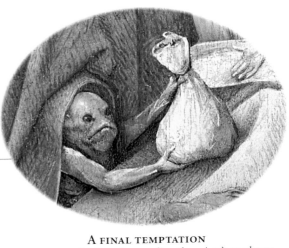

A FINAL TEMPTATION
A grotesque devil, understanding the miser's weakness, proffers a bag of gold in the hope of securing the miser's soul. We are left to draw our own conclusions as to the outcome of this human drama, but the gesture of compulsive greed made by the dying man, still eager for material gain, suggests the battle is already lost.

UNSEEN CRUCIFIX
At the heart of this painting is the battle for the miser's soul. His guardian angel pleads – perhaps in vain – for his salvation, and attempts to guide the dying man's attention to the small crucifix away off to the upper left, unseen by the miser and ignored.

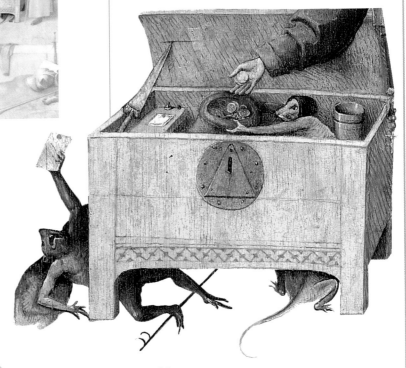

MONEY – THE FOCAL POINT
Lust, gluttony, and material greed were ranked among the worst of vices and were popular subjects of 15th-century religious sermons. The strongbox is given a prominent position, as the cause of the miser's possible damnation. He does not seem to see, as Bosch ensures we do, that the strongbox is alive with malicious, verminous creatures from the underworld, and that he carrries his key next to his rosary in vain.

SELF-PORTRAIT?
In the foreground, a small demon looks sideways at us amidst the miser's discarded silks, a face often seen in Bosch paintings, lean, pinched, and unhopeful. It has been suggested that this is a sardonic portrait of Bosch himself.

irreligious, since prominent among them are a monk and a nun, but they are all those who live "in stupidity". Bosch laughs, and it is a sad laugh. Which one of us does not sail in the wretched discomfort of the ship of human folly? Eccentric

90 Hieronymus Bosch, Death and the Miser, c. 1485/90, 93 x 30.5 cm (36½ x 12 in)

and secret genius that he was, Bosch not only moved the heart but scandalized it into full awareness. The sinister and monstrous things that he brought forth are the hidden creatures of our inward self-love: he externalizes the ugliness within, and so his misshapen demons have an effect beyond curiosity. We feel a hateful kinship with them. *The Ship of Fools* is not about other people, it is about us.

A MORAL TALE

Another of Bosch's panel paintings, *Death and the Miser (90)*, serves as a warning to anyone who has grabbed at life's pleasures, without being sufficiently detached, and who is unprepared to die. Who can feel indifferent to this fable? In a long and concentrated format Bosch sets out the whole painful scenario.

The naked and dying man has been a man of power: at the bed's foot, but sundered now by a low wall, lies his armour. His riches have come through combat; the sick man has fought for his wealth and stored it close to him. He appears twice, the second time in full health, soberly dressed because he hoards his gold, dense with satisfaction as he adds another coin. Demons lurk all around, death puts a leering head around the door (notice the sick man's surprise: death is never expected), and the final battle begins. It is one he must wage without his armour. Behind him stands a pleading angel. Before him, even now proffering gold, lurks a demon. Above the bed, expectant and interested, peers yet another demon. The outcome of the story is left undecided. We hope desperately that the miser will relinquish empty possessiveness and accept the truth of death.

GRÜNEWALD'S DARK VISION

The final flowering of the Gothic came relatively late, in the work of the German artist, Matthias Grünewald (his real name was Mathis Neithart, otherwise Gothart, 1470/80–1528). He was possibly an exact contemporary of Dürer (see p.152), but while Dürer was deeply influenced by the Renaissance, Grünewald ignored it in his choice of subject matter and style. Much of his work has not survived to this day, but even from the small amount that has come down to us, it is possible to see Grünewald as one of the most powerful of all painters. No other painter has ever so terribly and truthfully exposed the horror of suffering, and yet kept before us, as Bosch does not, the conviction of salvation. His *Crucifixion (91)*, part of the many-panelled

PHILIP II
The Spanish King Philip II (1527–98) was an admirer of the work of Bosch and amassed a substantial collection of his paintings. The son of the Emperor Charles V, Philip brought Spain out of the Middle Ages and into the Renaissance era. He commissioned many works by Titian (see p.131).

PANEL PAINTINGS
While painting on wooden panels was widespread across Europe, the timber used varied. In Italy poplar was the most common. North of the Alps there was a greater choice of wood, and oak, pine, silver fir, lime, beech, and chestnut were all used. Italian panels were left rough at the back while Northern European panels were beautifully finished. Those from Bruges were often stamped with a seal.

WORLD'S END
As at the end of most centuries, a number of people feared that the world would end in 1500. As a result apocalyptic images of death were widespread.

91 Matthias Grünewald, Crucifixion, *c. 1510–15, 270 x 305 cm (8 ft 10 in x 10 ft)*

MEDIEVAL MEDICINE
Up until the Renaissance, medical knowledge was rudimentary. Diseases and ailments were usually treated with herbal cures, blood-letting by leeches, or by supernatural "cures". Superstition dictated, for example, that sickness could be avoided by carrying holy relics, or texts taken from the Bible. This illustration, dating from the 14th century, shows a very docile patient undergoing a primitive lobotomy operation.

Isenheim Altarpiece, is now kept in Colmar. It was commissioned for the Antonite monastery at Isenheim and was intended to give support to patients in the monastic hospital. Christ appears hideous, his skin swollen and torn as a result of the flagellation and torture that He endured. This was understandably a powerful image in a hospital that specialized in caring for those suffering from skin complaints.

The more accessible *Small Crucifixion (92)* engages us very directly with the actual death of the Saviour. The crucified Lord leans down into our space, crushing us, leaving us no escape, filling the painting with his agony. We are hemmed in by the immensities of darkness and mountain, alone with pain, forced to face the truth. The Old Testament often talks of a "suffering servant", describing him in Psalm 22 as "a worm and no man": it is of Grünewald's Christ that we think. In this noble veracity, Gothic art reached an electrifying greatness.

92 Matthias Grünewald, The Small Crucifixion, *c. 1511/20, 61 x 46 cm (24 x 18 in)*

CRUCIFIXION

This is the central panel of Grünewald's large, multi-panelled *Isenheim Altarpiece*. It is an extraordinary record of intense and disfiguring human suffering. Because he worked in a hospital, Grünewald based his image of suffering on the patients whose torments he witnessed. These were mostly sufferers from skin diseases, which were common at the time.

PHYSICAL PAIN
The crossbar of the crucifix is a simple, rough-hewn branch, bending under the weight of the dying man. Christ's arms are abnormally elongated and His hand, contorted into a physical scream, seems both a desperate reproach and a surrender to God.

FAMILY GRIEF
Divided from the stoic figure of John the Baptist by the monstrous dying Christ are the traumatized relatives and friends. Mary collapses into herself, either swooning from exhaustion or from a need to shut out the vision of her crucified Son. Grünewald originally painted her as an upright figure, but later arched her body into this pitiful state. She is supported by the despairing St John the Evangelist.

ST JOHN'S PROPHECY
St John the Baptist stands barefoot, wearing the animal skins that symbolize his time in the wilderness, and carrying a book. He seems unbowed by the horror of the moment and is unshakable in his prophetic conviction – inscribed against the night sky – "He will increase while I decrease". John delivers the Christian message of hope and redemption, balancing the desolation of the scene.

AGONY VISUALIZED
Grünewald takes the Gothic concern with suffering, sin, and mortality to its furthest extreme. Here in graphic detail is Christ the victim, physically repulsive in His brutalized condition and far removed from the heroic, athletically beautiful Christs of the Renaissance. Grünewald's vision is one of horror, a metaphor for the supreme cruelty and degradation of which humanity is capable, and by the same token, of the supreme mercy of Christ's benediction.

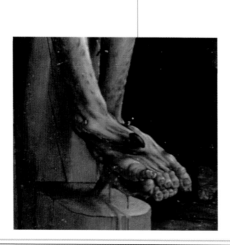

LAMB OF GOD
The lamb, used as a sacrificial animal by the Jews, was adopted by the early Christians as a symbol of Christ's sacrifice. It is associated with St John, who on seeing Jesus declared, "Behold the Lamb of God". The lamb normally holds a Cross and its sacrifical blood flows into a chalice.

THE ITALIAN RENAISSANCE

In the arts and sciences as well as society and government, Italy was the major catalyst for progress during the Renaissance: the rich period of development that occurred in Europe at the end of the Middle Ages. Because of the number of different fields in which it applied, "Renaissance" is a word with many layers of meaning. Accordingly, Renaissance painting cannot signify any one common or clearly definable style. As Gothic painting had been shaped by the feudal societies of the Middle Ages, with its roots in the Romanesque and Byzantine traditions, Renaissance art was born out of a new, rapidly evolving civilization. It marked the point of departure from the medieval to the modern world and, as such, laid the foundations for modern Western values and society.

Giovanni Bellini, **The Feast of the Gods,** *1514 (**detail**)*

Italian Renaissance Timeline

The Renaissance in Italy started gradually, its beginnings being apparent even in Giotto's work, a century before Masaccio was active (see p.46). The quest for scientific precision and greater realism culminated in the superb balance and harmony of Leonardo, Raphael, and Michelangelo. The influence of Humanism (see p.82) is reflected in the increase of secular subjects. In the final phase of the Renaissance, Mannerism became the dominant style.

Masaccio, Adam and Eve, 1427

Leonardo wrote that Masaccio "showed by his perfect works, how those who take for their inspiration anything but Nature – mistress of all masters – weary themselves in vain"; and in 1830, Eugène Delacroix wrote of him: "Born in poverty, almost unknown during the best part of his short life, he carried out singlehanded the greatest revolution ever known in painting." This revolution was his vision of the world: of mortal beings portrayed with honesty and tenderness, living and breathing in a terrestrial world of air, light, and space (p.83).

Piero della Francesca, Resurrection of Christ, c. 1450

Clarity and dignity characterize Piero's art. Influenced by Roman Classicism and Florentine innovation, his paintings combine complex mathematical structures with brilliant colour and crystalline light (p.102).

Leonardo da Vinci, Virgin of the Rocks, c. 1508

A true "Renaissance man", Leonardo was a great painter as well as a sculptor, architect, inventor, engineer, and an expert in such fields as botany, anatomy, and geology. His distinctively lyrical art reveals his compelling belief in nature as a source of inspiration (p.120).

1420	1440	1460	1480	1500

Fra angelico, beheading of st cosmas and st damian, 1438–40

This is part of the predella (a strip along the lower edge) of the altarpiece in the priory of San Marco, Florence. Fra Angelico's paintings have a delicate grace that belies their dynamism. There are elements of Gothic style, but the figures move in real, observed landscapes, and are defined by natural light (p.90).

Sandro Botticelli, Primavera, c. 1482

Botticelli is known best for his secular paintings – elaborate pagan allegories and mythological scenes. But his paintings are recognizable for their sheer beauty of line, free of discord. His art is notable for its peculiarly gentle, wistful melancholy. As he aged, this deepened to an anxious sadness; his figures became emaciated, sometimes with tortured expressions. This was possibly a reaction to contemporary political and religious tensions (p.94).

MICHELANGELO, IGNUDO (NUDE) FROM THE SISTINE CHAPEL, C. 1508–12
Michelangelo is another "giant" of the High Renaissance. However, in contrast with the lyricism of Leonardo's paintings, Michelangelo's art is characterized by gravity. Created on an epic scale, it is peopled with superhuman forms, of severe athletic beauty (p.122).

TITIAN, VENUS AND ADONIS, C. 1560
Titian was the greatest of the Venetian artists, and one of the world's supreme artists, with a profound influence on the development of Western painting. His late works are unsurpassed in their haunting and fragile beauty, strikingly suggestive of some 20th-century art (p.134).

EL GRECO, MADONNA AND CHILD WITH ST MARTINA AND ST AGNES, C. 1597–99
El Greco is the great religious Mannerist. His passionate vision surpasses the stylish manipulations of later Mannerists. After travels in Venice and Rome, he settled in Toledo in Spain. His work displays a mystic fervour that accurately represents the religious intensity of Counter-Reformation Spain (p.145).

CORREGGIO, VENUS, SATYR, AND CUPID, C. 1514–30
Correggio's imagery can seem too sweet for modern tastes. But beneath the outward charm is a tough appreciation of sensual truth (p.142).

1520	1540	1560	1580	1600

TINTORETTO, THE CONVERSION OF ST PAUL, C. 1545
The Venetian artist Tintoretto was a leading late Renaissance painter. After studying briefly under Titian, he evolved a distinctive, dynamic style with startling contrasts of colour and tone, sweeping vistas, and dramatic movement. His paintings exhibit a religious intensity and a passionate "expressionism" that move him into the realm of Mannerism, away from the Classicism of the High and Early Renaissance (p.134).

RAPHAEL, BINDO ALTOVITI, C. 1515
Raphael was a successor to Leonardo, whose early influence on him was profound. Raphael was also attracted to classical art, so that his paintings possess heroic grandeur, and his portraits a new, graceful spontaneity (p.128).

THE EARLY RENAISSANCE

The name "Renaissance" – meaning "rebirth" – is given to a period of broad cultural achievement spanning three centuries. The idea of rebirth lies at the heart of all Renaissance achievement: artists, scholars, scientists, philosophers, architects, and rulers believed that the way to greatness and enlightenment was through the study of the Golden Ages of the ancient Greeks and Romans. They rejected the more recent, medieval past, which constituted the Gothic era. Instead of this, inspired by Humanism, they looked to the literary and philosophical traditions, and the artistic and engineering achievements, of Greco-Roman antiquity.

BRUNELLESCHI AND FLORENTINE ARCHITECTURE
The cupola of Florence's Cathedral is considered to be the greatest triumph of the architect Filippo Brunelleschi. It has a diameter of 45 m (150 ft), and the marble ribs on the exterior exert a powerful centripetal force which supports the whole structure. Its eight faces are held in place by the continuously self-supporting masonry system, which is in itself a remarkable feat of structural engineering. The dome was completed in 1418, becoming the focal point of the city and proclaiming Florence to be the cultural capital of the Renaissance.

HUMANISM
Humanism was an important cultural movement of the Renaissance, in which prime importance was given to human reason rather than to God's revelation. Erasmus (see p.154) was its great theorist. Classical Latin and Greek texts were the main sources, but Humanist education also included the liberal arts, such as grammar, rhetoric, poetry, and ethics. Humanistic thinking was brought to the world of diplomacy by Machiavelli, and to architecture by Alberti (see p.88).

Renaissance painting began in Italy in the middle of the 13th century, and its influence rapidly spread throughout Europe, reaching its peak at the end of the 15th century. Renaissance artists believed their art was a continuation of the great antique tradition of Greece and Rome, an insight that came originally from Giotto (see p.46). With his joyful spiritual vision, Giotto is like the Gothic artists. But his ability to present stories from the Bible as very naturalistic, human dramas and his way of depicting his figures as solid, weighty characters were Renaissance qualities. Giotto showed what could be done, how an artistic vision could encompass the exciting new understanding of Humanism and Classicism, which were to be so important to Renaissance artists. With antiquity as a model and Giotto as a guide, painters of the early Italian Renaissance entered a new phase of pictorial representation, based on the reality of human existence.

MASACCIO AND FLORENCE
Of course the transition from Gothic to Renaissance did not happen overnight, but it can come as a surprise to see that the next great Italian painter after Giotto (who died in 1337) was not born until 1401, and therefore not active until nearly a century after Giotto's death. This gap is largely explained by the Black Death (see p.58), the first spread of which devastated Europe in the 14th century, reaching Italy first in 1347 and sweeping across Europe over the next four years. The consequences were far-reaching, and in addition to the massive physical loss, medieval society underwent great changes. Artistic revolution in the North, in the Low

93 Masaccio, **The Virgin and Child,** *1426, 135 x 75 cm (53 x 29½ in)*

Countries (see pp.60–70), was leading painting in new directions through its increasing naturalism, secularism, and technical mastery. In the South, it seemed as if Giotto had never been. Miraculously, there was a second spring with the birth of the Florentine painter,

Masaccio (Tomasso de Giovanni di Simone Guidi, 1401–28). It is Masaccio who is the revolutionary founder of Renaissance painting. Of the Italian painters, he was the one who really saw what Giotto had initiated, and made it accessible to all who followed.

Masaccio is forever young because he died when he was 27, yet his art seems to be outstandingly mature. His name is a nickname, meaning something like "Tom the Hulk", and his art is hulking too. But it is the hulk of genius, monumental, strong and convincing, true heir to the humanity and spatial depth of Giotto. One of his early works, painted for a church in Pisa, has an almost architectonic concentration. In *The Virgin and Child* (93), the central panel of a now scattered polyptych (multiple painting), the Madonna is sculptural in her blocky dignity, seated on a throne of classic weight, shadowed and austere, with her Child completely stripped of Byzantine kingliness. This Jesus is a real baby, sucking his fingers and staring into space. It represents the antithesis of the courtly refinement of the International Gothic style of Gentile da Fabriano, for instance (see p.56). Yet the pathos is heightened, not diminished: there is strength and vulnerability, beautifully combined, and even the angel musicians have a chubby earnestness.

LINKS WITH SCULPTURE

As Giotto was influenced by the sculpture of the Pisanos (see p.46), so was Masaccio by their Florentine sculptural descendants as it were, the two senior artists: Donatello (Donato di Niccolo, 1386–1466, see right), and Lorenzo Ghiberti (1378–1455, see p.102, column). The influence of sculpture on early Renaissance painting, and inherently on the development of the Western tradition in painting, cannot be overstressed. Masaccio's understanding of three-dimensional form, architectural space, and of perspective owed a great debt to the technical and scientific achievements pioneered by Donatello, Ghiberti, and the Florentine architect Brunelleschi (Filippo di Ser Brunelleschi, 1377–1446, see column, left). Sculptural realism lies at the heart of Renaissance painting, to culminate in the epic monumentality of Michelangelo's art during the High Renaissance (see p.120).

As Giotto translated Pisano's carvings into pictorial form, Masaccio drew inspiration from Donatello's freestanding sculptures and reliefs, and applied sculptural considerations to his paintings: creating images of convincingly solid objects, in a feasible space, with optical perspective. More significantly, he applied the sculptor's understanding of the effects of real light falling onto objects, and filtering through spaces, surpassing Giotto's already monumental leap towards understanding and reinventing the world through painting.

From now on the lovely play that can characterize the finest Gothic art (though less often that of Giotto or Duccio) has disappeared. Masaccio lives in a wholly serious world. His *Adam and Eve Expelled from Paradise (94)*, in Florence's Brancacci Chapel, wail with unselfconscious horror, blinded with grief,

94 *Masaccio*, **Adam and Eve Expelled from Paradise,** *c. 1427, 205 x 90 cm (81 x 35½ in)*

DONATELLO'S DAVID

Donatello was one of a group of brilliant sculptors who led the way for painters in the early Renaissance (see also p.105). He visited Rome, where he was inspired by the freedom of movement achieved in the nude figures of classical sculpture, and afterwards (c. 1434) created this bronze figure of the young King David. This overtly sensual work was one of the first nude statues of the Renaissance.

RESTORATION OF FRESCOES

Time and the elements, in particular modern pollution, have caused serious deterioration in the surface of many of the frescoes produced during the Renaissance. As a result, to repair the damage and to prevent more from occurring, many famous works, including Masaccio's Brancacci Chapel frescoes and Michelangelo's Sistine Chapel ceiling (see p.122), have been substantially restored. This has resulted in some controversy as not all art critics and historians are in agreement that all the work has been sensitively carried out. Some argue that the tonal values of the work have been ignored.

THE TRINITY

The doctrine of the Trinity – of God as three separate beings, yet remaining one entity – lies at the heart of the Christian "mystery". It is first mentioned in Matthew's Gospel (28: 19), as comprising Father, Son, and Holy Spirit. Masaccio's *Trinity* was commissioned for the church of Santa Maria Novella in 1425. It was covered over in 1570 with a panel painting by Vasari (see p.98), and only rediscovered in 1861.

MOTHER OF CHRIST
Mary the Virgin is the only one of the non-divine beings who looks directly out at us. She stands upright and dry-eyed, and points with a gesture both implacable and supplicating, towards her crucified Child and gives the viewer a concentrated glance of terrible reproach.

THE TRINITY
Masaccio's Trinity is part of a Renaissance pictorial tradition in which the Father is generally depicted as an aged and bearded patriarch, standing behind and above the crucified Son. He is often shown supporting both ends of the the crossbar of the crucifix, thus echoing His Son's sacrifice. Between them flits the white geometry of the Holy Spirit, traditionally depicted as a dove (see also p.101). The Spirit is the third person of the Trinity, but is here perhaps the most eye-catching in the sheer brilliance of the white smudge that bisects the fresco.

THE DONORS
The figures of the Trinity, and of Mary and St John, appear as solidly real as the two donors. Yet the donors are both included in and excluded from this timeless scene. Spatially they belong: they share the same scale (traditionally donors were shown on a specially reduced scale) and are bathed in the same light that illuminates the interior of the vault. But symbolically the donors remain "outside" the scene, because they have been positioned on a lower step, as though on the predella (a painted border strip) of an altarpiece, which locates them firmly in the world of the viewer.

PERSPECTIVE
Vasari recorded his admiration for Masaccio's Trinity when he described its sophisticated spatial structure as: "a barrel vault drawn in perspective, and divided into squares with rosettes which diminish and are foreshortened so well, that there seems to be a hole in the wall". Masaccio had interpreted Brunelleschi's (p.82) theories of perspective with such clarity, that in the past it was believed that Brunelleschi was actually directly involved in the production of the painting.

majesty we can well accept that these two figures are divine. Divinity is by definition a mystery, something we cannot comprehend, but Masaccio makes the mystery of the Trinity humanly accessible. Below the great central vertical pole of the Trinity, symmetrically fanning out on either side, are the four non-divine actors in the drama. Only one – Mary – is looking directly out of the picture. Balancing the figure of Christ's mother, Mary, on the other side of the Cross is St John, equally massive, equally solid, though he is looking not towards us, but towards Christ.

Beyond them, sealing in the picture, are the donors – large, profiled, solidly present as our representatives. At the very bottom of the painting there is a seventh character: the skeleton, representing Adam and Everyman. This is the human truth which underlies all religious dogma. Above the skeleton, on the stone wall of the narrow tomb in which it lies, is written the inscription "I was once what you are and what I am you will become". The universal nature of Masaccio's *Trinity*, encompassing the wide realm of mortal decay and spiritual salvation, belongs to a medieval tradition.

There is an immense authority about this young artist. *St Peter Healing with His Shadow (96)* is one of a pair of scenes from the Brancacci Chapel cycle, situated at either side of the altar. (The other is *The Distribution of the Goods of the Church*, and the pair share a common perspective.) St Peter strides towards the viewer down a narrow street of houses built in the Florentine style. One man in his entourage, wearing the short smock of a stonecutter, might be intended as a portrait of Donatello; another, younger man, his beard not yet grown, might be Masaccio's self-portrait (he is positioned facing directly out of the picture in the manner of self-portraits of the time). Peter's shadow is rendered with remarkable confidence in view of the fact that, prior to this, no technique for painting shadows had been developed. The cripples are depicted with a vividness and individuality astonishingly advanced for the early 15th century.

Masaccio's concerns with the true appearance of things earned him this singular appraisal from the art historian Vasari (see p.98):

95 Masaccio, The Trinity, *1425, 670 x 315 cm (22 ft x 10 ft 4 in)*

unaware of anything but their loss of happiness. Eve is so sheerly ugly as she screams aloud from misery that we are startled into attention and into pity.

MASACCIO'S TRINITY

What distinguishes Masaccio is his majesty; there never was a more massive, more dignified, more noble and yet more human painter. The wonder of this painting of *The Trinity (95)* is that it shows us six *human* images. Central are Father and Son. Although they are in the most moving way human (a real, suffering Jesus showing compassion for His fellow men and women as He dies, and a real Father upright in His splendid dignity as He holds up the Crucifix and shows us His surrendered Son) in Their

THE BRANCACCI CHAPEL

Several of Masaccio's frescoes cover the upper walls of the Brancacci family chapel in the church of Santa Maria del Carmine in Florence. This cycle of frescoes became a model for Florentine artists in the late Renaissance, including Michelangelo (see p.120).

OTHER WORKS BY MASACCIO

Crucifixion of St Peter (Staatliche Museen, Berlin-Dahlem)

Virgin with St Anne (Uffizi, Florence)

Tribute Money (Brancacci Chapel, Florence)

96 Masaccio, St Peter Healing with His Shadow, *1425 (detail of fresco)*

"With regard to painting we are indebted first of all to Masaccio, who first painted people's feet actually standing on the ground, and by doing so eliminated that awkwardness, common to all artists before him, of having the figures standing on tiptoe. We must also be grateful to him for having given his figures such liveliness and relief that he deserves the same credit as if he had invented Art itself".

THE "SMALLER" ART OF MASOLINO

Masaccio's greatness can best be seen if we compare him with Masolino (Tommaso di Cristoforo Fini da Panicale, 1383– c. 1447), nearly 20 years his senior, with whom he often worked. (It has been suggested that "Masolino", also a nickname, was coined to mark the difference between "Big Tom", Masaccio, and "Small Tom", Masolino.) He is unfairly seen as small, but only in comparison. On his own, he is still temperamentally in the Gothic era, as we

98 Masaccio, St Jerome and St John the Baptist, *c. 1428, 115 × 55 cm (45 × 21½ in)*

99 Masolino, St Liberius and St Matthias, *c. 1428, 115 × 55 cm (45 × 21½ in)*

see in his graceful *Annunciation (97)*, in which he shows us his love of the decorative and elegant, flowing line that is truly Gothic. But when paired with the bigger Tom, Masolino too stretched out into the true Renaissance.

The best proof of Masolino's ability to grow can be seen in a comparison between two panels, *St Jerome and St John the Baptist (98)* and *St Liberius and St Matthias (99)*, which hang to either side of an altarpiece. All four saints have a hulking presence typical of Masaccio – they certainly stand with their feet flat on the ground – yet it is now fairly certain that the former panel is largely by Masaccio, while the latter is mainly the work of Masolino. (Previously, both were attributed to Masaccio.)

DOMENICO THE INNOVATOR

The Venetian artist Domenico Veneziano (Domenico di Bartolomeo di Venezia, active c.1438–61) was one of the most important painters of the early Renaissance, working in Florence. His importance lies not so much in his personal achievement, as in the breadth and significance of his influence – for he was the teacher of Piero della Francesca (see p.100).

What we find so beautifully in Domenico is a splendour of light that emanates from a single source, breathing air into the space and unifying forms within it. He gives us the first radiant indication of that water-born silveriness that is one of the Venetian gifts to the visual world. Domenico had also a dazzlingly original mind. We admire – rightly – the great Masaccio; we love the limpid Domenico. His *St John in the Desert (100)* is a magical work. Light pours in blinding clarity over a glittering barrenness,

97 Masolino, Annunciation, *probably c. 1425/30, 148 × 115 cm (58¼ × 45 in)*

100 Domenico Veneziano, St John in the Desert, c. 1445, 28.5 x 32.5 cm (11¼ x 12¾ in)

THE MARZOCCO
This heraldic lion, known as the Marzocco, and the *fleur de lys* that it holds, were symbols of the Republic of Florence. The sculpture was made by Donatello in 1418–20. It was commissioned for the papal apartments at Santa Maria Novella, but is now in the Bargello Museum in Florence.

with the tender, naked saint the only softness to be seen. He is stripping off his worldly clothes, like a young athlete getting ready for the race. That the race is very present to him, and that it is a contest of the spirit is sublimely clear. But if it is an all-demanding vocation to which this slender youth is called, it is one lived in the exhilaration of a high plateau.

There is a strange relationship between this classical-looking nude, with his medieval golden halo, and his setting in a landscape reminiscent of Netherlandish (even Byzantine) art; and this juxtaposition illustrates the meeting of the spiritual, pagan, and physical worlds. This is a deeply Renaissance way of visualizing the story, as we can see if we compare it with the painting of the same subject by Giovanni di Paolo (c.1403–83). This is Giovanni's *St John the Baptist Retiring to the Desert (101)*, an archaic and bewitching Gothic fantasy that sends the youthful saint out like a young adventurer to seek his heavenly fortune.

101 Giovanni di Paolo, St John the Baptist Retiring to the Desert, c. 1454, 30 x 39 cm (11¾ x 15½ in)

PERSPECTIVE: SCIENCE INTO ART

The Renaissance concept that most gripped the Florentine artist Paolo Uccello (Paolo di Dono, 1397–1475), whose name is also a nickname (*uccello* means "bird" – given to him for his love of birds), was not so much that of light as perspective. Significantly, he was apprenticed with the architect Ghiberti (see p.102, column) at the beginning of his career.

In a story recounted by Vasari, Uccello once worked all night on this science, whereby the confusion of the world could be ordered into submission. His wife reported him crying out in ecstasy, "Oh, how great is this perspective!" and, on being called to bed, saying that he would not leave his "sweet mistress perspective". He seized upon it with an intellectual passion that might have produced a rather rigid art.

Put very simply, the art of perspective is the representation of solid objects and three-dimensional space in accordance with our optical perception of these things (and in direct opposition to a purely symbolic or decorative form of representation). We see the world "in perspective": objects appear smaller as they recede into the distance; the walls of a corridor or an avenue of trees, for instance, appear to converge as they stretch into the distance. The laws of perspective are based upon these converging lines meeting eventually at a single, fixed "vanishing point", which may be visible – such as when an avenue of trees stretches as far as the eye can see – or is an imagined "vanishing point" as when the converging lines of a room continue, in our imagination only, beyond the far wall.

One of Uccello's greatest works, which demonstrates his fascination with perspective, is *The Hunt in the Forest (102)*. Everything in it is organized upon a distant and almost unseen stag, a vanishing stag: the vanishing point. The bright little hunters, with their horses, hounds,

ALBERTI

The Florentine artist, architect, and antiquarian Leon Battista Alberti (1404–72) was one of the first to construct a formula of perspective that could be applied to two-dimensional paintings.

102 Paolo Uccello, **The Hunt in the Forest,** *1460s, 75 × 178 cm (29½ × 70 in)*

and beaters, run from all sides among the slim, bare trunks of a darkly wooded landscape. While all this activity is frenzied, it is exquisitely purposeful and sane. Throughout this painting, we feel Uccello's comfort and his poetry.

Uccello was not the first Florentine to explore perspective. Brunelleschi, the architect who built Florence Cathedral's revolutionary dome (see p.82), demonstrated linear perspective as an element in architectural design in about 1413. However, it was Leon Battista Alberti (see left) who pioneered its application to painting. His 1435 treatise *On Painting* had a widespread influence on contemporary artists. How widespread it was is something that we can never really prove. The fact remains that after Uccello, Brunelleschi, and above all Alberti, every artist had become alerted to the potential of this astonishing new insight.

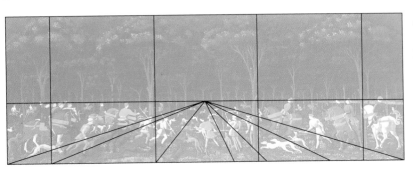

THE VANISHING POINT
That Uccello's Hunt in the Forest *demonstrates an effective rendering of perspective is shown in this miniature version. Lines have been added artificially to draw attention to features of the general composition that lead the eye to the vanishing point. At this point, the leading stag is disappearing into the forest.*

UCCELLO'S STUDIES
The complex perspective framework of Uccello's paintings was the result of meticulous study. In this drawing of a chalice he tackles the perspective problems of drawing a rounded object in three-dimensional space.

103 *Fra Angelico,* **The Beheading of St Cosmas and St Damian,** *c. 1438–40, 37 x 46 cm (14½ x 18 in)*

THE DEVOUT ART OF FRA ANGELICO

The Dominican monk Fra Angelico (Fra Giovanni da Fiesole, c. 1400–55) was active at about the same time as Masaccio. He painted with great religious gravity and in remarkably luminous tones, but he is insufficiently seen as the bold experimenter that he truly was – not in theme, but in manner.

Despite the implications of his name, there is a satisfying humanity about Fra Angelico that takes pleasure in the substance of the material world. No questions are left unanswered in his *Beheading of St Cosmas and St Damian (103).* It is a scene of intense chromatic brightness, every form and hue bathed in the relentless light of a summer morning. The landscape is wholly realized, from the clarity of the white towers to the tall, dark cypresses and the receding swoops and rises of a hilly countryside. The two saints wait, blindfolded against the brightness and horror, and the three already decapitated sprawl in the messy scarlet of their blood, each head rolling on the grass in its hoop of halo. It is real death, painted without recourse to melodrama, but seen with the half-smile of a total believer.

It is tempting to look at the *Virgin and Child Enthroned with Angels and Saints (104)* and regard it as charming but conventional, since the graceful, sinewy lines and strong local colour are derived from the Gothic tradition. But a closer look reveals that Fra Angelico was fully aware of the progressive tendencies in painting – of perspective and use of light especially – and the

SAN MARCO AND THE DOMINICANS

The Dominican order, of which Fra Angelico was a member, moved to the convent of San Marco in Florence in 1436. It was funded by Cosimo de' Medici, who also donated more than 400 classical texts to the library. It was at San Marco that Fra Angelico painted many of his best-known frescoes, including *The Annunciation*.

LUCA DELLA ROBBIA

Much admired in his time, Luca della Robbia (1400–82) was a Florentine sculptor. He carved the beautiful marble *cantoria* (choir gallery) for Florence Cathedral in 1431–38. The carvings illustrate the 150th Psalm and depict angels, boys, and girls playing musical instruments, singing, and dancing.

OTHER WORKS BY FRA ANGELICO

The Madonna of Humility (National Gallery of Art, Washington)

The Annunciation (Convent of San Marco, Florence)

St James Freeing Hermogenes (Kimbell Art Museum, Fort Worth, Texas)

Virgin and Child with St Dominic and St Peter Martyr (Church of San Domencino, Cortona)

Virgin and Child (Cincinnati Art Museum)

104 Fra Angelico, The Virgin and Child Enthroned with Angels and Saints, *c. 1438–40, 220 x 229 cm (7 ft 3 in x 7 ft 6 in)*

105 Fra Filippo Lippi, Virgin and Child, c. 1440–45, 215 x 244 cm (7 ft 1 in x 8 ft)

We peer past the agonized figure on the Cross to attempt – in vain – to decipher the carpet. Equally, past the reverential angels beside the throne, in a naturalistic landscape, we see light catching the tips of trees, glancing off leaves, escaping past the trunks to reveal a distant land. The total effect is anything but conventional.

SACRED AND PROFANE

All the same, Fra Angelico was the model of a good monk, just as Fra Filippo Lippi (c.1406–69) was not. Giovanni da Fiesole chose in his young maturity to become a monk, and his admiring brethren called him the "Reverend Angel" (*Fra Angelico*). In the 19th century he was thought to be a saint. But young Filippo (Lippo) was left an orphan and brought up by the Carmine monks in Florence: no other calling was suggested to him, though it became scandalously clear that he had no capacity for a life of frugal chastity. It is a story with a happy ending, in that he eventually met a woman to cherish (incidentally, a nun who had been "conventized" in much the same unthinking fashion as he was encouraged in his choice) and both were dispensed from their vows, and their marriage blessed.

Lippi's version of the *Virgin and Child (105)* surrounded by angels and saints may be compared with that of his truly devout brother in religion (see p.91). Lippi painted his version some years after Masaccio produced his frescoes in the Brancacci Chapel in Florence (see p.85), and these were a crucial influence on Lippi's work.

OTHER WORKS BY FRA FILIPPO LIPPI

Virgin and Child (Walters Art Gallery, Baltimore)

Madonna and Child (Uffizi, Florence)

Adoration in a Wood (Staatliche Museen, Berlin-Dahlem)

sculptural influence on his representation of physical space is pronounced. There is a strong formal patterning, real bodies stand in true relation to one another, and there is an unconventional delight in the near-primitivism of the animals in the carpet and in the tiny but significant Crucifixion that looms sternly up in the centre.

106 Fra Filippo Lippi, Annunciation, c. 1448–50, 68 x 152 cm (27 x 60 in)

However, the monumentality of form Lippi learned from Masaccio was to be tempered with delicacy and sweetness, similar to that found in Fra Angelico's paintings, and the serene mystical quality of his later paintings reveal growing Netherlandish influences in Italy.

Lippi's Virgin has a rounded physical presence, statuesque and forbidding despite its fullness, and the chubby Child looks rather disparagingly down on the kneeling St Frediano. The angels too are heavily present, crowded in upon one another in a confusion of light-filled space. There is too much going on. The marbled walls behind push down on us, and the jewelled brightness of material and form takes on an almost claustrophobic weight. But when he simplifies his scene, it is rare to find a painter more moving than Fra Lippi.

His *Annunciation (106)* is a heavenly little work, with diaphanous veilings exquisitely rendered, and a lovely tenderness in the pure and gentle girl and her angelic messenger. This panel is thought to have been part of the bedroom furniture of some great noble, possibly Piero de' Medici (who patronized Lippi). The Medici family emblem – three feathers in a diamond ring – appears carved in stone beneath the vase of lilies, and in the companion piece, *Seven Saints (108)*, all the saints are "connected" with the Medici: name saints of the family males. The seven sit dreamily on a marble garden seat, only St Peter Martyr, with his emblematic hatchet in his head, looking glum.

That saints in general are happy seems a congenial belief to Filippo. His own son, the model for many of the Infant Jesus images, was himself to become a painter and likewise express a fundamental well-being. But Lippi junior, Filippino

(1457–1504), was orphaned at ten and brought up by Botticelli (see p.94), who had been taught by Lippi senior. Filippino's work shows that Lippi tendency to happiness, shadowed by the Botticelli sense of human frailty. There is a quivering gentleness in Filippino that is uniquely his own. *Tobias and the Angel (107)* is a moving work, but it floats ethereally before us, scarcely seeming to acknowledge the earth.

107 Filippino Lippi, **Tobias and the Angel,** *probably c. 1480, 32.5 x 23.5 cm (12¾ x 9 in)*

COSIMO DE' MEDICI
The Medici family dominated Florentine political life for much of the 15th and 16th centuries. The glorious epoch of the family began with Cosimo (1389–1464) who commissioned work from Ghiberti, Donatello, and Fra Angelico. His descendant, Cosimo I (1519–1574), depicted above, became Duke of Florence in 1537. He was a skilled but ruthless soldier who managed to annex the republic of Siena to Tuscany in 1555. He too was a great patron of the arts and had his own collection of Etruscan antiquities. This portrait, painted in 1537, is by Jacopo Pontormo (see pp.139–141).

108 Fra Filippo Lippi, **Seven Saints,** *c. 1448–50, 68 x 152 cm (27 x 60 in)*

NEO-PLATONISM

This was a school of philosophy in which elements of the classical Greek systems of Plato, Pythagoras, and Aristotle were combined. It was first established in the 3rd century, but during the 15th century it was revised and made compatible with Christian belief. Neo-Platonism entailed a view of the universe in which ideas were more important than things, and the belief that the soul is endowed with virtues and is capable of an inner ascent to God. Cosimo de' Medici founded the Platonic Academy of Florence in 1459, employing the foremost theorist and classics translator of the time, Marsilio E. Ficino.

ANATOMICAL EXACTITUDE

The work of the Florentine artist Antonio Pollaiuolo (c. 1432–98) and his brother Piero (c. 1441–94/96) influenced that of Botticelli. According to Vasari (see column, p.98), Antonio was one of the first artists to carry out dissections of the human body in order to study the underlying systems and structures. *The Martyrdom of St Sebastian*, completed in 1475 and from which this detail is taken, clearly shows the results of this research.

BOTTICELLI: LYRICAL PRECISION

After Masaccio, Sandro Botticelli (Alessandro di Moriano Filipepi, 1444/5–1510) comes as the next great painter of the Florentine tradition. The new, sharply contoured, slender form and rippling sinuous line that is synonymous with Botticelli was influenced by the brilliant, precise draftsmanship of the Pollaiuolo brothers (see below, left), who trained not only as painters, but as goldsmiths, engravers, sculptors, and embroidery designers. However, the rather stiff, scientifically formulaic appearance of the Pollaiuolos' painting of *The Martyrdom of St Sebastian* (see left), for instance, which clearly

109 Sandro Botticelli, **Primavera**, *c. 1482, 315 x 205 cm (10 ft 4 in x 6 ft 9 in)*

follows anatomical dictates, finds no place in the paintings of Botticelli. His sophisticated understanding of perspective, anatomy, and the Humanist debate of the Medici court (see p.82) never overshadows the sheer poetry of his vision. Nothing is more gracious, in lyrical beauty, than Botticelli's mythological paintings

Primavera and *The Birth of Venus* (see p.96), where the pagan story is taken with reverent seriousness and Venus is the Virgin Mary in another form. But it is also significant that no-one has ever agreed on the actual subject of *Primavera (109)*, and a whole shelf in a library can be taken up with different theories;

> **"** *... [Botticelli] appears almost as if haunted by the idea of communicating the unembodied values of touch and movement.* **"**
> **B. Berenson,**
> *The Italian Painters of the Renaissance,* 1896

MYTHICAL FIGURES

Botticelli's *Primavera* is an allegory on the harmony of nature and humankind and contains many mythical figures including Venus (the link between nature and civilization) and Mercury. At the extreme right of the painting, the figure of Zephyr (the west wind of spring) is seen chasing Chloris, who is then transformed into Flora, the goddess of flowers. A blindfolded Cupid shoots his arrows at the Three Graces (the handmaidens of Venus) who were believed to represent the three phases of love: beauty, desire, and fulfillment. This illustration shows a woodcut of Cupid, who was one of the most popular figures in Renaissance art.

THE BIRTH OF VENUS

This secular work was painted onto canvas, which was a less expensive painting surface than the wooden panels used in church and court pictures. A wooden surface would certainly be impractical for a work on such a scale. Canvas is known to have been the preferred material for the paintings of non-religious and pagan subjects that were sometimes commissioned to decorate country villas in 15th-century Italy.

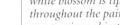

WOODED SHORE

The trees form part of a flowering orange grove – corresponding to the sacred garden of the Hesperides in Greek myth – and each small white blossom is tipped with gold. Gold is used throughout the painting, accentuating its role as a precious object and echoing the divine status of Venus. Each dark green leaf has a gold spine and outline, and the tree trunks are highlighted with short diagonal lines of gold.

THE WEST WIND

Zephyr and Chloris fly with limbs entwined as a twofold entity: the ruddy Zephyr (his name is Greek for "the west wind") is puffing vigorously, while the fair Chloris gently sighs the warm breath that wafts Venus ashore. All around them fall roses – each with a golden heart – which, according to legend, came into being at Venus' birth.

THE SHELL

Botticelli portrays Venus in the very first suggestion of action, with a complex and beautiful series of twists and turns, as she is about to step off her giant gilded scallop shell onto the shore. Venus was conceived when the Titan Cronus castrated his father, the god Uranus – the severed genitals falling into the sea and fertilizing it. Here what we see is actually not Venus' birth out of the waves, but the moment when, having been conveyed by the shell, she lands at Paphos in Cyprus.

NYMPH

The nymph may well be one of the three Horae, or "The Hours", Greek goddesses of the seasons, who were attendants to Venus. Both her lavishly decorated dress and the gorgeous robe she holds out to Venus are embroidered with red and white daisies, yellow primroses, and blue cornflowers – all spring flowers appropriate to the theme of birth. She wears a garland of myrtle – the tree of Venus – and a sash of pink roses, as worn by the goddess Flora in Botticelli's Primavera *(p.94–95).*

110 Sandro Botticelli, **The Birth of Venus,** *c. 1485–86, 175 × 280 cm (5 ft 9 in × 9 ft 2 in)*

but though scholars may argue, we need no theories to make *Primavera (109)* dear to us. In this allegory of life, beauty, and knowledge united by love, Botticelli catches the freshness of an early spring morning, with the pale light shining through the tall, straight trees, already laden with their golden fruit: oranges, or the mythical Golden Apples of the Hesperides?

At the right Zephyr, the warm wind of Spring, embraces the Roman goddess Flora, or perhaps the earth nymph Chloris, diaphanously clad and running from his amorous clasp. She is shown at the moment of her metamorphosis into Flora, as her breath turns to flowers which take root over the countryside. Across from her, we see Flora as a goddess, in all her glory (or perhaps her daughter Persephone, who spends half her time beneath the earth, as befits the patron saint of flowers) as she steps forward clad in blossoms. In the centre is a gentle Venus, all dignity and promise of spiritual joy, and above her, the infant Cupid aims his loving arrows. To the left, the Three Graces dance in a silent reverie of grace, removed from the others in time also, as indicated by the breeze that wafts their hair and clothes in the opposite direction from Zephyr's gusts. Mercury, the messenger of

the gods, provides another male counterpart to the Zephyr. Zephyr initiates, breathing love into the warmth he brings to a wintry world, and Mercury sublimates, taking the hopes of humanity and opening the way to the gods.

Everything in this miraculous work is profoundly life-enhancing. Yet it offers no safeguards against pain or accident: Cupid is blindfolded as he flies, and the Graces seem enclosed in their own private bliss. So the poetry has an underlying wistfulness, a sort of musing nostalgia for something that we cannot possess, yet something with which we feel so deeply in tune. Even the gentle yet strong colours speak of this ambivalence: the figures have an unmistakable presence and weight as they stand before us, moving in the slowest of rhythms. Yet they also seem insubstantial, a dream of what might be rather than a sight of what is.

This longing, this hauntingly intangible sadness is even more visible in the lovely face of Venus as she is wafted to our dark shores by the winds, and the garment, rich though it is, waits ready to cover up her sweet and naked body. We cannot look upon love unclothed, says *The Birth of Venus (110)*; we are too weak, maybe too polluted, to bear the beauty.

LORENZO DE' MEDICI
Succeeding in 1469 as head of the Medici family, Lorenzo *"Il Magnifico"* (the Magnificent) was a courageous, if autocratic, leader. He was a patron of the arts and assisted many artists, including Michelangelo and Leonardo da Vinci. Botticelli had some patronage from Lorenzo, but his chief patron was a cousin of *Il Magnifico* called Lorenzo di Pierfrancesco de' Medici, or "Lorenzino".

111 Sandro Botticelli, The Adoration of the Magi, *c. 1485–86, 175 x 280 cm (5 ft 9 in x 9 ft 2 in)*

THE MAGI

The Gospels speak of wise men from the east coming to Bethlehem, led by a star, when Christ was born. In the 2nd century these wise men (Greek: *magos*) became the subject of popular legends. They were thought to be kings, names were invented for them, and they were depicted as representing the three ages of man (youth, maturity, and old age). One was usually black, personifying Africa. By the 16th century, the Magi had acquired royal retinues, often including the family of the painter's patron.

GIORGIO VASARI

Although a competent painter and architect, Vasari (1511–74) earned lasting fame as an art historian and critic. This illustration shows the frontispiece of his most famous work, known as *The Lives of the Artists.* Published in 1550, the book issued the first real critical appraisal of artists as individuals and gave biographical details about them. Vasari also established the Accademia del Disegno, one of the first academies of art in Europe, which was supported by the great patron Cosimo de' Medici.

Botticelli accepted that paganism, too, was a religion and could bear profoundly philosophical significance. His religious paintings manifest this belief by converging all truths into one.

He seems to have had a personal devotion to the biblical account of *The Adoration of The Magi (111)*, setting it in a ruined classical world. This was not an uncommon Renaissance device, suggesting that the birth of Christ brought fulfilment to the hopes of everyone, completing the achievements of the past.

But no painter felt this with the intensity of Botticelli. We feel that he desperately needed this psychic reassurance, and that the wild graphic power of his *Adoration*'s great circles of activity, coming to rest on the still centre of the Virgin and her Child, made visible his own interior circlings. Even the far green hills sway in sympathy with the clustered humans as if by magnetic attraction around the incarnate Lord.

Botticelli was not the only Florentine to be blessed or afflicted by an intensely anxious temperament. In the 1490s, the city of Florence was overtaken by a political crisis. The Medici government fell, and there followed a four-year period of extremist religious rule under the zealot Savonarola (see column, facing page). Either in response to this, or possibly out of some desire of his own for stylistic experimentation, Botticelli produced a series of rather clumsy-looking religious works – the *San Bernabo Altarpiece* is an example.

THE STRANGE WORLD OF PIERO DI COSIMO

Piero di Cosimo (1462–1521) did not live, like Botticelli, in the enlightened ambience of the Medici court. He was a man who actively required some sort of seclusion so as to conserve his energies and explore his preoccupations. (He even went so far as to live on boiled eggs, we are told, cooking them 50 at a time, so as to be free of the mundane concerns of the mere body.) Yet in *The Visitation with St Nicholas and St Anthony Abbot (112),* he displays a wonderful sense of the body, its weight and presence. When he shows the Virgin Mary, still bewildered by the angelic annunciation of her sacred pregnancy, coming to greet her elderly cousin Elizabeth, also blessed with a miraculous pregnancy, the two women approach each other with a touching reverence.

Each is primarily conscious of the child in her womb, and Elizabeth is about to cry out to tell Mary that the unborn John the Baptist within her has leapt for joy at the nearness of the unborn Jesus. Piero merely shows us the two touching each other with a wondering reverence, yet the profundities are all the more present for being unexpressed.

But, as in all Piero's pictures, there are strange elements here. The women are flanked by two elderly saints: St Nicholas, identifiable by the three golden balls at his feet (the dowry he anonymously threw into the house of an impoverished father of three marriageable daughters, see p.53); and St Anthony Abbot, whose unromantic emblem of a pig rootles happily in the background. To the right, behind Elizabeth, a furious scene, swarming with violence, depicts the massacre of the innocents, and in the shadows behind Mary, we find a quiet and almost insignificant nativity. Do the saints, engrossed in their reading and writing, "see" these things in their minds? What is actually happening and what is imagined?

Piero leaves us with engrossing problems to ponder. "The strangeness of Piero's brain," as Vasari (see column, left) described it, is seen even more in his non-religious paintings like this mysterious *Allegory (113)*, with its mermaid, comical white stallion, and winged maiden, standing on a tiny island and holding the beast by a thread. We look with delight, but never find an answer. Piero's interest in animals and the exotic is revealed in many of his paintings. He included a snake in his *Portrait of Simonetta Vespucci*, a satyr and a dog in *Mythological Scene*, and various animals in his *Hunting Scene*.

113 Piero di Cosimo, Allegory, c. 1500, 56 x 44 cm (22 x 17⅓ in)

SAVONAROLA
This medallion of the Dominican friar, reformer, and martyr Girolamo Savonarola (1452–98) was made by Ambrogio della Robbia. As prior of San Marco, Savonarola strongly criticized the Medici government. Then, in 1494, Piero de' Medici's regime was overthrown and Savonarola became the effective leader of Florence. He set up a popular government, based on a council of 3,200 citizens, which aimed to enforce religious observance in all aspects of daily life. Unfortunately, in the years that followed, the city was afflicted by famine, plague, and war, which so reduced his popularity that he was asked to leave. He was declared a heretic, and in 1498 he was hanged and his body burned.

112 Piero di Cosimo, The Visitation with St Nicholas and St Anthony Abbot, c. 1490, 184 x 189 cm (6 ft ½ in x 6 ft 2 in)

MAJOLICA WARE
A type of tin-glazed earthenware known as majolica ware (or maiolica ware) was popular in Italy during the Renaissance. The name is derived from Majorca, the island off Spain through which the pottery was originally imported from North Africa and the Near East. This example is by Nicola da Urbino, one of the finest Majolica painters.

THE DUKE OF URBINO

One of Piero della Francesca's patrons was the first Duke of Urbino, Federigo da Montefeltro, whose portrait he painted (above). The Duke led several armies during the territorial battles of the 15th century, but was also a renowned scholar. His palace at Urbino was one of the important small courts of Italy and contained his extensive library.

THE MISERICORDIA

The Compagnia della Misericordia was founded in Florence in the 13th century to carry out missions of mercy, such as transporting the sick to hospital, and the dead to burial. In 1445, the organization commissioned Piero della Francesca to paint an altarpiece for Borgo Sansepolcro. The central figure in the work is the Madonna of Mercy, who was patroness of the Misericordia. The organization is still in operation today.

PIERO DELLA FRANCESCA'S SOLEMN GENIUS

The "other" Piero is far better known, and with justice. It can come as a shock to learn that the present admiration for Piero della Francesca (c. 1410/20–92) is of comparatively recent origin. His intensely still and silent art went out of fashion not long after his death, and its sublime restraint of expression was seen as inadequacy. Yet Piero della Francesca is one of the truly great masters of all time. He was born in the small town of Borgo Sansepolcro in Umbria, central Italy. In Piero's wide vision we can see the lovely defining light and sculptural form of Masaccio (see p.82) and Donatello (see p.83), brilliant clarity of colour, together with a new interest in "real" landscape, that was influenced by his master Domenico Veneziano (see p.86) and by Flemish artists. When his eyes dimmed in later life, Piero turned increasingly to his other abiding interest, mathematics, and as a branch of mathematics, perspective (see p.88). He was also a theorist, and, like Alberti (see p.88), wrote two treatises on the mathematics of art.

RELIGIOUS LANDSCAPES

The Baptism of Christ (114) takes place in an eternal dimension, even though those little streams and terraced hills are purely Umbrian. Piero's admiration of ancient art, which he studied in Rome around 1450, is manifested in the dignity and classical form of Christ, and of St John and the angels. The tall and slender column of manhood that is Jesus, Son of the Most High, is paired with the tall and slender column of the tree. The tree in turn is aligned with the majestic figures of the waiting angels. John the Baptist is another vertical, a slightly inclining one, solemnly performing his sacramental baptism with water from the river that, as told in legend, has stopped flowing at Christ's feet. A disrobing penitent, leaning forwards, both continues and varies the vertical theme. A group of theologians debates, clothes brightly reflected in the stilled water.

The invisible element, the Holy Spirit, is all-pervading, as a pure, crystalline early morning light, and in material form as a dove hovering horizontally with outspread wings, sanctifying the baptism with golden rays (only barely visible now), that shine down over Christ's head. The dove is the only presence in the baptismal group that could be reflected in the limpidity of the waters, but is not; it is unseen by all eyes but our own. There is such poetry in the sunlight and the high sky, the flowers, and the simple brightness of the garments, that it is impossible not to believe, as Piero does, that we who contemplate the scene are literally blessed.

114 Piero della Francesca, The Baptism of Christ, *1450s, 168 x 117 cm (66 x 46 in)*

Even a detail like the great over arching mass of foliage in the trees overhead seems to be weighted with holy significance. But Piero never presses home any symbolism, he never intrudes to put forward an interpretation. It has been remarked that everything in this picture is mathematically calculated to give the maximum impact, and one can even draw diagrams to show the underlying intelligence behind the structure. But our response comes immediately, affected unconsciously by this intelligence. Piero has that rare gift: he is effective – his pictures work; and he affects – we are moved by them.

THE BAPTISM OF CHRIST

This was originally the central panel of a large triptych. The rest of this triptych was painted by Matteo di Giovanni in about 1464. Piero's natural, almost casual depiction of this solemn ritual belies the work's sophisticated composition, and though its structure can be reduced to strict mathematical proportions, it is one of Piero's least mathematically controlled paintings.

ANGELS

The compact trio of angels is divided from the mortal world by the tree. They stand together with a charming degagé air, holding hands, their large and lovely flat feet planted solidly on the grassy meadow. The angels are witnessing Christ's baptism and affirm its importance with serene certainty. Piero shows us only a glimpse of the wing of the far angel, in which a few flecks of gold are still visible, and the landscape visible beneath.

CHRIST

The ritual anointing is performed in the deep, silent absorption of prayer, signified by the quiet concentration of John and Jesus. Christ's body has the whiteness of a bleached shell, His outer cleanliness echoing His symbolic purification through baptism – presided over by the Holy Spirit in the form of a white dove. A kind of spiritual force field separates John from Christ. He moves towards Christ, yet his free hand does not enter the unbroken divide between them.

BENDING FIGURE

The half-naked figure standing at the river's edge in the middle distance is stripping off his clothes in readiness for his own baptism. His nakedness is symbolic of his humility before the Almighty, and contrasts sharply with the extravagant and even kingly headgear and costume of the high priests, who stand farthest away and are given the smallest stature in Piero's hierarchy. The identity of the penitent is hidden – a temporary concealment hinting at the new life he will enter into after baptism. His body – like Christ's – is bathed in a brilliant white light.

DISTANT TOWN

Piero shows us the small town of Borgo Sansepolcro, with its fortified towers appearing piteously small and insignificant in the distance. Piero's treatment of the distinctly Umbrian landscape immediately distinguishes him from his contemporaries and displays an unprecedented naturalism. It reveals the extent to which Piero was influenced by Netherlandish art.

THE LEGEND OF THE TRUE CROSS

Several early Italian Renaissance frescoes depict the medieval legend that traces the history of the Cross from its beginnings as a branch of the Tree of Knowledge in the Garden of Eden until its recovery by the Emperor Heraclius in the 7th century. In Piero's version (see right), King Solomon orders the branch to be used in the building of his palace. However, because the branch is too large, it is used instead as a bridge across a stream. When the Queen of Sheba comes to visit Solomon, she worships the wood and then explains how she has had a vision that the wood will one day be used as the Cross for Christ's Crucifixion.

THE BAPTISTERY DOORS

In 1401, a competition was launched to produce a set of panels for the east doors of the Baptistery, a building next to the cathedral in Florence. Seven sculptors, including Brunelleschi (see column, p.82), were chosen to compete, using the Sacrifice of Isaac as a theme. The winner was Lorenzo Ghiberti (1378–1455). The subject was changed to the Life of Christ. This took Ghiberti 20 years to complete, and was finally installed on the north doors. Ghiberti then began the work that was actually installed on the east doors. These ten bronze panels, which include the one shown above, were called the "gates of Paradise" by Michelangelo.

PIERO'S MASTERPIECES

Although Piero has a claim to being the perfect painter, every one of whose paintings are wonderfully good, his greatest work is the fresco that makes magnificent the church of St Francis in the town of Arezzo, near Piero's birthplace. *The Story of the True Cross (115)* runs around the walls, telling all aspects of the legend, from the supposed beginning of the Cross as a

116 Piero della Francesca, **Resurrection of Christ,** *early 1450s, 225 x 205 cm (7 ft 5 in x 6 ft 9 in)*

tree growing in Paradise, up to the miraculous Finding of the Cross by St Helena, the mother of Constantine the Great. The story is legend from start to finish, yet Piero treats it with such reverent solidity that archetypal truths are revealed. When the Queen of Sheba, proceeding in stately fashion toward her encounter with Solomon, "adores the wood of the Cross", the quiet passion of that bending neck tells us of the meaning of adoration, and its loveliness.

Although she and her maidens are cut from the same cloth pictorially (tall, willowy, swan-necked beauties) it is only the queen who understands the challenge of the holy and prostrates her regal self. Behind her the pages gossip, beside her the maids of honour look interestedly on. She alone has understood the full dimensions of the finding. As ever in Piero, there is an air of silence so profound as to halt all movement in its tracks, and immortalize the scene that is depicted.

Another work, the *Resurrection of Christ (116),* has actually been described as the greatest picture ever painted (its only rival for this honour being Velázquez's *Las Meninas,* see p.194). The two masterpieces are utterly different, Piero's having a unique sublimity. Its gravely heroic Christ, impassive and heraldic, enters life as a sombrely compassionate Conqueror, lifting the sleeping world up onto a new plane of being. It was painted for the town hall of Borgo Sansepolcro – Italian for "the Holy Sepulchre."

examples of work by Donatello (see pp.83, 105). Many of Mantegna's paintings take on the appearance of a pictorial bas-relief akin to Donatello's and Ghiberti's sculpted panels (see p.102), and these works subsequently influenced High Renaissance painting, notably that of Raphael (see p.125).

For some, this sculptural bias has made Mantegna's art seem bloodless. It is severe, monumental, thought out from within. But it can strike us as all the more impressively emotional for that very need, experienced so intensely, to protect himself from the vulnerability of self-exposure. The task is impossible, since every major artist can only create from his own heart, and the attempt to conceal is as revealing as the desire to expose. Mantegna had left Padua to be court artist at Mantua when he painted *The Death of the Virgin (117)*, a great tableau where emotion is frozen into a sort of icy

115 Piero della Francesca, The Story of the True Cross, c. 1452–57, 335 × 747 cm (11 ft × 24 ft 6 in)

SOLIDITY IN MANTEGNA'S ART

There is something of Piero's silent massiveness in Andrea Mantegna (1431–1506), the first great artist from northern Italy. He belongs to the Florentine tradition in that his art showed the expressly Florentine concerns with scientific debate and classical aspiration, but as the leading artist of northern Italy he belonged also to that of nearby Venice. He is first heard of as a young man in Padua, struggling, by means of a lawsuit, to free himself from his teacher and adoptive father, Francesco Squarcione.

A sort of lonely freedom is basic to Mantegna's temperament, as we understand it, and there is something rather appropriate in his dual attempt to gain his legal independence and to plot with fierce intellectual clarity the frescoes on the walls of the Eremitani chapel. Although nearly all this work was destroyed or damaged during World War II, enough remains to indicate the almost awesome originality of his painterly approach.

The irony is that Mantegna would have claimed not originality, but a rigorous conservatism, and his art is a rejection of the more relaxed, painterly styles that were emerging in Venetian art. He may have benefitted from the teaching of Squarcione, who did at least possess an unrivaled set of antique drawings, but the sculptural quality of Mantegna's art makes it far more likely that he was influenced by local

117 Andrea Mantegna, The Death of the Virgin, c.1460, 54 × 42 cm (21¼ × 16½ in)

passion. The Apostles gathered around the bier are heavy with minutely observed grief. The Virgin is revealed with direct, personal simplicity in the humiliation of death. The drama is framed and given its context by the vast Mantuan landscape, which gleams in remote perfection behind the window. The waters lie still, the ramparts offer the pretence of human inviolability, and the serene sun bathes lakes, palaces, priests, and the dead Virgin in the same quiet light.

PERSPECTIVE SKILLS

This fresco was painted on a ceiling of the Gonzaga Palace in Mantua by Mantegna in 1465–74. In creating the illusion of an opening to the sky, the artist makes humorous use of Albertian perspective (see p.89), especially in the foreshortening of the winged figures.

OTHER WORKS BY PIERO DELLA FRANCESCA

Madonna of Mercy (Borgo Sansepolcro)

Federigo da Montefeltro (Uffizi, Florence)

The Nativity (National Gallery, London)

St Jerome in the Desert (Staatliche Museen, Berlin-Dahlem)

SINOPIA

This was a technique of using red ochre to draw initial guides for fresco painting. Each day, a section of the sinopia was plastered over and painted. The 1966 flood in Florence damaged a number of Renaissance frescoes. As part of the restoration work, some were removed from the walls on which they were created, thereby exposing the sinopia. This provided insight into the artists' working practices and showed that they often introduced changes between the drawing of the original guides and the final representations.

118 Andrea Mantegna, **Portrait of a Man,** *probably c. 1460, 24 x 19 cm (9½ x 7½ in)*

people's oppressor. Her expression is remote and impassive, and we perceive her extreme detachment of will in the way she averts her head, refusing to confront emotionally the reality of what she has done, as she passes the head to her shrinking attendant. She has resolutely turned her back on the pathos of Holofernes's dead foot, which rises up behind her like an accusing ghost. On one level, the painting is all calmness and immobility; on another, there is a revulsion of spirit so violent that there has to be a total psychological distancing.

This wonderful paradox, Mantegna's special gift, is fortuitously duplicated for us, for he painted another version *(119)*, in sombre richness of colour. The stony non-colour of the tent and the figures contained within its shade changes to a harmony of radiant pinks, oranges, ochres, and blue-greens. One work, in Washington *(120)*, emphasizes the distancing; the other, in Dublin *(119)*, the intensity. Both have a still and stately beauty that is unforgettable.

THE GONZAGA FAMILY
The Gonzaga court at Mantua was an important centre for the arts. Ludovico Gonzaga was a generous patron who had travelled to the Medici court, to gain ideas about leadership. This inspired him to undertake a plan of urban renewal, commissioning Alberti (see column, p.88) to build several churches. Another artist to benefit from Gonzaga patronage was Mantegna. The illustration above is a detail from a family portrait of the Gonzagas that he completed in 1474.

PORTRAITS OF THE GONZAGAS

Mantegna was commissioned to paint portraits of members of the influential Gonzaga family in Mantua. Even in these intimate pictures, which are unique for their historical immediacy, he always contrives to show us both the actual, which we can recognize, and the hidden ideal, which we can revere.

This is apparent even in this small-scale work, the *Portrait of a Man (118)*, where the unknown sitter is strongly individual and yet recalls to us the moral imperatives of duty and courage.

MANTEGNA'S GRISAILLE

In his love for the solid reality of sculpture, Mantegna went so far as to perfect a form of grisaille (monochrome painting that imitates the effect and colour of stone relief). The texture resembles stone, yet in his hands it was fully alive. He might have chiselled out the dramatic panel of *Judith and Holofernes (119)*, where the Junoesque heroine stands impassively before the rigid folds of the tent in which she has murdered her

119 Andrea Mantegna, **Judith and Holofernes,** *1495–1500, 48 x 37 cm (19 x 14½ in)*

120 Andrea Mantegna, Judith and Holofernes, c. 1495, 30 × 18 cm (12 × 7 in)

DONATELLO'S JUDITH

As a close personal friend of Cosimo de' Medici, Donatello was given the artistic freedom to produce this highly controversial sculpture of Judith slaying Holofernes in 1456. The Jewish heroine who murdered the Philistine (Assyrian) general Holofernes to protect her people was meant to symbolize humility overcoming pride, but the bronze was considered too disturbing by many Florentines, who petitioned successfully for its removal from the Piazza della Signoria.

OTHER WORKS BY MANTEGNA

Crucifixion
(Louvre, Paris)

St Sebastian
(Kunsthistorisches Museum, Vienna)

Dead Christ
(Brera Gallery, Milan)

Virgin and Child with the Magdalen and St John the Baptist
(National Gallery, London)

Dido
(Montreal Museum of Fine Arts)

The Dead Christ with Two Angels
(Statens Museum for Kunst, Copenhagen)

RENAISSANCE VENICE

Painting that was produced in Renaissance Venice belonged to the northern Italian tradition and had an identity and genealogy all its own. While Venetian artists also explored problems of perspective and mathematics, and were unavoidably influenced by the fertile art of Medician Florence – the heartland of the Renaissance – there emerged in Venice a new, essentially "painterly" tradition. Venetian painting showed less concern with sculptural form and hard-edged delineation, placing more emphasis on colour and nuances of light. From the beginning, it contained a peculiarly gentle lyricism, quite distinct from the Florentine tradition.

The artist great enough to lead painting into its next phase, and in doing so, greatly influence the course of Western painting since, was Giovanni Bellini (c. 1427–1516). He belonged to a family of artists, composed of his father Jacopo (c. 1400–70/71) and his brother Gentile (c. 1429–1507). The two brothers were taught by their father (who had been a pupil of Gentile da Fabriano, see p.56) in accordance with the artistic tradition in Venice, in which skills were passed down through generations. The two generations of Bellinis became the most influential group of artists in northern Italy; and just as the early Renaissance

is bound up with 15th-century Florentine culture, the Bellinis were responsible for the distinctly Venetian heritage of the High Renaissance of the late 15th to early 16th centuries.

INFLUENCE OF MANTEGNA

Although Mantegna (see p.103) stands alone, he had, in fact, a close and fruitful relationship with the Bellini family of Venice. (He was even a literal relation, in that he married Nicolosia, sister to Giovanni and Gentile. She does not seem to have softened him much – he remained litigious and over-sensitive to the end.) But the hard beauty of

121 Andrea Mantegna, **The Agony in the Garden,** *c. 1460, 63 x 81 cm (25 x 32 in)*

Mantegna's own work certainly affected that of his brothers-in-law. Giovanni Bellini is one of the supreme painters of all the ages, able to accept the spare majesty of Mantegna and yet transform it into his own subtle sweetness. Sometimes we can actually watch influences being absorbed.

Both painters, coincidentally, have a version of *The Agony in the Garden* in the National Gallery, London. Mantegna's *(121)* is thought to have been painted about five years before Bellini's, and the younger artist, Bellini, always regarded his own work as lesser in quality. Yet the contest is very close; both paintings have a gaunt and rocky landscape setting, appropriate for the austerity of the drama. Both excel in figural perspective, showing the sleeping Apostles in abrupt foreshortening. Both have the praying Christ half turned away, isolated on His jut of stone, bare feet vulnerable in His absorption upon His Father and His fate. In both paintings we see in the distance the approaching figures of the soldiers coming to arrest Jesus, led by the betraying disciple Judas.

But the two works are subtly different. It is not just that Mantegna is far more interested in the actual geophysical structure of the rocks, but that Bellini's world *(122)* is less aggressive, less confrontational. It may only be a question of degree, yet it modifies the feeling of the picture, makes it more tender, more visually ambiguous. It is here that Bellini's greatest gift is displayed, his sense of light in all its specificity.

It is sacred "time" in Mantegna, the "hour" of which Jesus spoke, removed from the mundane time of the normal day. Mantegna's sky, like his frozen and brooding city, is eternal. But Bellini shows us a real city faintly glimmering into visibility beneath the gentle skies of early morning. Light is beginning to flood with its warmth the cold night where Jesus has laboured in painful prayer, and the Angel of Consolation, solid in Mantegna, floats solitary and ethereal in Bellini, a dawn apparition that will dissolve into cloud.

The mature Bellini understood light with mystical fervour. It had a sacred significance for him, one that he could share with us without ever lapsing into the explicit. Bellini is an extraordinary artist, a man sensitive to beauty, aware of the significance of form, and inspired by a passionate love, both of the visible and the invisible, that makes his work moving on every level. There is no Bellini painting that we cannot respond to with joy and a deeper understanding of what our existence is all about.

BELLINI FAMILY

The Bellinis formed one of the most prominent and successful families of Renaissance painters. Father Jacopo's silverpoint sketchbook was the inspiration for many of Giovanni's paintings, which in turn inspired the young Giorgione and Titian. It featured mythological characters (such as Perseus with the head of the Gorgon, shown here), as well as classical, biblical, and imaginative subjects.

122 *Giovanni Bellini*, The Agony in the Garden, *c. 1460, 81 x 127 cm (32 x 50 in)*

123 Giovanni Bellini, **The Madonna of the Meadow**, *c. 1500–05, 67 x 86 cm (26½ x 34 in)*

ST JEROME

This detail from *St Jerome* by Ghirlandaio (see p.121) shows equipment used to copy ancient texts. Jerome was a popular figure in Renaissance art as he symbolized the ideal of the Humanist scholar. His great achievement was to translate the Bible into Latin.

The Madonna of the Meadow (123) may appear to be a typical Madonna, albeit a very enchanting one. But it is, in its understated manner, almost a revolutionary painting. Scholars have always pitted Florence against Venice, ever since Vasari, the great early art historian (see p.98), quoted his hero, Michelangelo, as lauding form above colour, and deploring the Venetian concentration on the latter. In this sense, Giovanni Bellini is the "first" Venetian painter.

He initiates in us the awareness of a magical, enveloping brightness, a palpable light in which all colours shine at their loveliest. In this colour-world, there is no longer man and woman in the midst of nature, but humanity as part of nature, another expression of its truth. The very texture of the harsh soil, the low lattices, the defended well, all have an undemonstrative integrity that has some mysterious, inexplicable connection with the strong pyramid of Mother and Child at the centre of the picture.

Madonnas are a common idiom in Renaissance painting. There was hardly an artist who did not attempt this great theme. We can understand why. The wonderful thing about the Madonna and Child theme is that it appeals both to the specifics of Christianity (where the humanity of Christ is a central mystery) and to the human values on which all religion is based, throughout the world.

Every painter had a mother. Every psyche has been affected by this fact. To explore this fundamental of human existence had an irresistible fascination for the artist. No-one has ever been more sensitive to this fundamental subject than Bellini. Every one of his Madonnas has an aesthetic and a spiritual force that makes them all memorable. He understands, at an elemental level, the meaning of motherhood and childhood, and this is the basis of the conviction that we see behind his Madonnas. This is only a sample, but an excellent one.

MADONNA OF THE MEADOW

Bellini was famed for his paintings of the Madonna and Child. From his 65-year-long career, no fewer than 14 of the major works that survive are on this, his favourite theme. It is one of the most ancient of all religious subjects, yet Bellini was able to invigorate what had become a formula, an icon, with a fully convincing depiction of both the sacred and the human.

HARBINGER OF DEATH

A large raven broods heavily over the meadows: a reminder of the ever-present figure of death. Death, however, assumes a small scale in comparison to the monumental serenity of the Madonna and Child, who affirm life after death. The bird perches high up in the small, thin, leafless trees that sway imperceptibly against the luminous pallor of the sky. Though its role is symbolic, the bird is integrated into the natural order of life.

VENETIAN LANDSCAPE

On the right, divided from death by the towering figure of Mary, are the sober activities of life. Despite the gloomy presence of death, the daily life of the natural world goes calmly on. A farmer tends to the livestock in the field. Above them, an insubstantial line of cloud drifts slowly over the softly gleaming ramparts of the little city, whose concerns of government and commerce are rightly distanced from the great theme of life and death that Bellini dwells upon. And this is no walled garden, with cherubim and angels floating amid exotic flowers and cultivated hedgerows, but the real, solid world – Bellini's world – in the province of Venice.

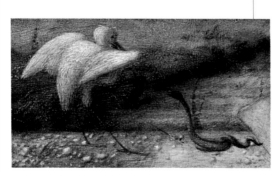

MORTAL STRUGGLE

Easy to miss in the middle distance, and on the side of death, is a little egret fighting with a snake. Wings raised in a threatening gesture, the egret circles the snake. This combat symbolizes the fight between good and evil. It may also refer to Christ's struggle before His sacrifice, and the reason for His sacrifice – the serpent's entry into the Garden of Eden. (It is interesting to note that there is a pair of egrets in the foreground of Mantegna's Agony in the Garden, see p.106.)

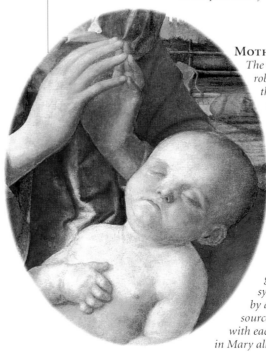

MOTHER AND CHILD

The blue and russet of Mary's robes are intensifications of the material world that surrounds her: earth and sky. She sits on bare earth, not as a queen enthroned in majesty (think of Duccio's Maestà, p.42), but as the Madonna of Humility, a 14th-century tradition. Though her robes form a pyramid and her scale is monumental, her humility appears real, and no mere pictorial convention. This is Bellini's greatness; the uniting of the symbolic and the real, united by a common and natural light source, in chromatic harmony with each other, so that we believe in Mary all the more implicitly.

MUSIC IN THE RENAISSANCE

This painting by Lorenzo Costa, dating from c. 1500, shows a lute player and singers performing a *frottola*; a simple song for one or a group of voices with an instrumental accompaniment. During the 16th century it became the prevailing form of refined music. The *frottola* later developed into the madrigal.

OTHER WORKS BY BELLINI

Pietà
(Brera Gallery, Milan)

St Francis in Ecstasy
(The Frick Collection, New York)

Virgin and Child Between St John the Baptist and St Catherine
(Accademia, Venice)

The Doge Leonardo Loredan
(National Gallery, London)

Virgin and Child
(Museum of Art, New Orleans)

124 Giovanni Bellini, St Jerome Reading, c. 1480/90, 49 x 39 cm (19½ x 15½ in)

There is this same magical involvement in his *St Jerome Reading (124)* where the centre of attention is not the noble saint, still less his attendant lion comfortably snuggled at his back, but the wonderful white hare, nibbling at the leaves with the same disinterested attitude as the saint brings to his mental fodder, his book. St Jerome, that renowned scholar, is oblivious, but the little animal is bright in the wintry sunlight, and makes us aware of the beauty of the created world, with its rocks, leaves, lagoons, and stones.

A splendid Bellini, *The Feast of the Gods (125)*, was modified into even greater splendour by no less an artist than Titian (see p.131). It is still quintessentially Bellini: all the gods are characterized and something of their legends and relationships given pictorial form, all in a golden light of high classical dignity. Another sign of his greatness as an artist is that having led the way for Giorgione and Titian (who heralded an entirely new phase of painting), the aging Bellini allowed himself to be led by the younger artists and, adapting his own style, produced masterpieces even in his eighties.

125 Giovanni Bellini, The Feast of the Gods, 1514, 170 x 188 cm (5 ft 7 in x 6 ft 2 in)

Oil paint and the flemish influence in Venice

If Bellini eventually outgrew Mantegna's influence, there were other, perhaps lesser artists, who were guided by it on their way to achieving their own summits, and to remaining there.

The Sicilian artist Antonello da Messina (c. 1430–79) is a rather perplexing figure, mainly because Vasari falsely credited him with the sole popularization in Italy of van Eyck's use of oil (see p.64). Antonello is the first important artist from southern Italy, but he did not belong to any Southern school; instead he found his influences abroad, in Flemish art.

Because the influence of Flemish art is strikingly visible in his paintings, Antonello provides an important bridge between Italy and the Netherlands. His visit to Venice in 1475, where he came into close contact with Giovanni Bellini, was to play a major role in the history of Venetian painting.

Some people, then, consider that Antonello introduced oil painting techniques, after they had already been mastered by the Flemish artists, to Venice. Others take the view that he had a sophisticated knowledge of the medium, having learned it in Naples, where he probably studied under a Flemish-influenced artist, and that this made the crucial impact on artists who were already experimenting with oil paints. The argument is not a terribly important one. Whatever the case, the result of this meeting of

126 *Antonello da Messina,* Portrait of a Young Man, *c. 1465, 35 x 25 cm (14 x 10 in)*

127 *Antonello da Messina,* Virgin Annunciate, *c. 1465, 45 x 34 cm (17¾ x 13½ in)*

the traditions was that, in Italy, oil painting techniques were pioneered exclusively by Venetian artists before they spread to other artistic centres. Antonello himself needs no spurious claims to attention. From the example of Piero della Francesca (see p.100), and especially Mantegna, he learned the importance of solid truth-telling. His forms are almost too clear and sharp; in them we see a "Flemish" intense scrutiny of detail contrasted with an Italian broad generosity of form. He bathes his forms in the most romantic of lights.

His *Portrait of a Young Man (126)* is lit from within, despite the unexceptional and pudgy face, and in a great work like the *Virgin Annunciate (127),* there is a concentrated simplicity that makes the Virgin affect us with immense impact. Interestingly, the artist presents the Virgin as a devotional portrait, rather than showing the Annunciation itself.

Modern anatomy

In 1543 the Flemish professor Andrea Vesalio (1514–64) wrote his *De Humani Corporis Fabrica* which became the first standard work of modern anatomy. It has been suggested that the drawings in the book were produced in Titian's studio in Venice.

FASCINATION WITH EXTERNALS

Carlo Crivelli (1430/5–c. 1495) also belongs to a Venetian artistic family. Like Antonello da Messina, he, too, has a clear cut manner that is unmistakable, influenced by Mantegna but applying the fine wire of his outline in an almost mannered style. "Fashion" is the word that springs to mind.

Crivelli's art reveals an ardent interest in externals and their lucid perfections – perhaps also partly owing to the Flemish influence of Antonello – but never in the actual spiritual substances involved (surprisingly, since he painted only religious subjects).

It is rather in material substance that Crivelli excels, enthralling us with the rotundity of a pear or the angular swirl of a damask skirt, winning us over to share his delight in gorgeous things. When he attempts an emotional theme we may feel embarassed, but on his own level, he is superb. His *Madonna and Child Enthroned, with Donor (128)* soars aloft with such elegance

128 Carlo Crivelli, Madonna and Child Enthroned, with Donor, c. 1470, 130 x 55 cm (51 x 21½ in)

and wit (note the dragon-like arms of the throne: brutality subdued to the service of religion) that we may miss the tiny, kneeling donor. He is tacked onto the real interest of the artist, which is not holiness and people praying, but shapes and their self-assured interplay.

Cima da Conegliano (Giovanni Battista Cima, c. 1459/60–1517/18) lived all his life in the environs of Venice, in the small provincial town of Conegliano (from which his name is derived). The strongest influence on him was that of Mantegna, though from early in his career he was also influenced by Giovanni Bellini. Cima is not a great painter, and his work developed very little throughout his artistic life, but he has a spontaneous innocence, a sense of the fitting,

129 Cima da Conegliano, St Helena, c. 1495, 40 x 32.5 cm (16 x 12¾ in)

and a technical amplitude as well, that make his work very appealing. *St Helena (129)* is a fine example of his work. She is tall and stately, with her slender Cross on one side and a slender living tree on the other, and dominates the green hills before which she appears. The hills are crowned by little cities where, we sense, her discovery of the True Cross (see column, p.102), however apocryphal, has changed the lives of the citizens. It is not by accident that she looms so large. Her stature is built into the picture's meaning as much as are her queenly bearing and her severe self-possession.

130 *Cosimo Tura,* **Madonna and Child in a Garden,** *c. 1455, 53 x 37 cm (21 x 14½ in)*

THE FERRARESE SCHOOL

Tura and Cossa, artists in the independent city state of Ferrara (see column, p.115), were also admiring contemporaries of Mantegna. Cosimo Tura (c. 1430–95) is perhaps the greater of the two, with his highly original and easily recogniz- able blending of the suave and the exciting. Like Crivelli, he rarely goes deep, but he gives us a superbly integrated surface, with a similar metallic wiriness and hard-edged control. There is wit and a tenderness in *Madonna and Child in a Garden (130)*, exquisite in its form and its daring chromatic contrasts. The Virgin steeples her long, thin fingers over the sleeping child, as if to make a refuge for him, and the rosy blooms that cluster behind her, like a cushioned

throne, make us conscious that both these tender creatures of God are in need of cushioning: there are dark gleams from the night background, caused only by light catching on fruit and leaf, but the effect is subtly sinister.

Francesco del Cossa (c. 1435–c. 1477) has humanized this insouciant austerity. Though Cossa was Ferrarese, his *St Lucy (131)* belongs to the Florentine tradition, infused with the hard-edged contours of Mantegna and tinged with the peculiar metallic quality of his contemporary, Tura – though the effect is a softer one, largely due to its being painted in the more gently luminous medium of oil paint.

Cossa's St Lucy is so monumental, so luminously afloat in her golden air, it takes us time to realize her spray is not composed of flowers, but two stalked eyes. The original Lucy was wrongly credited with being martyred by having her eyes torn out (see column, right), and this grisly emblem always accompanies her depiction.

ST LUCY

This early Christian, Italian martyr captured the imagination of several Renaissance artists. She is said to have survived many tortures, including burning, having her teeth pulled and her breasts cut off, before being killed by a dagger through the throat.

A legend grew that she died from having her eyes pulled out, but this was a misinter- pretation of her symbol of the eyes. The symbol in fact derived from her name, meaning "light".

131 *Francesco del Cossa,* **St Lucy,** *after 1470, 79 x 56 cm (31 x 22 in)*

CASSONI

The workshops of Renaissance painters were busy for much of the time in the production of objects other than paintings and altarpieces, such as plates, chests (*cassoni*), beds, and coats of arms. *Cassoni* were carved, inlaid, painted chests for storing linen, clothes, and household items. Brides often used them to keep their trousseaux and many *cassoni* were decorated with narrative paintings and family coats of arms.

THE FLIGHT INTO EGYPT

After being warned in a dream that Herod was seeking to kill the infant Jesus, Joseph took Mary and the Child away to Egypt until after Herod's death. The story of their journey to Egypt was a popular theme in Renaissance art and often contained guardian angels and a dramatic evening landscape.

The last of the great Ferrarese artists, Ercole de' Roberti, maintained the Mantegna–Tura–Cossa sobriety and classic formality. *The Wife of Hasdrubal and Her Children (132)* may be an unusual subject (see column, left), but we respond immediately to the solidity of these three human creatures, anguished, in frantic motion, yet still with a semi-sculptural stillness.

CARPACCIO: THE STORY-TELLER

Vittore Carpaccio (1455/65–1525/26), though essentially Venetian, was clearly influenced by the great artists of the Ferrarese school, and also by Giovanni Bellini's brother, Gentile. Carpaccio had probably been taught by the Bellini patriarch, Jacopo, and was an assistant to Giovanni. The element that is peculiarly his own is that of story-telling, of which he had an instinctive mastery. The delicacy of detail in his work may suggest a medieval naïveté, yet he is a highly sophisticated painter who can use narrative simplicities as a pleasurable means to his ends.

Carpaccio can rise above the picturesque. *The Flight into Egypt (133)* may not present us with wholly serious actors: Mary is most sumptuously clad and has obviously used some of her rose-red silks to fashion a tunic for St Joseph. But all lightheartedness is forgotten in the glory of the setting. In a sunset sky of striking verisimilitude we see why Carpaccio gives us the impression of being, despite all, a major artist. The light bathes an ordinary lakeside town and its surroundings – unimpressive, undramatic, and yet completely satisfying and convincing. There can be a delib-

132 Ercole de' Roberti, The Wife of Hasdrubal and Her Children, *c. 1480/90, 47 × 30.5 cm (18½ × 12 in)*

133 Vittore Carpaccio, The Flight into Egypt, *c. 1500, 72 × 112 cm (28¼ × 44 in)*

134 Vittore Carpaccio, **The Dream of St Ursula,** *1494, 275 x 265 cm (9 ft x 8 ft 8 in)*

erately Gothic charm in Carpaccio's legend cycles, as in the wholly delightful *Dream of St Ursula (134)*. This is one of a series of paintings Carpaccio produced for the confraternity of St Ursula. She was a legendary Breton princess who led a pilgrimage to Rome with 11,000 virgins who had converted to Christianity. The story ends with the massacre of the entire company by villainous Huns (see column, p.70). The neat little bed, and the sleeping saint have

an enamelled charm that will happily survive her coming martyrdom, signified by the entering angel bearing the symbolic palm. Carpaccio's meticulous recording of the material world has provided historians with insight into the material reality of 15th-century Venice. This faithful representation of the visible world, composed of many tiny parts, reappears in the work of another Venetian artist in the 18th century, Canaletto (see p.234).

(see column, p.70)
(see p.234)

FERRARA

During the Renaissance Ferrara became a lively centre for the arts and the court of the Este family encouraged individual artists from throughout Italy. Many impressive secular buildings were built in the city during the 15th century including the Palazzo dei Diamanti.

THE HIGH RENAISSANCE

Since Renaissance means "new birth", it is obvious that it cannot stand still. Once something is born, it begins to grow. But never has there been growth as lovely as that of painting as it matured into the High Renaissance. Here we find some of the greatest artists ever known: the mighty Florentines, Leonardo da Vinci and Michelangelo; the Umbrian, Raphael; and, equal in might, the Venetians – Titian, Tintoretto, and Veronese.

By a happy chance, a common theme links the lives of four of the famous masters of the High Renaissance – Leonardo, Michelangelo, Raphael, and Titian. Each began his artistic career with an apprenticeship to a painter who was already of good standing, and each took the same path of first accepting, then transcending, the influence of his first master. The first of these, Leonardo

135 Andrea del Verrocchio, **The Baptism of Christ,** *c. 1470, 180 x 152 cm (5 ft 11 in x 5 ft)*

mathematical excellence, scientific daring ... the list is endless. This overabundance of talents caused him to treat his artistry lightly, seldom finishing a picture, and sometimes making rash technical experiments. *The Last Supper*, in the church of Santa Maria delle Grazie in Milan, for example, has almost vanished, so inadequate were his innovations in fresco preparation.

Yet the works that we have salvaged remain the most dazzlingly poetic pictures ever created. The *Mona Lisa (136)* has the innocent disavantage of being too famous. It can only be seen behind thick glass in a heaving crowd of awe-struck sightseers. It has been reproduced in every conceivable medium: it remains intact in its magic, for ever defying the human insistence on comprehending. It is a work that we can only gaze at in silence.

Leonardo's three great portraits of women all have a secret wistfulness. This quality is at its most appealing in *Cecilia Gallarani (137)*, at its most enigmatic in the *Mona Lisa*, and at its most

> *"The first object of the painter is to make a flat plane appear as a body in relief and projecting from that plane."*
>
> Leonardo da Vinci

136 *Leonardo da Vinci,* Mona Lisa, *1503, 77 x 53 cm (30½ x 21 in)*

da Vinci (1452–1519), was the elder of the two Florentine masters. He was taught by Andrea del Verrocchio 1435–88), an engaging painter whose great achievement was his sculpture (see p.116, column). Verrocchio also had considerable influence on the early work of Michelangelo (see p.120). Verrocchio's best-known painting is the famous *Baptism of Christ (135)*, famous because the youthful Leonardo is said to have painted the dreamy and romantic angel on the far left, who compares more than favourably with the stubby lack of distinction in the master's own angel immediately beside him.

LEONARDO: RENAISSANCE POLYMATH

There has never been an artist who was more fittingly, and without qualification, described as a genius. Like Shakespeare, Leonardo came from an insignificant background and rose to universal acclaim. Leonardo was the illegitimate son of a local lawyer in the small town of Vinci in the Tuscan region. His father acknowledged him and paid for his training, but we may wonder whether the strangely self-sufficient tone of Leonardo's mind was not perhaps affected by his early ambiguity of status. The definitive polymath, he had almost too many gifts, including superlative male beauty, a splendid singing voice, magnificent physique,

137 *Leonardo da Vinci,* Cecilia Gallarani, *c. 1485, 54 x 39 cm (21¼ x 15½ in)*

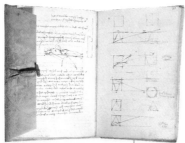

LEONARDO'S THEORIES

Between 1473 and 1518 Leonardo wrote a series of papers which were then collected together as his *Treatise on Painting*. One section, written in 1492, is devoted to linear perspective. The page shown here demonstrates his technique for transferring a figure onto the sides of a curved vault. This technique prefigured the later style known as *trompe l'oeil* (paintings that "deceive the eye").

INVENTIVE SKETCHES

Leonardo's sketches reveal a man with endless imagination and scientific interest. As well as anatomical studies and caricature, he also produced many mechanical drawings, inventing objects as diverse as war engines, water-mills, spinning machines, tanks, and even helicopters (shown above).

confrontational in *Ginevra de' Benci (138)*. It is hard to gaze at the *Mona Lisa*, because we have so many expectations of it. Perhaps we can look more truly at a less famous portrait, *Ginevra de' Benci*. It has that haunting, almost unearthly beauty peculiar to Leonardo.

A WITHHELD IDENTITY

The subject of *Ginevra de' Benci* has nothing of the Mona Lisa's inward amusement, and also nothing of Cecilia's gentle submissiveness. The young woman looks past us with a wonderful luminous sulkiness. Her mouth is set in an unforgiving line of sensitive disgruntlement, her proud and perfect head is taut above the unyielding column of her neck,

and her eyes seem to narrow as she endures the painter and his art. Her ringlets, infinitely subtle, cascade down from the breadth of her gleaming forehead (the forehead, incidentally, of one of the most gifted intellectuals of her time). These delicate ripples are repeated in the spikes of the juniper bush.

The desolate waters, the mists, the dark trees, the reflected gleams of still waters, all these surround and illuminate the sitter. She is totally fleshly and totally impermeable to the artist. He observes, rapt by her perfection of form, and shows us the thin veil of her upper bodice and the delicate flushing of her throat. What she is truly like she conceals; what Leonardo reveals to us is precisely this concealment, a self-absorption that spares no outward glance.

138 Leonardo da Vinci, Ginevra de' Benci, c. 1474, 39 x 37 cm (15½ x 14½ in)

GINEVRA DE' BENCI

Leonardo's exquisite portrait of Ginevra de' Benci was described by Vasari (see p.98) as a "beautiful thing". It was originally larger, but was cut down (because of damage) to this powerfully compact format by later owners. The back of the panel depicts a wreath of laurel and palm encircling a juniper sprig (see right). The three are connected by a scroll bearing the inscription "She adorns her beauty with virtue".

JUNIPER LEAVES
The young woman's name, Ginevra, is related to the Italian word ginepro, *meaning juniper. Appropriately, Leonardo has set her pale, marble-like beauty against the dark, spiky leaves of a juniper bush. She is well described by spikiness, we may imagine, and the bitter appeal of the gin that comes from the juniper berry is also adumbrated by this setting.*

RESERVED CHARACTER
Ginevra's rose-pink cheek and lips are painted with supreme delicacy and restraint. This effect is so subtle, so cool, that it admirably conveys her inner restraint, her firm control over her emotions. Her heavy, half-closed lids cast a shadow over the irises of her eyes, and the almost total absence of reflected light serves to reduce the communication between us and her. A slight cast in her left eye accentuates the lack of focus in her expression, and her gaze is directed over our shoulder.

SKIN UNDER THE BODICE
Ginevra's skin is rendered with absolutely smooth, "invisible" brush strokes. This is achieved by working wet-in-wet, and by the use of glazes and loose, "oily" paint, so that the colour and contours of each brush stroke blend imperceptibly to form a continuous, uninterrupted surface. It is seen through her diaphanous bodice, which is given only the slightest definition. If it were not for the gilt pin holding it together, we would perhaps not notice it at all.

INSUBSTANTIAL LANDSCAPE
In contrast to the woman, with her firm, sculptural presence, the middle-distance landscape quivers with uncertainty, rendered with thin, fluid paint. Each brushmark is visible over the next, and the trees are merely thin stalks, their trunks painted with delicate, tremulous brush strokes. This part of the picture is a prime example of Leonardo's sfumato (see p.116).

> *"... I cannot live under pressures from patrons, let alone paint."*
>
> Michelangelo, quoted in Vasari's *Lives of the Artists*

MACHIAVELLI

The Florentine statesman Niccolo Machiavelli (1469–1527) is remembered as the author of *Il Principe* (The Prince, 1532), a rational analysis of political power. His main argument was that a ruler must be prepared to do evil if he judges that good will come of it. After his death he developed a reputation as an amoral cynic and this was reinforced by criticism from his enemies in Church and State. In the present century a more balanced view prevails.

139 *Leonardo da Vinci*, Virgin of the Rocks, c. 1508, 190 x 120 cm (75 x 47 in)

INTERIOR DEPTH

We can always tell a Leonardo work by his treatment of hair, angelic in its fineness, and by the lack of any rigidity of contour. One form glides imperceptibly into another (the Italian term is *sfumato*; see column, p.116), a wonder of glazes creating the most subtle of transitions between tones and shapes. The angel's face in the painting known as the *Virgin of the Rocks (139)* in the National Gallery, London, or the Virgin's face in the Paris version of the same picture, have an interior wisdom, an artistic wisdom that has no pictorial rival.

This unrivalled quality meant that few artists actually show Leonardo's influence: it is as if he seemed to be in a world apart from them. Indeed he did move apart, accepting the French King Francis I's summons to live in France. Those who did imitate him, like Bernardino Luini of Milan (c. 1485–1532), caught only the outer manner, the half-smile, the mistiness *(140)*.

The shadow of a great genius is a peculiar thing. Under Rembrandt's shadow, painters flourished to the extent that we can no longer distinguish their work from his own. But Leonardo's was a chilling shadow, too deep, too dark, too overpowering.

MICHELANGELO: A DOMINANT FORCE IN FLORENCE AND ROME

Michelangelo Buonarroti (1475–1564), on the contrary, exerted enormous influence. He, too, was universally acknowledged as a supreme artist in his own lifetime, but again, his followers all too often present us with only the master's outward manner, his muscularity and gigantic grandeur; they miss the inspiration. Sebastiano del Piombo (c. 1485–1547), for example, actually used a drawing (at least a sketch) made for him by Michelangelo for his masterwork, *The Raising of Lazarus*. Masterwork it is: yet how melodramatic it appears if compared with Michelangelo's own painting,

Michelangelo resisted the paintbrush, vowing with his characteristic vehemence that his sole tool was the chisel. As a well-born Florentine, a member of the minor aristocracy, he was temperamentally resistant to coercion at any time. Only the power of the pope, tyrannical by position and by nature, forced him to the Sistine and the reluctant achievement of the world's greatest single fresco. His contemporaries spoke about his *terribilità*, which means, of course, not so much being terrible as being awesome. There has never been a more literally awesome artist than Michelangelo: awesome in the scope of his imagination, awesome in his awareness of the significance – the spiritual significance – of beauty. Beauty was to him divine, one of the ways God communicated Himself to humanity.

140 *Bernardino Luini*, Portrait of a Lady, c. 1520/25, 77 x 57 cm (30½ x 22½ in)

141 *Domenico Ghirlandaio,* **The Birth of John the Baptist,** *c. 1485-90 (detail of fresco panel)*

Like Leonardo, Michelangelo too had a good Florentine teacher, the delightful Domenico Ghirlandaio (c. 1448–94). Later, he was to claim that he never had a teacher, and figuratively, this is a meaningful enough statement. However, his handling of the claw chisel does reveal his debt to Ghirlandaio's early influence, and this is evident in the cross-hatching of Michelangelo's drawings – a technique he undoubtedly learned from his master. The gentle accomplishments of a work like *The Birth of John the Baptist (141)* bear not the slightest resemblance to the huge intelligence of an early work of Michelangelo's like *The Holy Family (142*; also known as the *Doni Tondo).* This is somehow not an attractive picture with its chilly, remote beauty, but its stark power stays in the mind when more accessible paintings have been forgotten.

142
Michelangelo,
The Holy Family,
c. 1503, 120 cm (47 in) diameter

POPE JULIUS II
On becoming pope in 1503, Julius II reasserted papal authority over the Roman barons and successfully backed the restoration of the Medici in Florence. He was a liberal patron of the arts, commissioning Bramante to build St Peter's Church, Michelangelo to paint the Sistine Chapel, and Raphael to decorate the Vatican apartments.

THE SISTINE CHAPEL

All the same, it is the Sistine ceiling that displays Michelangelo at the full stretch of his majesty. Recent cleaning and restoration have exposed this astonishing work in the original vigour of its colour. The sublime forms, surging with desperate energy, tremendous with vitality, have always been recognized as uniquely grand. Now these splendid shapes are seen to be intensely alive in their colour, indeed shockingly so for those who liked them in their previous dim grandeur.

The story of the Creation that the ceiling spells out is far from simple, partly because Michelangelo was an exceedingly complicated man, partly because he dwells here on profundities of theology that most people need to have spelt out for them, and partly because he has balanced his biblical themes and events with giant *ignudi*, naked youths of superhuman grace *(143)*. They express a truth with surpassing strength, yet we do not clearly see what this truth actually is. The meaning of the *ignudi* is a personal one: it cannot be verbalized or indeed theologized, but it is experienced with the utmost force.

SEERS AND PROPHETS

There is the same power, though in more comprehensible form, in the great prophets and seers that sit in solemn niches below the naked athletes. Sibyls were the oracles of Greece and Rome (see column, left). One of the most famous was the Sibyl of Cumae, who, in the *Aeneid*, gives guidance to Aeneas on his journey to the underworld. Michelangelo was a heavyweight intellectual and poet, a profoundly educated man and a man of utmost faith;

144 Michelangelo, The Erythraean Sibyl *from the Sistine Chapel ceiling, 1508–12*

143 Michelangelo, Ignudo *from the Sistine Chapel ceiling, 1508–12*

his vision of God was of a deity all "fire and ice", terrible, august in His severe purity. The prophets and the seers who are called by divine vocation to look upon the hidden countenance of God have an appropriate largeness of spirit. They are all persons without chitchat in them.

The *Erythraean Sibyl (144)* leans forward, lost in her book. The artist makes no attempt to show any of the sibyls in appropriate historical garb, or to recall the legends told of them by the classical authors. His interest lies in their symbolic value for humanity, proof that there have always been the spiritual enlightened ones, removed from the sad confusions of blind time.

The fact that the sibyls originated in a myth, and one dead to his heart (which longed for Christian orthodoxy) only heightens the drama. At some level we all resent the vulnerability of our condition, and if only in image, not reality, we take deep comfort in these godlike human figures. Some of the sibylline seers are shown as aged, bent, alarmed by their prophetic insight.

THE ERYTHRAEAN SIBYL

In the Sistine Chapel, sibyls from the ancient Greek and Roman culture are "twinned" with Old Testament prophets. The God of the Jews spoke to the prophets. The sibyls, too, were wise women with superior spiritual inspiration, capable of explaining God's message to all humanity. The prophets proclaimed to the Jews alone, whereas the sibyls prophesied to the Greeks. The Erythraean Sibyl lived in the town of Erythrae in Ionia (in what is now southwest Turkey). There were many others, such as, for instance, the Egyptian Sibyl.

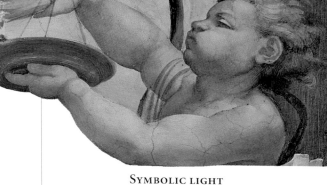

SYMBOLIC LIGHT
The cherub holds a lit torch, and the flame that issues from it looks almost like a fiery bird, the Holy Spirit come before His Pentecostal time. Significantly, the sibyl has not needed to wait for the lamp to be lighted: her light is from within, and her sureness of vision is contrasted with a dim little cherub, who rubs his eyes with baby fists.

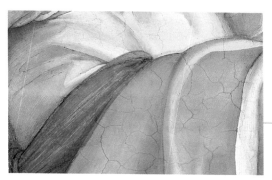

FLOWING ROBE
Michelangelo's original colours are believed to have had a startling, luminous quality. The Sistine Chapel frescoes gradually darkened with the passage of time and in the present century three attempts have been made – the latest from 1980 to 1990 – to restore their original appearance.

PENSIVE HEAD
The sibyl leans forward, lost in her book. She turns the page with the calm deliberation of one who "sees", one in command, touched by divine clairvoyance. She is inspired and infallible, and her stately head is undaunted by what she reads. Her role as illuminator and interpreter "to spread good tidings to all the nations" (Mark 16: 15) is evidenced by the opened book, turned outwards for all to see.

TURNING THE PAGES OF TIME
The great stature of the pacific sibyl reassures us at a subliminal level, and maybe all the more effectively for that. She needs only one muscular arm to turn the pages of the future; the other hangs in relaxation. She is poised to rise and act, yet remains still, concentrating on her reading. The book rests on a lectern covered with a blue cloth, symbolizing its divine content. The colours sing in splendour, pinks glazed to whiteness by the intensity of the light.

145 Michelangelo, The Last Judgment, *west wall of Sistine Chapel, 1536–41, 1463 x 1341 cm (48 x 44 ft)*

The implicit sense of God's majesty (rather than His fatherhood) is made explicit in the most alarming *Last Judgment (145)* known to us. It is Michelangelo's final condemnation of a world

he saw as irredeemably corrupt, a verdict essentially heretical, though at that time it was thought profoundly orthodox. His judging Christ is a great, vengeful Apollo, and the power in this terrible painting comes from the artist's tragic despairs. He paints himself into the judgment, not as an integral person, but as a flayed skin, an empty envelope of dead surface, drained of his personhood by artistic pressure. The only consolation, when even the Virgin shrinks from this thunderous colossus, is that the skin belongs to St Bartholomew, and through this martyr's promise of salvation we understand that perhaps, though flayed alive, the artist is miraculously saved.

As grandly impassive as the Erythraean Sibyl is the heroic Adam in *The Creation of Adam (146)*, lifting his languid hand to his Creator, indifferent to the coming agonies of being alive.

INFLUENCES ON RAPHAEL

After the complexities of Leonardo and Michelangelo, it is a relief to find Raphael (Raffaello Sanzio, 1483–1520), a genius no less than they, but one whose daily ways were those of other men. He was born in the small town of Urbino, an artistic centre (see p.100), and received his earliest training from his father. Later, his father sent him to Pietro Perugino (active 1478–1523) who, like Verrocchio and Ghirlandaio, was an artist of considerable gifts. But while Leonardo and Michelangelo quickly outgrew their teachers and show no later trace of influence, Raphael

MICHELANGELO'S DAVID

Michelangelo began work on the colossal figure of David in 1501, and by 1504 the sculpture (standing at 4.34 m/14 ft 3 in tall) was in place outside the Palazzo Vecchio. The choice of David was supposed to reflect the power and determination of Republican Florence and was under constant attack from supporters of the usurped Medicis. In the 19th century the statue was moved to the Accademia.

146 Michelangelo, The Creation of Man *from Sistine Chapel ceiling, 1511–12*

147 Pietro Perugino, Crucifixion with the Virgin, St John, St Jerome, and St Mary Magdalene, *c. 1485, centre 101 × 57 cm (39½ × 22½ in)*

had a precocious talent right from the beginning and was an innate absorber of influences. Whatever he saw, he took possession of, always growing by what was taught to him. An early Raphael can look very like a Perugino. In fact, Perugino's *Crucifixion with the Virgin, St John, St Jerome, and St Mary Magdalene (147)* was thought to be by Raphael until evidence proved it was given to the church of San Gimigniano in 1497, when Raphael was only 14. It is undoubtedly a Perugino, calmly emotional, and pious rather than passionate. A fascinating context for this scene of quiet faith is the notorious unbelief on the part of the artist, who was described by Vasari as an atheist. He painted what would be acceptable, not what he felt to be true, and this may account for the lack of real emotive impact.

EARLY RAPHAEL

There are still echoes of the gentle Perugino in an early Raphael like the diminutive *St George and the Dragon (148)*, painted when he was in his early twenties; the little praying princess is very Peruginesque. But there is a fire in the knight and his intelligent horse, and a nasty vigour in the convincing dragon that would always be beyond Perugino's skill. Even the horse's tail is electric, and the saint's mantle flies wide as he speeds to the kill.

148 Raphael, St George and the Dragon, *1504–06, 28 × 22 cm (11 × 8½ in)*

150 Raphael, The Alba
Madonna, *c. 1510,
95 cm (37½ in)
diameter*

POPE LEO X

As the second son of the
Medicean ruler Lorenzo
the Magnificent (see p.97),
Pope Leo X (1475–1521)
had an easy passage to high
office. He is best remem-
bered as a patron of the
arts and he established a
Greek college in Rome.
He encouraged the work
of artists such as Raphael
(who painted this portrait).
Despite his undoubted
inadequacies as the
spiritual head of
Christendom, his under-
standing of the human
need for great art and
architecture made him of
central importance. Such
worldliness undoubtedly
helped provoke the
Reformation (see p.169).

Raphael spent
his first sojourn in
Florence (1504–08) to
sublime purpose. At that time
Leonardo and Michelangelo were both working
there, and as a result Raphael adopted new
working methods and techniques –
particularly influenced by Leonardo
– and his paintings took on a more
vigorous graphic energy. We may
think we see a hint of what he took
from Leonardo in a work like the
Small Cowper Madonna (149), with
its softness of contour and perfection
of balance. Both faces, the Virgin's
almost smiling, almost praying,
wholly wrapped up in her Child,
and that of the Child, wholly at
ease with His Mother, dreamily
looking out at us with abstracted
sweetness, have that inwardness
we see in Leonardo, but made
firm and unproblematic. Behind
the seated figures we see a tranquil
rural landscape with a church
perched on a hill.

149 Raphael, **Small Cowper Madonna**
(detail), 1505, 60 x 45 cm (24 x 17 ½ in)

RAPHAEL'S LATER WORK

Raphael returned to the subject of the Madonna
and Child several times, each time in an intimate,
gentle composition. *The Alba Madonna (150),*
on the other hand, has a Michelangelic heroism
about it; tender as always in Raphael, but also
heavy; masses wonderfully composed in tondo
form; a crescendo of emotion that finds its
fulfilment in the watchful face of Mary. The
world stretches away on either side, centred on
this trinity of figures, and the movement sweeps
graciously onwards until it reaches the furthest
fold of Mary's cloaked elbow. Then it floods
back, with her bodily inclination towards the
left, and the meaning is perfectly contained:
love is never stationary, it is given and returned.
Raphael's life was short, but while he lived he
was one of those geniuses who continually
evolve and develop. He had an extraordinary
capacity (like, though greater than, Picasso's)
to respond to every movement in the art world,
and to subsume it within his own work.

THE ALBA MADONNA

Like Bellini, Raphael became a *Madonniere* – a painter of
Madonnas. Depicted like Bellini's *Madonna of the Meadow*
(see p.109) in an open landscape, *The Alba Madonna* is an example
of the Renaissance "Madonna of Humility" tradition. However,
all comparison with Bellini ends here, and it is the influence of
Michelangelo that is more evident in *The Alba Madonna*, not least
in its tondo format – derived from Michelangelo's *Holy Family*
(c. 1503), which Raphael saw in Rome (see p.121).

CHRIST CHILD
The Alba
Madonna *is not
as representative of Raphael's
treatment of the subject as the*
Small Cowper Madonna *(see
left), which exhibits all the
sensual warmth of human
love that exists between a
mother and her baby. Here
the Christ Child is depicted
as a kind of baby crusader –
upright and courageous,
a child with a man's
understanding of the
difficulties of human
existence. By compar-
ison, the chubby figure
of St John, dressed in
a drab lamb's fleece
to remind us of his
future in the
wilderness, appears
unsophisticated and
truly childlike.*

HEROISM
*The relatively
close tonal range
and restrained palette
of* The Alba Madonna *is
perfectly suited to her self-contained, gentle heroism. It is wholly
unlike the rosy glow and brilliant hues of the Small Cowper Madonna.
The Alba Madonna's whole demeanour, as well as her quietly mournful
gaze, expresses dignity, spiritual strength, and solidity. She meditates
on a small wooden cross that symbolizes Christ's Crucifixion.*

MADONNA'S FOOT
*The military style of the sandal
worn by the Madonna emphasizes
her warrior-like demeanour. Like
her Son, she assumes an heroic stance.
The ground on which she sits is
sprinkled with small flowers, some
in bloom. The petals are painted
delicately over the primary layer of
green earth. The flowers that St John
has gathered are anemones that
grow behind him. Round the picture
from where he kneels are a white
dandelion, what could be another
anemone, a plantain, a violet, and
three lilies, not yet in flower.*

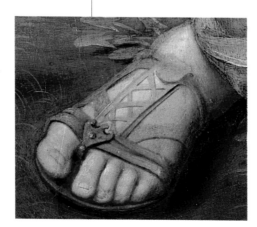

UMBRIAN COUNTRYSIDE
*Beyond the statuesque figure of
the Madonna, in the open Umbrian
landscape, is a small wood filled with
odd, tightly-foliaged trees. Beyond the
wood, still further into the distance,
are tiny horsemen. The activities of
the horsemen, too minute to make
out, are reduced almost to nothingness
by the giant-like form of the Madonna,
her remote gaze echoing their physical
distance and their essential irrelevance.*

*151 Raphael, Bindo Altoviti, c. 1515,
60 x 44 cm (23½ x 17⅓ in)*

Since Vasari (see p.98) described the picture commissioned by *Bindo Altoviti (151)* as "his portrait when young", historians have liked to think that this radiant youth was Raphael himself. He was indeed said to be unusually handsome, pensive, and fair, which is exactly what this portrait shows us. But it is now agreed that it is Bindo when young, and since he was at this time a mere 22 (and Raphael 33, with only five years left to him), this is not an "imagined" youth but the real boy who takes up so self-conscious a stance before the painter.

Raphael is one of the most acute of all portraitists, effortlessly cleaving through the external defences of his sitter, yet courteously colluding with whatever image the ego would seek to have portrayed. This duality, looking beneath the surface and yet remaining wholly respectful of the surface, gives an additional layer of meaning to all his portraits. We see, and we know things that we do not see; we are helped to encounter rather than to evaluate.

Bindo Altoviti was beautiful, successful (as a banker), and rich: rather like Raphael himself. There may have been some feeling of fellowship in the work, as the noble countenance is sensitively fleshed out for us. Half the face is in shadow, as if to allow the sitter his mystery, his maturing, his private destiny. The lips are full and sensual, balanced by the

152 Raphael, The School of Athens, 1510–11, 772 cm (25 ft 4 in) wide at base

deep-set eyes with their confrontational stare, almost defiant.
The ruffled shirt is half-covered by
the young man's locks, calculatedly
casual, at odds in their dandyish
profusion with the plain beret and
the rich but simple doublet. He
holds a darkened hand dramatically
to his breast, maybe to show off the
ring, maybe to indicate psychic ease.

But Raphael has not given him
the real world for his setting. Bindo
Aldoviti stands in a nowhere place
of luminous green, outside the scope
of time in his eternal youth, fearless
because he is protected by art from
human uncertainties.

There is an aptness in the areas
of darkness in which the great
doublet sleeve loses itself. For all
his debonaire poise, this is a young
man threatened. For the viewer
who knows how short Raphael's
own life was to be, the thought that
this might be a self-portrait
is seductively plausible. There is a
sense in which every portrait is one
of the self, since we never escape
our own life enough to see with
divine vision what is objectively there: this
shows us both men, painter and banker,
"when young".

Raphael is out of favour today; his work seems
too perfect, too faultless for our slipshod age. Yet
these great icons of human beauty can never fail
to stir us: his Vatican murals can stand fearlessly
beside the Sistine ceiling. *The School of Athens
(152)*, for example, monumentally immortaliz-
ing the great philosophers, is unrivalled in its
classic grace. Raphael's huge influence on succes-
sive artists is all the more impressive considering
his short life.

THE HIGH RENAISSANCE IN VENICE

There is always a happy sureness, a sense of
belonging, of knowing how things work, in
Raphael, and it is this confidence that seems
most to distinguish him from that other genius
who died young, the Venetian Giorgione
(Giorgio da Castelfranco, 1477–1510).

Giorgione achieved far less than Raphael (and
his life was still shorter). Even the few works said
to be by him are often contested, yet he has a
hauntingly nostalgic grace found nowhere else
in art. He trained in the workshop of the great
Venetian painter Giovanni Bellini (see p.107),
whose softness of contour and warm, glowing
colour continue in Giorgione's work. He does

153 **Giorgione**, The Tempest, 1505–10, 83 x 73 cm (32½ x 28¾ in)

not belong, as Raphael does, to this world, not
even in the rarefied way that we find in his great
successors, Titian (see p.131) and Tintoretto (see
p.134). His alliance is to another spirit, yet one
to which we instinctively respond, even if we do
not always understand the logic of his works.

The Tempest (153) is one of the most argued-
over works in existence. Its importance in
relation to the development of Venetian painting
lies in the predominance of landscape for its
own sake. Fortunately, everyone accepts that
this painting is by Giorgione, but who is this
motionless soldier, brooding quietly in the storm,
and who the naked gypsy, feeding her child and
apparently unaware of any company? Attempts
to read the scene as a novel version of the Flight
into Egypt are usually foiled by the inexplicable
fact of the woman's nakedness. Despite this,
countless scenarios have been provided, all
ingenious and all of them making some sense.

Elucidation has not been helped by scientific
analysis, which reveals that the first draft of the
work included a second naked woman, bathing
in the stream. The "real meaning" may elude us,
but perhaps that elusiveness is the meaning.
We are shown the world lit up with the startling
clarity of a sudden flash of lightning, and in that
revelation we are able to behold mysteries that
were hitherto concealed within the darkness.

**BALDASSARE
CASTIGLIONE**
This portrait by Raphael
is of the Renaissance
diplomatist and writer
Baldassare Castiglione.
He was employed in the
service of a number of
Italian dukes in the early
16th century. His treatise
Il Cortegiano, published in
1528, described the court
at Urbino and defined
the correct etiquette for
courtiers to learn. Another
feature of the book was
its popularization of
Humanist philosophy
(see p.82, column).

154 Giorgione (finished by Sebastiano del Piombo), **The Three Philosophers,** *c. 1509, 121 x 141 cm (47½ x 55½ in)*

The Three Philosophers (154) shows the potency of this lyrical richness. The actual subject-matter seems not to have mattered to the artist. He apparently began by intending a picture of the Magi (see p.98), the three eastern kings who saw the star at Christmastide and journeyed to the manger. The Magi were also believed to be astronomers, star-gazers, and from this Giorgione travelled mentally to the concept of philosophical search, plotting the stars with a sextant and pondering on their meaning.

Here too are the three ages of man, with the work being embarked upon by the serious youth, held mentally and debated by the man of maturity, and stored in material form by the elderly sage, glorious in his silken raiment.

Every detail of the three has a psychological significance: the boy is dressed in springtime simplicity, and he is solitary, as is often a youthful circumstance. Who can share his dreams and hopes? The two adult men turn inwards to themselves, seeming to converse, yet both as lonely as the passionate boy. They are elders, no longer fervent, but they bring to their problem a weighty earnestness.

The philosopher at the centre has the look of a man of affairs as he holds his hands free for work. Beside him, the older man grasps the visible signs of his thinking, a sky chart. The three human figures occupy only a half of the

The intensely poetic nature of the few undoubted Giorgiones brought a quality into Venetian High Renaissance art that it was never completely to lose. Even though finished by Michelangelo's friend, Sebastiano del Piombo,

BIRTH TRAYS

Like *cassoni* (see p.114), birth trays were another unusual form of Renaissance art. These colourfully painted wooden trays were used to carry gifts to new mothers and were then preserved as family heirlooms. This example from the first half of the 15th century depicts the Triumph of Love. Its 12-sided shape is typical of the period.

155 Giorgione, **The Adoration of the Shepherds,** *c. 1505/10, 91 x 111 cm (36 x 43½ in)*

picture, though. The rest – the part that gives them their significance – is tree and rock. In the rock is a dark cave, and beyond it, a rich landscape burnished by the late sun.

Two possibilities are open: to venture into the unknown, the dark cave, or to move out into the familiar beauty of the countryside; to go within, into the spirit, or to go without, into the world and its rewards. Each man, alone, faces the invitation, seriously debating the wiser course, not consulting, but responsibly considering.

It is the landscape, with its autumnal ambience, that gives the work its poignancy. Scholars tells us that the old man's beard suggests to them the philosophies of Aristotle, that the middle figure wears the oriental dress reminiscent of Islamic thought, and that the sextant in the boy's motionless hand indicates the new natural philosophy that we now call "science", but the information, true or not, seems irrelevant. The point is the poetry, the touch of interior gravity, the choice.

FORERUNNER OF TITIAN

A perfect example of Giorgione melting into Titian, who certainly finished some of Giorgione's paintings after his early death, is *The Adoration of the Shepherds (155)*, also called *The Allendale Nativity*. The balance of opinion now gives this solely to Giorgione, but it could equally be by Titian. In a way, the subject of the painting, or at least the focus of the artist's greatest interest, is the evening light, and this emphasis on light and landscape, first influenced by Giorgione, remained one of Titian's most enduring concerns. It unifies all it touches, and although there are certain activities taking place in the background, the overriding impression is of stillness and silence.

The business of the normal world has come to a stop. Parents, Child, and shepherds seem lost in an eternal reverie, a prolonged sunsetting that will never move to clocktime. Even the animals are rapt in prayer, and the sense of being shown not an actual event, but a spiritual one, is very persuasive. Giorgione transports us beyond our material confines, without denying them.

TITIAN: THE "MODERN" PAINTER

Titian (Tiziano Vecellio, c. 1488–1567), who was Giorgione's successor, was destined to have one of the longest life spans in artistic history – in contrast to Giorgione and Raphael – and was one of those few very fortunate artists (Rembrandt and Matisse were two others) who changed and grew at every stage, reaching a climactic old age. The early Titian is wonderful enough; the later Titian is incomparable.

Before working with Giorgione, Titian spent time in the workshop of Giovanni Bellini (see p.107). Bellini's mastery of oil painting techniques, which had transformed Venetian painting, was of huge importance to Titian's art – and by the same token, to the direction of subsequent Western painting. It is in Titian's paintings that we find a freedom prophetic of the art of today: the actual material of the paint is valued for its inherent expressive qualities – in harmony with, but distinct from, the narrative of the paintings. Titian is perhaps the most important of all the great painters of the Renaissance. Unlike his predecessors, who were trained as engravers, designers for goldsmiths, and other crafts, he devoted all his energies to painting, and as such was a forerunner of the modern painter.

156 *Titian,* Christ appearing to the Magdalen (Noli me Tangere), *c. 1512, 109 x 91 cm (42¾ x 36 in)*

Christ Appearing to the Magdalen (Noli me Tangere) (156) shows the youthful Titian delighting in the human interplay between the ardent Magdalen, all rich and spreading drapery, and the austere Christ, who withdraws from her with infinite courtesy.

Christ almost dances in resurrection freedom; she is recumbent with the heaviness of earthly involvements. A little tree tells us that newness of life has only just begun, and a great world stretches away towards the blue hills, remote, witnessing, leaving Mary Magdalene to her own choices. There is a touch of loneliness in the picture, a hint, too, of Giorgionesque nostalgia for a lost poetry. But fundamentally the mood has an earthly vigour.

OTHER WORKS BY TITIAN

Sacred and Profane Love (Borghese Gallery, Rome)

Bacchanal of the Andrians (Prado, Madrid)

Venus of Urbino (Metropolitan Museum of Art, New York)

The Rape of Europa (Isabella Stewart Gardner Museum, Boston)

Franciscan Friar with a Book (National Gallery of Victoria, Melbourne)

A Young Man (Staatliche Museen, Berlin-Dahlem)

TITIAN SELF-PORTRAIT

This painting was completed by Titian towards the end of his life when he was revered as an artist of great magnitude. He had revolutionized oil painting techniques, and was to be a great influence on artists such as Tintoretto and Rubens. He was ceremonially buried in Santa Maria dei Frari in Venice.

NOLI ME TANGERE

Titian's painting (see left) depicts the biblical story of Christ appearing before Mary Magdalene after His Resurrection. He forbids her to touch Him (*Noli me tangere*) but asks her to tell the disciples that He is risen. Mary mistook Him for a gardener, so He is shown holding a hoe.

RANUCCIO FARNESE

Ranuccio Farnese (1530–65) was the grandson of Pope Paul IV, and belonged to one of the most influential families in Italy. This portrait was painted in 1542. By then he already held the privileged position of Prior of the Order of the Hospital of St John of Jerusalem (the "Knights of Malta"), whose emblem, the Maltese Cross, is emblazoned on his cloak. Titian painted another portrait of a young aristocrat in 1542, the infant Clarissa Strozzi. Both pictures evince a warm sympathy for youth. They are full of the poignant realization of the tension between the playful world of childhood and the adult responsibilities awaiting the sitter in later life.

VISION OF YOUTH

At the top of the painting, above the curving swell of the satin, Titian admits the true reality of the unadorned boy, who belongs still to the realm of childhood. He has a child's fresh, unmarked skin, and his eyes are bright with reflected light. Bashfully, he does not meet our gaze, and his still-unformed mouth expresses an habitual amusement. In sharp contrast to the military paraphernalia weighing him down, we see the tender chubbiness of an untried adolescent.

MILITARY SYMBOL

The heraldic cross on Ranuccio's coat is given a metallic sheen. Thick white paint has been dragged over the graduated greys of the cross and has been applied unmixed, to create the sharpest highlights. This is the Maltese Cross, the emblem of the Knights of Malta, an order of chivalry founded in the 13th century. The order's original purpose was to administer a hospital in Jerusalem for soldiers wounded in the Holy Land while on service in the Crusades.

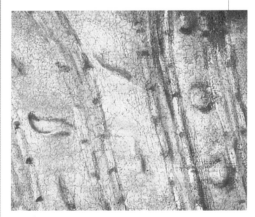

BOY'S TUNIC

The immediate focal point of this marvellous painting is the boy's brilliant red and gold satin tunic, contrasting with the warm, peachy flush of his cheeks. The rich cloth dazzles and shimmers in the light falling on the boy's chest, the red almost bleached out so that bright gold and silver remains, like the plumage of a bird. We are reminded of the tender vulnerability of the boy by the many small crimson slits that, in conjunction with the weapons, create an undercurrent of violence and pain.

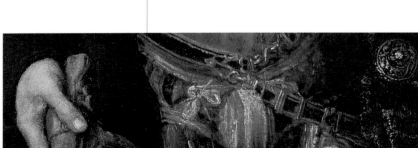

BELT AND CODPIECE

At the bottom of the painting we see the attributes of manhood – the prominent, highlighted codpiece, closed but potent for the future: many family hopes hang upon this and his putative heirs – and the clutter of belts and sword, whose steely glint is picked out in small, dot-like strokes. Titian's portrait is built upon the contrast between the innocence of youth (Ranuccio is about 12) and the outward trappings of someone belonging to one of Italy's most powerful aristocratic families.

157 *Titian*, Ranuccio Farnese, *1542, 90 x 74 cm (35 x 29 in)*

VENUS AND OTHER MYTHS

Mythological subjects featured strongly in Titian's later work, especially in the *poesie*, a series of paintings he made for Philip II of Spain. Venus is a particularly popular figure in Renaissance art appearing in the works of Botticelli, Giorgione, Bronzino, and Correggio as well as Titian. The Roman goddess of love and fertility, Venus is the mother of Cupid, the little god of love.

ITALIAN BANKING

The first modern bank had opened in Venice in the 12th century. However, during the Renaissance, Florentine banks became the most important in Europe, many having branches around the continent. The influential Medici family owed much of its wealth and power to its banking activities. These gold florins (above) were minted and circulated in Renaissance Florence.

TITIAN'S PORTRAITURE

This portrait *(157)* from Titian's middle years shows an artist of far greater depth of spiritual insight. Now he is not revelling in the sheer technique that turns thought into image; now he is painting from his own depths, and we feel the image arises almost spontaneously.

Ranuccio Farnese (157) portrays a very young man, splendid in his courtly attire. A silver cross gleams on one breast and light sparkles on the poignard below it. But the heraldic and warlike aspects are in shadows: what is real to the boy is the glove in his other hand, a hand visibly bare,

prepared to take on the burden of living, both unafraid and unprotected. He has not yet grown into his years, and the look of expectancy on the young face is full of an unformed innocence.

We admire the dignity that Titian has seen as appropriate, but we are also touched by the all-enveloping blackness in which Ranuccio is like a small, lighted candle.

Titian's insight is almost frightening in its realism. What he does do, with superb technical skill, is show us the truth of an individual with all the attendant weakness, and yet produce a picture that is supremely beautiful.

158 Titian, Venus and Adonis, c. 1560, 107 × 136 cm (42 × 53½ in)

THE LATE TITIAN

At the very end of his life, Titian painted many mythological scenes, as deeply poetic as those of the long-dead Giorgione, but with a deeper and sadder tone. Sometimes he would repeat a composition, as if seeking the total expression of some unrealized vision. One such repeated theme is that of *Venus and Adonis (158)*, in which the goddess of love pleads with the young and beautiful Adonis to stay with her, knowing in prophetic insight that he will be killed while

hunting. Adonis will not listen, will not – typical of inexperience – believe that he can die. He is every young man going off to war or to adventure, and Venus is every woman striving to hold him back. There is a painful irony in that she is the one being who is most desired of all men, most lovely of the gods and most loved; but the excitement of the hunt has greater charm for Adonis even than sexual bliss, and he impatiently rebuffs her. There is even a sense of older woman/younger man, another irony, since Venus is immortal and Adonis merely thinks himself so, with tragic results.

It is the quivering colour tones that make late Titian so marvellous, the soft and shimmering beauty of the flesh. Venus shows us her superb back and buttocks, beguilingly rounded, full of promise. Adonis is a hard and virile counterpart to her softness. Her coiled hair suggests her deliberateness – this is no dishevelled lady of the bedchamber, and indeed they are sleeping out-doors, under a brooding sky. The great hounds, wiser than their master, sense something amiss, and even Cupid weeps with pity.

EMOTIONAL INTENSITY

So supreme an artist is Titian that it is surprising to read that Ruskin, that most insightful of Victorian critics, thought he was surpassed by Tintoretto (1518–1594). Tintoretto's original name was Jacopo Robusti, but he came to be known as *Il Tintoretto*, meaning "little dyer" after his father's profession. In a city as small as Venice, all artists knew one another, and it is no

PUTTI

Nude children, often winged, known as *putti* (plural of the Italian *putto*, meaning a little boy) appeared in many early Renaissance paintings and sculptures. Often meant to depict angels and cupids, they originally graced the art of the ancient Greeks and Romans. This bronze statue of a *putto* with a dolphin was fashioned by Verrocchio c. 1470. (see p.116).

159 Tintoretto, The Conversion of St Paul, c. 1545, 152 × 236 cm (5 ft × 7 ft 9 in)

160 *Tintoretto,* **The Last Supper,** *1592–94, 366 x 569 cm (12 ft x 18 ft 8 in)*

surprise to learn that Tintoretto, about 30 years Titian's junior, declared his ambition was to combine Titian's colour with Michelangelo's drawing. "Drawing", as Michelangelo would haughtily agree, is hardly the word to use for Venetian chromatic unities: form coalesces out of light, very softly. Tintoretto, though, was an almost "hard" Venetian, in that he painted in a fury of inspiration, dashing down his first ideas and scumbling them into a whole.

The passion of his attack makes its tempestuous presence seen: there is constant excitement and a sense of the tremendous. Only a gigantic talent could hold this trembling emotion and keep it both genuine and humble, and all the major Tintorettos do indeed affect us with their total honesty and their overwhelming emotional force. A very early work, painted when he was in his twenties, *The Conversion of St Paul (159),* shows this extravagance of imaginative power.

Most painters show the conversion of St Paul as dramatic, since the not-yet saint was thrown bodily from his horse and received the divine message lying terrified on his back. But none of the other works has the wild turbulence of Tintoretto's scene. The whole visible world breaks into chaotic disfunction, as the divine

erupts into our normality. On the right, a horse stampedes away with rider and streaming banners, on the left another horse screams and rears, while its stricken rider is dazzled by the heavenly brightness above. Mountains surge, trees toss, men stagger and fall, the skies darken with ominous clouds. Paul lies in the centre, overshadowed by his fallen horse. But he does not panic; he stretches out his desperate hands, passionate for salvation.

Many of his most potent images are still in their Venetian settings. *The Last Supper (160)* is still in the chancel of San Giorgio Maggiore (see right). It is an idiosyncratic version of the Last Supper, the meal commemorated every time the Eucharist (Holy Communion) is celebrated. Little is shown of the interaction between the Apostles (we have to look hard to find Judas, usually a focal point). Tintoretto's one interest is in the gift of the Eucharist, and although many things are happening around this miracle, with cats, dogs, and servants included in the scene, all is insubstantial except for Christ and the Food of Heaven. There is a feeling that only Christ is truly real. Angels flicker and fade in the flashes of His glory, and human presence takes on some sort of nebulous coherence only when

**PALLADIAN
ARCHITECTURE**
The influential architect Andrea Palladio (1508–80) produced a number of buildings in Vicenza, but perhaps his most famous work is San Giorgio Maggiore in Venice. Begun in 1565, the church has the facade of a classical temple.

CHRIST AT THE SEA OF GALILEE

The contrast between Duccio's picture (see p.44) of the scene in which Christ first summons Peter and Andrew, and Tintoretto's extraordinary painting could not be greater. Once again we see Christ at the Sea of Galilee, here in the middle of a violent storm. He stands on the water and calls to His amazed Apostles. But as Duccio's panel painting was all certainty and calm – the moment of revelation, frozen in time and silent – Tintoretto's canvas reveals an uncertain world, filled with danger, doubt, and confusion.

THE BOAT AND FISHERMEN

The painting is largely composed of sharp, jagged shapes and wild zigzagging movement. Not least among these is the boat, whose mast is exaggeratedly curved into a thorn shape, bending almost to breaking point in the wind. The fishermen are picked out in rough, dry daubs of paint. Only two have halos: Peter (with the brighter halo), who, with all sense of personal danger lost, leaps into the water towards Christ, and another Apostle, who steers the boat towards the shore.

STILL POINT

Amidst the violence of the storm, only the figure of Christ and the upright tree are still. All else is in turmoil. The little branch growing out of the side of the tree is flowering – a symbol of hope – and seems untroubled by the violent storm. Its grey-green leaves and tiny white petals are painted with single, thick daubs of paint.

STORMY SEA

The thrashing waves echo the drama of the storm-filled sky, with its glancing, flashing light and rolling clouds. Earth colours have been added to the greens and greys of the turbulent waves, and the warm red ground shows through linking the water to the solid earth, thereby increasing its sense of destructive might. The sharp zigzag of waves, razor-edged with thick white paint, leads our eye back and forth between Christ and the boat, and gives the impression of the earth opening up.

VISIONARY FIGURE

Christ's robes are rapidly painted, with great bravura (His halo is a quick white swirl). The thick, creamy paint forming his lower robes gives them solidity, and their strange metallic pink is made by crimson glazes over the top. Tintoretto's Christ belongs to an essentially visionary world: His body lacks substance. His feet are merely outlines in white paint, with the green of the sea showing through, and His finger melts into the distant shore.

161 Tintoretto, **Christ at the Sea of Galilee,** *c. 1575/80, 117 x 169 cm (46 in x 66½ in)*

haloed with holy brightness. There is not a moment's pretence of realism, only of underlying and sacred meaning. We either take this to heart or find it too intense.

A late Tintoretto shows *Christ at the Sea of Galilee (161)*. It is a work of immense emotional intensity. Far from presenting a frozen moment in time, it shows more than could be conveyed in a flickering instant. It is as if life could never stay still long enough to reveal what is sacred. Instead, Tintoretto paints a timeless scene of confrontation. Christ stands on the surface of a wildly tossing sea and calls His disciples. He is taut with summons, a solitary figure of majestic instancy, beckoning His divine invitation.

The Apostles are a dim mass of anxious humanity, battered by the wild sea, helpless under the storm clouds. The voice of Jesus releases them from their fearful anonymity. Peter leaps joyfully into the waters, eyes fixed only on Jesus. The ugly trenches of the waves lie between servant and Master, but Tintoretto has no doubt at all that the two will meet. Violence is powerless in the presence of God, and in consequence has no authority over a seeker after God. Tintoretto shows nature as a thing almost

of torn paper, threatening and yet defanged. In an interesting touch, we are not shown the face of Christ, only His averted profile. Peter, who looks upon Him fully, can dare the leap of faith.

Even in a lovely secular work like *Summer (162)*, there is an ecstatic, spring-like vitality in Tintoretto's paintings that makes the very corn "immortal wheat" in the words of the 17th-century English cleric and mystic poet Thomas Traherne. This earthly image is reminiscent of the third great Venetian artist, Veronese.

162 Tintoretto, **Summer,** *c. 1555, 106 x 194 cm (42 x 76 in)*

VERONESE'S MATERIAL WORLD

Veronese (Paolo Caliari, 1528–88) has been called the first "pure" painter, in that he is practically indifferent to the actuality of what he paints, and totally taken up with an almost abstract sensitivity to tone and hue. His works glow from within, decorative art at its noblest.

Veronese may not be as profound an artist as Titian or Tintoretto, but it is easy to underestimate him. His fascination for the way things look, their capacity for ideal beauty, raises his art to a high level. He shows not what is but what, ideally, could or should be, celebrating materiality with a magnanimous seriousness.

To take the superficial so earnestly is to raise it to another order of being. His *St Lucy and a Donor (163)* does not really show us a martyr; he expects us to know the story of this saint and provide the context ourselves. What he does show is the glory of young womanhood, all satins and silks and sunlit beauty. Her lovely face is enraptured, slightly timid, and a closer

163 Paolo Veronese, St Lucy and a Donor, *probably c. 1580, 180 x 115 cm (71 x 45 in)*

164 Paolo Veronese, The Finding of Moses, *probably 1570/75, 58 x 44.5 cm (23 x 17½ in)*

inspection of the martyr's palm, held away from her, as if reluctantly received, shows her usual emblem, an eye. But the allusion could not be more reticent, more present for form's sake. We see the elderly donor more as an admirer in the worldly way than as a devotee of her cult. The work is one of great amplitude, of confidence, and bodily delight.

The Finding of Moses (164) shows the same healthy and hopeful nature: there is an obvious and unaffected pleasure in the sheer opulence of the dress of Pharaoh's daughter and of her maidens. Everybody, including the infant Moses, is good-looking, elegant, and happy. The characters in the scene all look refreshingly uncomplicated. Trees balance the landscape to left and right. The lady looks affectionately at the attractive child. The biblical scene as such has solemn overtones, but not for Veronese. What delights him is its beautiful humanity.

It is easy to underestimate Veronese, to see him as a superb decorator producing colourful tableaux. But he carries decoration to the point where it reveals the intensity of experienced beauty and becomes powerful art in its own right. Veronese's work glows out at us with an awareness of the potential of a material world that is supremely beautiful.

THE ITALIAN MANNERIST PERIOD

Like "Renaissance", the term "Mannerism" applies to a broad and diverse movement, and to a certain artistic standpoint, rather than any one style. It developed out of the High Renaissance, which was in decline by the early part of the 16th century, and lasted roughly 60 years, between 1520 and 1580. Mannerist art was influenced by the work of such High Renaissance artists as Michelangelo and Raphael (who died in 1520).

The word "Mannerism" is derived from the Italian word maniera, which in the 16th century meant "style" in the sense of elegance. Because of this implication of elegance, Mannerism has long been a somewhat misleading term that has caused much confusion and disagreement among art historians. Nevertheless "style", in this sense of the word, does constitute a crucial element of Mannerism, while Mannerist painting is also often highly "mannered" in the modern sense of the word. Mannerist painting is characterized by its self-consciously sophisticated, often contrived or exaggerated elegance, its heightened or sharp colour combinations, its complex and highly inventive composition, and the technical bravado and the free-flowing line favoured by its painters.

EARLY MANNERIST PAINTING IN FLORENCE

The High Renaissance was exceptionally rich in minor painters, artists whose work often slid imperceptibly into Mannerism as they exaggerated their styles, intent upon creating excitement in the viewer. Even if this sounds contrived and self-conscious, there is nevertheless an emotional charge in the great Mannerists that can be highly effective.

Rosso (Giovanni Battista di Jacopo, 1494–1540) was known in France, where he emigrated, as Rosso Fiorentino, "the Florentine". He was a deeply neurotic man, and his art was almost wantonly a flouting of normal expectations. He employed bold, dissonant colour contrasts, and his figures often filled the entire picture frame. *Moses and the Daughters of Jethro (165),* for example, is a fantastic jumble of nude bodies – huge, agitated, Michelangelo-like wrestlers, with a pale, terrified, half-stripped girl standing aghast amidst the carnage. Rosso is painting an idea of violence, rather than specifics, and he does so succinctly and expertly.

Pontormo (Jacopo Carucci, 1494–1556) was also an over-sensitive and neurotic man. He was sometimes known to withdraw completely from the world in order to live in seclusion. Like Rosso, his art is excitable and strange, striking us with a sort of enjoyable agitation.

Pontormo and Rosso were taught by the gifted Florentine Andrea del Sarto (1486–1531), whose soft forms, gentle colours, and emotional gestures provided a counterbalance to the rigorous athleticism of Michelangelo in Rome. His smudgy sweetness was influential, moving the Classicism of the High Renaissance towards a new Mannerist expression.

THE LAURENTIAN LIBRARY

In 1523 the Medici family commissioned Michelangelo to design a library that would hold 10,000 books and manuscripts. This, the Laurentian Library, became a forerunner of Mannerist architecture. It was 1559 before Michelangelo designed the staircase, which is recognized as a masterpiece of decorative architecture inspired by classical forms.

165 Rosso, **Moses and the Daughters of Jethro** c. 1523, 160 × 117 cm (63 × 46 in)

The essentially monochrome *Portrait of a Young Man (167)* is a good example of the subtle use of colour in Andrea del Sarto's work – and some contemporaries rated him as one of the four best painters of his time.

Pontormo's masterpiece is his *Deposition (166)*, painted for the altarpiece of a private chapel in Florence. Its strangely luminescent quality and lucid, unearthly light were created partly to compensate for the darkness of the chapel, but also reflect the work's emotional intensity. There is an overriding sense of vulnerability and loss; and this makes the contrast between the beautifully

167 Andrea del Sarto, Portrait of a Young Man, c. 1517, 72.5 x 57 cm (28½ x 22½ in)

athletic, long-limbed, classical bodies and the facial expressions of anxiety and confusion all the more pitiful. Pontormo's portrait of *Monsignor della Casa (168)* is brilliantly observed, with the prelate's long, aristocratic face giraffe-like above his auburn beard. He is hemmed in by the walls of his room, rigid and defensive, challenging the onlooker with his arrogance, and yet so pleasingly decorative to view.

166 Pontormo, Deposition, c. 1525/28, 312 x 190 cm (10 ft 3 in x 6 ft 3 in)

168 Pontormo, Monsignor della Casa, c. 1541/44, 102 x 79 cm (40 x 31 in)

169 Agnolo Bronzino, Eleanora di Toledo, *c. 1560,
85 x 65 cm (34 x 26 in)*

BRONZINO'S CHILL VISION

Pontormo was the teacher and almost foster-father of the strangely brilliant Agnolo Bronzino (1503–72). In Pontormo's reclusive moods Bronzino, too, was barred entrance. This may have been because Pontormo, who was deeply religious in a fanatic manner, picked up disturbing undercurrents in his protégé's work. There is a cold brilliance in Bronzino that can be very unappetizing, even when we admire his skill.

The court did not find him unattractive, however: his icy and rather bitter portraits were much admired in his day, and he became the leading Mannerist painter in Florence. His portrait of *Eleanora di Toledo (169)* shows her opulently dressed, dripping with costly pearls and grimly displeased.

Bronzino's *Allegory with Venus and Cupid (170)* used to be known as *Venus, Cupid, Folly, and Time.* It was commissioned by Cosimo I of Florence as a present for Francis I. The painting was described by Vasari as a many-sided allegory about sensual pleasure and a variety of unspecified dangers that lurk beneath the surface. Some have seen it as referring to incest, inherently perverse. But in 1986 a doctor suggested an extremely plausible explanation of the allegory, arguing that it was a reference to syphilis. The tortured figure on the left is an intricately worked illustration crammed with the clinical symptoms of the disease and one or

two of the side effects of treatments that were used in the 16th century. The allegory, by this reading, is that illicit love is attended by Fraud, who offers a honeycomb. A child representing the deceived will rushes to enjoy pleasure. The result of the ignorant embrace is syphilis. Time exposes the sickness by pulling away the blue backcloth, to reveal the truth that is hidden from Venus and Cupid.

SPIRITUALITY OF CORREGGIO

A Renaissance painter with a Mannerist mind was Correggio (Antonio Allegri, c. 1489–1534), who lived in Parma. He was one of the very great artists, intensely physical and yet steadily aware of light and its spiritual significance. Correggio was a follower of Mantegna (see p.103), and that inner solidity keeps his excesses reasonable and, still more, lovable.

A turning point in the development of Correggio's artistic identity came after a stay in Rome as a young man, where he saw at first hand the work of Michelangelo (see p.120) and Raphael

CONTEMPORARY ARTS

1542
University of Pisa founded by Cosimo de' Medici

1548
Hotel de Bourgogne, the first roofed theatre, opens in Paris

1553
The violin begins to develop into its modern form

1561
The English philosopher Francis Bacon is born

1578
The catacombs of Rome are discovered

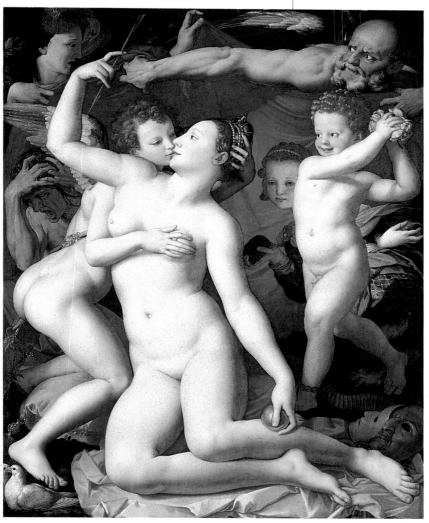

170 Agnolo Bronzino, An Allegory with Venus and Cupid, *c. 1545, 146 x 116 cm (57½ x 45½ in)*

171 Correggio, The Mystic Marriage of St Catherine,
c. 1510/15, 28 x 21 cm (11 x 8¼ in)

leans forward with an expression of deep reverence. Indeed the whole painting, small but emotionally expansive, is infused with a profound awareness of the sacred.

Correggio was important as a precursor to the Mannerism movement, rather than a Mannerist artist himself. In fact, his greatest contribution to Mannerism and the Baroque (see p.176) are his wonderful illusionistic ceiling frescoes, painted inside the domes of great churches in Parma.

Unfortunately, these frescoes defy reproduction. We have to stand inside Parma Cathedral, looking up into the light-filled *Assumption of the Virgin*; we have to be there in the church of San Giovanni Evangilista, tilting our heads in awe at *The Vision of St John the Evangelist*. Only experience enables us to appreciate the skill of foreshortening and the over-whelming impression of actuality, which were to culminate in the technical wizardry of the Mannerists.

THE ELEGANCE OF PARMIGIANINO
Parmigianino (Girolamo Francesco Maria Mazzola, 1503–40) was an artist of the utmost elegance, subsuming all reality in sheer grace. *The Madonna with the Long Neck (173)* is his best-known and most typical picture. Mary is a swanlike lady, set amid a wholly improbable scene of ruins and curtains, elongated not only

OTHER WORKS BY CORREGGIO
Salvator Mundi (National Gallery of Art, Washington)
Adoration of the Shepherds (Gemäldegalerie, Dresden)
Assumption of the Virgin (dome fresco, Parma Cathedral)
Jupiter and Io (Kunsthistorisches Museum, Vienna)
Holy Family with the Infant St John (Los Angeles County Museum of Art)

(see p.124). He soon became the leading artist in Parma. His *Venus, Satyr, and Cupid (172)* has a complete sensual abandon, yet there is an innocence in its fleshliness, a feeling of living in the age before the Expulsion from Eden. Each body reflects the moonlight individually and differently, the proportions subtly wrong, but thereby all the more morally reassuring.

There is precisely the same sort of fleshly sweetness in his religious pictures, such as *The Mystic Marriage of St Catherine (171)*. The legend, that Catherine had a vision in which the Child Jesus betrothed her with a ring, is no longer thought of as literally true, yet it has a deeper meaning, one of consecration, and above all, of the vow of chastity. St Catherine kneels, oblivious to her saintly partner, who

172 Correggio, Venus, Satyr, and Cupid, 1524/25,
190 x 124 cm (6 ft 3 in x 48½ in)

*173 Parmigianino, **The Madonna with the Long Neck**, 1534–40, 215 x 132 cm (85 x 52 in)*

GRINDING
PIGMENTS

This red ochre drawing by Parmigianino shows a workshop assistant grinding pigments. During their apprenticeships the artists learned to identify, grind, and blend the pigments. In oil painting the pigments would be suspended in vegetable oils derived from linseed, walnuts, sunflower seeds, poppy seeds, or other plant sources. Using a build-up of different-coloured pigments on the canvas imparted a light and liquidity that would be impossible using egg tempera.

ISABELLA D'ESTE

Recognized during the Renaissance for her exceptional talent and intellectual ability, Isabella d'Este (1474–1539) was a great patron of literature and art. She gathered a coterie of intellectuals, one of whom was Baldassare Castiglione (see p.129), to educate her, and employed the great artists of the time, including Correggio. There are portraits of her by a number of artists, notably Leonardo and Titian (shown above).

of neck but of person, with a long, elegant Child on her lap, insecurely posed but unworryingly so, since this is a world where the vulgarities of gravity do not apply. A long-legged angel, ravishingly beautiful, is only the first of a throng of similar exquisites. Everything sweeps upwards, like the background pillar, as if floating heavenwards and bearing us all along in its sweep.

DOSSI IN FERRARA

Dosso Dossi (c. 1490–1542), from Ferrara, is touched with the same light of fantasy as Parmigianino (see p.142). He was Court Painter to Lucrezia Borgia (see column, left), and there has been speculation that it is she who was the inspiration behind the magical *Circe and Her Lovers in a Landscape (174)*. It is an enchanting picture in a double sense, not least because of the possible initial misreading of Circe's body. Her left leg is modestly cloaked, but at first it can seem strangely absent, as if she strides across from another world into ours. The men magicked into animals have both pathos and humour, with a touch of cruelty congenial to the Borgia ménage. Yet Circe has a yearning face, and perhaps the strongest note in the picture is one of sadness and desire.

LOTTO IN VENICE

There is this same strain of sadness in Lorenzo Lotto (c. 1480–1556), a highly idiosyncratic painter who mingles his sadness with a disinterested human curiosity. He always gives us a slanting view, provocative and thoughtful, coloured by

175 Lorenzo Lotto, St Catherine, c. 1522, 57 x 50 cm (22½ x 20 in)

Giovanni Bellini's continuing influence in Venice. Lotto is famous especially for his portraits, where his weird and original insights found splendid scope, but even in an apparent religious image, there is the same enigmatic and offbeat inventiveness. *St Catherine (175)* tilts her charming head to one side and regards us thoughtfully. She has generously hidden from us her spiked wheel, covering it with the rich folds of her green mantle, and she rests her hands comfortably on its rotundity. The artist clearly suspects that her neck cross is essentially as much adornment as is her pearled crown, yet we believe totally in her. We may not believe in this Catherine as a saint, but that she is a real woman whom Lotto painted comes across with great clarity.

BECCAFUMI IN SIENA

Domenico Beccafumi (1485–1551) was the last great Sienese artist of the High Renaissance, just as Dossi was the last great Ferrarese. He is not an easy painter, with his sudden transitions from dark to light, his oddly proportioned figures, and his unusual acidic colours reminiscent of the Florentine Mannerist Rosso Fiorentino (see p.139). Beccafumi's figures can seem to loom up at us, disconcertingly, and his use of perspective, though sophisticated,

174 Dosso Dossi, Circe and Her Lovers in a Landscape, c. 1525, 101 x 136 cm (39½ x 53½ in)

176 Domenico Beccafumi, **The Fall of the Rebel Angels,**
c. 1524, 345 × 225 cm (11 ft 4 in × 7 ft 5 in)

is personal to himself. *The Fall of the Rebel Angels
(176)* is a tangle of dimly lit forms, hallucinatory
in its horror, yet shot though with the memories
of Sienese graciousness (see p.43).

EL GRECO: PASSIONATE VISIONARY

The greatest Mannerist of them all is the Spanish
painter El Greco (Domenicos Theotokopoulos,
1541–1614, called "El Greco" because he was
born in Crete). His artistic roots are diverse:
he travelled between Venice, Rome, and Spain
(settling in Toledo). The Christian doctrines
of Spain made a crucial impact on his approach
to painting, and his art represents a blend of
passion and restraint, religious fervour and
Neo-Platonism, influenced by the mysticism
of the Counter-Reformation (see p.176, 187).

El Greco's elongated figures, ever straining
upwards, his intense and unusual colours, his
passionate involvement in his subject, his ardour
and his energy, all combine to create a style that
is wholly distinct and individual. He is the great
fuser, and also the transfuser, setting the stamp
of his angular intensity upon all that he creates.
To the legacies of Venice, Florence, and Siena, he
added that of the Byzantine tradition, not necessarily in form but in spirit (although he did in
fact train as an icon painter in his early years in

177 El Greco, **Madonna and Child with St Martina and
St Agnes,** *1597–99, 194 × 103 cm (76 × 40½ in)*

Crete). El Greco always produces icons, and it is
this interior gravity of spirit that gives his odd
distortions a sacred rightness.

The *Madonna and Child with St Martina
and St Agnes (177)* sweeps us up from our
natural animal level, there at the bottom with

St Martina's pensive lion and St Agnes' lamb, balancing with unnatural poise on the branch of her arm. Martina's palm of martyrdom acts like a signal, as do the long, impossibly slender fingers of Agnes.

We are drawn irresistibly up, past the flutter of cherubic wing and the rich swirl of virginal robe, kept to the pictorial centre by those strangely papery or sheet-like clouds peculiar to El Greco. Up, up, rising through the curve of Mary's cloak until we are drawn to the heart of the work, the Child and, above Him, the oval serenity of the Madonna's countenance. We are continually on the move, but never left to our own devices. We are guided and directed by El Greco, with praying figures at the corners to hold us in the right position.

UNRESOLVED QUESTIONS

Such a dramatic and insistent art can seem too obtrusive: we may long to be left to ourselves. But this psychic control is essential to El Greco, the great – in the nicest sense – manipulator. Even when we cannot really understand the picture, as in the *Laocoön (178)*, we have no doubt that something portentous is taking place and that we are diminished to the extent we cannot participate. The literal reference to the Trojan

priest and his sons is clear enough (see p.20). But who are the naked women, one of whom seems to be double-headed? Even if the extra head is indicative of the work being unfinished, it is still uncannily apposite. *The Laocoön* was overpainted after El Greco's death, and the "second head" that looks into the painting was obliterated, while the two standing frontal nudes were given loincloths. Later, these features were restored to the form that we see now.

The serpents seem oddly ineffectual, thin and meagre; we wonder why these muscular males have such trouble overcoming them. And we feel that this is an allegory more than a straightforward story, that we are watching evil and temptation at work on the unprotected bodies of mankind. Even the rocks are materially unconvincing, made of the same non-substance as the high and clouded sky.

The less we understand, the more we are held enthralled by this work. It is the implicit meaning that always matters most in El Greco, that which he conveys by manner rather than by substance, gleaming with an unearthly light that we still, despite the unresolved mysteries, do not feel to be alien to us. No other of the great Mannerists carried manner to such height or with such consistency as El Greco.

178 El Greco, Laocoön, c. 1610, 137 x 173 cm (54 x 68 in)

LAOCOÖN

El Greco's painting depicts events best known to us from Virgil's *Aeneid*, but El Greco probably knew them from the Greek writer Arctinus of Miletus. Laocoön tried to dissuade the Trojans from letting in the treacherous wooden horse (which led to the sacking of Troy). In the Arctinus version Laocoön, a priest, was killed by serpents sent by Apollo for breaking his priestly rule of celibacy (in Virgil the gods intervened openly on the Greek side).

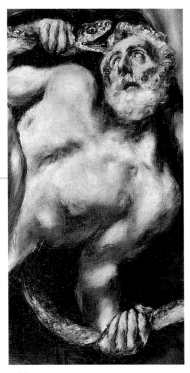

MYSTERY WITNESSES
The figures who appear to watch the scene with indifference are a mystery. One, a woman, seems to be two-headed, with one head looking out of the painting. The figures could be Apollo and Athena, come down to witness the judgment on Laocoön.

COILED SERPENT
El Greco's wonderful circular invention of the boy wrestling with the serpent creates a powerful physical tension. We are kept in suspense as to whether the boy will end the same way as his brother lying dead on the ground. El Greco's unique and unorthodox style admits an unprecedented freedom. Around the boy's outstretched arm there is a broad band of black, which has no spatial "meaning" as such, and which emphasizes the rigidity of the arm and the desperate efforts of the boy. The line flows around the strange, stone-coloured figures.

A SPANISH TROY
The allegorical horse in the middle distance trots towards the city, which is spread out under a glowering, doom-laden sky. It is a beautiful landscape, in which the vibrant, red-earth ground is covered with a lattice of silvers, blues, and greens. However, this is not the ancient city of Troy, but El Greco's home town of Toledo in Spain. El Greco painted Laocoön during the time of the Spanish Catholic Counter-Reformation, and his allegorical drama, of transgressing mortals and vengeful gods, set unequivocally in his own modern Spain, is an indication of the orthodoxy of the artist's religious beliefs.

THE EPONYMOUS SUFFERER
The anguished head of Laocoön is an example of the artist's characteristic light, rapid, feathery brushwork. Where skin meets skin – in between toes, lips, nostrils – he has applied crimson or vermilion, breathing life and a suggestion of life-blood into the death-like steely greys of the flesh.

THE NORTHERN RENAISSANCE

Having closed the Gothic chapter with the anguished realism of Matthias Grünewald, in order to concentrate on that most momentous of movements, the Italian Renaissance, we now return to the North, picking up the thread where we left off.

The 16th century heralded a new era for painting in the Netherlands and Germany. Northern artists were influenced by the great innovations in the South; many artists travelled to Italy to study; and the Renaissance concern for bringing modern science and philosophy into art was also evident in the North. There was, however, a difference of outlook between the two cultures. In Italy, change was inspired by Humanism, with its emphasis on the revival of the values of classical antiquity. In the North, change was driven by another set of preoccupations: religious reform, the return to ancient Christian values, and the revolt against the authority of the Church.

Pieter Brueghel, **The Wedding Feast,** *c. 1567–68 (detail)*

NORTHERN RENAISSANCE TIMELINE

The Renaissance in the North crystallized around the intense vision and realism of Dürer's work. Other painters in both Germany and the Netherlands followed the Northern impulse for precise observation and naturalism in the fields of landscape painting (Patinir and Brueghel) and portraiture (Holbein). As in Italy, the Northern Renaissance ended with a Mannerist phase. Mannerism was to last about a generation longer in the North than it did in Italy, where it was outmoded by 1600.

ALBRECHT DÜRER, MADONNA AND CHILD, C. 1505
Dürer's work is characterized by an intense scrutiny that enabled him to depict the innermost depths of his subjects. He sees through to the heart of his subject, whether his theme is portraiture or religious (p.153).

LUCAS CRANACH, CRUCIFIXION WITH THE CONVERTED CENTURION, 1536
In the course of his long career, Cranach developed two styles. Popular paintings such as nudes were sold privately to wealthy patrons, and court paintings were produced on official commission. These were either portraits or religious works. This Crucifixion, which alludes to the Gospel story of the centurion, shows Cranach tackling the task of devotional work. His sincerity is compromised by his own personal commitment to Humanism and his support for the Reformation, which questioned the value of religious imagery (p.158).

1500	1515	1530	1545

JOACHIM PATINIR, CHARON CROSSING THE STYX, 1515–24
Elements of Gothic style are visible in Patinir's work from the early Northern Renaissance. Charon, the mythical ferryman, is taking his passenger to Hades, the Greek equivalent of Hell, which is depicted as a war-torn landscape with burning buildings and tortured, despairing people in the manner of Hieronymus Bosch (see p.72). This work is, at the same time, an early foreshadowing of the Northern landscape tradition (p.166).

HANS HOLBEIN THE YOUNGER, CHRISTINA OF DENMARK, 1538
In the work of Holbein, we find the other face of portrait painting, in contrast to that of Dürer. Holbein was able to show the surface, without close inquiry into the inner life of the sitter. This distanced approach suited his work as a court and diplomatic portraitist to Henry VIII of England. Christina was not a queen but the Duchess of Milan and a member of the Danish aristocracy. She granted Holbein an audience of only three hours in which to sketch for this powerful picture (p.160).

JOACHIM WTEWAEL,
THE JUDGMENT OF PARIS, C. 1615
Wtewael was one of the leading Mannerist painters in the Northern Netherlands. His work shows a preoccupation with elegant figure painting, in which the subjects are invariably seen in distorted poses and a characteristically acidic range of colours. This scene has the typically artificial Mannerist setting, a fantasy woodland populated with elegant creatures (p.165).

SCHOOL OF FONTAINEBLEAU,
DIANA THE HUNTRESS, C. 1550
The Gothic castle at Fontainebleau outside Paris was developed by King Francis I (1514–47) as a cultural and artistic centre. The king employed artists and sculptors from Italy, and Fontaine-bleau became an entry point through which Southern influence made its way into Northern Europe. The poets of the school of Fontainebleau treated Diana as the most important of the gods, more so even than Venus. The way Diana is painted shows well the sinuous line and decorative pose that appeared in so much Mannerist art (p.164).

PIETER BRUEGHEL, THE
WEDDING FEAST, 1567–68
This is one of a number of works in which Brueghel took as his theme the life of the contemporary peasant. For a sophisticated intellectual, it was an extraordinary achievement to enter so profoundly into the crude vitality of these scenes. Despite their rough humour, Brueghel's peasant scenes exude an almost guilty compassion for the degradation in which the peasants lived (p.168).

| 1560 | 1575 | 1590 | 1610 |

PIETER BRUEGHEL, HUNTERS IN THE SNOW, 1565
It was part of Brueghel's universality that he excelled in landscapes as well as focusing closely on human nature. In 1565 he painted a series of landscapes linked to months of the year, thus continuing the tradition of calendar illustrations seen in the "books of hours" (see p.55). In the books of hours, peasant activities were shown in alternate panels with scenes from court life. In Brueghel's series, only the peasant scenes are known, at least today. Another of this series is Gloomy Day (see p.171).

BARTHOLOMEUS SPRANGER,
VULCAN AND MAIA, C. 1590
Frankly sensuous poses, attenuated figures, and a strong element of fantasy make this a quintessential work of Mannerism (p.165).

DÜRER AND GERMAN PORTRAITURE

Dürer was so great an artist, so searching and all-encompassing a thinker, that he was almost a Renaissance in his own right – and his work was admired by contemporaries in North and South alike. The 16th century saw the emergence of a new type of patron, not the grand aristocrat but the bourgeois, eager to purchase pictures in the newly developed medium of woodcut printing. The new century also brought an interest in Humanism and science, and a market for books, many of which were illustrated with woodcuts. The accuracy and inner perception of Dürer's art represent one aspect of German portraiture; another is seen in the work of that master of the court portrait, Holbein.

Impressive though others may be, the great German artist of the Northern Renaissance is Albrecht Dürer (1471–1528). We know his life better than the lives of other artists of his time: we have, for instance, his letters and those of his friends. Dürer travelled, and found, he says, more appreciation abroad than at home. The Italian influence on his art was of a particularly Venetian strain, through the great Bellini (see p.106), who, by the time Dürer met him, was an old man. Dürer was exceptionally learned, and the only Northern artist who fully absorbed the sophisticated Italian dialogue between scientific theory and art, producing his own treatise on proportion in 1528. But although we know so much about his doings, it is not easy to fathom his thinking.

Dürer seems to have united a large measure of self-esteem with a deep sense of human unfulfilment. There is an undercurrent of exigency in all he does, as if work was a surrogate for happiness. He had an arranged marriage, and friends considered his wife, Agnes, to be mean and bad-tempered, though what their real marital relations were, nobody can tell. For all his apparent openness, Dürer is a reserved man, and perhaps it is this rather sad reserve that makes his work so moving.

The Germans still tended to consider the artist as a craftsman, as had been the conventional view during the Middle Ages. This was bitterly unacceptable to Dürer, whose *Self-portrait (179)* (the second of three) shows him as slender and aristocratic, a haughty and foppish youth, ringletted and impassive. His stylish and expensive costume indicates, like the dramatic mountain view through the window (implying wider horizons), that he considers himself no mere limited provincial. What Dürer insists on above all else is his dignity, and this was a quality that he allowed to others too.

Even a small and early Dürer has this momentousness about it. His *Madonna and Child (180)*, which manifestly follows the Venetian precedent of the close-up, half-figure portrait, was once thought to be by Bellini. To Dürer, Bellini was an example of a painter who could make the ideal become actual. But Dürer can never quite believe in the ideal, passionately though he longs for it. His Madonna has a portly, Nordic handsomeness, and the Child a snub nose and massive jowls. All the same, He holds His apple

179 Albrecht Dürer, Self-portrait, 1498, 52 x 40 cm (20½ x 16 in)

180 Albrecht Dürer, Madonna and Child, c. 1505, 50 x 40 cm (20 x 16 in)

DÜRER WOODCUTS
In 1498 Dürer produced his first great series of woodcuts: a set of illustrations for the Apocalypse (the Book of Revelations). He would complete more than 200 woodcuts during his lifetime. The illustration above is a detail of one of these, *The Four Horsemen of the Apocalypse*. This is an allegorical representation of War, Hunger, Plague, and Death.

ART IN GERMANY AND THE LOW COUNTRIES
During the High Renaissance a number of Italian artists visited Northern Europe, but were generally critical of Northern art. Despite this, the North had a strong tradition of learning and the arts. There were many lively centres of artistic and intellectual achievement such as Vienna, Nuremberg, and Wittenberg. Certainly by Dürer's time a Renaissance in the North was overdue.

in exactly the same position as in Dürer's great engraving of Adam and Eve, and this attitude is pregnant with significance. The Child seems to sigh, hiding behind His back the stolen fruit that brought humanity to disaster and that He is born to redeem. On one side is the richly marbled wall of the family home; on the other, the wooded and castellated world. The sad little Christ faces a choice, ease or the laborious ascent, and His remote mother seems to give Him little help. Beautiful though the work is in colour, and fascinating in form, it is this personal emotion that always makes Dürer an artist who touches our heart, somehow putting out feelers of moral sensibility.

There is an almost obsessive quality about a great Dürer. One feels the weight of a sensibility searching into the inner truth of his subject. It is this inwardness that interests Dürer, an inner awareness that is always well contained within the outer form (he is a great portrait painter) but which lights it from within.

Having rejected the Gothic art and philosophy of Germany's past, Dürer is the first great Protestant painter, calling Martin Luther (see column, p.156) "that Christian man who has helped me out of great anxieties". These were secret anxieties, that hidden tremulousness that keeps his pride from ever becoming complacent. Although there is no reason why any Catholic artist should not have painted *The Four Apostles (181)*, nor why such an artist should not equally have chosen first John and Peter (indisputably biblical Apostles), then Paul and Mark (mere disciples, not ordained by Christ in the Gospel story, though they were great preachers of the Word), it strikes a definitely Protestant note.

These four embody the four temperaments: sanguine, phlegmatic, choleric, and melancholic. Dürer had a consistent interest in medicine and its psychological concomitants, since in some way he found humankind mysterious.

GERMAN WOOD SCULPTURE

German art of the 16th century was greatly influenced by the medieval tradition of detailed wood carving. In the 16th century the stylistic emphasis shifted towards more linear and animated figures, and limewood became the most popular carving wood. This example, known as *The Virgin of Sorrows*, is by the great southern German artist Tilman Riemenschneider, one of the supreme wood carvers of Renaissance Germany.

ERASMUS

Desiderius Erasmus (1466–1536), the Dutch Humanist and philosopher, was one of the leading figures of the Northern Renaissance. He travelled widely and became a professor at both Oxford and Cambridge Universities, where he met many of Europe's most influential intellectuals. He prefigures the religious teachings of Luther but came to abhor the extremism of the reformers themselves. This bizarre, doodled self-portrait is in one of his noteboooks.

181 Albrecht Dürer, The Four Apostles, 1523–26, 215 x 75 cm (85 x 29½ in) (each panel)

THE FOUR APOSTLES

Together the four Apostles make a whole, just as the four temperaments meet within an individual. Dürer is depicting many things at once: the wholeness of humanity, the unity that makes a church, the need to live united without a hierarchy, the interests of various kinds of men. The painting is infinitely satisfying, full, strong, almost sculptural in its awareness of space. The four stand against a black background, heroic in their individualism and their comradeship.

JOHN AND PETER

John is the sanguine man, hopeful and at peace, his ruddy cheeks matched by the full, flowing red of his cloak and by the auburn curls on his handsome head. As the writer of one of the Gospels, he holds a book. Peter, the phlegmatic, holds his papal keys impassively. He stands with bald head shining, face inexpressive, his body hidden behind John's impressive bulkiness. (There is surely a touch of acid wit in so diminishing the impulsive Peter, the appointed Keeper of the Keys.)

PAUL AND MARK

Mark is the choleric man, with angry eyes aglare. He is looking away to the right, almost as if to ward off danger. Masking him is the melancholic Paul, a tall brooder, who holds his Gospel closed and is watching us suspiciously out of the corner of his eye. Paul is visually redeemed by the amplitude of his flowing white garments, so creamy and so heavy that they fall in deep, shadowed folds. Shadows are part of melancholy, yet they have great dignity.

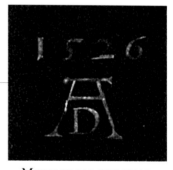

MONOGRAM AND YEAR

Dürer's distinctive "AD" monogram appears on virtually all his work. As if to emphasize his non-Italian, Germanic identity, he usually ignored the common practice of adding a Latin phrase to the signature. On the rare occasions when he did, he described himself as "Albertus Durer Noricus" – Albrecht Dürer of Nuremberg.

JOHN'S GOSPEL

St John's normal attribute is a chalice, the cup used at the Last Supper and, in symbolic form, at communion. Dürer departs from tradition by using St John's Gospel as an attribute. The open page shows the first words of a chapter, which on close inspection prove to be the German text of Luther's Bible translation, another indication of Dürer's Protestant sympathies.

182 Albrecht Dürer, **The Painter's Father,** *1497,*
50 x 40 cm (20 x 16 in)

MARTIN LUTHER
This portrait of the religious reformer Martin Luther (1483–1546) is by Cranach. In 1517 Luther drafted 95 theses opposing the contemporary emphasis on ritual and denouncing the decadence of the Church. In 1521 Luther (then under house arrest) translated the New Testament into German. By 1546 much of Germany had been converted to Protestantism.

Dürer came from a Hungarian family of goldsmiths, his father having settled in Nuremberg in 1455. In *The Painter's Father (182)* Dürer shows the face with respectful sensitivity. The technique is pencil-like, precise, and enquiring; the description achieved has a hard brilliance. However, the rest of the picture may be incomplete, or not all Dürer's work. The rudimentary background is a far cry from the detailed one in Dürer's own *Self-portrait* (see p.152), and the sitter's clothing is hardly more than sketched in.

THE SEDUCTIVE NUDES OF CRANACH

Lucas Cranach, the Elder (1472–1553), born one year after Dürer, is as self-determined as Dürer but without his spiritual concentration. From an early stage in his career, Cranach was able to obtain copies of Dürer's woodcut prints, and his familiarity with these was to have lasting influence on his painting, with its sharp definition and brilliant colour.

Cranach was almost two painters in one – artistically schizophrenic, as it were. His most popular works are the decidedly seductive nudes with which he delighted his aristocratic patrons. These coy creatures have the rare distinction of fitting in with modern tastes, being slender, free-spirited, and even kinky. They have a sort of refined sexuality, but it is also cold and teasing: we are tempted to think that Cranach did not really care for women and may even have feared them. His *Nymph of the Spring (183)* has hung

FONTIS NYMPHA SACRI SOM
NVM NE RVMPE QVIESCO ·

up her hunting arrows, but the presence of a pair of partridges (birds of Venus) suggests that it is the human heart that she hunts. A distinctly diaphanous wisp of silk draws attention to her loins by "covering" them, she wears her jewellery provocatively, and she is clearly only pretending to be asleep, propped up on the thick, sensual velvet of her dress. She sprawls before us, part of the landscape and in a sense its essence. A Latin inscription on the upper left reminds us that this is a nymph of a sacred

fountain. She is not a secular image, despite her alluring nakedness. We are warned not to break, not to shatter her holy slumbers. Love, Cranach is telling us, is something we have to approach with delicate reverence. A meaningful landscape surrounds her. Close by is the mysterious, symbolic cave in the rock – again, an image of sacred sexual symbolism, the female hollow. Beyond that there is the world of commerce and battle, church and family, in which the sacred realities of sex are played out in actual life.

183 Lucas Cranach, the Elder, **The Nymph of the Spring,** *after 1537, 48 x 73 cm (19 x 29 in)*

CRANACH'S COURT PAINTINGS

The other Cranach was also in great demand at the German courts, these being the excessively (and superficially) religious mini-courts of the Germanic states. He had a large workshop, which was busied with the production of copies of his more successful or popular pictures. His religious scenes are not always very convincing, even if the orthodoxy is impeccable: the soldier in his *Crucifixion with the Converted Centurion (185)*, a Teuton down to his monstrous feathered hat and studded armour, seems out of place beneath the Cross.

His portraits of these same Teutons, though, when the religious trappings are left aside, can be hypnotically powerful. He painted a great many court portraits, always ornately extravagant and materially decadent in mood. The fanatic precision of the dress, the elaboration of neck-laces and rippling hair, and, above the grandeur, the wistful child face, make his *Princess of Saxony (184)* one of the most appealing images of the

185 Lucas Cranach the Elder, The Crucifixion with the Converted Centurion, *1536, 50 x 35 cm (20 x 14 in)*

child in art. She is both regal and vulnerable, a princess in her splendid attire of golden chains and her scarlet-and-white dress, and a child in her open-eyed and wondering innocence. Cranach perplexes the eye with the intermingling of her soft, waving hair with her golden chains, an apt symbol for a princess.

HANS HOLBEIN THE YOUNGER

Cranach's little girl, over-dressed and over-decorated, makes an interesting contrast with Holbein's little boy *(186)*, who carries the splendour of his attire without question. The boy is, of course, not some anonymous Saxon, however noble, but the only son of the mighty King Henry VIII of England.

Hans Holbein (1497/8–1543) was educated in his father's studio in Augsburg, but early in his career he left his native Germany for Basle in Switzerland. It was in Basle that Holbein met the reformist scholar Desiderius Erasmus (see column, p.154). Erasmus provided an entry to English court circles, where Holbein eventually received royal patronage from King Henry VIII.

The English penchant for the portrait found its complete satisfaction in Holbein's shrewd, subtle, and respectful eye, his infinitely accurate and yet ennobling hand. The small Edward was the apple of his fearsome father's eye.

184 Lucas Cranach the Elder, A Princess of Saxony, *c. 1517, 43 x 34 cm (17 x 13½ in)*

186 *Hans Holbein, the Younger,* **Edward VI as a Child**, *probably c. 1538, 57 × 44 cm (22½ × 17⅓ in)*

FREDERICK THE WISE
Lucas Cranach spent most of his career as the Court Painter to Frederick the Wise, Elector of Saxony. The Electorate of Saxony was an independent state with a hereditary title (although part of the Holy Roman Empire, see p.157) which Frederick inherited in 1486. He was an intelligent, forward-thinking man who founded the University of Wittenberg and invited Luther to lecture on religious reform. He was also a great patron of artists and poets.

Holbein shows him as an apple: round, sweet, wholesome, red. It is hard to believe that Edward, who died at 15, was genuinely so bouncing a baby, but Holbein makes us credit both his health and his natural dignity. This is a princely baby, the all-important son whom Henry had sought with such savage desire in a marital history that left its mark on Europe. Holbein's intense interest in human personality, the facial characteristics that distinguish one individual from another, might seem to have little scope in dealing with a child. A child, after all, is not yet a fully achieved personality: he or she is essentially potential. Yet it is precisely this potential that Holbein shows. This face has all the soft indeterminacy of a baby, united into the hard reality of a ruler. It is the child as future king, royal child, Edward VI.

HOLBEIN AS COURT PAINTER

Holbein left the city of Basle in 1526 to go to England, where he became Court Painter to Henry VIII. His first visit lasted seven years and he painted many portraits of the English aristocracy. As Court Painter he was employed to paint the prospective wives of the king, but only managed to complete pictures of Anne of Cleves and Christina of Denmark, whom Henry did not marry (shown above). He also painted a mural of Henry VIII with Jane Seymour. This hung in the Whitehall Palace, but was destroyed when the palace burned down in 1698.

OTHER WORKS BY HOLBEIN

An Englishman
(Kunstsammlung, Basle)

A Woman
(Institute of Art, Detroit)

Sir Thomas Godsalve and his son John
(Gemäldegalerie, Dresden)

Henry VIII
(Fundaçion Thyssen-Bornemisza, Madrid)

A Merchant of the German Steelyard
(Royal Collection, Windsor)

Lady Margaret Butts
(Isabella Stewart Gardner Museum, Boston)

187 Hans Holbein, the Younger, The Ambassadors, *1533, 207 x 210 cm (6 ft 9½ in x 6 ft 11 in)*

An elaborate vanitas

In his portraits of the adult rich and powerful, we see the full extent of Holbein's scope. *The Ambassadors (187*, originally named *Jean de Dinteville and Georges de Selve*) is a memorial to two extremely wealthy, educated, and powerful young men. Jean de Dinteville (on the left) was the French ambassador to England in 1533, when the portrait was painted, and was aged 29.

On the right is Georges de Selve, an eminent scholar who had recently become a bishop; he was just 25. He was not a diplomat at the time of the painting, but later became French ambassador to Venice, at that time ruled by Spain.

This picture fits into a tradition of works that show learned men with their books and instruments. Between the two Frenchmen stands a table that has an upper and a lower shelf.

Objects on the upper shelf represent the study of the heavens, while those on the lower shelf stand for the educated pursuits on earth. At the left end of the upper shelf is a celestial globe – a map of the sky – in a frame that can be used to calculate astronomical measures. Next to it is an elegant portable brass sundial. Next is a quadrant – a navigational instrument for calculating the position of a ship as it travels, by measuring the change in the apparent position of fixed stars. To the right of this is a polyhedral (multi-sided) sundial, and then another astronomical instrument, a torquetum, which, along with the quadrant, was used for measuring the position of heavenly bodies.

Almost unnoticed, in the top left corner of the painting, a silver crucifix is seen, representing the goal of salvation, not forgotten amid the splendour and advanced scientific knowledge.

On the lower shelf at the left is a book, which proves to have been a recent guide to arithmetic for merchants (published in 1527). Behind it is the globe, representing geographical knowledge. The set square emerging from the book probably represents the skill of map-making. The lute was the chief courtly instrument of the time and stands for the earthly love of music. At the end of the bent-back tip, one string can be seen to be broken, representing the sudden breakage of death. Beneath the lute, next to a pair of compasses, is a copy of a Lutheran hymn book. The flutes beside them were popular instruments for all levels of society.

To this grand image of youth in its prime, Holbein has slashed across the foreground his reminder of human mortality. We realize that this strange shape, when viewed from a certain angle, is actually a human skull that has been cunningly distorted by stretching it sideways in so-called anomorphic projection.

Renaissance miniatures

In the 16th century Henry VIII relaunched the 15th-century fashion for miniature paintings. Nicholas Hilliard (1547–1619) became the most successful miniature portraitist, using his skills as an artist and as a jeweller to create exquisite masterpieces. Generally, miniaturists concentrated on the head and shoulders only, and used bright colours for details. This simple miniature is of Richard Hilliard, the artist's father.

Nicolaus kratzer

Holbein and Nicolaus Kratzer struck up a friendship in 1527 when working together on a ceiling in Greenwich Palace. Kratzer was an astronomer and an astrologer, and is said to have lent Holbein the instruments we see in *The Ambassadors.* In 1519 he was appointed "Astronomer and Deviser of the King's Horologes" and in this post he encouraged Henry VIII to popularize science and mathematics. This portrait is by Holbein and shows Kratzer working on a polyhedral sundial.

Most of Holbein's portraits are of lords and ladies, but there are a few that reveal more of his private life. One such is the haunting *Portrait of the Artist's Wife with Katherine and Philipp (188)*. Artists have always painted their families, but this is the saddest version on record. He lived very little with his wife and children in Basle (the reasons for this may have been political, religious, or financial), but this tragic little trio have all the withering marks of the unloved.

The dim-eyed wife presses down on the children, plain, pale little beings, all unhappy and all ailing. Holbein, that superb manipulator of the human face, cannot have meant to reveal their wretchedness and expose his neglect with such drastic effect. It is as if his art is stronger than his will and for once Holbein is without defences.

We might describe him as an un-Germanic German, since he left for Switzerland when he was still a teenager and then worked in England for Henry VIII. While Dürer and those influenced by Dürer (which includes practically all

189 **Hans Holbein, the Younger,** Sir Brian Tuke, *c. 1527, 49 × 39 cm (19½ × 15½ in)*

German Renaissance artists except Holbein) had an intense interest in the personal self of the sitter, Holbein was essentially discreet. A court painter *par excellence*, he always maintains a dignified distance. We see the sitter's exterior, what he or she looked like, but we never pass into the inner sanctuary. The sole exception, which is what makes it so extraordinarily interesting, is this painting of his wife and children. Here his courtly shield is down, perhaps because of the artist's personal sense of guilt. He was not a good husband or father, and while he can carry off any other portrait with superb technical aplomb, he catches his breath and opens the inner door when he paints the family that he abandoned and neglected.

A much more characteristic Holbein is *Sir Brian Tuke (189)*, with his clever, sensitive face, his air of unflinching probity, the tenseness of his half-smile and his clenched hand. A folded piece of paper on the table quotes a biblical passage in which Job appeals to God for rest from anxiety. We would know, without having sufficient knowledge to recall that Tuke served Henry VIII, that here was a man who was noble but imperilled – though in fact, he flourished.

Holbein's work is never cold nor lacking in involvement, as we can see in *The Ambassadors*, *Christina of Denmark*, and *Sir Brian Tuke*; but he protects his sitters from psychological exposure and, indirectly, protects himself. What a contrast with Dürer, who always leaves both the sitter and himself open to the most personal scrutiny.

188 **Hans Holbein, the Younger,** The Artist's Wife with Katherine and Philipp, *c. 1528, 77 × 65 cm (30½ × 26 in)*

To take one example of Reni's religious work, *Susannah and the Elders (214)* is a painting that confounds the ignorance of prejudice. The story is about a Jewish heroine who is surprised when bathing by two religious elders, who try to blackmail her into immorality. Susannah displays the opposite of surface piety: she faces her tormentors with the indignation of the innocent. She sees no reason for fear, trusting in God and her own blamelessness.

Reni is equally powerful in mythological works. *Deianeira Abducted by the Centaur Nessus (215)* is a work of thrilling majesty. Hercules is on a journey with his wife, Deianeira, when they come to a river, where the ferryman is the centaur Nessus. He takes Hercules across first, then tries to ravish Deianeira. The picture shows him ready to gallop off with her on his back. Bodies gleam in the sunlight: the man-beast hard and straining, the abducted woman vulnerable in her fleshly softness. Garments fly, clouds gather, a great equine leg is paralleled by the slender human form, the nearness underscoring the cruel unlikeness. Deianeira casts an anguished glance upward to the gods, one arm reaching out for help. On every level, visual and emotional, this is a painting that learns from Raphael and Caravaggio alike.

HUMAN DRAMA IN GUERCINO

Like Reni, Guercino (Giovanni Francesco Barbieri, 1591–1666) also fell into disrepute. Perhaps this is even less reasonable, for he is one of the great narrative painters, a draughtsman of infinite ability and a superb colourist as well, especially in his earlier years. The name by which we know him was a sort of nickname and is best translated as "Squinty". It indicates a disability, but no man ever used a squint to better effect. He was influenced by the Carracci, and like the Carracci also, by Venetian painting.

Character, interaction, passions in conflict: these are things that Guercino portrays with total confidence. *Christ and the Woman Taken in Adultery (216)* makes its point mainly through the gestures of the hands, as Jesus and the accusers signal their difference of principle (see column, below right). The noble head of Christ, imperturbably calm amid the hubbub, is just sufficiently unidealized to make the incident seem credible. Guercino shows us divine love as a great force of compassion, infinitely demanding and infinitely forgiving.

Guercino is an intensely dramatic artist, playing with light and shade with dazzling skill. We are moved by meaning in his work, but also by its sheer visual beauty.

> *"A great draughtsman and a most felicitous colourist; he is a prodigy of nature, a miracle."*
>
> **Carracci on Guercino in a letter of 1617**

THE WOMAN TAKEN IN ADULTERY

This story is told in St John's Gospel. Temple officials and members of the Pharisee sect try to trick Jesus into giving judgment (so that they can accuse Him of usurping authority). They bring before Him a woman who has been caught in the act of adultery, punishable in Roman law by stoning. Jesus pauses, writing with one finger in the dust, then replies, "He that is without sin among you, let him cast the first stone." At this the accusers leave the scene. Jesus finally says to the woman, "Go, and sin no more."

216 Guercino, Christ and the Woman Taken in Adultery, c. 1621, 98 x 122 cm (38½ x 48 in)

FLEMISH BAROQUE

In the 17th century, Flanders was the main stronghold of Catholicism in an otherwise Protestant northern Europe. It remained under Spanish rule when the Northern Netherlands won independence, and the greatest outside influences on Flemish art were Spain and the Counter-Reformation. This is clearly seen in both Rubens and van Dyck.

For a century, Spain had been the major military force in Europe. It had used its power to back up the might of the Catholic Church in Northern Europe – precisely where Catholicism was under the strongest attack from the Protestant Reformation. In the Netherlands, when the North won its independence, Flanders remained within the Catholic fold, in an ever closer relationship with Spain. The two Catholic countries had in common the religious idealism of the Counter-Reformation, and, linked as they were by their history, they shared similarities in their art. At the start of the 17th century, as a result of this consolidation with Spain, industry in Flanders flourished, and the arts, which were centred in Antwerp, benefited from the increasingly prosperous culture.

The greatest of the Northern Baroque painters was the Antwerp-based Peter Paul Rubens (1577–1640). He has something of Domenichino's largeness of spirit (see p.183), but greatly magnified. The wonderful mixture of Italian grandeur and Flemish lucidity, and feeling for light, climaxes in the paintings of Rubens. His work is infused with a kind of Catholic Humanism that admits sensuous delight along with religious sentiment, and it has an energetic, optimistic spirituality.

In 1600 Rubens went to Italy to study. He travelled widely over the next decade, notably to Spain, where he became friends with a Spanish artist who was 22 years his junior and who was of perhaps even greater stature: the incomparable Velázquez (see p.194).

Rubens wrote, "I consider the whole world to be my native land," and this confident generosity of spirit, this cosmopolitan view of the world, is manifested in his works. So expansive was his genius that he easily took the elements that he admired of the High Renaissance masters and assimilated them into his own strongly independent vision. His paintings reveal a supremely confident use of colour – always rich and generous – that he learned from studying the works of the great Venetian, Titian. His figures have a massiveness of form that runs in a clear line back to Michelangelo.

RUBENS' RELIGIOUS WORKS

Rubens spent some time in Rome and the influence of his Italian contemporary, Caravaggio (see p.176), proved to be an enduring one. This revealed itself most emphatically in Rubens' religious paintings, to which, in true Baroque form, Rubens gave popular appeal and an utterly physical presence. We cannot always tell from an artist's religious painting how personal is his faith: probably we can never tell, faith being so

217 *Peter Paul Rubens*, **Descent from the Cross**, *1612–14, 420 × 310 cm (13 ft 9 in × 10 ft 2 in)*

222 *Peter Paul Rubens,* Marchesa Brigida Spinola Doria
1606, 152 × 99 cm (60 × 38¾ in)

Venus, innocently amazed at her victory. It has
been remarked that her surprise is justified; that
Juno, with her back arched above her furs, is the
true winner. (The third goddess, Minerva, seems
to look on with amused curiosity.) The legend
takes on a special significance, quite apart from
preceding the Trojan war. What interests this
supremely balanced painter is the encounter
between what could have been a vulgar youth
and an unclad queen. Rubens lends the scene
dignity and graciousness.

JORDAENS – RUBENS' SUCCESSOR
Rubens ran a workshop in Antwerp, with a large
stable of assistants. One artist who is known to
have worked with him in Antwerp is Jacob
Jordaens (1593–1678), who gained a great deal
from his association with Rubens and flourished
over the years, producing coarse-grained but
vital works. Jordaens' *The Four Evangelists (221)*
is painted with vigour: the thick brushwork is
very different from Rubens' technique.

Jordaens worked best as a painter of genre
works and typically chose modest subjects; but
after Rubens' death in 1640 it was he who filled
the post of Antwerp's leading artist, perpetuating
Rubens' influence and producing a great many
public works over his long career.

VAN DYCK'S GRAND ELEGANCE
The closest to Rubens in gift, and at times
in style, in the North, was Anthony van Dyck
(1599–1641). In his youth, Rubens had a very
aristocratic elegance that reminds us of van
Dyck. An example from his early twenties is
his regal-looking portrait of *Marchesa Brigida
Spinola Doria (222)*, in which the face, gentle in
its self-assurance, proclaims the work of Rubens.

Van Dyck can manage just as much grandeur,
skilfully deploying all his arts to make his own
Marchesa (223), of the great Grimaldi family,
appear almost immortal in her lofty state. In his
portraits, van Dyck suppresses the "earthiness"
and animal vitality so forceful in Rubens'
paintings, and in its place we find an elegance
and psychological presence that his aristocratic
subjects doubtless found pleasing. The slave
who holds the parasol is humankind: the lady
is on another plane – yet not quite. Somehow van
Dyck manages to make us believe in his lady,
with a subtlety not evident in Rubens' portrait.

223 *Anthony van Dyck,* Marchesa Elena Grimaldi, *1623,
241 × 133 cm (95 × 52 in)*

PETER PAUL RUBENS
Rubens (1577–1640)
made an early start to
his career, becoming a
Master of the Guild of
St Luke at Antwerp in
1598. From 1609–21
he was Court Painter to
Albert and Isabella, the
rulers of the Spanish
Netherlands (see
opposite), with an
annual salary of 500
florins (guilders). After
Albert's death in 1621
Rubens became an
adviser and diplomat
for Isabella. He also
worked in Paris on a
cycle of pictures for
Marie de' Medici (see
p.188). In 1629 he visited
the court of Charles I
of England, winning the
praises and confidence
of the king.

VAN DYCK
The great 17th-century
master portrait painter
Sir Anthony van Dyck
(1599–1641, shown
above) achieved renown
as an artist in the service
of royalty and the
aristocracy. His patrons
included Prince William
of Orange (see p.215)
and Charles I of
England (see p.192).
The elongated figures
of his subjects, with
their air of remoteness
and self-confidence,
established a pioneering
"English" portrait
tradition.

224 Anthony van Dyck, **Charles I of England out Hunting,** *c. 1635–38, 266 × 207 cm (8 ft 8½ in × 6 ft 9½ in)*

Portrait painting was a lucrative business, and van Dyck really excelled at it. Like Rubens (in whose Antwerp workshop he briefly worked) he travelled extensively, enjoying an illustrious career before settling in 1632 in England. It was at the court of Charles I, that doomed monarch, that his gifts flourished, influencing generations of portrait painters in England and throughout the rest of Europe. The diminutive king featured in many of van Dyck's paintings, in a variety of symbolic roles, sometimes in armour, and sometimes on horseback. One portrait in the Louvre, *Charles I of England out Hunting (224),* is the greatest piece of public relations ever created. By sheer force of genius, van Dyck presents us with an icon of the heroic, of the grave scholar king who yet loves the chase. Noble tree, noble seat, noble monarch: van Dyck integrates the three into a most memorable image. Charles knighted him, and we feel he deserved it.

SPANISH BAROQUE

Painting in 17th-century Spain was profoundly influenced by the Church, at least partly because of the religious zeal of the Spanish Hapsburg dynasty. King Philip II and his two successors, Philip III and IV, maintained religious orthodoxy by means of the dreaded Spanish Inquisition, a council for the persecution of all forms of "heresy", including Protestantism. Spanish Baroque art was largely devotional in nature, though the period can boast a little court painting and some mythological, genre, and still-life work.

Despite the tense atmosphere of religious conformity presided over by the Hapsburg régime, Caravaggio's liberating influence (see p.176) is fairly widespread in Spanish painting in the early part of the 17th century. Caravaggio's rich contrasts and dark palette were well suited to the Spanish tradition, in which a tendency towards grim and graphic realism was already well established, especially in religious sculpture (see column, p.198).

"Caravaggism" found an early exponent in Jusepe de Ribera (1591–1652), who painted with dark colours and, often, disturbingly sinister undercurrents. Ribera went to Italy – first to Rome, where he absorbed Caravaggio's influence, then to Spanish-ruled Naples. He remained in Italy for the rest of his life and enjoyed great success. There is more piety, and sensual pleasure, in Ribera's religious paintings than in those of Caravaggio and, equally, a deeper level of pain and suffering. There is a terrifying degree of pain in this mythological work *(225)*, in which Apollo punishes Marsyas by skinning him alive. Marysas, who was a skilled flautist, had challenged Apollo to a music contest, but had lost. As victor, Apollo was allowed to choose the punishment.

Ribera found his models among urchins and beggars, and portrayed them as they really were. His beggar-boys, even his philosophers, confront us with all their physical imperfections: rotting teeth, deformed limbs, dirty skin, and aged flesh, breathing a harsh and unprecedented social realism into 17th-century painting.

DON QUIXOTE
Miguel de Cervantes (1547–1616) was the most successful Spanish novelist of the 17th century. His most famous work, *Don Quixote*, was written while he was in prison in Seville. The novel is a satire on the current fashion for chivalry but also portrays the theory of the human ideal and the frailty of man. The two characters represent the many fluctuating features of insanity, and the detailed descriptions of the Spanish countryside give the book a powerful resonance. By 1605 the book was in print in Madrid; this illustration (above) shows the popular 1608 edition.

225 *Jusepe de Ribera,* **The Flaying of Marsyas,** *183 × 234 cm (6 ft × 7 ft 8 in)*

PHILIP IV OF SPAIN

Although he was a discerning patron of the arts, King Philip IV of Spain (1605–65) took little interest in politics. He left the administration of his realms to his minister, Count Olivares (1587–1645). Velázquez (1599–1660) became Court Painter in 1623. The king often ordered several variants of one picture (usually, only the colours of the clothes would be altered). Since Velázquez was notoriously slow in his work, a studio of copyists was employed to reproduce the master's work. This portrait of the young king may be by Velázquez, or merely by a copyist.

OTHER WORKS BY VELAZQUEZ

Cardinal Don Ferdinand of Austria (Prado, Madrid)

The Rokeby Venus (National Gallery, London)

The Infanta Maria Teresa (Kunsthistorisches Museum, Vienna)

The Moorish Kitchen Maid (National Gallery, Edinburgh)

Count Olivares (The Hermitage, St Petersburg)

The Infante Balthasar Carlos (The Wallace Collection, London)

The Painter Juan de Pareja (Metropolitan Museum of Art, New York)

VELAZQUEZ: SPANISH GENIUS

When Diego Velázquez (1599–1660) first made his bid for painterly glory (barely out of his teens) he was influenced by Caravaggio (see p.176). There is the same surety of form and control of light, but beyond this, all real comparison ends. Velázquez was unique, one of the very greatest of painters, and he developed a vision of human reality that owed little to outside influence.

The only image of royalty comparable to the van Dyck portraits of the Stuart King Charles I (see p.192) is that given by Velázquez of the Hapsburgs, whom he served as Court Painter; but, again, the comparison is a superficial one. Velázquez did not merely glorify his king and court, though he did that as a matter of course; he was also oddly intent on rising in social status. In time he did win his way to a mild friendship with Philip IV. The king was a poor politician (see left), but his saving grace was that he did appreciate the genius fate had sent him as Court Painter and rewarded him accordingly.

The sheer beauty of Velázquez' court paintings, official statements in an age without photography of what the monarch and entourage looked like, undoes all attempts at labelling. *Las Meninas (226)* ("the maids of honour") is now hung in pride of place, behind bulletproof glass, visibly the greatest treasure of its great museum, the Prado, Madrid.

226 Diego Velázquez, Las Meninas, 1656, 318 x 276 cm (10 ft 5 in x 9 ft ½ in)

LAS MENINAS

At one level, this picture is easy to read: at the centre is the little princess, the Infanta Margarita Teresa, with her maids clustered round her, her tutors, page, and dwarf in attendance, and her gigantic dog. From the dog we work our way up by stages to the distant reflection of the king and queen. Here is the whole world of the inner court, presented obliquely, in reverse order of importance. Painted for the king's private summer quarters, this work is both a portrait of his young daughter and a sophisticated, innovative tribute to the king himself. It portrays a single moment, each figure responding to the entrance of the king.

MINIATURE PORTRAITS
In the rear mirror, our attention drawn to it by the silhouetted courtier, we see a reflection of the king and queen. Whether it actually reflects them, or the painting Velázquez is working on, nobody knows for certain. Secure in their position, the royal pair can easily afford to become a mere reflection behind their child. Even as pale shadows, they can dominate, surely the subtlest of compliments.

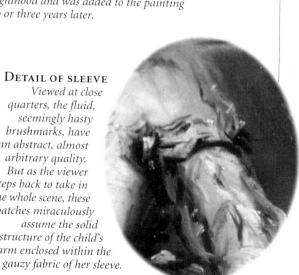

SELF-PORTRAIT
The painter, Velázquez himself, stands at the far left, intent upon a canvas looming impressively upwards, while the large copies of Rubens' paintings behind him are diminished (there is irony here) by the shadows. The red cross on Velázquez' chest signifies his subsequent knighthood and was added to the painting two or three years later.

DETAIL OF SLEEVE
Viewed at close quarters, the fluid, seemingly hasty brushmarks, have an abstract, almost arbitrary quality. But as the viewer steps back to take in the whole scene, these patches miraculously assume the solid structure of the child's arm enclosed within the gauzy fabric of her sleeve.

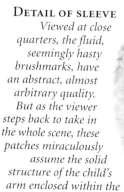

COURT LIFE
There is a sense of life as actively lived, life held still for a passing moment – not a moment of special significance, however; merely one of the thousands passing every hour: and this one lives on. The figures of the Infanta's entourage appear and recede in a vast cave of shadows. All have been identified as historical personages except for the man standing quietly on the right.

COURT JESTERS

Since medieval times, dwarves were employed as jesters in the courts of Spain. Philip IV's favourite was a dwarf named Sebastiano de Morra. The dwarves' feelings as human beings were generally ignored, and they had to endure the jokes and insults of the courtiers. It was usually the king who chose the names of his jesters, often giving them mock titles of ludicrous grandeur.

Earlier in his career, Velázquez had contributed to the grand projects inaugurated by Philip IV. These included a splendid new palace, the Buen Retiro, built in 1631–35, in whose many rooms some 800 paintings were hung. Its principal ceremonial room, known as the Hall of Realms, contained 27 paintings by Spanish artists, including Velázquez' *Surrender of Breda*, along-side a number of works by Zurbarán (see p.197). The king's next project was the Torre de la Parada, a hunting lodge in the grounds of the Pardo Palace. Velázquez, despite the king's increasing interest in foreign artists, contributed portraits of the young crown prince Balthasar Carlos, and two of the court dwarves, one of whom, *Francisco Lezcano (228)*, is shown here.

228 Diego Velázquez, Francisco Lezcano, 1636–38, 107 x 83 cm (42 x 32½ in)

Velázquez' use of paint intrigued his royal friends. They pointed out to one another, quite intelligently, that his pictures had to be viewed at a distance, when the rough and apparently glancing dabs of colour would suddenly, miraculously, integrate themselves into the image. Lace, gold, the glitter of light jewels, the rosy flush of a young cheek, the weary droop of an aged head: Velázquez could catch them all and hold them for us to see. He could do this with a religious image: no *Christ on the Cross (227)* has a more mournful human dignity than his.

He could teach us that the court dwarf *(228)*, who often used to serve as a jester (see left) and a figure of fun, had the same tragic dignity and unalienable humanity as the dying Jesus.

He could take a theme from mythology and show us that paganism, too, is a religion and so draws its force from the movements of the human spirit. *The Forge of Vulcan (229)* is a masterpiece of contrasts between two kinds of being. On the one hand, there is the luminous, epicene, and effeminate youth, visitant from another world, blandly confident of his ability to make himself understood. On the other, there is the team of blacksmiths, male to their core, wiry, and astonished – and yet at the same time clearly unimpressed. The two worlds meet with mutual incomprehension and with mutual disesteem, yet Velázquez laughs so low in his chest that the joke may go unheard.

227 Diego Velázquez, Christ on the Cross, 1631–32, 248 x 169 cm (8 ft 1 in x 5 ft 6½ in)

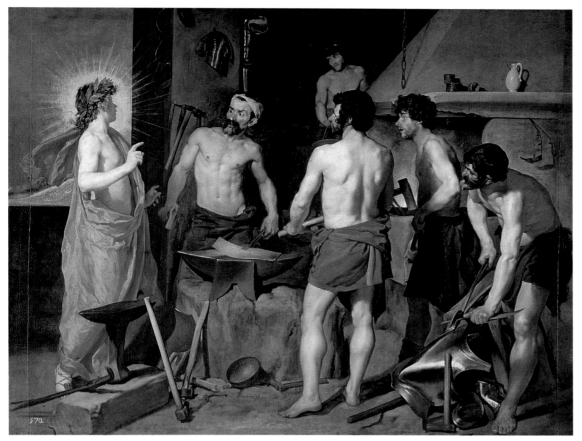

229 *Diego Velázquez*, **The Forge of Vulcan**, *1630, 223 x 290 cm (7 ft 4 in x 9 ft 6 in)*

ZURBARAN: A SACRAMENTAL CALM

Francisco Zurbarán (1598–1664) was a contemporary of Velázquez and worked in Velázquez' native town of Seville. The two were largely unlike in style, except that Zurbarán's paintings display that pleasing solidity of form and plasticity of paint found in Velázquez' early work (see p.196). It is in still life that we find Zurbarán at his finest. *Still Life with Oranges (230)* has a sacramental monumentality, a modest certainty of the value of things, the fruit laid out on an altar, the flower silent beside the humble mug, three images bathed in sunlight and conveying an indescribable sense of the sacred.

230 *Francisco Zurbarán*, **Still Life with Oranges**, *1633, 60 x 107 cm (23½ x 42 in)*

In 17th-century Spain, religious sculpture became an important artistic movement. One famous example is the *Dead Christ* in the Capuchin Monastery at El Pardo, carved by the sculptor Gregorio Fernandez and commissioned by Philip III. Christ's body lies on an altarcloth and the drama of his pain is realistically re-created with open wounds and streaks of red blood against the brown wood of the body. The carvings, which were often carried in church festival processions, became increasingly popular as the cult of the Passion developed. The obsession with realism culminated in the use of real hair, eyelashes, and eyebrows on the figures' faces.

231 **Francisco Zurbarán,** The Lying-in-state of St Bonaventura, *c. 1629, 250 x 225 cm (8 ft 2 in x 7 ft 5 in)*

The Lying-in-state of St Bonaventura (231) has the same weight of lucid significance, of "event" that is uneventful. The work hovers between time and eternity, intent upon the unseen that gives the seen its meaning. The human actors in the drama (and we might say that the dead saint is the most vital of these) are spotlit against profound darkness. The mystery of our journey from birth to death becomes almost tangible.

MURILLO: A FORGOTTEN MASTER

The next great 17th-century Spanish master after Velázquez and Zurbarán is another artist who lived in Seville, Bartolomé Esteban Murillo (1617–82). Sadly, Murillo is easy to misjudge; at his weakest, which is not all that infrequent, he has a softness that can only be called sentimental. The mistake is to take the weak Murillo as the only Murillo. It is true that he is never as strong or as deep as Velázquez or Zurbarán, but he has his own gentle strengths and depths. Murillo can make us catch our breath with his unworldly but convincing images.

Murillo is often accused of being too soft, too anodyne, perhaps because of our modern desire to face life whole, with all its cruelty. It is a wish that runs contrary to Murillo's personal world of family love and understanding.

Some of our surprise may come from the realization, unexpected, that sweetness can be made to work. *The Holy Family (232)*, with its tenderly involved St Joseph and the absence of anything resembling heavy symbolism, has a charm that increases the longer the picture is looked at. The small mongrel and the cosseted child are both painted with the insight of love.

But we can perhaps best appreciate the genuine if not monumental gifts of this artist in one of his rare secular works. *Two Women at a Window (233)* is a splendid image, reticent, creamily beautiful, certain of its own understanding of the two figures. One of them is almost certainly a duenna – an older woman employed by the family to be both a governess and a chaperon. She is laughing, but we are not shown her laughter: only her creased-up cheeks, flushed with mirth. Her twinkling eyes assure us that what makes the young woman smile to herself, unaffected, makes the older woman crinkle up with sardonic glee. She sees more, and understands with sharper wit, than the pretty child, and Murillo shows us this with the most delicate understatement.

In this wonderful picture, the great strong vertical of the shutter, and the equally strong horizontal of the window ledge, frame the two women. The girl, who is the emotional centre of the picture, looks out at life with ironic detachment, but Murillo, and the older woman, know that her practical options are severely circumscribed.

232 *Bartolomé Esteban Murillo,* The Holy Family, *1650, 144 x 188 cm (56½ x 74 in)*

233 Bartolomé Esteban Murillo, Two Women at a Window, c. 1670, 127 × 106 cm (50 × 41¾ in)

A DUTCH PROTESTANT VISION

The United Provinces of the Northern Netherlands claimed their independence in 1579, but it took 30 years of armed conflict to drive the Spanish from their soil. A treaty was signed in 1648, and this Protestant region, with its Reformation affinities and Northern realist heritage, now evolved its own tradition. Life was lived out in a dramatic atmosphere, first of revolution and later of the fight to defend the hard-won freedom. A new order began, based on social justice and spiritual austerity. Churches were stripped bare for Calvinist worship, and in painting, there was renewed emphasis on realism and simple, everyday things.

THE UNITED PROVINCES

This name was first used in 1579, when the Protestant states of the Northern Netherlands declared independence from Spanish rule. Warfare raged until the truce of 1609 (see p.186). It took 39 years for Spain and the other Catholic powers to recognize the new Protestant state and finally sign the Treaty of Münster (in 1648). Holland was the richest of the United Provinces and its name has come to be used for the whole country, though the official name today is the Netherlands.

THE BLINDING OF SAMSON

The story of Samson is told in the Old Testament book of Judges. Samson's enemies, the Philistines, seeking a chance to kill him, enlist Delilah to seduce him. She succeeds in getting him to give away the secret of his enormous strength (his hair), and while he is asleep, she lets them cut off his hair. As a consequence, his strength deserts him, leaving him helpless. The Philistines put out Samson's eyes and imprison him. Eventually he manages to exact revenge by pulling down the pillars supporting the roof of the house in which he is being held.

It can be difficult to realize that Rubens (1577–1642, see p.186) and Rembrandt (van Rijn, 1606–1669) were contemporaries, their lives overlapping for the first half of the 17th century. Both lived in the Low Countries, though Rubens was based at Antwerp in Flanders, and Rembrandt at Amsterdam in the North, in the country that was known then as the United Provinces, and today is called "the Netherlands" or, more conversationally, "Holland".

Rubens seems to belong to an older age, more classical and international. Rembrandt is emphatically a Dutchman, and his vision comes primarily from himself and not from antiquity. Both are magnificent, but it is Rembrandt to whom we feel closest, perhaps because of his fascination for the self-portrait, which makes us able to "read" him at every stage of his emotional life. The human face fascinated him from the beginning, a fortunate circumstance that brought him many lucrative commissions. However, it is never the externals that intrigue Rembrandt, whether in his own face or that of others. It is the inner workings of the mind, an obsession that eventually lost him his successful position and the respect of his peers. Yet in Rembrandt's paintings, the two worlds of inner and outer are not in opposition. It is precisely through the body, so wonderfully conjured up in the medium of paint, that Rembrandt unveils to us the nature of the sitter, even the passing moods, as well as the deep-seated attitudes.

Rembrandt was a miller's son; in other words, he came from a middle-class background. This was significant of his times, for alongside the independence struggle, Dutch society was changing and the middle class was growing. As it grew it created a strong new demand for realistic paintings, such as serious institutional portraits and images of working life. Rembrandt was one of those born painters who started young and was recognized almost at once. His earliest work, with its love for melodrama and keen interest in the humanity of his models, is essentially merely a hint at what is to come. His painting of a biblical story, *The Blinding of Samson (234),* is superbly done; we flinch involuntarily from the sinister, silhouetted shape of the sword about to jab into a defenceless eye, and we tremble to see the tumultous violence that is raging within the dark and claustrophobic spaces of the cave. Samson writhes in anguish, Delilah flits away, half-gloating, half horrified, and the pressure builds up so high that it threatens to topple over into farce. We can see the same "overweight" of story in the early self-portraits, too.

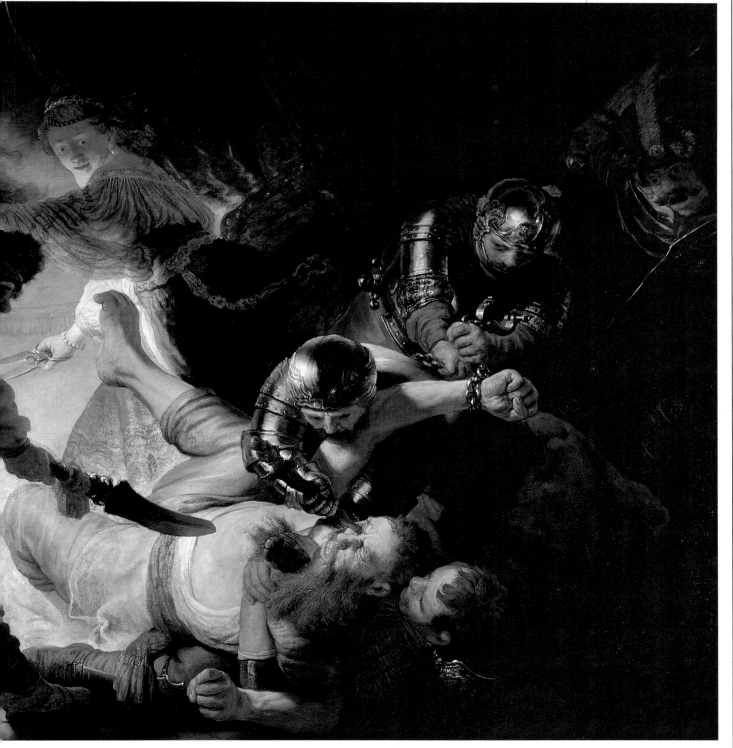

234   Rembrandt, The Blinding of Samson, 1636, 236 x 300 cm (7 ft 9 in x 9 ft 10 in)

The *Self-portrait at the Age of About 21 Years (235)*, dark and secretive, shows Rembrandt in early adulthood, perhaps deliberately acting the part of the "artist". In his mid-life self-portraits he is more reflective, obviously successful, and quietly confident, gazing dispassionately out at us. A late work *(236)*, ten years before his death in relative poverty, shows a face stripped of all pretensions, looking earnestly, not at us, but at himself, judging himself not unkindly but with disinterested truthfulness. It is one of the most moving confessions of personal inadequacy ever made, great art won from personal failure.

PORTRAIT INTERPRETATION

Rembrandt is essentially a master story-teller. Sometimes, even in the portraits, he simply puts into our grasp the materials of the "story" and trusts us to enter into it by ourselves. *Portrait of a Lady with an Ostrich-feather Fan (237)* haunts us with its tranquil sadness, its bravery and

235 **Rembrandt**, Self-portrait at the Age of About 21 Years, *c. 1627, 20 x 16 cm (8 x 6¼ in)*

wisdom. Where do we see all this? Why should we be certain that the unknown lady has a history of sorrow and of exceptional joy? Rembrandt merely puts her before us, with light lingering as if with love on the once-beautiful face, the acceptant hands, the great, free sweep of the feather. Sometimes, though, he plays out

236 *Rembrandt,* **Self-portrait,** *1659, 84 x 66 cm (33 x 26¼ in)*

237 *Rembrandt,* **Portrait of a Lady with an Ostrich-feather Fan,** *c. 1660, 100 x 83 cm (39 x 32½ in)*

REMBRANDT'S ETCHINGS
Etching is a method of engraving in which the image is scratched onto a waxy coating on a metal plate, using a needle. The plate is then immersed in acid, which eats ("etches") into the metal where the image has been scratched. The technique is more versatile than the earlier metal-engraving process, as it enables the artist to alter the tone during the procedure. Etching reached its greatest heights as an art form with Rembrandt, who made his first etching in 1628. He enjoyed experimenting with different-textured papers and inks, and often reworked his etchings several times. His etchings cover a variety of subjects, including portraits, biblical stories, and scenes of daily life.

238 Rembrandt, Joseph Accused by Potiphar's Wife, 1655, 106 x 98 cm (41¾ x 38½ in)

the story for us, counting upon our educated knowledge of the context. *Joseph Accused by Potiphar's Wife (238)* is an incident from the book of Genesis that has intrigued many artists. Old Potiphar, his young wife, and a handsome young Jewish slave: the outcome is as might be expected, except that Joseph is one of the heroes, and he repulses his master's wife and her advances. Woman scorned that she is, the wife accuses Joseph of attempted rape.

Rembrandt makes no distinction here between virtuous and vicious: all merit his compassion. Central is the wife, shifty of eye, false of gesture, clearly not really expecting to be believed. Sad in the shadows, Potiphar listens, and as clearly, does not believe. He knows his wife, and knows his servant. Chivalry ties his hands. The miracle

is that Rembrandt makes us see all this marital interplay, and the sorrow of it, neither party able to be truthful with each other, yet hating the falseness. Ignored amid the passionate privacies of husband and wife, Joseph waits for his public disgrace. He is wholly unassertive, unaggressive, and – most movingly – unself-pitying. He too understands that Potiphar cannot afford to ignore his wife's histrionics, and in a sense, it is only Joseph, the victim, who is capable of accepting the situation. Without a single overt sign, Rembrandt makes us aware that Joseph commits his cause to God, and rests in peace. The wife is isolated in her finery, concerned only with herself. Even the hand meant to gesticulate towards her rapist is not directed at him, but at his red cape hanging over her bed. Her other hand

THE QUESTION OF ATTRIBUTION
In recent years many paintings that were thought to be by Rembrandt have been reattributed to other artists who worked in his workshop. Since the beginning of the 20th century over a third of the 988 "Rembrandts" have been reattributed. Experts check the colour, brushwork, and subject matter to confirm the correct artist. Today many of Rembrandt's old workshop assistants are gaining new respect for having produced renowned paintings.

presses painfully to her breast. She is suffering, not only from her sexual rejection by a younger man, but from her own awareness of her life. Rembrandt involves us in her personality, just as he does in the unbelieving husband, who reaches out, not to her, but to her chair, the material realm where these two have their only contact. Joseph is lost in the gloomy vastness of the chamber, yet a faint nimbus (an emanation of light) enhaloes him.

Rembrandt has allowed light and colour to tell us the meaning of the event and make it move us with its inextricable human complexity and its profound sadness, redeemed only by blind faith in an unseen Providence.

A TENDER UNION

Perhaps the greatest and most profound of all Rembrandt's works is the mysteriously entitled "*Jewish Bride*" *(239)*. This is the 19th century title, since Rembrandt left the work unnamed, and it is a suitable title because no viewer can help but be stirred by the picture's sense of the sacred, and the biblical garb suggests that the couple are Jewish. Who these two people are we shall probably never know, but they are clearly married. Both are past their first youth; they are plain in looks and rather careworn, though splendidly attired.

The husband enfolds his wife with an embrace of heartbreaking tenderness. One hand is on her shoulder and the other on the gift of his love, the golden chain that hangs on her breast. This chain is gold, it is his gift; it is still a chain. It is this aspect of love, that it binds, that its wonder is inseparable from its weight, that seems to preoccupy the woman. She is weighing up the responsibilities of loving and being loved, of receiving and of giving. It is not by chance that her other hand rests upon her womb, since children are the ultimate responsibility of married love.

Love binds, love weighs, love is the most serious experience that we can ever know in our life. It is Rembrandt's awareness of this profound truth, and the glorious visual beauty with which he makes it accessible to us, that makes the "*Jewish Bride*" so unforgettable.

239 Rembrandt, "The Jewish Bride", 1665–67, 122 x 168 cm (48 x 66 in)

"THE JEWISH BRIDE"

"The Jewish Bride" is one of Rembrandt's late works, and one of his most beautiful. Its superb harmony, of red and gold and warm browns, is built around the most profound and compassionate insight into human relationships. It received its current title only in the 19th century, a title that implies that this could be an imaginary portrayal of one of the celebrated biblical marriages: Tobias and Sarah, for instance, or Isaac and Rebekah. But the couple's dress and jewellery, together with the powerful sense of two distinct, living personalities, suggests rather that it is a portrait of an unknown couple.

CARING EMBRACE
This is surely one of the most tender of all paintings. Few depictions of mortal love reveal such depth with such subtlety. His hand lies flat across her bosom, symbolically as well as physically tender. Her hand rests on his, with the gentlest pressure, both acknowledging and returning his caress but again delicately, as though the full significance of their union lies deeper within.

AUTHENTIC EXPRESSION
Despite the opulence and beauty of the wedding costumes, the overwhelming impact of this great painting lies in its simple emotional authenticity. The groom is a little care-worn, his hair is thinning, and there are lines around his mouth and eyes. He makes no grand displays of devotion, and there is no sense of male victory but rather a quiet certainty as he inclines his head towards her, lost in thought almost as though listening to her thoughts. They do not formally address us as witnesses to their betrothal, and the intimacy is such that we feel we are intruding upon a very private moment.

SHIMMERING SLEEVE
The great billowing sleeve swells out like soft golden armour. The paint is heavily built up, and Rembrandt has used short, staccato brush strokes to recreate the many little pleats and folds that shimmer in the light. Touches of thick, white paint provide the brightest points. Thick, encrusted paint glints and shimmers across the surface of the canvas, and one senses that their costumes are stiff and heavy, expensively brocaded. The bride's jewellery is picked out in dots and blobs of paint, again highlighted with white.

240 *William Heda,* Still Life, *1637, 45 x 55 cm (17¾ x 21½ in)*

THE TULIP TRADE

The tulip first appeared in Europe around the mid-16th century, imported from Turkey by the Austrian ambassador. Trading began in 1634 and speculating on future bulbs eventually led to the great crash in 1637, when investors lost huge sums of money. At one stage during the tulipmania a single bulb could sometimes attract extortionate amounts. This illustration shows one of the oldest types of tulip, the Gesneriana.

THE DUTCH STILL-LIFE TRADITION

Humankind, fashioned from earth and spirit, and forever struggling towards the goal of integration, fascinated Rembrandt; still life did not greatly attract him, yet in his own milieu we find some wonderful examples of this genre.

A still life may be said to make a statement, while Rembrandt asks a question. And yet there is infinite curiosity in a work like Heda's (Willem Claesz, 1597–1680). His *Still Life (240)* of a tablecloth, silvery in the light, gleaming with goblets and glasses and wide plates and littered with the remnants of a meal, is painted with the utmost dignity and respect.

De Heem (Jan Davidsz, 1606–1683/84) paints a *Vase of Flowers (241)* as time defied, nature held eternally in a radiant present for our delectation; it is the other pole of the genre. Heda is silent, and de Heem sings aloud with pleasure: both enhance for us the meaning of the ordinary, achieving the same effect, in their own smaller fashion, as does Rembrandt. One might suspect that something in the Dutch temperament responds to the quietness of a still life. It demands from the artist the ability to discard the heights and lows of drama; which suggests, does it not, the flatness of the Dutch landscape?

RADIANT TRANSPARENCY

One of the glories of a great still life is that it is as great in the parts as it is in the whole. This is the aftermath of a meal, but the uneaten nut is a whole world in itself, the fallen glass has a radiant transparency, and we can pick out every detail of the scene with increasing pleasure. Notice how the light gleams on the edge of the knife blade, how the tankard changes in tone when we see it through the bell-shaped end of the glass. Heda shows refraction changing the outline of the tankard and the play of light.

241 Jan de Heem, Vase of Flowers, *c. 1645, 69 x 57 cm (27 x 22½ in)*

DELFT POTTERY

Initially Delft pottery was simply an imitation of imported Chinese pottery, but by the end of the 17th century it had acquired its own independent reputation. Delft ware is blue and white, and as well as dishes, tiles, and vases, more unusual pieces were made, such as this water cistern in the shape of a house. Examples of Delft pottery can be found in countries that once belonged to the Dutch empire, such as Surinam in South America, and Indonesia.

OTHER WORKS BY VERMEER

The Little Street
(Rijksmuseum, Amsterdam)

A Lady with Her Maid
(The Frick Collection, New York)

Interior with an Astronomer
(Louvre, Paris)

Interior with a Music Lesson
(The Royal Collection, Windsor Castle)

Head of a Girl with a Pearl Earring
(Mauritshuis, The Hague)

Interior with a Girl at a Window
(Gemäldegalerie, Dresden)

THE SILENCE OF VERMEER

There is something about the reverent awareness of the still life painter that reminds one of the great solitary of 17th-century Holland, Jan Vermeer (1632–75). He was not literally solitary, having 11 children and a powerful family of in-laws, but none of the hubbub that must have filled his small house is ever evident in his miraculous paintings, far less any suggestion of family.

Vermeer does not need brightness in his paintings. *Woman Holding a Balance (242)*, for example, has the shutters almost closed, with light stealing obliquely round the edges. It catches the downy fur on the lady's jacket, the decorated linen that falls gracefully round her tilted head, the pearls gleaming on the shadowed table. It glances off a finger here and a necklace there, but it insists only on its silence. Silence "expresses" the purity of what exists: pure because it exists. This picture has some symbolism in that the lady is testing her empty balance, and the picture behind her shows the *Last Judgment* (see right).

But the meaning is equally in the "balance" that we experience in the actual painting: darkness and light are held in dynamic equilibrium, and in fact the picture as a whole displays a variety of balances – warm human flesh against the silky and furry garment, the unstable human hand against the frozen certainties of metal.

242 Vermeer, Woman Holding a Balance, *c. 1664, 42.5 x 38 cm (16¾ x 15 in)*

WOMAN HOLDING A BALANCE

This painting is also known as *Woman Weighing Gold*. It is a solemn, allegorical work, in which a young woman stands before the symbols of her material wealth, weighing them for their value, whilst behind her, in the painting on the wall, the figure of Christ can be seen "weighing" souls. The young woman is clearly pregnant, and it is significant that the two strongest accents of warm orange/gold do not emanate from her jewels or her gold but from the small window, high up in the wall, from which the light falls directly onto her stomach. It is tempting to read deeper meaning into this, as comparisons with annunciation paintings (see for example pp.50, 63, 86, and 92) unavoidably spring to mind.

JUDGMENT DAY
The painting on the wall is a version of the Last Judgment *possibly by the 16th-century Flemish altarpiece painter Jean Bellagambe (c. 1480–c. 1535). The air of serenity and contentment in the quiet room contrasts with the pitiful chaos of the damned, who are painted as flat, dim silhouettes behind the intensely vital, living form of the woman.*

MOOD OF CONTEMPLATION
Her knowing expression, with gently tilted head and almost closed eyes, shows her to be more than just idly enjoying her treasures. Rather, she is at a moment when she contemplates the meaning of value itself. She is dressed richly but simply, her head covered by a plain white hood that is "beaded" with drops of light. On the wall opposite her is a mirror, suggestive of her quiet self-contemplation.

A SIMPLE BALANCE
The woman will weigh her gold and pearls on a delicate brass balance with a gesture of infinite grace. The balance is rendered so finely that in parts it is barely visible, and touches of glimmering light shine on the empty pans. This is appropriate since we are again reminded of the other, final weighing depicted behind her.

FAMILY VALUABLES
A rich blue tablecloth has been pushed back, and scattered over the table-top, spilling out of jewellery boxes, is her collection of pearls and gold. Each little orb consists of a single droplet of light, made from individual touches of paint that are jewel-like in themselves. The flat coins, or gold weights, are given a sense of roundness by just the slightest highlight.

Boats are moored and no obstacle presents itself. It is the utter ordinariness of the scene that is so piercingly evocative of the Paradise world. Even when Vermeer paints a *Kitchen Maid (244)* he bathes the kitchen in a quiet radiance. She is merely pouring out milk, but there is a sense of luminous stillness, of time gently slowed, of body translucent with soul, of secular holiness. The simplicities of her yellow bodice and her blue working apron gleam out at us, not beautiful in themselves, but beautiful because light makes all it shines on share its own brightness. Her plain, broad, peasant face is lost in absorption with her task, rather as we think Vermeer must have been as he painted her. He is one of the artists who is immediately accessible, which makes his years of neglect all the more astonishing.

HALS' BRAVADO

Frans Hals (c.1582/83–1666) also knew neglect, but his case is not the same as Vermeer's. We can sympathize with the bewilderment, for example, of the wealthy Coymans family at seeing the finery of young *Willem Coymans (245)* depicted by a rash dribble of paint, with rough slashes pleating his linen sleeve and a rather brutal sensuality lightly informing his face. Willem himself, however, may well have liked his portrait very much indeed (Hals' patrons tended to be delighted with his versions of them).

Willem has a daredevil gallantry, a look of dissipated splendour that any young man might find highly appealing to his self-esteem. Hals does not delve deep into personality like Rembrandt (see p.200) or contemplate all sitters under the noble light of Vermeer (see p.208).

243 Vermeer, View of Delft, *1658, 100 x 117 cm (39 x 46 in)*

CAMERA OBSCURA
The camera obscura (Latin, "dark chamber") was a device used to create an accurate reproduction of a panoramic view or an interior. A pinhole would be made in one side of the box, allowing light to enter. The rays would cross as they passed through the hole and would then fan out, creating an upside-down reduced image on the wall. The artist could then paint a scene with accurate perspective. Vermeer is thought to have used a cubicle-type camera obscura to paint his interiors. A portable camera obscura known as the tent-type (shown above) was also popular.

We come to believe that Vermeer's pictures have a reality – not like everyday reality, but greater, less fragile. It is his unique triumph to concentrate with absolute – or so it seems – optical fidelity on the minutiae of material things. Every texture has its complete integrity in painterly form. He elides, of course, but we are unaware of it, and this sense of total truth, offered to us through a reverence for what is bodily present, effortlessly acquires a sense of the spiritual.

TRANSCENDING THE CITY
The French writer Marcel Proust, who centred his whole literary work upon the recovery, alive and powerful, of memory, thought *View of Delft (243)* the greatest work ever painted. On one level, it appears so unassuming: a topographical setting-out of the appearance of this Dutch city. Vermeer is not inventing, only describing. But he takes the bare facts of the city and its approaches and, without manipulation, renders them transcendent.

That city shining out at us across the water is both Delft and the heavenly Jerusalem, the city of peace. It offers profound variety, not in extravagance but in its simple mixture of roofs and towers, of churches and houses, of sunlit areas and swathes of lovely shadow. Overhead, the sky arches, the rain clouds lift and disperse, the lofty area of blue almost visibly grows.

The tiny figures on the near quayside are vital: they are us, not in the holy city yet, still sundered and yearning, but with great hope.

244 Vermeer, Kitchen Maid, *1656–61, 45 x 40 cm (17¾ x 16 in)*

245 *Frans Hals,* Portrait of Willem Coymans, *1645, 77 × 63 cm (30½ × 25 in)*

ALLA PRIMA TECHNIQUE
Until the 17th century most artists who used oils underpainted their surfaces first, to achieve a consistent surface. Frans Hals was one of the pioneers of the *alla prima* (Italian for "at first") technique in which the paint is applied directly to the ground without underpainting. The effect of this technique is clearly visible in the broad brush strokes and spontaneous textural qualities of much of Frans Hals' work. With the development of better pigments in the 19th century the technique became more popular.

He first made his reputation with a series of portraits, ranging from the celebrated *Laughing Cavalier* to a variety of low-life sketches of gypsies and drunkards, which were all painted in the years 1620–25 and were all delightful renderings of the nuances of expression in the sitters' smiling or leering faces. Hals' family came from Antwerp in Flanders and moved to Haarlem, in the Protestant North, when he was just a child. One is tempted to imagine what he would have produced had he stayed in the Catholic South, where his inclination towards extravagant display would certainly have found a wider field of expression than that of portraiture. Hals paints what he sees, with a sort of daredevil carelessness. He leaps upon the tightrope of pictorial art, rarely stumbling, but astonishing us with his emphatic facility. He achieves "the mostest with the leastest", to adapt the words of an American general.

Much of the work of Hals appeals to us because of its light, virtuoso quality, but in his impoverished old age he rose to a gravity that puts the stamp of greatness on his work.

246 *Frans Hals,* **The Women Regents of the Haarlem Almshouse,** *1664, 170 × 250 cm (5 ft 7 in × 8 ft 2 in)*

His *Women Regents of the Haarlem Almhouse (246)*, painted shortly before the artist's own almshouse death, is a totally serious picture. He has forgotten the ego that spurred him on to witty bravura. Here he shows us not merely the outward look of these tired and elderly women, but something of their individual personalities, and something of their corporate attitude to the responsibilities of their office.

DUTCH GENRE PAINTING

Pieter de Hooch (1629–84) has the uneasy distinction of making us aware of how great is Vermeer. De Hooch is a semi-Vermeer – all the ingredients but lacking the magic. It is as if some of Frans Hals' worldly confidence had seeped into the work, making it parochial.

Yet of course, it is the celebration of the parochial that gives de Hooch his charm, a very real charm, inadequate only in comparison with the very greatest of his contemporaries. *A Dutch Courtyard (247)* has an enchanting immediacy, with its occupants "snapped" as if by a camera. The sense of reality is seductive; at any moment the girl, we feel, will go inside through the open door, and we will go with her. The illusion is of a merely temporary pause in activity, of daylight and weather, of work and play.

This feeling of time held still and on the point of moving forward is also the beauty of *The Skittle Players Outside an Inn (248)* by Jan Steen (1626–79). Much of his work has a coarse vitality,

247 *Pieter de Hooch,* **A Dutch Courtyard,** *c. 1660, 68 × 58 cm (27 × 23 in)*

248 *Jan Steen*, The Skittle Players Outside an Inn, *c. 1652, 33 x 27 cm (13 x 10½ in)*

249 Albert Cuyp, Herdsman with Cows by a River, *c. 1650, 45 × 74 cm (17¾ × 29 in)*

with peasants junketing and a general air of happy vulgarity. But this painting is marvellous, evocative of an evening in early summer, with the viewer made privy to a moment of calm enjoyment. Calm enjoyment is also the constant theme of Albert Cuyp (1620–91), the enjoyment being mostly on the part of cows, which are washed in a heavenly golden radiance, inhabiting a natural paradise on our behalf *(249)*. The herd stands peacefully in the peaceful waters, the ships move past them slowly into the light. It is essentially a communication of serenity. Sunlight and its bovine enjoyers do not seem the stuff of great art, and this is one of the enchantments of the Baroque. It makes its beauty out of the ordinary with great gusto. Often the focus is on the land or sea, flat fields becoming as spaciously beautiful as the romantic mountains of earlier or later art.

Jacob van Ruisdael (1628/9–82), can take a *Forest Scene (250)*, a tangle of trees and glimpsed water, a great dead horizontal of stricken branch and root, dark skies forming and humankind departing, and without tidying it up or making a moral, give us a moving depiction of the tangle of our complex and vulnerable lives. He has a greater weight than any other Dutch landscape artist. There is almost a sense of a tragic dimension, but never one without hope. His uncle, Salomon van Ruisdael (c.1600–70), works the same magic with river scenes.

Pieter Saenredam (1597–1665), focusing on another aspect of the workaday, takes us into the great spaces of church interiors, like

250 Jacob van Ruisdael, Forest Scene, *c. 1660/65, 105 × 131 cm (41 × 51½ in)*

251 Pieter Saenredam, **The Grote Kerk, Haarlem,** *1636–37, 60 x 82 cm (23½ x 32¼ in)*

The Grote Kerk, Haarlem (251). The play of light on these silent architectural masses has an almost Vermeerish profundity, a strange immediacy. It would be easy to get carried away into speculation about the meaning of "interiors", which these pictures seem to be about, and so it is useful to remember that Saenredam, who specializes in church interiors, somehow also manages to get the same "inner" quality when he paints church exteriors.

The Dutch seemed to have an insatiable love for the actualities of their surroundings: their Calvinism, however tolerantly held, makes the idea of explicitly religious painting unappealing, and we can feel a great weight of quasi-religious significance being quietly removed, to rest upon landscape, still life, and portraiture. There was still room for the so-called "history" painting genre, but the most popular narrative painting was that of Gerard Dou (1613–75).

Dou's works were small, exquisitely finished, and technically perfect. Although this praise sounds rather mechanical, there is no doubt that, at his best, Dou well deserved his reputation. These small, jewel-like pictures still delight and allure: it may be for the sheer contrast between their tiny size and their intensity of focus. Dou had been Rembrandt's pupil, but he seems to have taken little of the master's spirit. The cluttered but brilliant cave interior of *The*

Hermit (252) has Dou's own technical intricacy but nothing of Rembrandt's spiritual intensity, and they remain essentially genre works.

252 Gerard Dou, **The Hermit,** *1670, 46 x 34 cm (18 x 13½ in)*

WILLIAM III OF ORANGE
As Stadholder (ruler) of the United Provinces, William III of Orange (1650–1702) rescued his country from the hands of Louis XIV in the Franco-Dutch wars of 1672–79. He was a sincere Calvinist and a respected patron of the arts. He had grown up in the uncertain climate of the rule of the anti-Orange party led by Johann de Witt. In the revolution of 1672 he overthrew his enemies and became Stadholder. He became King of Britain and Ireland in the "Glorious Revolution" of 1688, when the Whigs and Tories invited him to invade the country and claim the throne for himself and his wife Mary (daughter of the British King James II).

THE GRAND TOUR
A favourite pastime of the young rich in the 17th and 18th centuries was to go on the Grand Tour. Accompanied by a servant, a young aristocrat would tour Europe, culminating in a stay in Italy to appreciate the arts of classical antiquity. This 18th-century caricature shows a horrified father meeting his fashionable returning son.

PIERRE PUGET

Recognized as the greatest French Baroque sculptor, Pierre Puget (1620–94) originally trained as a ship's sculptor in Marseilles. His earliest work is on the portals of the town hall in Toulon, completed in 1656. He created his most famous work, the *Milo of Crotona*, for Louis XIV's palace at Versailles. The sculpture shown above, *The Assumption of the Virgin*, is now kept in Marseilles.

FRANCE: A RETURN TO CLASSICISM

Dutch painters loved landscape, and they acquired great skill in its depiction, but the great names in landscape painting in the 17th century were French. Foremost among these were Nicolas Poussin and Claude Lorrain, who both lived for years in Italy and were strongly influenced by Italy's natural Classicism, however dissimilar they were in other ways.

The lure of Rome, the heartland of the Baroque style, was strong in the first half of the 17th century, so much so that the French painting tradition, which was classical at heart, was considerably weakened by the exodus of artists. Among these was Nicolas Poussin (1594– 1665), who enjoyed considerable fame in Rome and painted many important works there. It took the persuasive powers of Louis XIII and his Chief Minister, Cardinal Richelieu (see p.223), to entice Poussin back from Rome in 1640.

The King had made previous attempts to rejuvenate the French tradition in painting, but he had met with little real success. A tradition still existed, and was even growing, in France, and it was both delicate in palette and dignified in approach. But the French School did not develop until Poussin's arrival from Rome. His art drew on Carracci's legacy of Venetian harmony and ideal beauty (see p.182). In Italy, he had studied the High Renaissance masters, together with antique sculpture, and he was also influenced by the arch-classicist Domenichino (see p.183), who was 13 years his senior and who ran a successful workshop in Rome.

Poussin's art represents a rejection of the emotional aspects of Italian Baroque, but at the same time sacrifices none of the Baroque's spiritual intensity and richness – which distinguishes him from Neoclassical art (see p.256)

253 Nicolas Poussin, **The Holy Family on the Steps,** *1648, 68 x 98 cm (27 x 38½ in)*

In a sense, his aims in painting have more in common with those of the Renaissance artists (see pp.79–138). Poussin brought to the Baroque an austere, restrained Classicism, combined with a clear, glowing light.

He is an artist of the utmost intelligence, achieving total integration of every element within his pictures. But it is a visual intelligence, a massive understanding of beauty, so that what could be daunting in its orderliness is radiant with supreme grace. This great painterly intellect moves us rather than convinces us. In the words that John Donne, the 17th-century English poet, used to describe his beloved, it could be said of Poussin that his "body thought". It is this wonderful incarnation of vision in actuality that makes Poussin supreme.

AUSTERE BEAUTY

The Holy Family on the Steps (253) might seem, at first viewing, not a landscape work at all. This is, broadly, quite correct: the concentration is upon the five human figures in the centre. But they form a great equilateral triangle, based upon the long, low step that acts as a plinth and a barrier. Mary is a sacred plinth herself, a holy barrier that holds Jesus up for us to see but is His earthly safeguard. So protected, the naked Child leans down to His nude cousin, little John the Baptist, who is untended by his own mother, St Elizabeth, all of whose longing attention is fixed upon Mary's Child.

Balancing her, humbly seated in shadow, sits St Joseph, whose elegant feet emerge into astonishingly clear light. Three objects line the lower margin: a basket of fruit, symbolic of the world's fertility that will spring from this Family: a fertility of grace. Near Joseph, as if under his care, are two containers – a classical vase, reminiscent of the Greeks, and a box, which recalls the eastern kings and their costly gifts.

Material riches lie at the base, then, and from here the painting soars up, the eye being led by balustrade and pillar, to the porticos that open on infinity and the endless sky. The Holy Family is clearly not sitting on the steps of a real building: this is more an idealized version of an entrance, though it lacks symmetry. The glories of this world are asymmetrical; only the perfect balance of the Holy Family has the beauty of pure rationality. The centre is an apple offered to the Holy Child by our representative, John.

The fruit of the fall is here redeemed, and the discreet orange trees indicate that redemption has now happened. There is fruit galore, fruit for us all. Mary holds Jesus almost as if He is living fruit, and at once we pick up eucharistic resonances. In Poussin there is always subtlety

254 *Nicolas Poussin,* **Self-portrait**, *1650,*
97 x 73 cm (38 x 29 in)

upon subtlety, but at no time is it either forced subtlety or mere conceptual cleverness. He takes his concepts into his own depths, and there he finds their proper form. This painting is of an ascent, powered by the insistent verticals and made credible by the exquisite placement of continual stepping-stones of horizontals.

The austere *Self-portrait* in the Louvre *(254)* makes no concessions to vanity. Poussin looks out gravely, with his fleshy nose and secretive eyes, and his lips shut with that firmness so obvious in all his work. He encompasses himself with canvases that are also geometrical intensifiers. His background, he implies, is one of severe order. Yet the only actual picture we see – a young woman being embraced – has a romantic charm. The other rectangles of canvas, as well as the door, are blank, and all the frames are blank. While seeming to expose himself, Poussin is actually preserving his secrecy.

NICOLAS POUSSIN
Poussin aimed to achieve a unity of mood in each picture by developing his theory of modes. According to this theory, the subject and the emotional situation of the painting dictate the appropriate treatment. Poussin also used a miniature stage set to practice composition and lighting for his paintings.

THE SUN KING
Louis XIV of France
(1638–1715) reigned as an
absolute monarch at a
time of great growth and
development in the history
of France. He is known as
the Sun King because he
was seen as a new sun god
who shines upon everyone
and is omnipresent. The
king believed that his
powers were ordained by
God and that he was the
incarnation of the state.
He would make all
decisions by consulting only
a few very close ministers,
and his favoured style
(Classicism) was imposed
on all new buildings.
His most lasting symbol
(a monument to his own
splendour) is the Palace
of Versailles, which was
begun in 1669 and
became the residence
of the court in 1682.

**OTHER WORKS BY
POUSSIN**

*The Crossing of
the Red Sea*
(National Gallery of
Victoria, Melbourne)

*Venus Presenting Arms
to Aeneas*
(Art Gallery of
Ontario, Toronto)

The Nurture of Jupiter
(Dulwich Picture
Gallery, London)

*The Triumph
of Neptune*
(Philadelphia
Museum of Art)

Apollo and Daphne
(Alte Pinakothek,
Munich)

Acis and Galatea
(National Gallery of
Ireland, Dublin)

SHEPHERDS AND ARCADIA

To educated people in the 17th century the name
Arcadia readily evoked the pastoral tradition, that
easy-going genre of poetry that had developed
in parallel with epic writing since the time of
the classical Greeks. The tradition stems from
the carefree, open-air life that was supposedly
enjoyed by shepherds and shepherdesses, who
spent all summer guarding their flocks.
Consequently they had plenty of time in which
to play their flutes and compose love poems,
which they might sing to one another, perhaps
in a contest.

Best remembered of the pastoral poets were
Theocritus in Sicily and Virgil in Italy, whose
Eclogues are the best remembered of all. Arcadia
is mentioned in the *Eclogues*, and occasionally
in literature since the Renaissance.

The phrase "*et in Arcadia ego*" cannot be
traced to any known source in the classics. It
means either "I, the one who is dead, was once
in Arcadia too," or "I, Death, am in Arcadia
too." The Italian painter Guercino (see p.185)
made a painting with this same theme in 1620.

Poussin himself produced two paintings on
the "Death in Arcadia" theme. The first (the
Chatsworth version) was painted between 1630
and 1632. In it, a group of shepherds discovers
with shock that a tomb, with its disturbing
message, exists in their idyllic countryside.

They are shown leaning forwards in a tense
attitude, confronting the fearsome discovery.
In the version shown here (the Louvre version,
255), originally entitled *Happiness Subdued by
Death* and painted in 1638–40, the shepherds
form a more relaxed group around the tomb.
Instead of reacting dramatically they seem to
be pondering the meaning of the inscription.
Each of the four shepherds is expressing his or
her own personal emotional response. Without
overemphasis, Poussin makes us clearly aware of
those vulnerable humans in all their individuality.

Poussin's Arcadia is a silent place; even the
shepherds seem to be communicating by gesture
rather than by word. They seem to have found,
to their bewilderment, their first evidence of
death. It is evidence, too, that their beautiful
country has a history, has been lived in and
died in, and yet this history has been completely
forgotten. They puzzle out the inscription on
the tomb with wonder and fear.

What gives this picture its force, of course,
is its relevance to our own personal histories.
We pass a milestone in human maturity when
we come to an emotional understanding of death
and of our own relative insignificance in the
context of human history. Countless generations
lived before us and will live after us. In all the
magnificence of their youthful beauty, the
shepherds must accept this.

255 Nicolas Poussin, Et in Arcadia Ego, *c. 1638–40, 85 x 121 cm (33½ x 47½ in)*

ET IN ARCADIA EGO

Historically, Arcadia was the central plateau of the mountainous region of southern Greece and was inhabited by shepherds and hunters. But Arcadia was also an earthly paradise, a pastoral idyll celebrated by poets and artists as early as the 3rd century BC. It was the home of romantic love, ruled over by Pan, the rustic god of "all things": flocks and herds, woods and fields. Its native shepherds and shepherdesses shared their simple paradise with nymphs, satyrs, centaurs, and the bacchantes.

SILENT COMMUNICATION
The shepherds and shepherdess respond in different ways to the discovery of death. Some are content to ponder its significance, while others question and decipher. All, however, are silent, revealing their sadness or curiosity through individual gestures and expressions. One young shepherd looks up at the young woman beside him with an especially urgent communication, as though struck with sudden realization of his own immortality.

LANDSCAPE
Although this is one of Poussin's mature works, his treatment of the landscape is not as stylistically developed as is his treatment of form and colour throughout the rest of the painting. The line of trees and foliage serves primarily to enclose the scene and act as a backdrop to the main focus of attention, which centres on the discovery of a tomb.

"I TOO WAS ONCE IN ARCADIA"
The inscription is the central focal point of the whole work. All our attention is directed to it, reinforced by the puzzled gestures of the shepherds as they run their fingers over the tomb as though hoping to discover its mysterious identity. The painting takes on the nature of an elegy as they quietly and solemnly contemplate the significance of the words (see left).

CLASSICAL FORM
Poussin has not portrayed the simple and carefree shepherds and shepherdesses supposed to inhabit Arcadia, but instead classically formed, sober and dignified figures from antiquity. The young woman manifests the classical ideal, with her smooth brow and fine nose, the proportions of her head to her body, and above all, her noble, statuesque bearing. In her figure, we can see Poussin's distinctive late handling of colour. It is sharp, strong, and clear, and the artist's growing passion for order and clarity is paramount. The four figures form a tight cluster around the tomb, the balance equally distributed among them.

The Funeral of Phocion (256) shows Poussin's landscape art at its most profound. There is a story in this painting, one of those classic tales of great moral meaning that were so dear to him. Phocion was an Athenian general who argued for peace at a time when the majority were for war with Macedon. His enemies used Athens' democratic system to have him condemned.

Poussin shows this victim of judicial murder being carried to his burial by a mere two faithful slaves. They carry him through a world teeming with antique activity. Behind them the great city can be seen, with its temple, its domed capitol proclaiming Athenian order, its inhabitants peacefully busy at their rightful occupations.

Yet all this outward stability is made into a lie by the sad pair in the foreground, moving disconsolately through the wholly civilized terrain on their uncivilized task. Justice has been flouted, cruelty and envy have triumphed: the great pacific state apparatus grinds on with massive and unreal dignity. The eye is entranced by the sheer intelligibility and interest of the scene, by the nobility of the concept and the beauty of its execution. It is as intense as any poetry, yet the poetry is always epic. Poussin can daunt, but he is worth all our effort.

CLAUDE'S PASTORAL IDYLLS

Claude (Claude Gellée, 1600–82), whose Frenchness was marked by adding "Lorrain" to his name, was a fellow inhabitant of Rome with Poussin. Claude too is a very great artist, but not an intellectual. Where Poussin thought out a work, Claude used his intuition. One understood the classic world, the other entered it by imagination: both visions are wonderful.

Claude is forever making us free of the classical paradise-that-never-was (or at least, not literally) so that it is subliminally the essence of his work. He sees the landscape of the Roman Campagna (a low-lying plain surrounding Rome) as bathed in a golden light, a place in harmony with the nymphs or else with the heroes of the Bible. We feel it is much the same for Claude whether we gaze across the wooded hills with Paris and the three goddesses he must assess for the most beautiful in *The Judgment of Paris (257)*, or with the biblical Isaac and Rebekah, who have come to celebrate their marriage in *Landscape with the Marriage of Isaac and Rebekah (258)*. The "subject" is not what the title indicates. Paris and Isaac and Rebekah are excuses, pretexts for his venture into the lovely lost world of pastoral poetry.

256 Nicolas Poussin, The Funeral of Phocion, *1648, 47 x 71 cm (18½ x 28 in)*

257 Claude Lorrain, **The Judgment of Paris,** *1645/46, 112 x 150 cm (44 x 59 in)*

Both landscapes are made glorious by their trees, by the amazing sense they provide of immense spaciousness. The eye roams untrammelled to the distant hills and follows the curves of the shining waters. It is not a real landscape, but its power to arouse emotion is real.

To the modern eye, *The Marriage of Isaac and Rebekah* might seem to work better than the *Judgment of Paris* if only because Claude's great weakness is thought to be his painting of the human figure. In *The Marriage* the tiny human forms dancing and feasting in the glade are as removed from us in space as they are in time. We stand at a height looking down, and although in the Bible this marriage was an important event for the continuance of the "seed of Abraham", it is the landscape that matters here, that dwarfs the human celebrants into relative insignificance. Claude clearly recognized this by his very title. Yet the landscape, so shadowed, so immemorial, does not fight the theme of marriage; it reinforces it.

In *The Judgment of Paris* we are much closer to the drama. The four actors (five if we include the infant Cupid, who clings to his mother) are fairly large and also fairly individualized. The painting captures a moment at the start of the judgment. Juno, as queen, is the first of the three goddesses to speak, putting her case as the most beautiful to Paris. He is perching rather insecurely

on his rock, almost dislodged by the vigour of her approaches. Minerva, as befits a wise woman, abstracts herself from the scene and in so doing becomes its appropriate but unwitting centre. It is on her white body, as she leans forward to tie her sandal, that Claude's golden light so lovingly lingers.

258 Claude Lorrain, Landscape with the Marriage of Isaac and Rebekah, *1648,
149 x 197 cm (58¾ x 77½ in)*

259 Claude Lorrain, Landscape with Ascanius Shooting the Stag of Silvia, *1682, 120 x 150 cm (47 x 59 in)*

Very occasionally theme matters in Claude, as in his last painting, *Landscape with Ascanius Shooting the Stag of Silvia (259)*. Here again is the whole lovely expanse of nature, but this time it is all affected by the dreadful certainty that murder is to be done and the balance of the Italian pre-Roman peace destroyed. Claude homes in on the tension of the one moment when Ascanius would still be able, if he chose, to hold back the arrow. The world waits in fear, and stag and man are locked in puzzled questioning. We need not know the legend to guess what will happen. We have indeed destroyed our sacred stag and brought down upon ourselves the end of peace. All the tragedy of the daily newspaper is implicit in this great painting.

THE ART OF THE EVERYDAY

Poussin, sublime by nature, said that those who painted "mean subjects" did so because of "the weakness of their talents". This obviously has no reference to Claude, but it might indicate why the le Nain brothers and Georges de la Tour were relatively unappreciated. The le Nains took for their subject the humble lives of the peasants. *Landscape with Peasants (260)*, by Louis le Nain (1593–1648) has, in fact, a lovely sweep of dullish scenery that seduces by its resolute lack of excitement. Peasants stand or sit, quiet amid the quietness, unaffected as is the painter by any need to become "interesting".

260 Louis le Nain, Landscape with Peasants, *c. 1640, 47 x 57 cm (18½ x 22½ in)*

LIGHT AND DARKNESS

Georges de la Tour (1593–1652) did not exactly choose "mean subjects", but he painted with a light-and-shade duality that relates to the Caravaggesque tradition (see p.177), and he did so in a manner that verges on the simplistic. His forms are sparse, his design bare. He was a provincial painter, and his unusual freedom from accustomed conventions might well have seemed inadequate or "mean" to a classicist. *The Repentant Magdalen (261)* concentrates with semi-brutal fierceness on the legendary period that the Magdalen, who had been a sinner,

spent in lamenting her past. But it seems rather to be the picture of abstract thought. The Magdalen is shown as lost in profound musing, her hand caressing the skull, a "vanitas" motif, which is repeated in its mirrored reflection. The candle – the only source of light – is masked by the dome of bare bone, and the Magdalen does not so much repent as muse. With great daring, the major part of the picture is more darkness, with the young woman looming up out of the shadow like a second Lazarus. It is a work hard to forget, yet its power is difficult to explain. Vulgar? Or spiritually intense?

THE PHILOSOPHY OF DESCARTES

Regarded as the founder of modern philosophy, Descartes (1596–1650) was a French philosopher and mathematician. His *Discourse on Method*, published in 1637, explains the basis of his theory of dualism –"I think therefore I am". He argued that reason reigns supreme and that it is vital to systemize knowledge. The idea of God is so complex that no man could have invented it and so God must have planted the idea into man's mind.

261 Georges de la Tour, **The Repentant Magdalen,** *c. 1635, 113 x 93 cm (44 x 36½ in)*

CARDINAL RICHELIEU

Under Louis XIII, France was a weak country, with the Protestant population forming a state within a state. Richelieu (1585–1642) became Minister of State in 1624 and his first task was to reduce the power of the Huguenots. He was to remain a vital pioneering force in France until the ascendency of Louis XIV, and he survived many plots against his life. He died leaving Louis XIV in a position of absolute power over a stronger and more unified country.

ROCOCO

With Antoine Watteau we move into the Rococo era. This style evolved in France and became a dominant influence in 18th-century art through most of Europe. The word was not a flattering term (few art labels ever have been); it was coined in the early 19th century, deriving from the French word rocaille. *This was the name of a style of interior decoration that made use of shell patterns and other ornamental stonework. Rococo art was thought of as thin, airy-fairy, not the serious art of the past.*

The Rococo style emerged in the early 18th century as an exaggeratedly decorative variation of the Baroque. Perhaps, at first, only the French took it seriously; its first great champion was Jean Antoine Watteau (1684–1721). There is an underlying sadness in his pictures that gives a painful note to all his airs and graces, a wistfulness that belongs more to the 17th than the 18th century. Watteau was born in Flanders and lived most of his short life in exile in France. His work evinces a poignant sense of never belonging, of having no lasting stake in the world, that is

FETES GALANTES

Watteau arrived in Paris in 1702 and soon made a reputation as the inventor of a new artistic genre known as *fêtes galantes*. The name means "a feast of courtship" and was coined by members of the French Academy in 1717. It applies to any open-air scene with a mixed company, such as musicians, actors, and flirtatious lovers, all enjoying themselves out of doors.

Many of Watteau's contemporaries favoured the genre, using it to portray the manners and fashions of the aristocracy.

262 *Jean Antoine Watteau, "Embarkation for Cytherea", 1717, 129 × 194 cm (50½ × 76 in)*

specific to Watteau's own circumstances but has a moving relevance to us all. His training and early artistic development took place outside the confines of Paris, which is lucky for us, since the Parisian art world was becoming increasingly academic. He studied in Luxembourg under Claude Audran. Here he was fully able to absorb Rubens' great *Life of Maria de' Médici* cycle (see p.188), and we can see something of the sensual dynamism of Rubens – only in miniature form – in Watteau's delicate paintings.

LOVE AND PATHOS

Watteau was the inventor of a new art genre (though few ever could make his poetic use of it): *fêtes galantes*, in which lovers sang and danced and flirted, always on the edge of loss.

263 Jean Antoine Watteau, Italian Comedians, probably 1720, 63 x 76 cm (25 x 30 in)

This example, "*Embarkation for Cytherea*" *(262)*, is in fact misnamed, but has been so immemorially. It shows lovers leaving, not embarking for, the fabled isle of lovers, on which they have made their vows to the shadowy Venus who is hidden in the undergrowth. The act of taking vows has made them into inseparable pairs, but they leave with reluctance. Never again will love be so accessible and so certain: in leaving the seclusion of Venus and her bower they set all at risk and jeopardize their happiness. Watteau has no need to make this explicit. His pairs of lovers are satiated with fulfilment, yet move sadly and slowly. Love does not bring joy.

Watteau's other famous theme differs only at the literal level: his many scenes featuring the troupes of actors, Italian or French, who entertained the court. These two nationalities had different approaches to drama, but both traditions were based on the theme of love and its disappointments. *Italian Comedians (263)* has its jester and its gaily posturing actors, its pretty ladies, and its flirtations. But at the centre is the strange, tragic figure of Pierrot, taller than anyone else, starkly visible in his silken whites, motionless and heraldic.

There is even a blasphemous echo of Pilate presenting Christ to the mockery of the people, and it is impossible to say that Watteau did not explicitly intend this echo. No crown of thorns, but a crown of flowers lies neglected and rejected on the steps. All gleams, and there is laughter, but we are strangely chilled.

COMMEDIA DELL'ARTE

The Italian *commedia dell'arte* began as an anti-literary form of theatre based on improvisation, with juggling and acrobatics. It had a set of stock characters, the foremost of which were a rich, foolish old man and his clever servant Harlequin. Two others were Columbine and Pierrot, the latter being the embodiment of out-spoken simplicity. With its anti-establishment character it was banned by the French nobility in 1687. In 1716 the Italian actors were recalled by the Duc d'Orléans, Louis XV's Regent from 1713 to 1723. Scripts were eventually written for the *commedia dell'arte*; these had a delicate verbal style, and often an erotic undercurrent.

DIANA BATHING

Diana (known as Artemis to the Greeks) has several identities: as chastity, and more commonly, as the huntress, in which guise she appears in this painting. To the Romans, she had three personifications: Diana for the earth, Hecate for the underworld, and Luna for the moon – which explains the crescent moon she wears in her hair.

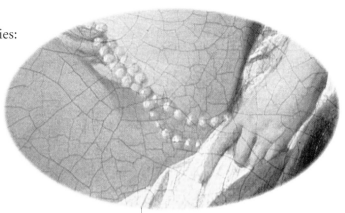

PEARLS

This detail reveals how the surface of the painting is covered in a network of fine cracks. The smooth, uninterrupted finish of Diana's perfect skin seems all the more delicate. Pearls suggest the moon, both in their gentle gleam and their lovely rotundity, and these are Diana's only ornaments. She needs nothing else, suggests Boucher, her godhead is apparent.

ATTENDANT NYMPH

Boucher has chosen to depict Diana after the hunt; to have shown her in active pursuit of game would not have suited his temperament at all. Instead, we are presented with what is essentially a boudoir scene, a fine young lady seated on her expensive silks and pampered by her handmaiden – except that this happens to be the goddess Diana, attended by a reverent nymph who dries her feet, and seated in a secluded woodland glade.

DIANA'S HOUNDS

Diana as the Huntress is shown with hunting dogs, arrows, and quiver. One of the dogs, alerted by a noise in the undergrowth, lifts its head and sniffs the air. This is an allusion, perhaps, to the doomed mortal, Actaeon, who, according to legend, accidentally stumbles upon the scene and, as punishment for beholding the naked goddess, is turned into a stag and devoured by his own dogs.

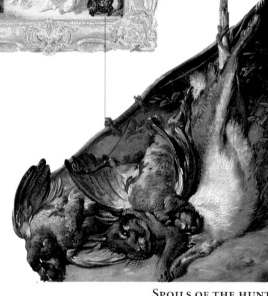

SPOILS OF THE HUNT

A rabbit and two doves have been strung onto Diana's dainty bow. Diana was often depicted in opposition to Venus, the goddess of love. Here, Venus' attribute of a pair of doves – symbols of love and lust – has been vanquished by chastity. The birds' earthy, vital nature contrasts sharply with Diana's unearthly, pure skin.

264 François Boucher, Diana Bathing, *1742, 57 x 73 cm (22½ x 28¾ in)*

BOUCHER'S SOLID STYLE

After Watteau came François Boucher (1703–70), a fuller and more solid painter, less magical but more robust. This contrast may be the outward reflection of the fact that he was in relatively better health than Watteau, whose constitution was frail. Boucher demonstrates the Rococo fear of the solemn, and his art – more than that of Watteau – reveals the truly Rococo spirit of decoration.

Yet, despite this ornamental spirit, Boucher's entrancing ladies, who are usually shown sweetly displaying to us their naked charms, are not trivial. At his best, Boucher succeeds in making us share in his worship of the female body, its vulnerable roundness, and its essential innocence. There is far more to Boucher than appears at first viewing. He is a great celebrator,

and a work like his masterpiece, *Diana Bathing (264)*, celebrates not only the firmly rounded goddess and her eager companion, but the civilized terrain of parkland as well. This is a cultured landscape, in which the savagery of nature has been tamed.

At the start of the 20th century Boucher was held in very low esteem, seen merely as a decorator and an artist of charm but little substance. His work in fact is very out of key with contemporary attitudes, especially feminism. Strangely, however, he has been creeping up in critical esteem as the spirit of his work – which is genuinely reverential – becomes more apparent to the discerning eye. Creative beauty in all its forms moved him emotionally and his eye dwells as lovingly on the dogs and the riverbank as it does on the nymphs.

Boucher never ogles, but – and in this respect he is akin to Rubens – lifts his hat and sweeps low the plumes. *Venus Consoling Love (265)* floats deliciously onto the canvas, one naked goddess and three naked children. They have an eerie similarity, all four, to the fatly feathered pair of nesting birds among the reeds. Nothing here is real or meant to be. But the sense of pleasure in ideal beauty is very real, and makes the work into much more than a triviality.

BEFORE THE REVOLUTION

Fragonard (Jean-Honoré, 1732–1806) followed Boucher. He came from the town of Grasse in southeastern France, which was and is the centre of the French perfume industry. Fragonard was a rapid and spontaneous painter. He was as skilled as his teacher Boucher in sharing his pleasure in young women and their bodies, but more alert to their emotions.

Fragonard had a keen and endearing sense of human folly, especially when set in the expanses of the natural world. In his *Blindman's Buff (266)* a children's game is merrily being played out by adults. Despite the light, bright and airy atmosphere there is a sense of foreboding in the painting. The gathering clouds that dominate

265 *François Boucher,* Venus Consoling Love, *1751, 107 × 84 cm (42 × 33 in)*

half the canvas suggest to us, yet surely not explicitly to the painter, that the French Revolution was to come before his death. The Revolution had very unfortunate consequences for Fragonard, as it ruined his patrons and deprived him of commissions. After 1793, despite previous success, he lived in obscurity for the rest of his life.

A Young Girl Reading (267) is aglow with the softest of umbers, the rich colour darkening and paling as it follows the girl's young contours. Her back is supported by a sort of maternal abundance of rosy pillow, but there is an almost horizontal element in the board under her arm except when her charming sleeve has overlapped its rigid outline. She is intent upon her book, as unprotected as any Boucher nymph.

The sweetness of *A Young Girl Reading*, its almost Renoirish charm (see p.298), should not blind us to its strength and solidity. There is a geometrical framework to the softness of the adolescent reader: a strong, vertical swathe of yellow-brown wall, and the gleaming horizontal bar of the armrest. It is this ability to transcend decoration that distinguishes Fragonard. Look at the girl's neck and bosom: delicious frills and ribbons, and the crinkling descent of the silks, yet there is the firm basis of a real, plump, human body. As in *Blindman's Buff*, the literal theme of this picture is held in an unstated context of solemnity. Like Boucher, Fragonard is more profound than he seems, and his genuine sensitivity is becoming increasingly apparent.

266 *Jean-Honoré Fragonard,* Blindman's Buff, *probably c. 1765, 216 × 198 cm (7 ft 1 in × 6 ft 6 in)*

267 Jean-Honoré Fragonard, A Young Girl Reading, c. 1776, 81 x 65 cm (32 x 26 in)

CHARDIN: WEIGHT AND SOBRIETY IN A ROCOCO ERA

Jean-Baptiste-Siméon Chardin (1699–1779), who is so unlike the pleasure-loving Fragonard, taught the young Fragonard before he found a more congenial mentor in Boucher.

Chardin is categorized as "Rococo" only by date, as it were. Despite his charming choice of subjects, frequently painting small children and young servants, he did not have it in him to create other than from his depth. *The Attentive Nurse (268)* simply shows a young nursemaid preparing the supper egg. She stands in the kitchen engrossed in her task, a coloured column of lovely rectitude. The table is laid as for a sacrament: the bread and the goblet take on a sacred significance, and the great white water jug has baptismal import.

None of the mysterious significance contained in *The Attentive Nurse* is overt. It is simply that the scene has overtones. The whites here – the cloth, eggs, jug, and towel – are so pure; and the pinky oranges in the petticoat and the bread, picked up and intensified in the floor and bowl,

SÈVRES PORCELAIN

In the early part of the 18th century hard-paste porcelain became highly fashionable. In 1738 Robert and Gilles Debois from Chantilly offered their porcelain-making services to the French royal household. They were paid 10,000 louis and given part of the castle at Vincennes to set up the factory. The company moved to Sèvres in 1753 and Louis XV and Madame de Pompadour began to commission work.

The Sèvres porcelain is identifiable by the richness of the colours and the quality and opulence of the gilt decoration. The three most popular colours were *bleu de roi* (dark blue), *bleu céleste* (light blue, illustrated above), and *rose Pompadour* (pink).

OTHER WORKS BY CHARDIN

Still Life with the Ingredients of Lunch
(Musée des Beaux Arts, Carcassone)

Vase of Flowers
(National Gallery, Edinburgh)

Girl with a Shuttlecock
(Uffizi, Florence)

The Governess
(National Gallery of Canada, Ottawa)

Soap Bubbles
(National Gallery of Art, Washington)

Woman Working on a Tapestry
(National Museum, Stockholm)

268 Jean-Baptiste-Siméon Chardin, The Attentive Nurse, *probably 1738, 46 x 37 cm (18 x 14½ in)*

269 *Jean-Baptiste-Siméon Chardin,* **Still Life with Game,** *c. 1760/65, 50 x 60 cm (20 x 23½ in)*

are so ruddy with the goodness of health, that we feel unable to accept the work at face value. Often in Chardin there are underlying moral messages or implications, as we see in *The House of Cards (270)* (life's instability and the child's ignorance of it) or *Soap Bubbles* (not illustrated – the uselessness, the vanity in the biblical sense, of most human activities). But, paradoxically, the more explicit the moral, the less its effect.

It is the implicit moralities, like the sacramental overtones of the nurse with her egg, or the similar message contained in one of the great still lifes *(269)* (from one of the greatest of all the still-life painters) that most move us. The slaughtered bird and hares, all small and harmless creatures, lie in solemn state on their altar of the kitchen ledge. A dusky shadow glimmers on the wall, and the slab seems lit from within. Chardin is paying homage to a ritual sacrifice, offered on our behalf. And not only the animals: the vegetable world, too, is one of sacrifice, and Chardin duly bows his head before it.

Chardin never ventured upon what his age would have considered a major theme: his work is essentially domestic, quiet, undramatic. It is his treatment that makes his themes major.

270 *Jean-Baptiste-Siméon Chardin,* **The House of Cards,** *c. 1735, 82 x 66 cm (32¼ x 26¼ in)*

TIEPOLO AND ITALIAN ROCOCO

The Italians also had their great Rococo artists, especially in Venice, where the sway and sparkle of the omnipresent waters make a fitting setting. Giambattista Tiepolo (1696–1770) is the quintessential master of this style; all the decorative vitality and glowing colour of the Venetian tradition finds its culmination in him. His exuberance is held under masterly control; he has a natural gaiety that is supremely imaginative and capable of flights of visual wit that have never been excelled.

Tiepolo's greatest work was done mostly in fresco. In these vast, soaring compositions the sheer extent of space to be covered draws from his stupendous best. There is, therefore, a pleasing congruity in his often being commissioned to paint ceilings. This he did with enormous panache and skill, something we may miss if we see his work in a museum, where it has been removed from above our heads and pallidly hung upon a wall.

But the great ceiling at the Museo ca Rezzonico in Venice *(271)* still remains in place, arching superbly over our heads and worth any amount of neck craning. It was painted to celebrate the marriage of two Venetian princely houses, the families of Ludovico Rezzonico and Faustina Savorgnan, which Tiepolo does in a delightful allegory. Ludovico, the bridegroom, leans expectantly forward, the lion of St Mark at his side, holding aloft the banner that shows the two coats of arms united into one. Apollo, the sun god, surges forward in his chariot, bringing the modest bride. Fame blows her trumpet, goddesses, *putti*, and birds rejoice, and in the distance the goddess of fertility, half concealed, contemplates the face of the child that will be conceived. The mirror of the future is still blank, but the glory Tiepolo has created makes it impossible to believe that there can be anything ahead but glory.

Tiepolo borrowed the motif of Apollo's chariot and horses from the ceiling of the Kaisersaal at the bishop's palace in Würzburg (see p.231), his masterpiece of 1750–53. Tiepolo brings the same radiant conviction to mythological subjects too. The theme of the painting that is currently entitled *Queen Zenobia Addressing Her Soldiers (272)* has been the subject of much speculation. It is now known to have been commissioned by the Zenobio family of Venice

271 Giambattista Tiepolo, **Allegory of the Marriage of Rezzonico to Savorgnan,** *1758*

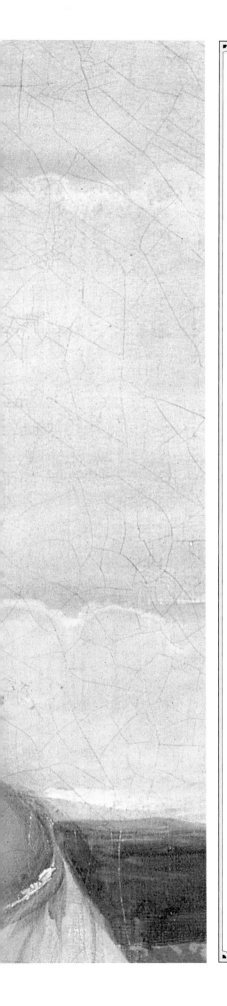

NEOCLASSICISM AND ROMANTICISM

Neoclassicism was born out of a rejection of the Rococo and late Baroque styles, around the middle of the 18th century. Neoclassical artists wanted a style that could convey serious moral ideas such as justice, honour, and patriotism. They yearned to re-create the simple, dignified style of the art of classical Greece and Rome. Some succeeded, but the movement suffered from a certain bloodlessness, a spirit of academic narrowness.

Romanticism began in the same era, but it was an approach that had to do with the modern rather than the antique, and it was about wildness and expression rather than control. Romantic artists had no fixed laws relating to beauty or the proprieties of subject matter. Instead, Romanticism was a creative outlook, a way of life.

A vast gulf existed between these two outlooks, and the debate between them was long and at times bitter; but in the end, Romanticism emerged as the dominant artistic movement of the first half of the 19th century.

Eugène Delacroix, An Orphan Girl in the Graveyard, 1824 (detail)

NEOCLASSICISM AND ROMANTICISM TIMELINE

Neoclassicism began in the middle of the 18th century (well before the Rococo style finally went out of use) and was in decline by the early 19th century. Likewise, early traces of Romanticism in painting are found in the 1740s; for instance, in Gainsborough. Romantic painting became a recognized movement by the 1780s, continuing into the mid-19th century.

JOHN SINGLETON COPLEY, THE COPLEY FAMILY, 1776–77
Copley's portrait of his own family is an example of the effects of European Neoclassical influence (chiefly that of Reynolds) on an artist arriving from the New World. When living in America, Copley had been known for his unvarnished but convincing realism. In England, in response to the prevailing fashion, he idealized and made his figures elegant, but in the event all too often diminishing his original insight (p.246).

SIR JOSHUA REYNOLDS, LADY CAROLINE HOWARD, 1778
Reynolds was England's leading academic painter and possibly the best portraitist. He is an eclectic painter, leaning heavily to the classic, which gives dignity to his pictures of contemporary aristocrats. Here he gives an atmosphere of grandeur, almost heroism, to a simple portrait of a child (p.244).

GEORGE STUBBS, MARES AND FOALS, 1762
By specializing, George Stubbs attained a degree of distinction that guaranteed him lasting fame. He dedicated himself to the horse, and this is one of his many horse pictures that leave humans out altogether. It gives a glimpse of these wild creatures as superior beings to whom the landscape truly belongs (p.247).

1740	1750	1760	1770	1780	1790

THOMAS GAINSBOROUGH, MR AND MRS ANDREWS, 1749
This unforgettable portrait haunts us with its startlingly original treatment. The poses and facial expressions are individual and convincing, and yet paradoxically the two figures are made to look like dolls or porcelain figures. They are positioned in the corner of the composition, allowing two-thirds of the painting to be devoted to landscape. Nature is an important element in all of Gainsborough's portraits, and he had a profound influence on the English landscape painters in the 19th century, notably Constable (p.240).

JACQUES-LOUIS DAVID, THE OATH OF THE HORATII, 1784–85
This was the first really famous image from the Neoclassical school. David was on the side of the Revolution when it came in 1789, and this subject evoked revolutionary patriotism. The composition is carefully orchestrated: for instance, the exaggerated weakness and softness of the women on the right contrast with the rigid, heroic pose of the three young men on the left (p.253).

JOHN CONSTABLE,
THE WHITE HORSE, 1819
This is one of the Suffolk scenes that have become part of the canon of great paintings in the English landscape tradition. Constable's work has a unique freshness. There is a brilliant use of broken colour, with an immediacy and convincing truth. With his robust, work-a-day scenes from the country-side near his home, Constable breached classical rules on what constituted the "correct" sort of landscape to paint (p.270).

FRANCISCO GOYA,
COLOSSUS, 1810–12
Goya was influenced, when first at the Spanish royal court, by the Neoclassicist, Anton Raphael Mengs, but over the years of his career he moved more and more in the direction of Romanticism. He is an artist of the very greatest stature and exercised considerable influence on the development of Romanticism throughout Europe. The Colossus is an example of Goya's ability to realize an image that seems to come from our inner consciousness, powerful but with no single, unambiguous message (p.252).

EUGENE DELACROIX,
DEATH OF SARDANAPALUS, 1827
Delacroix' Romanticism has a solid underpinning of the classic. Rubens and Géricault encouraged him to see the emotional effect of strong colour. This painting shows the energy and exoticism of his work, but he always retained a certain detachment and inner control (p.261).

1800	1810	1820	1830	1840	1850

JEAN-AUGUSTE INGRES,
THE BATHER, 1808
Ingres became the "high priest" of Neoclassicism in France. He had a special preference for the backs and necks of his nudes, often making them into prominent features of his paintings and frequently distorting them or elongating them in order to suit the needs of his highly sophisticated compositions. This was typical of the Neoclassical painters, for whom control over subject matter was central to their whole approach to art. Ingres' distortions went even further than in this example, but they were nearly always achieved in such a way as to make anatomical "falsehoods" seem as plausible as reality itself (p.256).

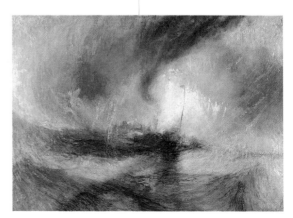

J.M.W. TURNER,
STEAMBOAT IN A SNOWSTORM, 1842
In Turner's seascapes we see to the full the emotive power of Romantic art. Yet, like all truly great artists, Turner retains control over what is happening in this painting. Here he shows a ship in mortal danger in a storm at sea. No matter how imaginative or extreme the subject, he is still aware of perspective and its imperatives (p.265).

THE BRITISH SCHOOL

In British painting of the 18th century there was a mixture of both the Romantic and the Neoclassical tendencies. On the one hand there was the marvellous lyricism of Thomas Gainsborough, always including the natural environment in his portraits, many of which were more in the way of being landscapes. On the other hand there was the educated, classical approach of Sir Joshua Reynolds, appealing to the ideals of polite society of his time – which was known, then as well as today, as the Age of Reason.

One of the artists who led English painting into its great period was Thomas Gainsborough (1727–88). He called himself "a wild goose at best", and it was this ravishing originality, within the bounds of gentlemanly appeal, that made him so popular. A supreme portrait painter, his great love was the landscape, and his finest works give us both. His achievements in landscape painting paved the way for Constable's radically naturalistic approach to landscape, and for the English Romantic tradition (see p.264). Gainsborough's

landscapes are reminiscent of Watteau's *fêtes galantes* (see p.224): whimsical, idyllic scenes, peopled with delicate creatures. In Gainsborough, however, these are transformed into large-scale lyrical landscapes, refreshing in their truth to nature. The most famous of Gainsborough's early portraits is the unconventional *Mr and Mrs Andrews (278)*. The young newlyweds pose in their ancestral fields, she in the height of fashion, scowling over her silks, he casual and somehow adolescent.

278 Thomas Gainsborough, Mr and Mrs Andrews, c. 1749, 71 x 120 cm (28 x 47 in)

A NEW STYLE OF PORTRAIT

The Andrews portrait takes its verve from its paradoxically real and unreal portrayal of the sitters, who appear doll-like, and yet are nonetheless totally convincing; and from its strikingly original composition. Its originality lies in the positioning of its subjects off-centre, flanked by an unidealized, genuinely 18th-century English landscape of farmland with its cornfield, sturdy oak tree, and changeable sky.

Their position emphasizes their status as landowners. They appear to be surveying the landscape around them, a landscape that plays an important part in its own right, no longer merely as a decorative, fanciful backdrop (as had been the custom for such outdoor portraits). The portrait is not finished. Mrs Andrews is believed to have made the rather odd request that she be painted holding a pheasant, which probably accounts for the blank patch in her lap. Gainsborough clearly finds the couple comic, yet he paints with an admirably straight face.

279 Thomas Gainsborough, The Painter's Daughters Chasing a Butterfly, late 1750s, 115 x 105 cm (45 x 41 in)

PATHOS AND CELEBRATION

As Gainsborough matured, his sensibility became more delicate, more "finely tuned", as did his confidence in his ability to catch a likeness. His lyrical landscape backgrounds, lightly sketched, became more idealized (though never unbelievable) and were executed with increasing freedom. Gainsborough is very sensitive to the pathos of beauty or heroism, graces that time will transform, and there can be a heartbreaking pensiveness in some of his portraits.

There is pathos, for example, in his repeated portraits of his two daughters, Molly (Mary) and Margaret, plain girls whom he dearly loved and whose future was to be unhappy – both were psychically fragile. Our foreknowledge of this unhappiness to come seems sublimely shared in his enchanting picture of them in their childhood: *The Painter's Daughters Chasing a Butterfly (279)*. Only the young chase the butterfly: the adult knows sadly that it is hard to catch, and may die as a result. For children, the chase itself is sheer pleasure without misgivings, and Gainsborough subtly expresses, at one and the same time, the happiness of innocence and the sadness of maturity.

Gainsborough was one of the great "independents" and his influence on portraiture was only limited. However, his landscapes were important as models for the young John Constable (see p.268), who wrote, "I fancy I see Gainsborough in every hedge and hollow tree."

RAMSAY THE CATALYST

Perhaps the greatest portrait painter in 18th-century Britain is the unfairly forgotten Scot, Allan Ramsay (1713–84). The English writer Horace Walpole, one of the shrewdest men of his age, remarked that "Reynolds seldom succeeds in women," whereas "Ramsay is formed to paint them." A great Ramsay is usually treasured by the family that originally commissioned it, and he has fallen from critical view for far too long.

This portrait, *Mrs Allan Ramsay (281)*, is of Ramsay's second wife, Margaret Lindsay (1726–82). The first Mrs Ramsay, Anne Bayne, had died in childbirth, thereby forever destroying Ramsay's confidence in the invulnerability of love. His second wife is very lovely, sweet and fresh, but he paints her with a touching anxiety, a haunting fear that her beloved life may fade away as inevitably as the flowers at her side.

Ramsay's delicate style introduced a blend of Baroque Italian Classicism, with French Rococo charm, into English painting. His personality – contrasting so noticeably with that of Hogarth, the pragmatic social commentator – gave impetus for change, and the active ingredients for this great period in British painting.

280 Thomas Gainsborough, Mrs Richard Brinsley Sheridan, 1785/86, 220 x 154 cm (7 ft 3 in x 5 ft ½ in)

THE PLAYWRIGHT'S WIFE

Pathos, again, is inherent in this portrait of *Mrs Richard Brinsley Sheridan (280)*. She had a tempestuous marriage with the great playwright Sheridan, as well as being renowned for her singing voice and her unearthly beauty. Her loneliness, and her elusive charm, are all conveyed to us in her portrait. Only the grave and lovely face is solid: all else is thin, diaphanous, unstable. Her mood is echoed by the wistful melancholy of the setting sun.

Full-length portraits, particularly of ladies placed in a natural setting, were a special tradition in 18th-century English and French painting; they were noticed on the continent, and copied, by Goya among others (see p.248).

281 Allan Ramsay, Margaret Lindsay, Mrs Allan Ramsay, early 1760s, 68 x 55 cm (27 x 22 in)

MRS RICHARD BRINSLEY SHERIDAN

The rather incompatible natures of the subject of this portrait and her husband (see column, p.242) meant that the former spent much of her time in the country, where she was happiest, while her wayward spouse stayed in London. She was an appropriate subject for Gainsborough's new, Romantic approach to portraiture, where all elements combine to express the gently melancholic mood of the sitter.

FACE
She is depicted as truly belonging in this environment, and her hair, caught by the wind, is treated in the same way as the leaves on the tree. Her plaintive expression (the focal point of the painting) and whole demeanour seem to express the wish she made to her husband to "Take me out of the whirl of the world, place me in the quiet and simple scenes of life that I was born for." Her wistful mood is echoed by the setting sun.

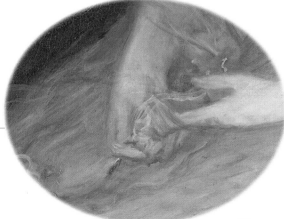

DISTANT TREE
A solitary tree in the distance has been superimposed over the sky. Its trunk is a few simple arabesques, and the fluffy clumps of foliage are all painted in the same direction. Pink underpainting is visible in the sky, which echoes the pinks and blues of her costume.

HANDS
In comparison to her face, her pale arms are relatively flatly painted, with virtually no modelling or shading. Her hands seem to lose themselves in the folds of her dress and scarf. The transparent scarf is composed of a network of fluid squiggles weaving in and out of her fingers. It unifies the figure into one single romantic gesture as it twists and tumbles down from around her shoulders and across her chest, falling through her arms and onto her knees and feet.

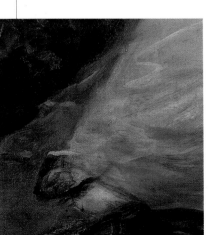

RHYTHM OF COLOUR AND FORM
The lightly suggested feet are subordinate to the major rhythms of the composition. Gainsborough has worked largely wet-in-wet, with loosely-woven layers of washes, a technique that produces softness of definition. At the speed of a glance, he has zig-zagged his brush down the expanse of her dress to her feet. Our eye moves automatically to the distant tree and then up and down through the foliage behind her, where her diagonal pose begins the circular rhythm anew.

RAEBURN: BRILLIANT PORTRAITIST

Raeburn, a fellow Scot, was clearly influenced by Ramsay, and at his peak is practically his equal. One would love to know whether it was the Rev. Walker himself or Raeburn who hit upon the wonderful pose of the skater *(282)*. This extraordinary image, with the dark outline of a minister in his sombre black, intent upon balancing his movement across the ice, has the superb background of mist and mountains. The man is so solid, the world so nebulous. He fixes his gaze adamantly upon the unseen and skates his way forward. We can see the muscles in play as his skates score the ice, and yet where he is going, and why this image is appropriate, baffles us still.

REYNOLDS' GRAND MANNER

Joshua Reynolds (1723–92), who was knighted for his great success as a portrait painter, is less sensitive than Gainsborough but more balanced. Unlike the latter, who had little formal education, and preferred the company of actors and musicians to scholars, Reynolds was decidedly

283 Sir Joshua Reynolds, Lady Caroline Howard, *1778, 143 x 113 cm (56 x 44½ in)*

an intellectual. From early on in his training, Reynolds had immersed himself in the art of the Renaissance, and he shared an interest in antiquity with the Italian and French Neoclassical artists. These influences led to his revival of the "Grand Manner", set in a modern context (see column, left). He was, without question, considered the leading portrait artist in Britain in his day, although, like Gainsborough, his passion lay outside the field of portraiture.

History painting was for Reynolds the highest form of art, and he contrived to instil Classicism and heroism into his portraits of the English ruling class. The threat to Reynolds' standing in England – especially from Gainsborough's popularity – did not arise until fairly late in the day, and Reynolds' influence on English art endured for many years. He became the first president of the Royal Academy on its foundation in 1768, and his enormous influence formed the basis for academic painting (see column, left).

Reynolds was an influential theorist whose lectures at the Royal Academy still make useful reading, and he encapsulates the aristocratic dignity of his age. He can hover alarmingly on the edge of the sentimental, especially in his idealization of childhood, but when he catches youthful freshness, he is very appealing. Here is one of the best examples of his portraiture: *Lady Caroline Howard (283)*, with her rosebush and her general air of simplicity, has a pensiveness that does not make extravagant claims, but lets us enjoy this quiet and rosy child.

282 Sir Henry Raeburn, The Rev. Robert Walker Skating, *mid-1790s, 73 x 60 cm (29 x 24 in)*

AMERICA AND ENGLAND: A SHARED LANGUAGE

If the forgotten Ramsay (see p.242) is arguably the greatest portrait painter of the time, then the equally overlooked American artist Gilbert Stuart (1755–1828), 42 years his junior, may be the most original. Stuart, as his name suggests, was originally of Scottish ancestry. He arrived in London at the age of 20 and trained under a fellow American, the hugely successful history painter Benjamin West (see right).

Stuart was also a great success in London. His work was so acclaimed that at a later stage it was even confused with that of Gainsborough. This is a double-edged compliment: he has his own style, which is almost recklessly truthful. His time may be too early to speak of a specifically American style, but there is a homespun brilliance in his work that we do not find in European artists.

There is superb observation in his *Mrs Richard Yates (284)*: what other artist would have dared show her vestigial moustache? The gradations of facial colour, too, and the alertness to the light glancing and dulling on her dress and cap, are all prophetic of the Impressionists (see p.294). After running into serious financial problems, Stuart returned to live permanently in America in 1793. He is probably known mainly because he painted George Washington, but despite his popularity he is not at his best as a public artist. It is the sheer domesticity of Mrs Richard Yates, a merchant's wife, that calls out his reserves of sensitive observation.

285 *Benjamin West*, Self-portrait, *c. 1770, 77 x 64 cm (30¼ x 25⅛ in)*

284 *Gilbert Stuart*, Mrs Richard Yates, *1793/94, 77 x 63 cm (30¼ x 25 in)*

HISTORY PAINTING: A POPULAR GENRE

A more famous, though less interesting artist than Gilbert Stuart is Benjamin West (1738–1820), whose enormous reputation as a history painter was gained in England rather than his native America.

West's style relied very much on accuracy of detail and historical fact, and he was influenced by Neoclassical artists such as Anton Mengs (see p.248) when he was in Rome in 1760. West's great historical dramas, which so impressed his contemporaries, leave us rather unmoved. They seem to be generated from the mind rather than the heart.

But the heart is always involved in painting a self-portrait, and here we see him at his best *(285)*. There is wishful thinking, perhaps, in this self-portrait – that of a quiet, elegant gentleman, dressed in the fashionable severity of urban style, contemplating us with aristocratic serenity. West's sketch seems an adjunct to his portrait and is in fact placed on the perimeter. Half his face and his body are deeply shadowed, with all this suggests of a divided and secretive persona.

ANGELICA KAUFFMAN

Angelica Kauffman was a friend of Joshua Reynolds and fellow member of the Royal Academy. She began as a fashionable portraitist, then became more interested in historical subjects. In the 1770s she painted a series of decorative murals for the architect Robert Adam. In 1781 she remarried and moved to Rome. This piece of Neoclassical Meissen ware (fine porcelain) is decorated with a portrait of Angelica Kauffman.

AMERICAN INDEPENDENCE

A disagreement between the government in London and the American colonists over increases in tax is seen as the initial catalyst of the American Revolution. George Washington (1732–99, shown above) was appointed Commander-in-Chief of the army and on July 4th, 1776 the Declaration of Independence was signed. George Washington proved to be an excellent leader and was inaugurated as the first president in 1789.

286 John Singleton Copley, The Copley Family, *1776-77, 185 x 292 cm (6 ft 1 in x 9 ft 7 in)*

COPLEY: AN UNFULFILLED TALENT

If Britain gave West the opportunity he needed, it both rewarded and damaged John Singleton Copley (1738–1815). His American works show a realism and a truthfulness that is marvellously alive. Moving to England involved him in the elegance of Neoclassicism and the influence of Reynolds' Grand Manner; but, for Copley, this was not a fruitful involvement.

The change is evident in *The Copley Family (286)*. In this painting, which was carefully worked up from preliminary studies, his father-in-law's face and hands and the glorious doll in the left-hand corner are examples of his early style. Here it is thrillingly convincing. For the remainder of the picture, Copley idealizes and abstracts, and the whole, though impressive, is somehow derivative: we have seen this kind of "Grand Manner" portraiture before in the work of Reynolds, Gainsborough, and West, for example. It remains a fascinating work, as much for its weakness as its strength. One of the weaknesses

287 George Stubbs, Mares and Foals, *1762,
100 x 190 cm (39 x 75 in)*

he himself were an honorary member of the species. Stubbs did not totally disdain to paint humans, who after all were the source of his equestrian commissions. But *Mares and Foals (287)* is one of his many pictures that has no human component. There is certainly no sentimentality either, yet these stately mothers and children, trustfully grouped together with artless poetry, evince a tender vision of nature at its most inspiring.

The horses group themselves with classic elegance against an archetypal English landscape. Stubbs is profoundly moved by their beauty and he communicates to us his own secret conviction that it is they to whom the landscape truly belongs. Thick-limbed humanity, with its clumsy trapping of clothes and its intrusive apparatus for living, is so inferior to these bare, gleaming creatures of the wild that yet honour us with their comradeship.

HORSE PAINTINGS
George Stubbs' (1724–1806) horse paintings are a testimony to the 18th-century gentleman's passionate interest in improved stock breeding techniques. The formal discipline of Stubbs' composition is Neoclassical in spirit but the artist's romantic perception of the horse is demonstrated by his move towards Romanticism in his later years. The implied and described violence in paintings, such as *A Horse Frightened by a Lion,* appeal strongly to our emotions.

288 George Stubbs, A Horse Frightened by a Lion, *1770,
94 x 125 cm (37 x 49 in)*

that is paradoxically a strength comes from our uncertainty as to where this family group is located. Are they inside – as is suggested by the brocaded sofa and the gilt-edged curtain, not to mention the expensive carpet? Or are they assembled outside – as seems to be indicated by the backdrop, with its distant hills and intrusive foliage? The two settings are cleverly linked. The carpet is patterned with leaves and there is a flower motif on the sofa.

GREAT EQUESTRIAN PAINTING

The one great Anglo-Saxon master of the century, George Stubbs (1724–1806), was, like Gainsborough, a lover of the portrait and the countryside, but all his passion is concentrated on the horse. Stubbs does not merely look at horses: in his time he dissected them (literally), meditated upon them, and entered into every aspect of this noble but non-human being, as if

Idyllic though it is, Stubbs does not cheat. The sky is darkening with storm clouds, and shadows already fall around the mares and foals. Only the very centre of the meadow, where they actually stand, is still sunlit.

Stubbs was equally sensitive to the vulnerability of animal life. *A Horse Frightened by a Lion (288)* comes straight from a Freudian nightmare. Blown by the wind, under some heavenly spotlight that gleams with eerie fierceness on its terrified body, a white horse halts in abrupt horror as a leonine head looks out at it from the darkness. It is a frozen tableau of fear. He leaves its outcome to our imagination.

OTHER WORKS BY STUBBS
Otho with Larkin Up (Tate Gallery, London)
Repose After Shooting (Yale Center for British Art, New Haven, Connecticut)
Portrait of Lady Laetitia Lade (Royal Collection, Windsor)
Returning from the Hunt (Museum of Art, San Antonio, Texas)

GOYA

The greatest artist of the 18th century, without any qualification, was a Spaniard – Francisco Goya. He was a man of irrepressible originality and determination. After initially being influenced by the German-born Neoclassical artist Anton Mengs, he developed in his own way and painted, above all, with a truly Spanish vision.

THE EARLY YEARS
This photograph shows the humble interior of Francisco Goya's birthplace. He was one of five children and was born (in March 1746) into a poor family in Fuendetodos, near Saragossa in northern Spain. Goya's first commission, at the age of 16 years, was to decorate a reliquary cabinet in the local church. It was not until he was 24 years old that he would depart for Italy in search of success at the academies.

JOHANN JOACHIM WINCKELMANN
Johann Winckelmann's (1717–68) doctrines on art theory were highly influential during the Neoclassical period. He developed a fervent love of classical antiquity and ancient art and wrote several treatises on the philosophy of art. He believed that classical art had "noble simplicity and grandeur" and argued that artists should apply ethical and aesthetic honesty to their work. One of Winckelmann's most ardent supporters and followers to apply these doctrines to his own art was Anton Mengs.

Anton Raphael Mengs (1728–79) was a founder of Neoclassicism, in association with Johann Winckelmann (see column, left). He is more significant to us today, however, for his extremely influential style of Neoclassical portraiture. Perhaps even more importantly, he was also the Court Painter to King Charles III of Spain. The king was a committed antiquarian and social reformer, and he had a natural preference for Mengs' serious, dignified, and pragmatic approach, which is admirably demonstrated in Mengs' *Self-portrait (289)*. It was Mengs who invited Goya to Madrid – in 1771.

GOYA: A SPANISH GENIUS

The influence of Mengs can be seen in the early work of Francisco Goya (1746–1828), particularly in his first portraits. Beyond that Goya fits into no category: his career spanned some 60 years, undergoing several metamorphoses, changing, and maturing in new ways right up to the mid-1820s. Goya seems to have worked solely from the centre of his own genius. With the hindsight of history we can see that his essentially personal

290 Francisco Goya, Marquesa de Pontejos, c. 1786, 210 x 127 cm (83 x 50 in)

vision of the modern world places him as an early Romantic (see p.259). His art was more in tune with the Baroque mixture of classical form and emotive personal expression – he cited Velázquez, Rembrandt, and Nature as his masters – than with the disciplined idealism of the Neoclassicists.

Goya possessed two outstanding gifts. He could pierce through the external façade of any sitter, to unmask the interior truth, a gift dangerous for any but the prudent. But he coupled with it a marvellous decorative sense, as is clear from his disarming portrait of the *Marquesa de Pontejos (290)*. His work has such sheer beauty that even those almost pilloried in his portraits seem not to have grasped what had happened, being overwhelmed by wonder of the paint.

289 Anton Mengs, Self-portrait, 1744, 73 x 55 cm (29 x 22 in)

291 *Francisco Goya*, The Family of King Charles IV, *1800,
280 x 336cm (9 ft 2 in x 11 ft ½ in)*

THE ROYAL FAMILY

In 1779 Goya was appointed to the position of First Court Painter under King Charles IV of Spain, who came to the throne in 1778. Court life under Charles IV was extravagant and self-indulgent, and full of personal intrigues. This miniature of the royal family in profile (above) was painted on silk by an unknown artist. It is of interest because of the way it shows the close resemblance between family members.

AN AMBITIOUS FAMILY PORTRAIT

The Family of King Charles IV (291), a portrait of the ruling Borbón family, who were haughtily remote from their countryfolk, shows the sitters for what they are: vain and pompous. Yet they continued to patronize Goya throughout his career. The portrait is breathtaking in its cruel insight and its beauty. The royals are spread out like a frieze, heavy, dull-faced, and self-satisfied, squashed together with little elegance and no style. We wince for them, we pity the poor, stupid king and his vixenish queen, and sigh over the impenetrable crassness of their stumpy heir. Then we look again, at the dazzle of attire, the silks and laces, the infinite delicacy with which decoration, ribbons, jewels, and sashes are found to be glittering, gleaming, blazing out at us with undiminished glamour.

In every portrait, Goya puts his finger on the living pulse of the sitter. He does so with such intensity of power that we positively need the decorative qualities to offset the impact. When we look at his *Thérèse Louise de Sureda (292)*, our eyes dwell with continual fascination on the chair with its wonderfully inconsistent canary shade, and on the dress, which is a gleaming

292 *Francisco Goya*, Thérèse Louise de Sureda, *c. 1803/04,
120 x 81 cm (47 x 31 in)*

TAPESTRY CARTOONS

Goya worked at various times between 1774 and 1794 at the Royal Tapestry Factory, painting cartoons – the paintings from which the weavers copied their tapestries. Many of the cartoons have been lost, but 63 of Goya's are known today, either in their original form as cartoons or as the finished tapestries. This photograph shows a tapestry of Goya's cartoon *The Vintage* on the loom. Weavers worked the tapestry from the back, studying the cartoon through the threads.

blue-black shot through with red and green – because the colour makes it possible, through its seductions, for us to accept the force of the sitter's implacable gaze. Doña Teresa was a friend of Goya's in that her husband (also a painter) was one of Goya's drinking companions. But she was a "friend" mainly in the sense that Goya knew her and, we suspect, disliked her. She is well rounded, a compact bundle of womanhood, but she is tense and angry. She will not submit to the painter, challenging him with her glare and her uprightness, carefully coiffured but not for the warmth of love's embraces. There can be no comparable portrayal of a woman at once so attractive and so hostile.

Goya made his living by working for royalty and the establishment, and his political views appear confused: they may necessarily have been ambiguous. But it is impossible not to believe that he had an inborn hatred of tyranny. His art suggests a vehement independence, and perhaps his greatest painting may be his version of a French war crime, the shooting of hostages after the Spanish people rose against Napoleon Bonaparte's rule in 1808. *The Third of May 1808 (293)* was painted six years after the event it portrays. This is only partly a patriotic picture, if it is that at all. It is not the French that Goya condemns but our communal cruelty. It is humankind that holds the rifles, but humankind at its most utterly conscienceless. The victims, too, are Everyman, the huddled mass of the poor who have no defender.

Goya manages to make us feel that we are both executioners and executed, as if the dual potential for good or evil that we all possess were animated before us. Intensity of fear, pain, and loss on one side, and the extremity of brutality on the other: which fate is the worse? Who is really destroyed in this terrible painting, the depersonalized French or the individualized Spanish? Behind the dying rises a hillock, bright with light; the soldiers stand in a shadowy and sinister no-man's-land. Meanwhile, in the central background, the city endures.

This is a very dark painting, psychologically, but the really dark works were to be painted later, in Goya's sick old age, when he was deaf and lonely, a prey to the irrational fears that are subliminally present in all his work, giving it a secret bite. He used these fears to create images of our darkest imaginings – not just his own, or they would fail to produce their terrible effect. Goya's last works have a ghastly sanity in their insanity, as if all demarcations had gone, and we had all fallen through into the abyss.

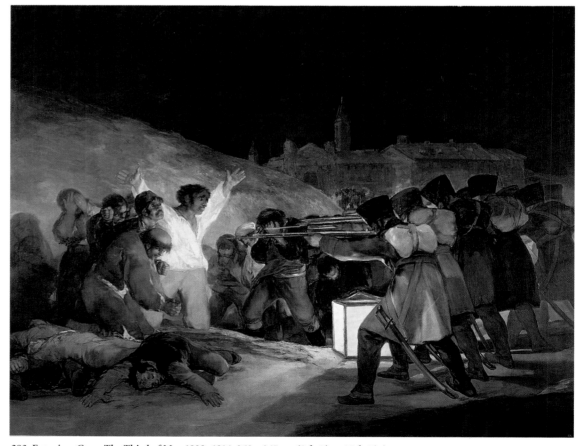

293 Francisco Goya, The Third of May 1808, *1814, 260 x 345 cm (8 ft 6 in x 11 ft 4 in)*

THE THIRD OF MAY 1808

The Third of May 1808 is one of a pair of paintings focusing on the brutal suppression and subsequent mass executions of Spanish civilians who had risen against French troops on May 2nd, 1808. Only when King Ferdinand VII was finally restored to power in 1813 did Goya quickly send him a petition asking to commemorate the "most notable and heroic actions or scenes of our glorious insurrection against the tyrant of Europe".

FIRING SQUAD
The soldiers are depicted as faceless automatons. Their bodies are locked together, like some form of destructive insect. They stand unfeasibly close to their victims, emphasizing the brutal and tragically ludicrous nature of the scene, and crudely mirror David's great Neoclassical painting, The Oath of the Horatii (see p.253). But whereas David's soldiers represent unity of will, Goya's represent only the mindless anonymity of the war machine.

CHRIST FIGURE
Our attention is immediately drawn to the man kneeling with outstretched arms, evoking the Crucifixion, about to be shot almost at point-blank range. However, his heroic gesture cannot detract from the overwhelming despair and mortal terror that is depicted all around him, and his white shirt, brightly lit by the soldiers' lamp, we know will shortly be splattered with red.

"GLORIOUS INSURRECTION"
Despite his declared intention to immortalize the "heroic actions" of his countrymen, Goya has instead produced an image of a slaughterhouse. A dead man, lying face down in a pool of blood, thrusts disturbingly into the foreground. He has been crudely foreshortened and appears twisted and mangled. His outflung arms suggest a supplication, mutely (and perhaps more eloquently) echoing the courageous, dramatic gesture of the next victim, who will shortly join the pile of corpses in the foreground.

GOYA'S DEATH

By 1825 Goya's health had deteriorated. He spent his remaining years in exile at Bordeaux in France. In 1826 he made the long, hard journey to revisit Madrid, after which his eyesight became so weak that he had to paint with the aid of a magnifying glass. Goya died on the night of April 15th, 1828 in Bordeaux, and remained buried there until 1901, when his body was moved to Madrid. Later, in 1929, it was exhumed again and moved to a tomb in the Hermitage of San Antonia de la Florida. This painting of the original Bordeaux tomb is by Goya's old friend Antonio Brugada.

OTHER WORKS BY GOYA

Don Manuela Silvela
(Prado, Madrid)

The Marqués de Castro Fuerte
(Museum of Fine Arts, Montreal)

The Duke of Osuna
(Frick Collection, New York)

The Duke of Wellington
(National Gallery of New Zealand, Wellington)

Isabel de Porcel
(National Gallery, London)

Young Woman with a Letter
(Musée Lille)

294 Francisco Goya, The Colossus, 1810–12, 115 x 105 cm (45 x 41 in)

The Colossus (294) has a subtitle, *Panic*. It shows all humanity in flight, streaming away like ants from unimaginable horror – an analogy for the monstrous destruction of war, one of the bloodiest in Spain's history (see column, p.250). Goya has visualized this dread for us, given it concrete form: a huge, hostile presence fills the sky, not yet looking down at the terrified masses below, merely flexing his muscles. Existence is not what we had thought: here are different rules and we do not know what they are. What we are contemplating is our common nightmare.

Goya gives this fear an awesomely convincing form. He is painting his own dreads, but his genius reveals them to be our own. They may in fact be more our own than we realize.

The Colossus is in fact looking away from the fleeing people: are we perhaps seeing more of a threat in this mysterious form than is literally there? He can even be seen as a protective Colossus, the native genius of Spain, arising in might to challenge Napoleon. Yet somehow this benign interpretation does not spring readily to mind.

There is a darkness in Goya, an anger, a wildness, that represents something within our hearts, repress it though we may. It is precisely this irrational fury of the imagination, prefiguring the Romantics – poets such as Shelley, Keats, and Byron, or composers such as Schumann or Berlioz – that gives Goya the edge over his contemporary, the great French Neoclassical artist Jacques-Louis David.

THE NEOCLASSICAL SCHOOL

Neoclassicism clearly proved to be a popular philosophy among artists in the middle of the 18th century. It manifested itself in a variety of national schools, in varying degrees of intensity. In England, it was found in a modified form, in the work of Reynolds and his followers. In Italy it was important, for Rome was the world centre for Neoclassical thought, attracting such personalities as the first "true" Neoclassicist, Anton Mengs. But Neoclassicism did not really become established as a coherent movement in the arts until it emerged in quintessential form in the late 18th century, in France.

In the middle of the 18th century, as in the middle of the 17th (see p.216), artists turned to Classicism in reaction against the frivolity of art of the previous generation. The 18th-century Neoclassicist philosophy was reformist in character, calling for a revival of ancient standards of seriousness, morality, and idealism. It was taken up readily by artists and writers who found themselves in the midst of social and political upheaval.

With the French Revolution (see column, p.255) breaking out in 1789, its potential for use in propaganda was not wasted. Jacques-Louis David's (1748–1826) style is nobly classical, the whole image so integrated that each section supports the other and there is a fine concentration of significance. The first great Neoclassical painting, painted in 1784–85, *The Oath of the Horatii (295)* is theatrical, but it is honestly so.

THE OATH OF THE HORATII

An argument between the peoples of Rome and Alba threatened to lead to war and so it was decided that each side (the Horatii and the Curatii) would send three men to fight for their city. After the battle only one man remained alive, Horatius. He discovered that his sister had been betrothed to one of the enemy Curatii. In revenge he slew his sister and was found guilty of murder but managed to get a reprieve from the death sentence. In art, the three brothers are usually shown swearing a sacrificial oath in front of their father.

295 Jacques-Louis David, The Oath of the Horatii, 1784–85, 335 × 427 cm (11 ft × 14 ft)

296 *Jacques-Louis David,* Madame Récamier, *1800, 175 x 244 cm (5 ft 9 in x 8 ft)*

NEOCLASSICAL SCULPTURE

The first fully Neoclassical sculptor was Antonio Canova (1757–1822), who began his career in Venice. He established a reputation as a unique modifier of the classical Greco-Roman style, his most famous piece being *The Three Graces.* He ran a large studio producing a wide range of pieces, including commissions for Napoleon and Wellington and the beautiful *Psyche Revived by the Kiss of Love* illustrated above.

All elements in the painting are geared towards facilitating our understanding of the drama: three brave Romans are vowing their lives away for their country. The uprightness of their intent is shown in the straightness of their outstretched arms as they receive swords from their father. Great symmetrical arches stabilize their act of taking the vow, setting it in a noble context. The austerity and clarity of the colours emphasize the selflessness and totality of their fervour.

The men are hard, concentrated, active; across the room huddle the women, soft, distracted, passive. The contrast between them is absolute, and it is in this uncompromising climate of absolutes that David feels most at home. When David painted *The Oath of the Horatii,* the Revolution was not far away, and the picture contains a clear reference to this.

Probably the works of David that are most compatible to present-day sensibilities are his portraits. Here we have no need to set him in his historical setting before we can respond fully: he is wonderful in the sheer conciseness of his vision. There are no superfluities, yet the bareness has a confident rightness about it.

Madame Récamier (296) is the epitome of Neoclassical charm. We see that she knows she has charm, and that she is almost consciously watching its effect upon the painter. Everything on and about her is sophisticatedly simple: she scorns, we feel, the vulgarity of devices, but she is all one living device, forcing us to accept her at her own valuation. David sees that she is lovely, and makes us see it as well: she reclines because she is sure of the power of her charm, secure behind the ivory chill of her pose. But he seeks to know her at a level below the conscious, and in that lies the forcefulness of the image.

A MARTYR OF THE REVOLUTION
The absoluteness of *The Oath of the Horatii* (see p.253), intrinsically overstated but subjectively real, is what makes *The Death of Marat (297),* a revolutionary icon. David was very involved in the Revolution, debating in the assembly with a furious excitement, and was intellectually swept away, along with many others. Marat, whom he here idealizes as a modern saint, was assassinated by the royalist Charlotte Corday, who prepared for her act with fasting and prayer.

The real Marat was a politician of particularly hideous appearance who was obliged to take frequent baths because of a severe skin infection. David shows him fair and martyred, struck down amid his labours for the common good. But the literal truth is unimportant here. David painted the truth he wanted to believe, a deliberate act of propaganda, and the sheer wanting, the passionate faith in the revolution and its sanctifying power, gives the work a gigantic force. If we forget Marat himself and generalize, here is an image of death in its purity. Everything conspires to recall the Christian martyrs – the dark background lightens to the right, as if heavenly glory awaited the dying saint. Yet this is brilliant legerdemain because at no point does David cheat by using Christian imagery: it is all done by subtle reminiscence.

THE FRENCH REVOLUTION

In 18th-century France, the poorest people were forced to assume the burden of the highest taxes whilst the aristocracy and clergy were exempted from payment. On July 14th, 1789, the masses (known as *sans-culottes*, illustrated above) attacked the Bastille (the royal prison) hoping to find a stock of weapons.

It was against this background that on August 4th, 1789, the Constituent Assembly voted to abolish the *ancien régime* (feudal society). In 1791 the royal family tried to flee Paris but were captured and the trial and execution of Louis XVI took place in January 1793.

297 Jacques-Louis David, The Death of Marat, *1793, 160 x 125 cm (63 x 49 in)*

MAXIMILLIAN DE ROBESPIERRE

A leading radical in the National Assembly and an early member of the Jacobin Club, Robespierre (1758–94) derived his ideas from the doctrines of Rousseau. On June 8th, 1794, Robespierre held "The Fête of the Supreme Being" which was stage-managed by Jacques-Louis David. This new religious group was based on the disestablishment of the church and the worship of nature as a deity.

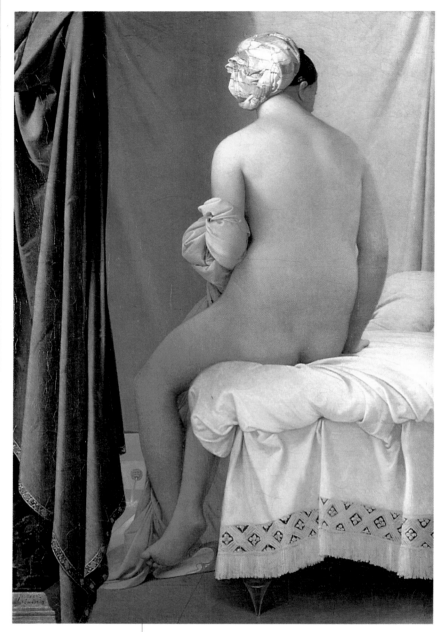

*298 Jean-Auguste Ingres, The Bather, 1808,
146 x 97 cm (57½ x 38 in)*

felt it ought to be, with additional vertebrae to provide the perfect elongation. *La Grande Odalisque (299)* is a superb example of this. A great curve of naked back sweeps from the line of her neck, outlining her backbone and ending in the voluptuous fullness of her buttock. She is like a glassy stream, breaking into a waterfall at the barrier of the jewelled fly-whisk, with the tumult of hands, legs, and feet flowing to the edge of the canvas.

Parmigianino, the Italian Mannerist painter, did much the same, lengthening the beautiful neck of his Madonnas (see p.142). But the Mannerists intended to excite by their use of forms; Ingres does not. His intention is to get us to accept his forms as actual, as classically perfect, and in their weird beauty they come close to it. *The Bather* (also known as *The Valpinçon Bather, 298)* is an example of this. It is a heavily sensual picture, the naked back exposed amidst the contrived setting of a great sway of olive-green drapery and the wonderful pillowy whites of a bed's edge.

OTHER WORKS BY INGRES

Portrait of Edme Bochet
(Louvre, Paris)

*Head of St John
the Evangelist*
(Metropolitan Museum
of Art, New York)

The Marriage of Raphael
(Walters Art Gallery,
Baltimore)

Portrait of Dr Defrance
(Bührle Foundation,
Zurich)

Apotheosis of Homer
(Art Gallery of
Ontario, Toronto)

NEOCLASSICISM'S GREATEST HEIGHTS

Ingres (Jean-Auguste Dominique, 1780–1867) studied under Jacques-Louis David, who was 32 years his senior, but eventually he emerged as the leading exponent of Neoclassicism in France. Ingres was greatly influenced by David, especially in his earlier works. Like David, Ingres was a strange man, almost fanatic in his meticulousness, so dedicated to the ideal that he could not accept the real if it fell below his aspirations.

Ingres was a passionate admirer of Raphael, the supreme classicist, and it almost seems that his whole art is a yearning for that earlier certainty represented by Raphael. He is renowned for painting the female back, not as it is, but as he

She has been given the name *The Bather* in an attempt to make sense of her position and her cap, but Ingres hardly needs the trappings. It is that heavy, dimpled back he needs, over-long in its luscious curvature, obsessing the artist and affecting the viewer through the force of his emotion. The same impossible curve distinguishes his Thetis. *Thetis Entreating Jupiter (300)*, in which the male is as impossibly broad as the female is supple, is a comic picture, quite unintentionally, because of this bodily fixation.

Ingres believed that "drawing is the probity of art", and his linear grace carries him magnificently through most hazards. But Thetis is stretching out an arm with elastic bones, a dislocated limb that halts us in our gaze and alerts us to the comely deformations the artist is trying to persuade us to accept. Ingres obviously feels that Jupiter has an iconic majesty, which has an odd truth to it, but the clam-like beauty at his knees undoes whatever faith we have managed for Jupiter. The picture fails, but so gloriously, so alarmingly, that it fascinates still.

300 *Jean-Auguste Ingres*, Thetis Entreating Jupiter, *1811, 350 × 257 cm (11 ft 6 in × 8 ft 5 in)*

THETIS AND JUPITER
The legend of Thetis entreating Jupiter is told in the *Iliad*. Thetis, the mother of Achilles, is sent by her son to Jupiter with a petition concerning his quarrel with Agamemnon.
In paintings the scene usually depicts Jupiter, sceptre in hand, enthroned on Mount Olympus. Thetis kneels before him and is seen imploring with the god to intervene in her son's fate.

299 *Jean-Auguste Ingres*, La Grande Odalisque, *1814, 91 × 163 cm (36 × 64 in)*

CONTEMPOARAY ARTS
1764
Mozart composes his first symphony at the age of 8 years
1792
Mary Wollstonecraft writes *A Vindication of the Rights of Women*
1804
The English Watercolour Society is founded
1813
Jane Austen writes *Pride and Prejudice*
1818
The Prado Museum is founded in Madrid
1826
The US Academy of Design is founded
1837
Dickens' *The Pickwick Papers* is serialized
1862
Victor Hugo writes *Les Misérables*

MARIE ANTOINETTE

After marrying the Dauphin in 1770, Marie Antoinette (1755–93) became Queen of France on the coronation of her husband Louis XVI in 1774. Unfortunately the miseries of France became identified with her extravagances. As a feminist Marie Antoinette supported female artists, including Vigée-Lebrun, and was involved in the march on Versailles in 1789. After the execution of her husband in 1793 she was placed under arrest and was guillotined in 1793.

THE FRENCH SALON

The Salon of 1667 was the first official art exhibition held in France and was limited to members of the Royal Academy. The term *Salon* derived from the Salon d'Apollon, in the Louvre, where the annual exhibitions were first held. Until the 19th century the limited number of artists who were allowed to show at these salon exhibitions had a monopoly on publicity and sales of art. This painting, *L'Innocence*, is by Adolph-William Bouguereau (1825–1905), who was one of the key supporters of the 19th-century salon.

301 Elisabeth Vigée-Lebrun, Countess Golovine, *c. 1797–1800, 83 x 67 cm (33 x 26½ in)*

ROYALIST IN REVOLUTIONARY TIMES

(Marie) Elisabeth (Louise) Vigée-Lebrun (1755–1842) was a clear-minded supporter of the monarchy. She fits uncomfortably within the revolutionary climate that so excited David. She understood Neoclassicism but transcended its formalities, delighting in the freedoms of the Baroque, with its strong, contrasting colours. A charming woman, she made friends with Marie Antoinette and had an instinct for the socially acceptable. At times, her insight can take her beyond this, as in her fine portrait of the

Countess Golovine (301). It is impossible not to warm to the completely feminine frankness of this Russian aristocrat, her ingenuous gesture with her scarlet cape and the seductive simplicity with which her rosy face smiles out at us beneath the carefully dishevelled black curls. This is a strong woman, for all her charm, and Vigée-Lebrun must have recognized an equal. At the outbreak of the Revolution, Vigée-Lebrun went into exile in Italy. She went to London in 1802, where she painted several important portraits, returning to Paris in 1805.

THE GREAT FRENCH ROMANTICS

THE GREAT FRENCH ROMANTICS

If applied to the arts today, the word Romantic suggests a certain theatricality and sentimental idealism. Its original meaning, however, had quite different associations. While Neoclassicism was associated with the culture of antiquity, the Romantic was associated with the modern world. Romanticism admitted the "irregular": the wild and uncontrolled aspects of nature (both animal and human, both beautiful and ugly). The necessary strategy for such expression was inevitably incompatible with the dogma of Neoclassicism and its fixed notions about beauty and subject matter.

The pastoral idyll suggested by some of the country scenes of Gainsborough (see p.240) was fast disappearing under the Industrial Revolution, while in France, revolution of a more violent kind brought irrevocable change to the social order. The grandeur and idealism of Neoclassicism were at odds with the realities and hardships of an increasingly industrial society. Prefigured by Goya (see p.252), Romanticism stands for an outlook, an approach, a sensibility towards modern life. France was its true home, and that of its earliest innovators, Théodore Géricault (1791–1824) and Eugène Delacroix (1798–1863).

If Ingres (see p.256) was the great Neoclassicist, these were the great Romantics. Their art was diametrically opposed to his, and in the bitter debate between the two schools, theirs proved the stronger. Ingres was concerned mainly with the control of form and with outward perfection as a metaphor for inner worth. The Romantics were far more interested in the expression of emotion – through dramatic colour, freedom of gesture, and by their choice of exotic and emotive subject matter. *The Raft of the Medusa (302)* was enormously important as a symbol of Romanticism in art.

JEAN-JACQUES ROUSSEAU

Jean-Jacques Rousseau, (1712–78) the political philosopher and author, had a great influence on the Neoclassical period. It was not until 1750 that he made his name as a writer with his *Discourse on the Sciences and the Arts* which argued that there was a schism between the demands of contemporary society and the true nature of human beings. His argument for "Liberty, Equality, and Fraternity" became the battle cry of the French Revolution.

302 Théodore Géricault, **The Raft of the Medusa,** *1819, 491 x 717 cm (16 ft 1 in x 23 ft 6 in)*

too trivial, too joyous, for such a scene. There is no space for the viewer in which to escape the terrible impact of that rough triangle of raft. It juts out at us, a blow in the solar plexus.

Disappointed with its tepid reception in France, Géricault took the painting to England, where he stayed for a few years, deeply impressed by Constable (see p.268).

Géricault's life was short but intense. He sought after the real with a hungry passion, but it was to make the real transcendent that he sought. There is a hypnotic power in his portraits of the insane, such as *Woman with the Gambling Mania (303)*. These tragic and haunted faces had some personal resonance for him. He is not regarding their sufferings objectively; there is a moving intensity of reaction. He makes us feel that the potential for these various imbalances are endemic to us all. It is our own possible future that we contemplate.

DELACROIX: THE GREAT ROMANTIC
Géricault had a preoccupation with death and the morbid that is absent in his contemporary, Delacroix, whose characteristic is a sense of the romantic fullness of being alive. After Géricault's death in 1824, Delacroix was regarded as the sole leader of the Romantic movement, but his art was very much his own, and soon transcended Géricault's early influence. Like Géricault, Delacroix received a classical training (in fact they first met as students of the Neoclassicist Pierre-Narcisse Guérin) but, despite much

303 Théodore Géricault, Woman with the Gambling Mania, c. 1822, 77 x 65 cm (30½ x 26 in)

GÉRICAULT'S RAFT
The raft carried survivors from a French naval ship, *La Méduse*, which sank en route to West Africa in 1816. The captain and senior officers took to the lifeboats and left a makeshift raft for the 150 passengers and crew. During 13 days adrift on the Atlantic, all but 15 died. Géricault's choice of this grim subject for a gigantic canvas went against traditional artistic rules. It also implied criticism of the government, for the appointment of this unseamanlike captain had been an act of political favouritism.

This radical work was accepted, but grudgingly, by the artistic establishment: the gold medal it won at the Paris Salon of 1819 was merely a way of denying Géricault the controversy he sought. Géricault forces us, almost physically, to accept the reality of human suffering and death. It is death in the most terrible conditions, anguished, tortured, long-drawn-out, without nobility or privacy. The drama is all in the physical details. It is as if Géricault eschews the use of colour as

304 Eugène Delacroix, An Orphan Girl in the Graveyard, 1824, 65 x 54 cm (26 x 21½ in)

SCHOPENHAUER
In the early 19th century, Arthur Schopenhauer (1788–1860) became a major influence on the philosophy of art. He argued that art was the only kind of knowledge that was not sub-servient to the will. He emphasized the active role of will as the creative but irrational force in human nature. After taking a teaching position in Berlin in 1820 he became a direct rival of Hegel but failed to attract enough people to his lectures. He retired to a reclusive life in Frankfurt accompanied only by his poodle but eventually earned a reputation as a philosopher. He was to be highly influential on future movements such as existentialism.

305 Eugène Delacroix, **The Death of Sardanapalus,** *1827, 391 x 496 cm (12 ft 10 in x 16 ft 3 in)*

criticism from the salons, he went on to develop a uniquely animated and expressive style, greatly influenced by Rubens (see p.186), employing a characteristically vivid palette that places him as one of the great colourists. He has an almost Rubensian energy, a wild and sometimes reckless vitality that is the exact visual equivalent of Byronism. Like Byron (see column, p.262) he can be histrionic at times, but generally he exults with the vigour of the truly great and carries the viewer uncritically away.

Delacroix is an extremely active artist. When he paints *An Orphan Girl in the Graveyard (304)*, she is not a tearful or passive orphan, but a vibrant young beauty, avid for life, alarmed and alerted by the nearness of death, but slack-mouthed and bare-shouldered as she looks away from the graves towards rescue. Her eyeballs have the gleam of a frightened horse, but the tenseness of her neck muscles is completely healthy. She is not a victim, despite her label.

The Death of Sardanapalus (305) shows Delacroix at his most brilliantly unpleasant – appropriately, for Sardanapalus was an Assyrian dictator. The gorge rises to see female slaves treated as chattels just like the horses and jewels. If sado-masochism is to be glorified, this is its glorification. Only Delacroix, with his almost innocent delight in movement and colour, could even attempt to carry it off.

Like Géricault, Delacroix exulted in horses, especially those from the exotic wastes of Arabia or Africa. But he did not share the younger Romantics' interest in contemporary, local reality. When he deals with modern events he distances himself by setting them in a far-away, exotic location. Such detachment sets him apart from the Romantic movement as such, though not from the Romantic attraction to the exotic. It also reveals his concern that art should still strive to attain the timelessness and seeming universality of the great art of the past.

OTHER WORKS BY DELACROIX

The Assassination of the Bishop of Liège (Louvre, Paris)

Education of the Virgin (National Museum of Western Art, Tokyo)

Hercules and Alcestis (Phillips Collection, Washington, DC)

Odalisque (Musée des Beaux Arts, Dijon)

Death of Valentino (Kunsthalle, Bremen)

The Lion Hunt (Chicago Art Institute)

Death of Ophelia (Neue Pinakothek, Munich)

LORD BYRON

One of Delacroix's great heroes was the poet George Byron (1788–1824). Byron had supported the Greeks in their struggle against the Turks since he visited Greece in 1809–10 and witnessed the terrible conditions in which they were living. With the outbreak of the War of Independence in 1821 Byron sailed to Argostoli to lead a private army of soldiers. Soon he became disillusioned with the internal fighting within his ranks and his efforts were overshadowed by mutinies and illness. He died of a fever on April 19th, 1824. This illustration shows Byron dressed in the national Greek costume.

TRAVEL JOURNALS

In the mid-19th century it became popular for artists to go on tours of distant countries. In 1832 Delacroix travelled to North Africa and filled seven notebooks with drawings and watercolour sketches like these studies (shown above) of the walls around Meknès. The experiences of his six-month tour of Morocco and Algeria fuelled his imagination for the next 30 years.

Delacroix spent time in Tangiers and Morocco, and he remained in tune with this romantic world all his life. He felt a temptation to the violent, the extreme, and exorcized it in his paintings of the Near East, rather than of his own periodically turbulent country. Here, in a wild swoop of motion and a rolling swirl of colour, he can show *Arabs Skirmishing in the Mountains (306)*. He claimed to have seen these attacks and even taken part, but their truest origin is in his imaginative bonding with the warriors. He is himself in all parts of the picture, in the frenzy of the horses, the manoeuvres of the fighters, their pain and anger, their courage and despair. He is at one with the landscape, wild and high, desolate, infertile, yet fiercely loved.

The citadel on the cliffs, though, remains, above the smoke and the fury, and that, too, is to be understood personally. Delacroix never loses himself in his greatest works but, with instinctive tact, leaves always a place for detachment. There is an inner stability that keeps the work from bluster, however near the edge it may go.

306 Eugène Delacroix, **Arabs Skirmishing in the Mountains,** *1863, 92 x 75 cm (36½ x 30 in)*

ARABS SKIRMISHING IN THE MOUNTAINS

Delacroix produced this painting a few months before his death in 1863. It has been suggested that it depicts a battle between the Moroccan Sultan's tax collectors and local rebels, and Delacroix may have come into contact with such incidents when he travelled to Meknès with the Moroccan foreign minister in 1832. (An entry in his diary of 1832 suggests this.) Historical details are, however, irrelevant to the real subject of the painting, which is a Romantic celebration of drama, colour, light, and of the exotic. It is primarily a story-teller's painting, reinvented 31 years after Delacroix's Moroccan journey, and whatever its connection with real events, it exists as a purely fictitious scene.

DISTANT ACTION
The gunmen fighting in the distance are picked out largely by their headdresses and guns, within the brilliant cloud of dust, or possibly heat haze. The livid, broken surface of the horse's flank (below), which provides a sharp focal point for the foreground, gradually gives way to a broader, more relaxed application of paint as the action recedes, culminating in the ghostly fortress on the mountain.

DISTINCTIVE BRUSHWORK
Delacroix's distinctive broken brushwork recalls the flame-like motion of El Greco's (see p.145) and contrasts utterly with his Neoclassical contemporary, Ingres (see p.256). The action of the narrative is imitated in the actual paint surface, through a kind of visual onomatopoeia. It is alive with writhing, swirling brushmarks, and there are no straight lines or flat, uninterrupted surfaces; the vegetation waves, and even the men's rifles seem animated.

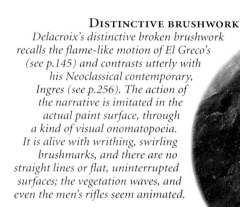

FALLEN HORSEMAN
The fiery red cloak of the fallen horseman, painted with impulsive sweeps, introduces a rhythm of colour that leads our eye along his body, up the path described by vegetation to the line of kneeling riflemen, where the direction is reinforced by the emphatic diagonals of their rifles. The sweeping movement then continues on, led by the galloping horseman, into the more distant action.

ROMANTIC LANDSCAPES

In their landscape paintings the Romantics gave free rein to their daring and their imagination. Art lovers in the 19th century may have lamented the lost rational serenity of the 17th-century master Claude Lorrain (see p.220), but many of them also saw that Turner was his equal. Turner's revelations of atmosphere and light answered the need for a new artistic language. Constable surprised the world with a new awareness of, and a new openness to, nature as it actually is, and not in any idealized or stylized form.

JOHANN WOLFGANG VON GOETHE

Germany's greatest poet, Goethe (1749–1832) pioneered Romanticism in German literature in the 1770s. He believed that great art must simulate the creative force of nature. In his later life he also studied various sciences including optics. Goethe's writings on art included a book on the theory of colour which opposed Newton's discovery that there were seven colours in the spectrum and argued that there were only six in natural daylight conditions.

The French were by no means the only Romantics: Germany was the original "land of the Goths". A touch of that heavy symbolism that so often characterizes German art is seen in Caspar David Friedrich (1774–1840). It is primarily the countryside that Friedrich sees as a symbol, a mute praise of its unseen and unseeable Creator. Germanic mysticism has never been very exportable, and Friedrich is only today being seen as a powerful, significant artist. Religious art without an explicit religion is not easy to paint, but Friedrich succeeds.

Monk by the Shore (307) has a daring simplicity. Three great bands stretch across it: sky, sea, land, with the one vertical note of the human being, who gathers the muteness of nature into himself and gives it a voice. "Monk" comes from the Greek for "alone", and it is this loneliness that Friedrich shares with us. In the sense of this picture, we are all monks and we all stand on the shore of the unknown.

THE ENGLISH ROMANTIC TRADITION

True Romanticism – in the sense of the broad movement that was bound up with the demise of Neoclassicism – necessarily belongs to France. On the other hand, speaking strictly chronologically, a Romantic tradition had emerged earlier in England than it did in France; in a way it had been there all along, in the form of a particularly English sensibility towards the landscape – exemplified in the paintings of Gainsborough (see p.240). This early sensibility reached its full Romantic expression in the works of England's two great landscape painters: Turner and Constable.

TURNER'S LANDSCAPES

Turner (Joseph Mallord William, 1775–1851) disturbed those who met him by conforming so little to the accepted idea of a great artist. He remained an unrepentant Cockney, not over scrupulous about cleanliness or correct pronunciation, but passionately intent on the things that mattered to him. He was recognized as great from the beginning, and his career was a source of baffled but resoundingly affirmative reactions throughout his life. If his pourings and soakings of paint were beyond comprehension, they bore the certain stamp of genius.

We associate Turner with colour, but his early work is dark, the actuality of the scene being an over-riding concern, and beyond this, its inherent drama. In mid-career, it is light itself that has begun to fascinate him. Place never loses its necessity, but it is as a focus for the light, as a precious receptacle, that it matters.

He was friendly with a group of English watercolourists who were at that time developing an art that was very much based on the atmosphere of a place, as well as its topographical fact. This new art form was called the "picturesque". Turner's early training was as a watercolourist, and he would eventually come to realize watercolour's special potential for freedom of expression in his oil paintings, creating a completely unprecedented new language.

Mortlake Terrace (308) is without obvious drama. There is an early summer evening, the Thames flowing gently by, pleasure boats venturing out, tall trees lining the terrace and swaying lightly in the breeze. Shadows fall across the short grass, a few bystanders watch, a small dog leaps onto the parapet. Nothing really happens, yet the drama is as vibrant as ever. It is light that

307 Caspar David Friedrich, **Monk by the Shore,** *1810, 110 x 170 cm (43 x 67 in)*

308 J.M.W. Turner, Mortlake Terrace, c. 1826, 92 x 122 cm (36½ x 48 in)

is the artist's preoccupation; all is a pretext for his enamoured rendering of this delicacy of sunlight. Light quivers in the air, it bleaches the far hills, it makes the trees translucent, it throws a dark, diagonal patterning on the dull turf that takes on an entranced quality; light hides the world, and reveals it.

The Napoleonic wars ended in 1815, and the Continent became accessible once more. Turner began his long series of travels in European countries. Particularly important were his trips to Italy: in 1819 he spent three months in Rome and then visited Naples, Florence, and Venice. He revisited Italy in 1829, 1833, 1840, and 1844. His understanding of the mechanics of light was greatly enhanced by the times he spent in Italy, especially Venice, and this is what marked the beginning of his last and greatest phase.

Steamboat in a Snowstorm (309) shows Turner at his most impassioned. We are presented with a whirlwind of frenetic energy, almost tactile communication of what it means to be in a storm at sea, and a snowstorm at that. The opacity of the driven snow, the dense clouds

309 J.M.W. Turner, Steamboat in a Snowstorm, 1842, 91 x 122 cm (36 x 48 in)

swirling from the smokestacks, the furious commotion of the water, all combine with almost frightening realism. And yet, take away the title, change the century, and we would think we were looking at an abstract.

This is the greatness of Turner, an almost reckless appreciation of natural wildness, controlled solely by the power of the artist's understanding. In controlling the scene, Turner seems to control nature itself, a godlike quality, and he communicates this orderliness to us. The viewer experiences the wildness, and yet is able to hold it in perspective. There can be few things more exhilarating than to encounter the full force of a great Turner.

EXHILARATION OF LIGHT
In Turner's work from this time until his old age, light has conquered so completely that all dissolves in its radiance. In these pictures, the Romantic glorification and love of nature's drama are shown to the fullest. It is here that the deeply poetic nature of Romantic painting first finds supreme visual form. As his rival John Constable (see p.268) put it, late Turners are as though "painted with tinted steam".

Approach to Venice (310) needs its title, since we are presented with a haze of coloured nothingness, through which there looms the bright accents of what we make out to be boats and a far-off steeple. The water is golden with light, but so is the sky: where does one end and the other start? There is no perspectival depth, just space, height, clouds, dazzle, glory.

The impression given is of immense exhilaration, almost ecstatic in its power; the natural is allied with the spiritual. Turner has torn the world into paper shreds and thrown them up to the sun: there they catch fire and he paints them for us, crying "Alleluia!"

Not until the 20th century, with Pollock, Rothko, and de Kooning (see pp.368–372) was there such a daring disregard for realism. Yet Turner knew precisely what he was aiming at. The clouds of glory, the lakes of light, the stone and mortar transformed into citadels of Heaven: these are not inventions. Few people have not seen the extravagances of glory that the sun produces with casual ease morning after morning. It was Turner's special gift to know that these extremes of light and colour demand from the artist an extremity of technique.

TURNER'S TECHNIQUE
This caricature by Richard Doyle entitled *Turner Painting One of His Pictures* was painted for the *Almanack of the Month* in 1846. It makes the point that Turner's love of chrome yellow, which he had used consistently since the 1820s, was still considered shocking by the public. Turner's use of luminous yellows, blues and pinks was his most characteristic feature.

310 J.M.W. Turner, **Approach to Venice,** *c. 1843, 62 x 94 cm (24½ x 37 in)*

Approach to Venice

Turner visited Venice several times. He painted *Approach to Venice* on what was probably his last visit there. As a late work it exceeds, stylistically, his earlier paintings of Venice, pushing further his daring with Romantic atmospherics and departing from the topographic reality of the Venetian sea- and townscape even more than before.

Distant city
The mysterious and unnamed procession of barges moves silently through water that, more than anything, resembles liquid gold, towards the shimmering, floating city of Venice. The distant city seems to be dissolving, no more on firm ground than the barges themselves, and takes on the quality of a mirage. Indeed, when this painting was exhibited in London, a critic for the weekly magazine The Spectator *wrote: "beautiful as it is in colour it is but a vision of enchantment".*

Darkening sky
Turner has created a canopy of orange and blue over the setting sun. These are the strongest touches of colour in the painting and suggest that the colours of the sunset have not yet reached their peak of intensity before they finally disappear. Over a smooth (and now heavily cracked) surface, these "abbreviated" clouds have been quickly and lightly rendered, and Turner has created a wonderful sense of transition as the sky moves rapidly from day to night.

Moonlight
ON THE WATER
Beyond the ostensible subject matter of Approach to Venice, *with its important-looking barges sailing towards Venice, is the real subject of the painting: the duel between sunset and moonrise. To the right of the canvas, the sun is setting in a spread of diffused, pale lemon light. To the left, casting its cooler reflection down the length of the picture, is the ascending full moon. When Turner first exhibited this painting, he accompanied it with these lines from a poem by Byron:*

> "The moon is up, and yet
> it is not night,
> The sun as yet disputes
> the day with her."

Layered surface
Turner habitually prepared his canvases with a thick layer of white oil ground, which would largely obliterate the "tooth" of the canvas. Over this smooth surface he would apply thin, pale washes of those colours that were to be used full strength later. This resulted in a fresh, glowing surface over which he built up subsequent layers. To the barge on the left he has added thick, crusted paint, which, having a jewelled effect, catches natural light falling onto the picture and provides areas of focus. Conversely, the shadows of the dark barge on the right have been applied with thin washes of black so that they appear to sink within the surface.

CONSTABLE – POETRY IN REALITY

Turner's Romanticism, though full of drama, is not melodramatic, and indeed "Romantic" does not preclude the humble and ordinary as we have already seen in Turner's treatment of a quiet sunset at Mortlake (see p.265).

Constable (1776–1837) is as intense as Turner and, in his less obvious manner, fully as daring, but he always reverences the factuality of what he paints. Since he sees those facts as purely poetic, there is no loss of intensity. Turner loved the grandiose and the magnificent. Venice was his natural habitat. Constable loved the ordinary, and his love and natural dwelling place was the flat land of his beloved Suffolk. He is the natural heir to Gainsborough's lyricism (see p.240), but

whereas Gainsborough was still largely concerned with extracting the beautiful and harmonious in the natural landscape, Constable saw the long meadows and winding canals, the old bridges, and the slimy posts by the rivers, as being inherently as lovely as anything the heart of man could desire. All his youth and all his hope of Heaven were intimately connected with these rural simplicities, already under threat from industry as he began his arduous and none too successful career as an artist.

Turner lived unmarried; Constable needed the solace of a wife to share his loneliness. Even shared, this loneliness is always discernible. The sun may shine and the trees wave in the breeze, but a Constable landscape carries a deep sense

311 *John Constable*, Wivenhoe Park, Essex, *1816,*
56 x 102 cm (22 x 40 in)

JOHN RUSKIN
The art critic John Ruskin
(1819–1900) took it upon
himself to rescue Turner
from obscurity. In 1843 he
wrote his treatise *Modern
Painters* in defence of
Turner, which he then
developed into a series of
volumes concerning artistic
tastes and ethics. Ruskin
belonged to the Romantic
school in his conception
of the artist as inspired
prophet and teacher. His
personal life, however,
was deeply unhappy
and he died a lonely
Christian socialist fighting
against the onslaught of
the Industrial Revolution.

**OTHER WORKS BY
CONSTABLE**
Hampstead Heath
(Fitzwilliam Museum,
Cambridge)

View at Epsom
(Tate Gallery, London)

Naworth Castle
(National Gallery of
Victoria, Melbourne)

*Coast at Brighton,
Stormy Weather*
(Yale Center for British
Art, New Haven,
Connecticut)

View of Salisbury
(Louvre, Paris)

The Watermill
(National Museum,
Stockholm)

Wooded Landscape
(Art Gallery of
Ontario, Toronto)

of loss and yearning. After the early death of his
beloved wife, this yearning becomes even more
apparent. Yet it is a resigned yearning and an
acceptance of life as it is, and of the consolation
given by the beauty of the material world, our
nearest image of lost Eden.

The intensity of Constable's poetry was not
obvious to himself: he believed that he was the
most throughgoing of realists. Even an early
work, though, like *Wivenhoe Park, Essex (311)*,
despite its conscientious fulfilment of the owner
of the park's desire to illustrate every aspect of
his property (which Constable found "a great
difficulty") is still a work of imaginative ardour.
The reality of all he portrays is evident: there
fish the Wivenhoe tenants, on the fish-stocked

lake; there wander the dairy cows, belonging to
the farm; there, tiny in the distance, is the family
in the trap; there in the background is the stately
home. Yet all this is bathed in a silvery sunlight,
so that the waters shimmer and the shadows
beneath the great, spreading trees entice the
viewer towards their shade.

Over the earth and water towers a pale and
clouded sky, hinting at rain to come, the blissful
rain that every estate needs. Peace and silence,
contentment and prosperity are all imagined
and realized in the actual details, so that
Wivenhoe Park is both real and ideal, both
in our world and removed from it.

SONGS OF INNOCENCE

As a child, the English poet William Blake (1757–1827) saw visions from which he drew lifelong inspiration. One of William Blake's most significant inventions was the printed book in which the illustrations were completely intergrated with the text, both being printed from a single metal plate.

The two mediums of poetry and engraving came together triumphantly in 1789 when he published his *Songs of Innocence.* This illustration shows the original title page. The fictional world of *Songs of Innocence* is Christian and pastoral with the innocence of childhood celebrated as a spiritual force. Five years later Blake wrote the antithesis of this idyll entitled the *Songs of Experience.* In his last years Blake produced some of his finest engravings, illustrating, among others, the book of Job.

312 John Constable, **The White Horse,** *probably 1819, 130 x 188 cm (51 x 74 in)*

THE UNTRADITIONAL CONSTABLE

"Constable's England" has become so familiar to us that it is difficult to understand the impression his paintings made on his contemporaries. His work has come to shape our conceptions of the beautiful in the English landscape, but his contemporaries were accustomed to a very different kind of representation of the natural landscape. There were set formulas, strictly adhered to, concerning the correct way to create distance, harmony, and mood. Constable's naturalistic, vivid greens, for instance, totally upturned these formulas, which were based on the use of warm browns in the foreground and pale blues in the far distance – and his depiction of the random or "unbeautiful" aspects of the landscape was counter to accepted standards of composition and to the conventions of appropriate subject matter.

When Delacroix (see p.260) visited England in 1825 he was enormously impressed with Constable's animated brushwork, and the optical freshness that resulted from his use of broken colour to create tone. On his return, Delacroix is believed to have reworked his large *Massacre at Chios,* enlivening the surface of the painting to make it echo its emotive subject.

It was his great "six-foot" canvases that Constable valued most, but modern taste finds even greater beauty in the studies and sketches with which he prepared for them. The wild passion of a Constable study has a marvellous vigour that the sedate control of the finished works may lack. *White Horse (312)* is such a magnificent picture, with the white streak of the horse uniting both sides of the river, the greenery almost palpable, the sense of actuality so piercing, that it is almost a shock to find that his oil sketches, such as *Dedham from Langham (313),* can be even more immediate and evocative, even more vital.

313 John Constable, **Dedham from Langham,** *c. 1813, 13.5 x 19 cm (5¼ x 7½ in)*

PREPARATORY SKETCHES

Constable adopted a systematic approach to painting from nature, making oil sketches on the spot then later working them up into larger works. *Dedham from Langham* was one of a number of preliminary sketches of the same scene. Constable said of it, "Nature is never seen, in this climate at least, to greater perfection than at about 9 o'clock in the morning of July and August when the sun has gained sufficient strength to give splendour to the landscape 'still gemmed with the morning dew'".

ENGLISH MYSTICISM

Romanticism provided an outlet for the spiritual expression and individuality that Neoclassicism, with its emphasis on the ideal and on stoic heroism, largely denied.

Both William Blake and Samuel Palmer worked primarily as watercolourists rather than as oil painters, yet both have the peculiarly English quality of nostalgic realism that is so pronounced in Constable. Both were poets, Blake (1757–1827) literally so (see column, p.270) and Palmer temperamentally, and there is a haunting awareness of time and its passing in their works.

Blake's *Job and His Daughters (314)* is a clumsy, archaic vision that is nevertheless extremely powerful. Blake later went on to illustrate the book of Job. His strange, visionary art found a more sympathetic response after his death, and he achieved cult status among the Pre-Raphaelites of the 19th century (see p.276). Blake's wood engravings contained the crucial element of mystery and innocence that his followers also admired in the paintings of the German primitives, and of the 18th-century Romantic group, the Nazarenes.

Samuel Palmer (1805–81) was an avid follower of Blake, nearly 50 years younger than him and influenced particularly by his few landscape works, which had been commissioned as illustrations

315 **Samuel Palmer,** Coming from Evening Church, *1830, 30 x 20 cm (12 x 8 in)*

for a school edition of Virgil's *Eclogues* (see p.218). Palmer's *Coming from Evening Church (315)* is just as naïvely independent of styles and schools as Blake's art, and has much the same spiritual innocence. Palmer developed a way of working with mixed media – such as Indian ink, watercolour, and gouache – that resulted in an intense luminosity, reminiscent of the medieval illuminated manuscripts (see pp.28-34).

Constable was an artist in the largest sense, as Blake and Palmer were not, but his influence continued in their work – in their particularly English strain of deeply personal love of the land, and in their awareness of its mystical importance to our spiritual well-being.

314 **William Blake,** Job and His Daughters, *1799–1800, 27 x 38 cm (10½ x 15 in)*

THE ANCIENTS

In 1826 Samuel Palmer (1805–81) moved to Shoreham in England and founded a group of artists known as The Ancients. The name of the group was derived from their passion for the medieval world and their concentration on pastoral subjects with a mystical outlook. Palmer's work was largely forgotten until the Neo-Romantics rediscovered him during World War II.

THE AGE OF IMPRESSIONISM

In the middle of the 19th century, painters began to look at reality with a new alertness. Academic conventions had become so solidified and entrenched that artists such as Gustave Courbet could see no point in them. He painted peasant life as it truly was, thereby shocking and alienating the art world establishment.

The label for this reaction was "Realism", but the next generation of artists ultimately found it too material a vision. They too rejected idealized and emotional themes, but they sought to go much further. Studio painting seemed in itself unnatural to them when the real world was "out there": it was there that they painted, outside, seeking to capture the fleeting effects of light and give the real impression of a passing moment. Rather contemptuously, they were known as Impressionists and their most characteristic figures were Claude Monet and Auguste Renoir, who captured the poetry of the here and now.

Auguste Renoir, **The Boating Party Lunch**, *1881* **(detail)**

AGE OF IMPRESSIONISM TIMELINE

Realism as a style was based upon a new attitude to social truth; it accepted the sordid conditions of real life. Impressionism was not social but personal, less "life" than "experience". If we want historical dates, it lasted from the first Impressionist exhibition of 1874 to the last in 1886, but artists escape these neat time boxes, and Impressionists reach back to the Realists and forward to the Post-Impressionists.

JEAN-FRANCOIS MILLET, THE GLEANERS, 1857
The village of Barbizon was the home of a group of artists who shared a common desire for a greater naturalism in landscape painting than that provided by Romanticism or academic painting. Millet shared this desire, painting peasants with a strong sense of their dignity, imbued with compassion for their laborious lifestyle (p.281).

SIR JOHN EVERETT MILLAIS, OPHELIA, 1851–52
The Pre-Raphaelites were a group of English artists who rejected the studio conventions of their day and harked back to medieval simplicities. Ophelia *is a fine example of their weird amalgam of specific detail and Romantic theme (p.276).*

CAMILLE COROT, VILLE D'AVRAY, C. 1867–70
Corot's long career began in the 1820s, during the Romantic era, and this painting is an example of his late work. It shows his deeply poetic response to the timeless qualities of classical landscapes, that nostalgic world of the lost paradise from which we are all inevitably barred. He taught the Barbizon painters how to see this world and make it real, and the Impressionists learnt from him too (p.280).

1850	1860	1870

GUSTAVE COURBET, BONJOUR MONSIEUR COURBET, 1854
Courbet, like the Pre-Raphaelites, believed in the importance of the specific, but far more flamboyantly. He himself was the centre of his art, and we see him here splendidly confident. It is not theories that make his paintings work, but sheer artistic power (p.283).

EDOUARD MANET, LE DEJEUNER SUR L'HERBE, 1863
Manet painted with a naked truth that stripped away the social pretences of his time. It was not the subject of his work that was startling (a picnic in the woods was a well-established theme), but its alarming realism, its refusal to pretend, to hide in an antique guise. He was not specifically an Impressionist, but his artistic discoveries were an enormous influence on Impressionism (p.284).

AUGUSTE RENOIR, THE BOATING PARTY LUNCH, 1881
While other Impressionists were fascinated with the ever-changing patterns of nature, Renoir was more interested in people. He took simple pleasure in whatever met his good-humoured attention and aimed to give the impression, the sensation, of his subject matter. This painting shows Renoir's skill in capturing delightful scenes of modern life and recording how the Parisians spent their leisure time. He also shows relationships between people – such as that of the pair on the right (p.298).

ALFRED SISLEY, MEADOW, 1875
Sisley came from an English family living in France, and can be considered the one true Impressionist. He never developed beyond it. His landscapes are not as robust as Monet's, but are subtle, lyrical, and peaceful. The place shown here is unimportant, but Sisley catches the quality of light and the changing shadows perfectly (p.301).

EDGAR DEGAS, FOUR DANCERS, C. 1899
Degas often exhibited with the Impressionists, although he studied the Old Masters throughout his life and was a superb draughtsman. This late work is a good example of how he could seize upon the unbalance of an actual scene in the real world, and make art from what he had found. He learnt this from photography and the strange magic of the Japanese printmakers (p.292).

1880	1890	1900

JAMES WHISTLER, NOCTURNE IN BLUE AND GOLD: OLD BATTERSEA BRIDGE, 1872–75
American by birth, Whistler moved to Europe and lived first in Paris, then London. Nocturne in Blue and Gold reveals his debt to the Impressionists. He had looked at them, but also, and more significantly, at the Japanese, with their use of a non-realistic, seemingly two-dimensional composition, and the skilful choice of a few highly significant details. Whistler was interested in the Realist and Impressionist movements, but took from them what he needed to create a decorative style that was his alone (p.302).

CLAUDE MONET, THE WATERLILY POND, 1899
A quintessential work of Impressionism, this is one of Monet's numerous waterlily studies, some of which border on the abstract with their floating shapes and surface reflections (p.296).

THE PRE-RAPHAELITES

*T*owards the middle of the 19th century, a small group of young artists in England reacted vigorously against what they felt was "the frivolous art of the day": this reaction became known as the Pre-Raphaelite movement. Their ambition was to bring English art (such as it was) back to a greater "truth to nature". They deeply admired the simplicities of the early 15th century, and they felt this admiration made them a "Brotherhood".

While contemporary critics and art historians worshipped Raphael (see p.125) as the great master of the Renaissance, these young students rebelled against what they saw as Raphael's theatricality and the Victorian hypocrisy and pomp of the academic art tradition. The friends decided to form a secret society, the Pre-Raphaelite Brotherhood, in deference to the sincerities of the early Renaissance before Raphael developed his grand manner. The Pre-Raphaelites adopted a high moral stance that embraced a sometimes unwieldy combination

THE PRE-RAPHAELITES

The Pre-Raphaelite Brotherhood was founded in London in 1848 and the members initially included Rossetti, Holman Hunt, and Millais, but would soon extend into a group of seven. The initials PRB were first used on Rossetti's painting *The Girlhood of Mary Virgin* in 1849 and were soon adopted by the other artists. John Ruskin (see p.269) initially criticized the brotherhood but later recognized the echoes of his own values in their work and published a spirited defence in *The Times*. Ruskin was the most articulate supporter of the movement amd had a profound influence on the artists.

OPHELIA

Shakespeare's plays provided a wonderfully rich source book for Victorian painters and had a great influence on several Pre-Raphaelite painters. Shakespeare's tragic story of Ophelia driven to madness and suicide by Hamlet's murder of her father, Polonius, was carefully recreated by Millais in 1851. The exquisite flowers floating on the surface of the water are not simply decorative and naturalistic but were chosen for their traditional symbolic meanings:

poppies – *death*
daisies – *innocence*
roses – *youth*
violets – *faithfulness and early death*
pansies – *love in vain.*

316 Sir John Everett Millais, Ophelia, *1851–52, 75 x 112 cm (30 x 44 in)*

of symbolism and realism. They painted only serious – usually religious or romantic – subjects, and their style was clear and sharply focused. It entailed a unique insistence on painting everything from direct observation.

The group initially caused outrage when the existence of their secret brotherhood became known after their first works were exhibited in 1849. They also offended with their heavily religious and realist themes that were so unlike the popular historical paintings. However, the Royal Academy continued to exhibit Pre-Raphaelite paintings, and after 1852 their popularity burgeoned. Their work, though certainly detailed and for the most part laboriously truthful, became progressively old-worldish, and this

317 William Holman Hunt, On English Coasts, 1852, 43 x 58 cm (17 x 23 in)

decision to live in the past, while deploying the judgments of the present, makes the work of an artist such as John Everett Millais (1829–96) appear disturbingly unintegrated. His *Ophelia (316)*, Hamlet's drowned lover, was modelled with painstaking attention on a real body in water, surrounded by a ravishing array of genuine wild flowers (see column, p.276).

Millais spent four months painting the background vegetation on the same spot in Surrey, England. He then returned to London to paint his model, Elizabeth Siddal, posing in a bath full of water, so determined was he to capture the image authentically. The result is oddly dislocated, as if the setting, girl, and flowers did not belong together, each keeping its own truth and ignoring that of the others.

LUMINOUS COLOUR

William Holman Hunt (1827–1910), a fellow art student and friend of Millais, was more alerted to the theatricalities of his age, and *On English Coasts (317)* is a political allegory on the theme of strayed and unprotected sheep. Yet the weirdly acidic colours, even though honestly come by, strike unpleasantly on the eye. We are constrained into belief, but against our will: the bright yellow is so garishly bright and so are the aggressive greens of the sea.

The Pre-Raphaelites achieved such intense luminosity in their work by painting pure colours onto a canvas that had been prepared with white paint, sometimes reapplied fresh before each day's work, so as to give the hues added brilliance.

CHARLES DICKENS
The English author Charles Dickens (1812–70) is considered one of the greatest novelists of the 19th century. His early life was one of poverty and hard work, but he managed to educate himself and find a job as a journalist for the *Morning Herald*. His first printed work, *Sketches By Boz*, was published in 1836 and from this date onwards he became a prolific writer, completing many serialized novels including *Hard Times*, published in 1865 (illustrated above). As an important literary figure, Dickens found ready listeners for his criticism of Millais' *Christ in the House of His Parents*. He objected to the imagery, and style, calling it "mean, odious, repulsive and revolting".

WILLIAM MORRIS

William Morris (1834–96) became a lifelong friend of Edward Burne-Jones whilst they were studying at Oxford University. Along with several other craftsmen, Morris founded a manufacturing and decorating firm in 1861. The firm produced works based on the ideal of a medieval guild, in which the artists both designed and executed the work.
Products included furniture, stained glass, tapestries, carpets, and wallpaper (illustrated above).

DANTE GABRIEL ROSSETTI

Rossetti (1828–82) was born into an intellectual and creative Italian family but spent most of his life in London. Throughout the 1840s his poetry and painting prospered and he completed many symbolic historical paintings. He met Elizabeth Siddal in 1850 whom he then married in 1860 after a troubled courtship. His wife, however, was weak and died only two years later, leaving Rossetti a broken man. For her burial Rossetti insisted on placing his complete poetry manuscripts in her coffin, which he then retrieved in 1869 by exhuming her body. He fell into depression and in 1872 attempted suicide but did not die. He lingered on in a alcoholic and drug-induced haze until his death in 1882.

LITERARY INFLUENCES

Dante Gabriel Rossetti (1828–82), the third founding member of the Pre-Raphaelites, became the recognized leader and even formed a second grouping of the brotherhood in 1857, after Millais and Hunt had gone their separate ways. Rossetti came from an artistic and versatile Italian family, and it was perhaps the confidence engendered by this background, and his dynamic personality, rather than his artistic talent, that earned him his prominent position.

Rossetti was a poet as well as a painter, and in common with the other Pre-Raphaelites, his art was a fusion of artistic invention and authentic renderings of literary sources. The brotherhood drew heavily from Shakespeare, Dante, and contemporary poets such as Robert Browning and Alfred Lord Tennyson – Rossetti in particular was greatly attracted to Tennyson's reworkings of the Arthurian legends. He specialized in soulful maidens of extraordinary looks for his romantic themes, using his beautiful but neurotic wife Elizabeth Siddal as his model. Her striking face, with its long-nosed, languid expression, appears in many pictures. After Elizabeth's

318 Rossetti, **The Day Dream,** *1880, 160 × 92 cm (63 × 36½ in)*

319 Edward Burne-Jones, **The Golden Stairs,** *1876–80, 270 × 117 cm (106 × 46 in)*

death, Rossetti's model was William Morris' wife Janey (a Siddal look-alike). She is the one we see in *The Day Dream (318)*.

Edward Burne-Jones (1833–98), who was a great influence on the French Symbolists (see p.321), was a friend of Rossetti and Morris. He places his introspective, medievalized heroines in *The Golden Stairs (319)* in a dreamlike never-neverland that comes close to his own unworldly convictions. This romanticized world may cloy, but there are many who feel at home in the serious play of the Pre-Raphaelites, and have no difficulty in responding to their themes.

REALISM IN FRANCE

Neither a Romantic nor a Realist, it was Camille Corot, who early in the 19th century, showed that these two approaches were not necessarily in opposition. He united great truth with great lyricism, but it was his astonishing truthfulness that ultimately made the greater impact. Honoré Daumier began to look at the social realities of his day with a boldness he had learnt from Corot, and so did the Barbizon School of painters. This Realism, now fully deserving its capital "R", came to its full maturity in the astonishing work of Gustave Courbet.

After the emotional extremes of the Romantics (see p.259), it comes almost as a relief to enter the gentler world of Corot's imagination (Jean-Baptiste-Camille, 1796–1875). Corot's style was far removed from the heroics of the Romantics. He saw the world, both natural and man-made, with an innocent truthfulness that greatly influenced the Barbizon School of artists, as well as practically every painter of landscape in the latter half of the 19th century.

In 1825 Corot went to Italy, a journey that influenced his approach to painting for the rest of his life; subsequently, it affected the whole development of modern landscape painting. It was in Italy that Corot first experienced the benefits of painting *en plein air* (see column, right), and his authentic depiction of light and nuance set a new precedent in French landscape painting. He came to place great importance on the Italian practice of making sketches *in situ*, valuing these for their spontaneity, truthfulness, and atmosphere. He was deeply responsive to the timeless serenity of the classical landscape; its quietness found a response within, and his Italian landscapes express this profound and lovely silence.

A View near Volterra (320) was not painted on the spot: Corot saw this view as he travelled in this strange region of Italy and some years later, referring to his original sketch, he painted it both as what he remembered and for what it meant to him. The truth then is emotional rather than factual, but it is truth nonetheless: the quiet rocks and sunlit foliage bear within them a sense of the antique. Many generations have lived on the sites of the ancient Etruscans

PAINTING EN PLEIN AIR

The French landscape painter Charles Daubigny (1808–79) was one of the earliest exponents of *plein air* (open air) painting and was to have a significant influence on the later Impressionist painters. The invention of metal paint tubes allowed long-term storage of oil paints, making trips into the countryside feasible using the new portable easels. Many of the Impressionists settled and painted in the riverside communities along the banks of the River Seine. This illustration shows Camille Corot (1796–1875) painting *en plein air* under an umbrella.

OTHER WORKS BY COROT

Morning near Beauvais (Museum of Fine Arts, Boston)

La Rochelle (Cincinnati Art Museum)

In the Dunes (Rijksmuseum, The Hague)

Souvenir of Palluel (National Gallery, London)

The Ferryman (Louvre, Paris)

Landscape at Orleans (Bridgestone Museum of Art, Tokyo)

Canal in Holland (Philadelphia Museum of Art)

The Happy Island (Museum of Fine Arts, Montreal)

320 *Camille Corot,* **A View near Volterra,** *1838, 70 x 95 cm (27½ x 37½ in)*

*321 Camille Corot, Ville d'Avray, c. 1867–70,
40 x 60 cm (19½ x 26 in)*

(see p.18), and their presence still lives on
subliminally. Corot paints the place and its feel,
evoking our own memories to unite with his.
The place is dreamlike, yet fundamental in its
solidity. No artist ever made mere substance
so spiritual as did Corot.

Corot can be so unassuming that his true
greatness is missed. He never dramatizes or
exaggerates, never strikes any kind of attitude.
Few painters have ever had such a mastery of
tone, of the imperceptible gradations by which
one colour melts into another. His landscapes
are often small but perfect, with a simplicity so
profound as to be totally satisfying. He may not
have beautified his undramatic countrysides but
the excitement is in the veracity of his vision.

Corot's early and less critically successful
landscapes paved the way for Impressionism. In
his later years, he would modify his art, painting
again and again an entrancing forest glade,
dappled and peaceful. This is the fashionable
Corot, and this too is lovely, but it is a declension
from the unique magic of his disregarded early
work. A typical and lovely example of late Corot
is *Ville d'Avray (321)*: feathery trees, pale sky,
pure white of the distant houses, silvery water,
and young people bright amidst all the flowers
and grasses. The one abiding component is a
contemplative stillness that Corot never lost.

DAUMIER THE SATIRIST
We do not know what Corot thought of the
French painters Daumier and Millet, but he
gave financial help to Daumier in his blind
old age, and to Millet's widow. Honoré Daumier

(1808–79) was greatly influenced by Corot's
work – though the caustic wit and the overtly
socio-political content of Daumier's caricatures
and lithographs (see column, left) would appear
to have little in common with the serenity of
Corot's art. Though he was acknowledged as one
of the most important cartoonists of the 19th
century during his lifetime, it is only since his
death that Daumier's qualities as a serious
painter have been recognized. His directness of
vision and lack of sentimentality in the way he
painted actual experiences make his works some
of the most powerful examples of Realism.

While Corot was comfortably well off and
never had to earn his living, Daumier struggled
throughout his career as a satirist to support
himself, suffering censorship and imprisonment
because of the subversive nature of his art. He
was a committed Republican with an intense
political passion for the poor, drawing such
strong caricatures that his own contemporaries
found it hard to take him seriously as a fine artist.
He gave Corot his painting *Advice to a Young
Artist (322)* in gratitude for an act of generosity
by Corot that released Daumier from financial
worry in his final years. Two men are alone in
the studio, the unmade bed the only sharp colour.
The young man is tense, the older man intent,
perhaps marking time while he finds the encourag-
ing yet sincere words to offer as advice. The
stress is wholly on personal interaction, with the
entire context conjured up out of just a few props.

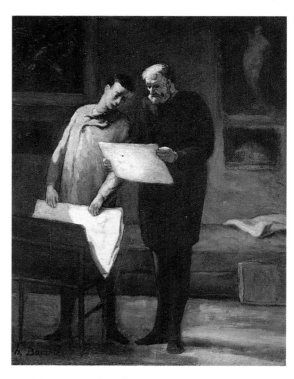

*322 Honoré Daumier, Advice to a Young Artist, probably
after 1860, 41 x 33 cm (16 x 12 in)*

MILLET AND THE BARBIZON SCHOOL

In the 1830s a group of landscape artists moved out of Paris to the small village of Barbizon on the outskirts of the Forest of Fontainebleau, where they were often joined by Corot. He was a great influence on the group, but they were also affected by Constable's landscapes (see p.268) in their desire for a greater naturalism and a truthful depiction of the countryside.

Jean-François Millet (1814–75) settled in Barbizon in 1849 and was soon associated with the School. Although in later life he turned to painting pure landscape, he is more famous for his peasant pictures, the truth of which arises from his own personal experience as the son of a farm labourer. Some now think these paintings sentimental, but they were considered radical in their day for their social realism. Millet was a sad and laborious painter, apt to see life as very dark – the temperamental opposite of Corot, with his luminous world of serenity and light – but people clearly responded to his art, although

they were still baffled by Daumier's. Millet's style was simplified, diluted, yet powerful, imbuing the ordinary with a strong sense of dignity and a monumental weight.

Millet's most famous work is probably *The Gleaners (323)*. We see three peasant women at work in a golden field: two of them are bowed in measured toil, assiduously gathering the scraps left behind by the harvesters, while the third binds together her pathetic sheath. Millet makes inescapable the realization that it is hard, back-breaking work. The women's faces are not only darkened by the sun, but seen as almost brutish, with thick, heavy features. Yet, beasts of burden though they are, he regards them with reverence. We feel awed at their massive power and the sheer beauty of the classical frieze they create silhouetted against the meadow. This is a setting of great natural loveliness: golden corn, peaceful sky, the rhythmic movement of distant labourers. The background is a pastoral idyll; the foreground a pastoral reality.

MILLET'S SKETCHES
Jean-François Millet (1814–75) was the most famous painter of rural life in 19th-century France. Although renowned as a painter, some of Millet's best works are his drawings, which invest the ordinary with depth and dignity. Millet is known to have said that he aimed "to make the trivial serve to express the sublime". Millet was admired by many artists including van Gogh (see p.316).

*323 Jean-François Millet, **The Gleaners**, 1857, 83 x 111 cm (33 x 44 in)*

THE PAINTER'S STUDIO

Dissatisfied with the space allotted to him at the Universal Exhibition of 1855, Gustave Courbet decided to establish his own pavillion called *Le Realismé* to show his works. One of the paintings exhibited was *The Painter's Studio* which proved that secular art could now convey the deep seriousness previously only expected from religious paintings.

There were many interpretations of the painting, including a theory that it was a covert denouncement of Napoleon III. Courbet, however, stated that it shows "all the people who serve my cause, sustain me in my ideal, and support my activity".

COURBET, THE GREAT REALIST

The Pre-Raphaelites' (see p.276) concept of Realism was a fundamentally different one, their work often displaying a superficial, outward impression of nature and expressing sentiments quite removed from reality. The greatest Realist, in a much truer sense, was the brash, anti-intellectual, and largely self-taught artist, Gustave Courbet (1819–98). He was by nature prone to rhetorical flourishes and was not as down-to-earth as he himself thought, but he had no tincture of the dreamy hankering after the past that characterizes the Pre-Raphaelites. Courbet's defiantly non-conformist stance and his commitment to concrete reality was an important influence on a subsequent generation of artists.

Courbet lived by his belief that artists should paint only "real and existing things", striding resolutely into the future and taking, he generally felt, possession of it. He was impressed by Caravaggio's robust expression (see p.176) and by the Dutch masters Hals (p.210) and Rembrandt (p.200). Their influences can also be traced in Courbet's own admirers. His landscapes are always vital with a savage sort of power and he prided himself on this uninhibited zest. The son of a rural bourgeois landowner, he was by nature a rough, coarse, and passionate man and he sublimated these qualities in his art. He called himself "a socialist, a democrat and a Republican and above all a Realist, that is to say a sincere lover of genuine truth".

Courbet's work has a heavy realism that is unflinching in its restless scrutiny. All his qualities, including an indefinable something that eludes the viewer, are present in his masterpiece, *The Painter's Studio (324)*. This is an intensely personal work, yet it keeps its secrets: nobody has ever quite discovered what is meant by its full title – *A Real Allegory Summing Up Seven Years of My Artistic and Moral Life*. Courbet claimed to have assembled, imaginatively, in this one canvas, all the significant influences of his life, some generalized and some apparently

324 Courbet, The Painter's Studio, *1855, 361 x 597 cm (11 ft 10 in x 19 ft 17 in)*

personified. The people are of all kinds and
conditions, all totally authentic, all centred
on the artist himself, who paints a ravishing
landscape while a nude model presses herself
affectionately against his chair. These visitors are
all guests, whom he seems to have invited for a
purpose. Courbet actually described this strange
allegory in a letter to his friend, the novelist Jules
Champfleury, writing that the figures on the left
were those who "live on death", while the figures
on the right "live on life".

Although the portraits on the right are
identifiable – Champfleury himself is depicted
among the onlookers, along with other elegant
Parisian friends of Courbet, such as the journalist
and socialist Pierre Proudhon and the poet Charles
Baudelaire (see p.286) – the characters on the
left, veiled in semi-darkness, could represent
people from Courbet's past or previous influences
in his life: there may even be a disguised portrait
of the Emperor Napoleon III. We may smile at
this naïve self-importance, yet we are also

325 *Gustave Courbet,* Bonjour Monsieur Courbet, *1854,
130 x 150 cm (51 x 59 in)*

impressed. Courbet had every right to see
himself as a major painter who understood
materiality so profoundly as to make it appear
to become more than it really was.

THE OMNISCIENT ARTIST

Courbet's vanity is not rare in those with creative talent, but few have put their weakness to
such effective use. *Bonjour Monsieur Courbet
(325)* shows the painter as he sees himself, very
handsome and virile, detached from the softness
of civilized living, striding forth along a country
lane. Courbet's devoted patron, Alfred Bruyas,
and his servant, bow reverentially to the artist as
if he is their superior, and it is clear that Courbet
heartily agrees. There is an innocent conceit
in the tilt of the artist's noble head, in the
condescension of his affable smile. The dusty
path, the bordering weeds and grasses, the dog –
every detail of this wholly ordinary part of
France is grasped completely in its truth and left
undramatized. We are drawn into what Courbet
saw and smelt and heard, not through any
dramatic overemphasis but from his enormous
painterly conviction.

This self-image of the artist existing above
and beyond the mediocrities of "bourgeois"
civilization was to find full expression in the
works and lives of the next generation of
painters, particularly Manet and Degas, who
benefited from Courbet's artistic advances and
laid the foundations of "modern" expression.

**OTHER WORKS BY
COURBET**

Hunters in the Snow
(Musée des Beaux
Arts, Besançon)

Reflection of a Gypsy
(National Museum of
Western Art, Tokyo)

Landscape
(National Museum,
Stockholm)

*Girls on the Banks
of the Seine*
(Petit Palais, Paris)

The Waterfall
(National Gallery of
Canada, Ottawa)

Woman with a Parrot
(Metropolitan Museum
of Art, New York)

The Grotto of the Loue
(Kunsthalle, Hamburg)

THE INFLUENCE OF MANET & DEGAS

Courbet's richness of colour and insistence on his own personal vision were immensely influential on other artists, teaching them to believe only what they could see with their own eyes. Manet abandoned the conventional practice of subtle blending and polished "finish", using instead bold colours to explore the harsh, realistic contrasts created by sunlight. Degas, influenced by photography and the simplicities of Japanese prints, adapted his skills as a draughtsman to create startlingly new compositions with his figures.

THE NEW PARIS

When Napoleon III became Emperor in 1851 he set about making Paris the new centre of Europe. Napoleon employed the architect Baron Haussmann (shown above) to redesign and rebuild central Paris, using a new network of interconnecting tree-lined boulevards. During the rebuilding he also created new parks, squares, and municipal buildings. Haussmann's ruthless plans displaced over 350,000 people and led to more social problems, including increased visibility of prostitution on the wide-open boulevards.

SALON DES REFUSES

The "Salon of the Rejected" was formed after the official 1863 Salon turned down over 4,000 paintings. The alternative salon was ordered by the Emperor Napoleon III, and many artists, including Manet, Cézanne, and Whistler were happy to find a place to show their rejected works. When the Salon des Refusés opened in May 1863, over 7,000 people visited on the first day, but the exhibition received very little critical acclaim. The Salon des Refusés inspired other artists to develop their own salons and increased the influence of art dealers. This illustration shows a contemporary cartoon parodying the jury system of the Salon.

326 Edouard Manet, Le Déjeuner sur l'Herbe, 1863, 206 x 265 cm (6 ft 10 in x 8 ft 8 in)

329 Edouard Manet, **The Bar at the Folies-Bergère**, *1882, 97 x 130 cm (38 x 51 in)*

ANTONIN PROUST
Manet and Proust were
schoolboys and students
together and were to
remain life-long friends.
In 1850 Manet and Proust
joined Thomas Couture's
art academy in Paris
and there developed their
animosity towards the
art establishment.
Proust's *Souvenirs de
Manet*, published in 1897,
is the source usually
quoted for some of Manet's
earliest sayings. It celebrates
their unfailing friendship
and expounds the glories
of Manet's genius. Manet
died in April 1883 after
six months of constant
pain. Proust was a main
speaker at his funeral
which was also attended
by many famous artists
including Monet,
Renoir, Pissarro, and Sisley.

the vague impressions of a foreground. It is
this new sensitivity to the fleeting, mobile reality
of time that Manet gave to other artists, and
which was so important to the progress of the
Impressionist movement.

THE FINAL MASTERPIECE
This sense of the small, fleeting moment held
perpetually still is supremely conveyed in
The Bar at the Folies-Bergère (329). Manet also
plays with the deceptiveness of space: there are
reflections that reflect falsely, and it is hard to
locate ourselves in the work. The barmaid
looks out with the sad dignity of the exploited,
as much a comestible as the wine in the bottles
or the fruit in the bowl. Like the exquisite vase
of flowers on the bar, she seems to have been
plucked and set before the viewer. Manet died
relatively young, and knowing this, we find
his late flower studies to be among his most
poignant works. There we find fragile flowers,
so lovely yet so mortal, contrasted with their
vases, also lovely but capable of indefinite
existence. There are deep emotions in Manet,
but never on the surface.

It is impossible to overestimate the haunting
beauty with which Manet embraces every detail
of this last great canvas, his valediction to the
world of high art, and it is fitting that this final
work is a scene from modern Parisian life.

FANTIN-LATOUR –
A PAINTER OF STILL LIFES
Manet had a particularly wide circle of friends
and artists including Monet, Renoir, Cézanne,
and Bazille, an early Impressionist painter who
died in 1870 in the Franco-Prussian war (see
column, p.286). There were other artists who
were friends with the Impressionists, but who
never quite crossed over into the fleetingness
of their world. Henri Fantin-Latour (1836–1904),
for example, who was especially famous for
the exuberant beauty of his
flower arrangements, always
remained a Realist, painting
his flowers with the objectivity
achieved from prolonged
contemplation. *Flowers and Fruit
(330)*, with its meticulous detail,
shows little awareness of the way
Manet, Monet, or Renoir would
dissolve the blooms into
iridescence. His group portrait
Homage to Delacroix (see column,
p.287) reveals Fantin-Latour's
friendship with some of the most
advanced artists of the day, yet
the dark, brooding colours and
the substantial feel of each figure
confirms his preference for
consistent, realistic images.

330 Henri Fantin-Latour, **Flowers and Fruit**,
1865, 64 x 57 cm (25½ x 22½ in)

331 Berthe Morisot, The Harbour at Lorient, 1869, 44 x 73 cm (17½ x 29 in)

BERTHE MORISOT

The Morisot family was part of Manet's social circle, and his brother (Eugène Manet) eventually married the beautiful Berthe (1841–95). Morisot learned from Manet how to catch the passing hour and make it stay still for her, how to render the exquisite delicacy of light without hardening it into what it is not. During her early years she was taught by Corot and was also in contact with Charles-François Daubigny, an artist of the Barbizon School (see p.281). She was influenced by their honesty in capturing the true, changeable atmosphere of the landscape as it truly appeared before their own eyes.

Morisot enjoyed an intense, mutually respectful relationship with Manet. This influence was offset by her affiliation with the Impressionist group, with whom she exhibited regularly (while Manet remained aloof). Her eventual adoption of a lighter Impressionist palette was itself of considerable influence on Manet's late works. Morisot is not a strong painter in the Manet sense, but only a strong woman could have forced this work through: women's art was universally derided at that time. *The Harbour at Lorient (331)* is one of her finest paintings, a truly Impressionist work, in which the landscape is not subordinate to the figure and all is painted with the same care and the same ease. Great areas of contrasting blue shimmer as still water reflects unstill sky, powerfully geometric diagonals anchoring the picture, and the wonderful freshness of the morning as a girl sits on the embankment, a blithely blurred image under her pink parasol. The world hovers at the corner of the eye, delightful and unobtrusive.

MARY CASSATT

The other important woman Impressionist, Mary Cassatt (1845–1926), was as upper-class as Morisot, but her family lived in Pittsburgh, America, not in Paris. It was after she came to France in 1868 to paint and exhibit with the Impressionist group that she became modestly well known. Her art has an amplitude, a solidity very different from Morisot's, and gender is one of the few things they have in common. Cassatt's grave dignity is never over-emphatic. Her *Girl Sewing (332)* is made beautiful by the sheer variousness of the soft light. It pinkens the path behind the young woman, glows red in the flowers, and plays with a cascading grace over her simple frock. We are held by her attitude of childlike endeavour, lips set in concentration, and by the sheer brilliance with which her physical presence is captured. Cassatt was also an accomplished and brilliant printmaker, and the widespread influence of Japanese prints is especially evident in her prints and drawings.

332 Mary Cassatt, Girl Sewing, 1880–82, 92 x 63 cm (36½ x 25 in)

Cassatt's art shows her interest in physicality. This is very understandable since it was Degas, not Manet, who was Cassatt's mentor. Degas (Hilaire-Germain-Edgar, 1834–1917), a cynic in later life and a misogynist at every age, was condescendingly surprised at Cassatt. He admitted her power, quite against his will. Yet this power of draughtsmanship, and the ability to make a body palpably real, is very much his own.

DEGAS AS DRAUGHTSMAN

Degas is a far greater painter than Cassatt, and his graphic powers have never been excelled: his genius for line combined with a rich colour sense to produce work that will always ravish the viewer. Like Manet, he was separate from the Impressionist group (though unlike Manet, he did exhibit with them). He was sceptical of studying nature for its own sake and was instead drawn to Classicism.

Degas remained remote from life as much through his wealthy upbringing as his temperament. That his temperament was that of a voyeur seems certain: he looked on, not only from a distance, but from a height. This was so instinctive to him that it rarely offends us. Such a curiosity is shown in *Madame René de Gas (333)*, painted when he visited a branch of the family in New

333 Edgar Degas, Madame René de Gas, 1872/73, 73 x 92 cm (29 x 36½ in)

DEGAS' DANCERS

Over half of Degas' paintings depict the young ballerinas who performed between the main acts at the Paris opera (see p.291). Although Degas painted the dancers in intimate behind-the-scenes situations, he viewed them with a cool detachment. Only one of Degas' ballet sculptures was exhibited (in 1881), and at the time it was considered unusually realistic because Degas dressed the sculpture in real clothes. This illustration shows a bronze sculpture of a young dancer based on a number of pencil sketches.

DEGAS AND HORSE RACING

In the mid-19th century horse racing became extremely popular in Parisian society. Both Manet and Degas were part of the well-bred racing fraternity and attended many of the races at Longchamp in the Bois de Boulogne. Degas preferred to depict the moments before the race began, such as those in the painting illustrated above. He produced over 300 works of art on the race course theme.

334 Edgar Degas, Four Dancers, c.1899, 151 x 180 cm (59½ x 71 in)

Orleans. His brother René had married a woman who went blind; Edgar Degas at least did not need to fear that the intensity of his stare would disturb her. He shows her gazing blankly, plump and well-dressed, and we sense what her darkened world is like. The picture is strangely indistinct except for the face, where she is truly "herself". For the rest, she exists in cloudy spaciousness, her skirts spreading widely around her, the couch a sketchy background, nothing on the wall except light. The tight constraint of her hairstyle, unbecomingly scraped back, gives a certain pathos. Degas is sensitive to her situation, yet full of admiration: "My poor Estelle... is blind. She endures this in an amazing way; she is seldom helped around the house".

There is a tragic irony in the fact that Degas himself was to suffer from poor eyesight and eventually became unable to paint at all. His later work, mostly painted in the more direct medium of pastel, has a wild, instinctive rightness, as if his hand "knew" what his eye could barely see. *Four Dancers (334)* is not in pastel, but the oil is used with a pastel-like freedom. He makes no attempt at obvious design. The dancers move out of the painting backwards so that we just glimpse them as they move away. This unbalanced

composition, learned from photography (see column, p.293) and Japanese prints, shows Degas' understanding of this effect. The viewer is intrigued, forced to accept the painter's logic rather than that of convention. The colours, too, are vivid, insistent, glaringly bright, and this is part of Degas' theme: the stage is at all times artificially lit and our distance from it makes the colours become both loud and blurred, creating an impression of distance and glamorous dazzle.

UNIDEALIZED NUDES

For one who so openly professed contempt for women, Degas was strangely fascinated by the female nude. But he also brutally demystifies it: the women he depicts are wholly unideal and lacking in individuality. Instead, his interest is in form, the figure being reduced to an animating agent. He loved, he said, to paint as if "through the keyhole", catching his subjects when they thought themselves unobserved. The pastel painting *Girl Drying Herself (335)* is typical. We see only the back of this young woman as she stands with gawky tension upon her clothes. It is the rosy gleam of the light that provides romance and the hollow and swell of her muscles as she dries herself with animal vigour.

335 *Edgar Degas, Girl Drying Herself, 1885, 82 x 50 cm (31½ x 20 in)*

DEGAS AND PHOTOGRAPHY

By the time of the Impressionists, technical advances had led to the development of the "snap-shot" camera. The availability of instant unposed photography, with blurrings and accidental cropping off of figures created a sense of spontaneity which the Impressionists also sought to achieve. Edgar Degas was inspired by the pioneer photographer, Eadweard Muybridge, whose freeze-framed photographs of humans and animals in motion revolutionized the depiction of movement in art. This illustration shows the type of camera used by Degas.

OTHER WORKS BY DEGAS

Dancers in Pink
(Museum of Fine Arts, Boston)

Woman Arranging Her Hair
(Ordrupgaard-Samlingen, Copenhagen)

Dancers in the Foyer
(Art Institute of Chicago)

The Repetition
(Burrell Collection, Glasgow)

Jockeys
(National Gallery of Canada, Ottawa)

After the Bath
(Bridgestone Museum of Art, Tokyo)

The Rehearsal of a Ballet
(Musée d'Orsay, Paris)

Nursemaids
(Norton-Simon Museum, Pasadena)

THE GREAT IMPRESSIONISTS

Impressionism was officially "born" in 1874, when the term was applied to a relatively diverse collection of artists who exhibited at the Salon des Refusés that year. Many of the works had a comparatively coarse, unfinished appearance, which gave a strong sense of immediacy that incensed the critics. Although these artists were all individualistic, with disparate ideas and attitudes, they were united in their desire to achieve a greater naturalism in art, and their work revealed a startling new freshness and luminosity.

Critics found the independent exhibitors an easy target, especially the younger artists, Monet, Renoir, Morisot, and Sisley. These artists established a pictorial style that continued to the end of the decade and, after their first shows, consciously adopted the "Impressionist" label (see column, left). Cézanne, Pissarro, Degas, Gauguin – even some mainstream Salon artists – also exhibited at the Impressionist shows. Degas, though he had little stylistic affiliation with the Impressionists, wanted to support an alternative salon that would undermine the monopoly of the official Salons and provide a public arena for an innovative kind of painting based on real life.

Degas' concentration on formal line rather than on the effects of colour make him quite different from his contemporaries, Monet and Renoir. Claude Monet (1840–1926), in particular, is the quintessential Impressionist, and as such his world is exhilaratingly beautiful. Monet's style, like that of the other Impressionists, was characterized by a light, colourful palette, and he often applied unmixed paints directly onto a canvas prepared with a pure white coating. This bright surface enhanced the luminosity of each colour and increased the broken, disharmonious appearance of the picture.

What fascinates Monet in *Woman with a Parasol (336)* (also called *Madame Monet and Her Son*) is not the identities of the models, but the way the light and breeze are held upon the canvas for our perpetual delectation. One summer's day a young woman stood on a small rise in the ground, grass and flowers hiding all sight of her feet. She seems to have floated here, borne along by her dappled sunshade, radiant in the sheer brightness of the hour. Her dress is alive with reflected hues, gleaming gold or blue or palest pink. The colours never settle down, any more than do her pleats and folds, which swirl against the glitter of the clouds and the intense blue sky. Monet saw this, held it still, and made it pictorially accessible to our eyes. We look up over the variegated grass with its luminous shadows, and we are dazzled.

THE SERIES PAINTINGS
Monet's contemporaries were used to controlling the motionless images they painted in their studios, so that their work corresponded not with what was actually seen in real life – which was never still – but with what was thought to be seen. Monet took away these comforting labels of certainty. He did this most alarmingly in his great series paintings, where he surveyed the same subject in different weather conditions at different times of day or seasons. As the

*336 Claude Monet, **Woman with a Parasol**, 1875, 100 x 81 cm (39 x 31 in)*

337 *Claude Monet*, Rouen Cathedral, West Façade, *Sunlight, 1894,*
100 × 66 cm (39¼ × 26 in)

Rouen Cathedral,
The Portal Seen from the
Front (Harmony in Brown)

Rouen Cathedral,
The Portal, Grey Weather
(Harmony in Grey)

Rouen Cathedral,
Morning Sun
(Harmony in Blue)

Rouen Cathedral,
The Portal and the Saint-
Romain Tower, Morning
Effect (Harmony in White)

MONET AT ARGENTEUIL

The suburb of Argenteuil, only a 15-minute train journey from Paris, was a popular destination for day-trippers. Monet lived in the town from 1871–78 and produced 170 paintings. Following the example of the earliest *en plein air* painter Charles-Francois Daubigny, Monet had a studio boat built (replica illustrated above). The boat had a cabin and a shaded open deck so Monet could work outside. Monet never sailed far in the boat and tended to moor on quiet stretches of the Seine.

During his time at Argenteuil the town hosted many international sailing regattas, providing inspiration for much of Monet's work.

OTHER WORKS BY MONET

Vétheuil
(National Gallery of Victoria, Melbourne)

Heavy Sea at Trouville
(National Museum of Western Art, Tokyo)

The Artist's Garden at Giverny
(Bührle Foundation, Zürich)

The Beach at Pourville
(Museé Marmottan, Paris)

La Grenouillère
(Metropolitan Museum of Art, New York)

Field of Poppies Near Giverny
(Museum of Fine Arts, Boston)

The Japanese Bridge
(Neue Pinakothek, Munich)

enveloping light changes, so do the forms that had hitherto been thought constant and permanent. Monet used his brilliant palette to capture the optical effects created by natural light across a landscape or a townscape, paying little attention to the incidental details and using highly visible, sketchy, "undiscriminating" brushwork to capture the scene quickly.

Rouen Cathedral had seemed an unchangeable reality, but as Monet painted that identical west front with its spires and entrance arches – always from the same viewpoint – he saw how it was constantly transformed by the light: now richly ruddy, the thick, crusty paint echoing the rough stonework, the welcoming gates very visible, the great picture window a mystery of dark appeal; then pale, shimmery, fluid, and shifting, almost without detail in the richness of the glare. He usually worked on several canvases at once, softening the stonework in dull weather with a harmonious palette of grey and heightening

it with white and cobalt blue when the sun was at its most brilliant. *Rouen Cathedral, West Façade, Sunlight (337)* makes its statement solely through this light. It was this sensitivity to the changing, transforming light – in the strictest sense, creative light – that was Monet's greatest gift as a painter. This, of course, was for him the great fascination of the series paintings, and he explored this fascination to the utmost.

Monet extended his pleasure to the mechanics of water gardens during the final years of his life, working directly with nature: at last he had the time and the money to create his own garden and paint it. Some of his final waterlily murals, painted on enormous canvases, are almost abstract with their floating shapes and surface reflections, but *The Waterlily Pond (338)* is held firmly in the world of actuality by the Japanese bridge that curves across the centre. Even here, without that unifying curve, we might read this riot of greens, blues, and golds as an abstraction.

338 Claude Monet, The Waterlily Pond, *1899, 90 x 92 cm (35 x 36½ in)*

THE WATERLILY POND

Monet moved to a house at Giverny in northwest France in 1883, and lived there for the rest of his life. His garden was his main source of inspiration during his remaining years, and in 1893 he increased its area by purchasing an adjoining site that contained a pond. Here he created his celebrated water garden. This is one of 18 paintings belonging to Monet's late series, in which the arched, Japanese-style bridge, that he had constructed over his waterlily pond, forms the central motif.

VERTICAL BRUSHWORK

This version of the waterlily pond reveals the garden in full summer, with dense, bright green foliage. Beyond the tense, arching curve of the bridge, the foliage is a soft mass of confusion: greens, blues, pinks, and purples merge in and out of one another, and definition is almost non-existent. However, the vertical rhythm of the brushwork prevents the foliage from melting into incoherence, and it helps maintain the strong formal structure, repeating the verticals of the bridge and the sides of the canvas.

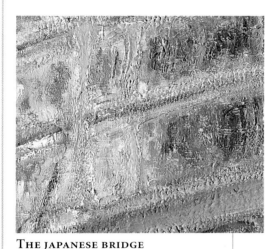

THE JAPANESE BRIDGE

In this detail we can see Monet's characteristic "dry" paint surface. A heavily loaded brush was dragged over the canvas where previous applications were allowed to dry first. The result is a richly-textured, encrusted surface, built up over time, which attracts light falling onto the canvas. The thick crust of paint imitates the solid structure of the bridge, standing out in sharp definition against the amorphous vegetation and transient light.

HORIZONTAL BRUSHWORK

The vertical rhythms of the foliage are continued into the deep shadows and bright reflections in the water. However, the unified downward movements of this brushwork are counterbalanced by bold horizontal brushstrokes, running from side to side across the canvas, which describe the receding bands of waterlilies stretched across the pond. These bands of colour are applied with thick sculptural paint over the top of the reflections and shadows in the water, "anchoring" them by asserting the flatness of the water's surface. This continuous criss-cross interplay of brushwork maintains a lively tension between the painting's two-dimensional abstract properties and its illusion of three-dimensional space.

MONET'S SIGNATURE

The effect of The Waterlily Pond *is an overwhelming sense of life, blocking out the sky and pushing in from all directions, almost vulgar in its lushness. Within the gloom of a deep shadow, not immediately visible amid such vibrancy, Monet's signature and the date of the painting can be found. The signature has been added in red, which has also been used to pick out individual flowers.*

339 *Auguste Renoir,* The Boating Party Lunch, *1881, 130 x 175 cm (51 x 69 in)*

CONTEMPORARY LIFE

Auguste Renoir (1841–1919) and Monet worked closely together during the late 1860s, painting the same scenes of popular river resorts and views of a bustling Paris. Renoir was by nature more solid than Monet, and while Monet fixed his attentions on the ever-changing patterns of nature, Renoir was particularly entranced by people and often painted friends and lovers. His early work has a quivering brightness that is gloriously satisfying and fully responsive to what he is painting, as well as to the effects of the light.

Renoir seems to have had the enviable ability to see anything as potentially of interest. More than any of the Impressionists, he found beauty and charm in the modern sights of Paris. He does not go deep into the substance of what he sees but seizes upon its appearance, grasping its generalities, which then enables the spectator to respond with immediate pleasure. "Pleasure" may be decried by the puritanical instinct within us all, but it is surely the necessary enhancer that

life needs. It also signifies a change from Realism: the Impressionists' paintings have none of the laboured toil of Millet's peasants, for example: instead they depict delightful, intimate scenes of the French middle class at leisure in the country or at cafés and concerts in Paris. Renoir always took a simple pleasure in whatever met his good-humoured attention, but he refused to let what he saw dominate what he wanted to paint. Again he deliberately sets out to give the impression, the sensation of something, its generalities, its glancing life. Maybe, ideally, everything is worthy of attentive scrutiny, but in practice there is no time. We remember only what takes our immediate notice as we move along.

In *The Boating Party Lunch (339)*, a group of Renoir's friends are enjoying that supreme delight of the working man and woman, a day out. Renoir shows us interrelationships: notice the young man intent upon the girl at the right chatting, while the girl at the left is occupied with her puppy. But notice too the loneliness, however relaxed, that can be part of anyone's

THE BOATING PARTY LUNCH

Renoir began this painting of his friends on the terrace of the Restaurant Fournaise in the summer of 1881. The restaurant was located in a village called Chatou, which was a fashionable destination for outings on the River Seine. We can identify most of the people: Monsieur Fournaise, the proprietor, standing on the left; Aline Charigot, Renoir's wife-to-be, seated on the left; Baron Barbier, in the top hat in the distance, and at the front right, Gustave Caillebotte, the artist.

experience at a lunch party. The man behind the girl and her dog is lost in a world of his own, yet we cannot but believe that his reverie is a happy one. The delightful debris of the meal, the charm of the young people, the hazy brightness of the world outside the awning: all communicates an earthly vision of paradise.

RENOIR'S PORTRAITS

One of Renoir's early portraits, *A Girl with a Watering Can (340)*, has all the tender charm of its subject, delicately unemphasized, not sentimentalized, but clearly relished. Renoir stoops down to the child's height, so that we look at her world from her own altitude. This, he hints, is the world that the little one sees – not the actual garden that adults see today, but the nostalgic garden that they remember from their childhood. The child is sweetly aware of her central importance. Solid little girl though she is, she presents herself with the fragile charm of the flowers. Her sturdy little feet in their sensible boots are somehow planted in the garden, and the lace of her dress has a floral rightness; she also is decorative. With the greatest skill, Renoir shows the child, not amid the actual flowers and lawns, but on the path. It leads away, out of the picture, into the unknown future when she will no longer be part of the garden but an onlooker, an adult, who will enjoy only her memories of the present now depicted.

340 Auguste Renoir, A Girl with a Watering Can, 1876, 100 x 73 cm (39 x 29 in)

341 Auguste Renoir, Bather Arranging Her Hair, 1893, 92 x 74 cm (36½ x 29 in)

RENOIR'S LATE STYLE

Although he may seem a happy hedonist, Renoir was in fact a serious artist. At one stage he changed his whole style, feeling that he had gone as far as he could with Impressionism and was in danger of becoming superficial. His late style is firmer, with a cleaner edge to his figures, and the last works have a classical solidity. In *Bather Arranging Her Hair (341)*, he has preserved the solid feel of the bodily form and irradiated it with luminous colour. The girl's lovely body is set out amid the disarray of her many-coloured garments: her corset, her hat, the white material draped around that round and rosy flesh. Renoir persuades us that the girl herself does the stripping and the presenting, and we feel she loves her body, as she should. He gazes worshipfully, not at her, the person, but at her body, the outer her, and he delights in painting her soft, glowing skin. Her bright but concentrated expression hints that the distinction would not mean much to her; she is an innocent country beauty.

DURAND-RUEL

Paul Durand-Ruel (1831–1922) was the first art dealer to give consistent support to the Impressionists. He was introduced to Monet by the artist Daubigny whilst in England during the Franco-Prussian war and became the sole financial backer of a number of the Impressionist artists. In 1886 he achieved a breakthrough with an exhibition of Impressionist works in New York and in 1905 his exhibition of hundreds of paintings brought the artists' work to London. Monet's international acclaim was due wholly to the support and investment of Durand-Ruel during the 1870s.

342 *Camille Pissaro,* Orchard in Bloom, Louveciennes, *1872, 45 × 55 cm (17½ × 22 in)*

CAMILLE PISSARRO

Camille Pissarro is seen as the patriarchal figurehead of the Impressionist movement and is the only artist to have had work shown at all eight of the Impressionist exhibitions. During the Franco-Prussian war (see p.286) Pissarro joined Monet in England and was influenced by the English landscape tradition of Turner and Constable. In 1872 he returned and settled in Pontoise where he became a friend and mentor of Cézanne. Pissarro's art centres on the people who work the soil and he is renowned for his paintings of peasant girls going about their daily chores.

CAMILLE PISSARRO

Camille Pissarro (1830–1903) was the patriarch of the Impressionists, not only because he was slightly older, but because of his benign and generous character. After meeting Corot in 1857, Pissarro was encouraged to abandon his formal training to paint in the open air and, despite his age, he became one of the most receptive of the Impressionists to new ideas. He was a passionate champion of progress, sometimes to the detriment of his own individual expression. He was the only artist to have shown work at all eight Impressionist exhibitions.

Pissarro was a dedicated painter and enormously prolific. He tended to stray in and out of pure Impressionism as the spirit took him, unconcerned with the rigours of style. He was the outsider of the group, perhaps, a man of mixed blood (Portuguese, Jewish, and Creole), and he was instinctively reponsive to the underlying architecture of nature. His paintings, with their almost naïve simplicity and unpolished surface, influenced Gauguin (see p.322), van Gogh (p.316), and Cézanne (p.310), who called himself the "pupil of Pissarro".

Orchard in Bloom, Louveciennes (342) is a work with bones under the painterly flesh: the path that we notice in the foreground leads us with a real sense of distance through the flowering brightness of impressionistic trees. There is a

343 *Camille Pissarro,* **Peasant Girl with a Straw Hat,** *1881, 73 × 60 cm (29 × 24 in)*

This is one particular day when the wind begins to rise at sea with all the emotions freshly to hand for the painter. The sun shines and the air of excitement runs all along the horizon, ending with the filling – and balancing – sails that punctuate the far right of the picture.

THOMAS EAKINS

If Homer is a supreme watercolourist, then Thomas Eakins (1844–1916) is a supreme oil painter of the American Realist tradition. *Breezing Up* is wonderful, but it seems just that slight shade less convincing than *The Biglin Brothers Racing (348)*, one of Eakins' greatest works. Eakins persuades us that we too would have seen this, had we stood in Philadelphia one summer's morning to watch the racers exercise.

349 *John Singer Sargent*, Mrs Adrian Iselin, *1888, 154 x 93 cm (61 x 37 in)*

We would not have seen this scene, of course: the Biglin brothers would have vanished from sight before we had time to notice how the sunlight catches doublet and oar, or how the distant riverbank is as dim and dense as foliage. Eakins has held the image and created a work of such atmosphere that when we look at the painting the moment seems full and long – not at all like a snap shot. In the light of this comparison, Homer's glimpsed sailors begin to seem far more impressionistic than at first sight.

SARGENT THE SOCIETY PAINTER

John Singer Sargent (1856–1925) is essentially known as a society painter and, except for his marvellous watercolours of nature, he painted almost only high society. Often there was a great swagger of fashionable dress, but *Mrs Adrian Iselin (349)* is too élite for such embellishments. She glitters before us in austere black with the domineering haughtiness of a *grande dame*. For those who think Sargent pandered to his sitters, he has faithfully depicted her large and ugly ear. At his best, Sargent could be as ruthless as Goya, and with something of his technical brilliance.

HENRY JAMES
In the work of the American writer Henry James (1843–1916) we see a change of subject matter as the author moved through three creative phases. In the first phase, which produced one of his most famous novels, *The Bostonians* (1886), James was concerned with the impact of American life on the more established European societies. In 1876 James moved to England and devoted his time and novels to the issues of English society. His novel *The Ambassadors* unites Anglo-American attitudes in his last period of creativity. Although an American he was very pro-English and took British citizenship during World War I.

JOHN SINGER SARGENT
The outstanding portrait painter of his time, John Singer Sargent (1856–1925) was an American citizen with a French education who came to work in England in 1885. His move to England was prompted by the scandal surrounding his exhibit at the 1884 Paris Salon. The painting, *Madame X*, was considered to be too provocatively erotic by the judges and was also quite obviously the portrait of a real woman, Madame Gautreau. Her mother begged Sargent to remove the picture but he fled to England. In his later years he was made official war artist of World War I.

POST-IMPRESSIONISM

Art history loves labels, and Post-Impressionism is the label for the diverse art that immediately followed Impressionism (this label roughly covers the period between 1886 and 1910). The Impressionists had destroyed forever an artistic belief in the objective truth of nature. Painters now understood that what we see depends on how we see, and even more when we see: the "objective view" was in fact subject to both perception and time. We live in an essentially fleeting and uncontrollable world and it is the glory of art to wrestle with this concept.

The greatest of all wrestlers was Paul Cézanne, who understood, as no artist before him ever had, the personal need of the artist to respond to what he saw and make a visual and enduring image of its wayward and multi-dimensional beauty. Another Post-Impressionist giant, Georges Seurat, sought a more scientific analysis of colour in his painting, though his art transcended his theories. Other artists chose to portray the world, not just by its physical, outward appearance, but by its inner, less tangible realities, exploring new symbolic associations with colour and line.

Paul Gauguin, Riders on the Beach, 1902 (detail)

POST-IMPRESSIONISM TIMELINE

Post-Impressionism is the name given to a group of painters in the last two decades of the 19th century. They have very little in common except their starting point – the Impressionists. Paul Cézanne, Paul Gauguin, and Vincent van Gogh are all geniuses of a high order, but the movement we call Post-Impressionism also embraces, in its capacious sweep, small groups such as the Nabis.

VINCENT VAN GOGH, THE ARTIST'S BEDROOM, 1889

Van Gogh used colour to convey emotion more than to represent objects: this painting carries a poignant message of loneliness, hinted at by the extra chair, waiting for an eagerly expected companion (Gauguin). This room is in the house at Arles that van Gogh shared with Gauguin from October 1888 to May 1889. He painted this scene in 1888 and made two copies of it in 1889 (this is one of them) when he was in the asylum at St Rémy (p.316).

EDOUARD VUILLARD, THE READER, 1896

To the Nabi artists it was important to show beauty in simple scenes, such as this superbly decorative painting with its assemblage of patterned fabrics (p.328).

1885	1890	1895

GEORGES SEURAT, THE LIGHTHOUSE AT HONFLEUR, 1886

Seurat was that rare thing, both scientist and artist. He was enthralled by the newly emerging science of optics and developed a style of painting called Pointillism, which used innumerable dots of colour. The eye combines these as we do in real life, but his vision was of a world supremely pure and controlled, painfully different from actuality (p.315).

HENRI DE TOULOUSE-LAUTREC, RUE DES MOULINS, 1894

The witty, searching art of Lautrec often depicted nightclub and drinking scenes, or portrayed the denizens of Parisian low life. Here, two prostitutes are shown queuing up for a medical examination, and the sadness and shame of their position in society are held up to our gaze. Lautrec was influenced by the Japanese and their complete freedom from conventional notions of composition; the centre of attention was often off-centre. His style was perfectly suited to poster art, to which he brought great new zest and life. In all his work there is a fluidity and passion that captures the vitality of city life (p.320).

EDVARD MUNCH, FOUR GIRLS ON A BRIDGE, 1889-1900

A strange man, Munch experienced overwhelmingly gloomy emotions. It was to express the intensity of these emotions that his art was directed. Personally he found the pain of life too much to bear, but artistically he struggled to express this pain and make beauty out of it. Symbolism struck a deep chord within him: with its high colour and formal simplicity, it offered him a refuge from his fears. This Nordic gloom lived on to influence Expressionism, which dominated Germanic art after World War I (p.325).

PIERRE BONNARD, THE LETTER, C. 1906

Bonnard was a leading member of the Nabis, who in some ways were a transitional movement between Post-Impressionism and the art of the 20th century. Bonnard was interested in oriental philosophy and mysticism. He was influenced by Japanese art, imitating the graphic simplicity of Japanese woodcuts. The Letter is a typical example of his many paintings of everyday life. The model is one who frequently appears in Bonnard's pictures, his partner and later wife, Marthe. She is portrayed with a wonderful concision, and Bonnard takes an uncomplicated pleasure in the patterns into which the image falls (p.326).

PAUL CEZANNE, LE CHATEAU NOIR, 1900/04

At all stages of his career Cézanne was a supreme master. This picture is a fine example of the Post-Impressionist tension between actuality and illusion, description and abstraction, reality and invention. We are forced to read it not only as a wooded landscape with a château, but equally as a flat plane, upon which colours of different chromatic and tonal values have been arranged (p.312).

1900　　　　　　　　　　　**1905**　　　　　　　　　　　**1910**

PAUL GAUGUIN, NEVERMORE, 1897

The English title Nevermore, *appearing in the corner of this painting, is the keynote of a poem,* The Raven *by Edgar Allan Poe, which was a favourite of the French Symbolists. However, the painting is not exactly an illustration of the poem. Poe writes about a devilish raven that prevents him from adoring his beloved, who is absent. For Gauguin the girl is the main feature in the painting, and the bird is reduced to a toy-like caricature. Gauguin is concerned to show the capacity of art to escape from rationality and naturalism, in order to describe more accurately the inner workings of the heart and mind (p.324).*

GUSTAV KLIMT, THE KISS, 1907/08

Gustav Klimt came from a family of artists and craftsmen, his father being a gold engraver. As one of Austria's most prominent artists he helped found two radical groups, the Vienna Secession and the Vienna Workshop. The Kiss is a gloriously decorative work, a fusion of two figures into one, with a suggestion of anxiety in the tense grip of the hands and the averted face of the girl (p.325).

POST-IMPRESSIONIST ARTISTS

Like the Renaissance, Impressionism made an irreversible difference, so that one naturally senses that all art since that time has been "after Impressionism". The artists who rejected Impressionism towards the end of the 19th century painted not only what they observed, but what they felt, finally setting painting free to deal with emotions as well as material reality. They experimented with new subjects and techniques, moving art closer to abstraction and winning tremendous freedom for the next generation of artists.

350 Paul Cézanne, The Artist's Father, *1866, 199 x 119 cm (78 x 47 in)*

Post-Impressionism was never a movement – the term was unknown to the artists involved during their own lifetimes (see column, p.311). It encompasses a group of artists with diverse styles and ideals who became dissatisfied with the limitations of Impressionism and departed from it in various directions. Never again could it be so taken for granted that painting has a direct relation to the exterior world.

CEZANNE'S EARLY WORK

Paul Cézanne (1839–1906) is certainly as great an artist as any that ever lived, up there with Titian, Michelangelo, and Rembrandt. Like Manet and Degas, and also Morisot and Cassatt, he came from a wealthy family – his was in Aix-en-Provence, France. His banker father seems to have been an uncultivated man, of whom his highly nervous and inhibited son was afraid. Despite parental displeasure, Cézanne persevered with his passionate desire to become an artist. His early paintings display little of the majesty of his late work, though today they are rightfully awarded the respect that he certainly never received for them.

His early years were difficult and his career was, from the beginning, dogged with repeated failure and rejection. In 1862 he was introduced to the famed circle of artists who met at the Café Guerbois in Paris, which included Manet, Degas, and Pissarro, but his awkward manners and defensive shyness prevented him from becoming an intimate of the group. However, Pissarro was to play an important part in Cézanne's later development (see p.300).

One of the most important works of his early years is the portrait of his formidable father. *The Artist's Father (350)* is one of Cézanne's "palette-knife pictures", painted in short sessions between 1865 and 1866. Their realistic content and solid style reveal Cézanne's admiration for Gustave Courbet (see p.282). Here we see a craggy, unyielding man of business, a solid mass of manhood, bodily succinct from the top of his black beret to the tips of his heavy shoes. The uncompromising verticals of the massive chair are echoed by the door, and the edges of

351 Paul Cézanne, Abduction, c. 1867, 90 × 117 cm (35 × 46 in)

ROGER FRY
The term
Post-Impressionism was
coined by the English
art critic Roger Fry
(1866–1934) to describe
the group of artists who
came immediately after
the Impressionists. These
artists were centred in
Paris and chose to reject
the Impressionists'
concentration on the
external, fleeting
appearances of their
world. Fry was curator
of the Metropolitan
Museum of Art in New
York between 1906 and
1910 and introduced the
Post-Impressionists to
Great Britain by exhibitions
which he arranged at the
Grafton Galleries in 1910
and 1912. Artists he
displayed included
Gauguin, Cézanne,
and van Gogh.

the small still life by Cézanne on the wall just behind: everything corresponds to the absolute verticals of the edges of the canvas itself, further accentuating the air of certainty about the portrait. Thick hands hold a newspaper – though Cézanne has replaced his father's conservative newspaper with the liberal *L'Evénement*, which published articles by his childhood friend, Emile Zola (see p.286). His father devours the paper, sitting tensely upright in the elongated armchair. Yet it is a curiously tender portrait too. Cézanne seems to see his father as somehow unfulfilled: for all his size he does not fully occupy the chair, and neither does he see the still life on the wall behind him, which we recognize as being one of his son's. We do not see his eyes – only the ironical mouth and his great frame, partly hidden behind the paper.

MYSTERY OF NATURE
Cézanne was in his twenties when he painted *The Artist's Father*. Wonderful though it is, with its blacks and greys and umbers, it does not fully indicate the profundity of his developing genius. Yet even in this early work, Cézanne's grasp of form and solid pictorial structures which came to dominate his mature style are already essential components. His overriding concern with

form and structure set him apart from the Impressionists from the start, and he was to maintain this solitary position, carving out his unique pictorial language.

Abduction, rape, and murder: these are themes that tormented Cézanne. *Abduction (351)*, an early work full of dark miseries, is impressive largely for its turgid force, held barely under his control. These figure paintings are the most difficult to enter into: they are sinister, with passion in turmoil just beneath the surface.

Cézanne's late studies of the human body are most rewarding, his figures often depicted as bathers merging with the landscape in a sunlit lightness. This became a favourite theme for Cézanne and he made a whole series of pictures on the subject. This mature work is dictated by an objectivity that is profoundly moving for all its seeming emotional detachment.

It was before nature that Cézanne was seized by a sense of the mystery of the world to a depth never expressed by another artist. He saw that nothing exists in isolation: an obvious insight, yet one that only he could make us see. Things have colour and they have weight, and the colour and mass of each affects the weight of the other. It was to understand these rules that Cézanne dedicated his life.

OTHER WORKS BY
CEZANNE
Basket of Apples
(Art Institute of
Chicago)

Mont Sainte Victoire
(Courtauld Institute,
London)

Still Life of Fruit
(Barnes Foundation,
Marion, Penn.)

The Card Players
(Metropolitan Museum
of Art, New York)

Poplars
(Musée d'Orsay, Paris)

Self-portrait
(Bridgestone Museum
of Art, Tokyo)

L'Estaque
(Bührle Foundation,
Zürich)

MONT
SAINTE-VICTOIRE

The Sainte-Victoire mountain near Cézanne's home in Aix-en-Provence was one of his favourite subjects and he is known to have painted it over 60 times. Cézanne was fascinated by the rugged architectural forms in the mountains of Provence and painted the same scene from many different angles.

He would use bold blocks of colour to achieve a new spatial effect known as "flat-depth" to accommodate the unusual geological forms of the mountains. Cézanne travelled widely in the Provence region and also enjoyed painting the coast at L'Estaque.

352 Paul Cézanne, Le Château Noir, 1900/04, 74 x 97 cm (29 x 38 in)

STRUCTURE AND SOLIDITY

From 1872, under Pissarro's influence, Cézanne painted the rich Impressionist effects of light on different surfaces and even exhibited at the first Impressionist show. But he maintained his concern for solidity and structure throughout, and abandoned Impressionism in 1877. In *Le Château Noir (352)*, Cézanne does not respond to the flickering light as an Impressionist might; he draws that flicker from deep within the substance of every structure in the painting. Each form has a true solidity, an absolute of internal power that is never diminished for the sake of another part of the composition.

It is the tension between actuality and illusion, description and abstraction, reality and invention that makes Cézanne's most unassuming subjects so profoundly satisfying and exciting, and which provided a legacy for a revolution of form that led the way for modern art.

The special attraction of still life to Cézanne was the ability, to some extent, to control the structure. He brooded over his apples, jugs, tables, and curtains, arranging them with infinite variety. *Still Life with Apples and Peaches (353)* glows with a romantic energy, as hugely present as Mont Sainte-Victoire (see column, left). Here too is a mountain, and here too sanctity and victory: the fruits lie on the table with an active power that is not just seen but experienced. The jug bulges, not with any contents, but with its own weight of being. The curtain swags gloriously, while the great waterfall of the napkin absorbs and radiates light onto the table on which all this life is earthed.

353 Paul Cézanne, Still Life with Apples and Peaches, c. 1905, 81 x 100 cm (32 x 40 in)

LE CHATEAU NOIR

The château in this painting derives its name from rumours about its owner, rather than from its appearance. It was built in the 18th century by an industrialist from Marseilles, who manufactured lampblack paint (derived from soot). He also used it to decorate the interior walls and furniture of the château. As a result, he was associated with black magic among the local people, who believed that the château was also home to the devil.

BROKEN LINE
Again, Cézanne emphasizes the physical, plastic reality of the painting. The jagged lines describing the overhanging branches are fragmented, beginning and ending in mid-air. They are valued as much for their formal role in maintaining the strong vertical, horizontal, and diagonal balance of the composition as for their descriptive function: Cubism's debt to Cézanne is paramount (see p.346). The impossibly rich, deep blues and greens of the sky, applied right up to and overlapping the branches, fight for dominance, creating a continuous tension between decorative flatness and spatial depth.

PATCH OF SKY
The deep blue of this patch of sky, visible through the trees, is painted with no concessions to illusory depth. The strong blue of the sky "jumps" forward over the quieter colours of the surrounding foliage, insisting that we read the picture not only as a wooded landscape with a château, but equally as a flat plane upon which colours of differing chromatic and tonal values have been arranged.

BRUSHWORK
This detail shows us Cézanne's characteristic diagonal brushwork, and the way in which he counterbalances the disjunctures created by his abstract treatment of space (see above) with a unifying application of paint. Cézanne thus realizes his belief that a painting should be both structurally convincing and formally independent. The slanting, generally equal-sized brushmarks range across the surface of the canvas and, as such, must do the job of describing form through relative values of colour alone, in a process that Cézanne called modulation.

THE CHATEAU
The slender, Gothic-arched windows of the château reveal nothing but the intense blue of the sky. The complementary relationship of the yellow building and the blue windows emphatically affirms the colour harmony of the work, and its ambiguity between "solid" sky and "ephemeral" stone. The building seems in turn both impressively permanent, and also a shallow façade through which the blue hills and sky are visible. It is an intensely blue painting, made even bluer by the intervals of yellow ochre, and united by the more neutral greens.

SEURAT AND DIVISIONISM

It is possible, though perhaps improbable, that Georges-Pierre Seurat (1859–91), had he lived longer, might have been in the league of Cézanne. Like the great Masaccio at the beginning of the Renaissance (see p.82), like Giorgione (p.129) and Watteau (p.224), he died tragically young – yet after just a few years of painting he left us some marvellous work. He believed that art should be based on a system and developed Impressionism towards a rigorous formula. He invented a method he called optical painting – also known as Divisionism, Neo-Impressionism, or Pointillism – in which dots of colour laid beside one another blend together in the viewer's eye. He believed that these dots of intense colour, placed schematically in precise patterns, could imitate the resonant effects of light falling onto various colours more accurately than the more random, intuitive practice of the Impressionists. Seurat's systematic approach was based on his study of the new theory of colour science. As a theory it sounds daunting, and in the hands of imitators it does daunt, being a theory that is more poetic than literal in its truth. A silent and secretive young man, Seurat perhaps needed this theory psychologically, and he made wonderful use of it in his paintings.

Seurat differed from the Impressionists in more than just his scientific approach. He was influenced by Ingres (see p.256) and the great Renaissance artists, and his work has a gravity that relates more to the classical tradition than to the casual intimacy and transience of Impressionism. And though, like the Impressionists, Seurat worked on small studies in the open air so that he could faithfully record the effects of light on the landscape, his large compositions were produced entirely in the studio according to his own strict laws of painting. To the themes already well mapped out by the Impressionists, such as city life, seascapes, and

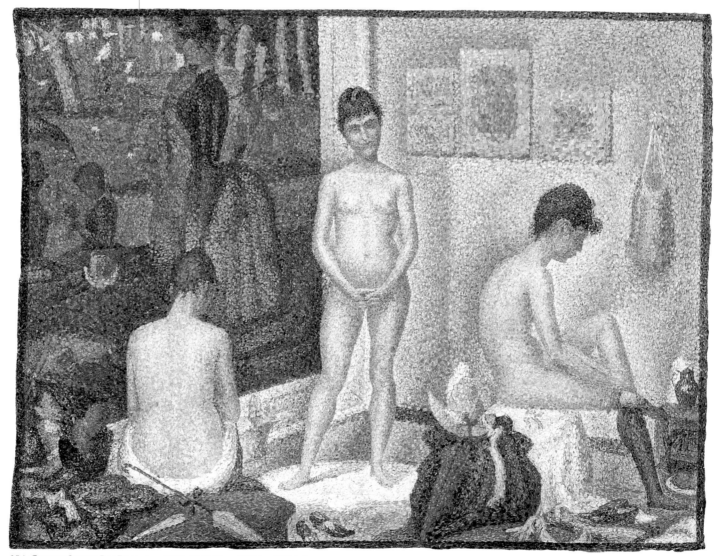

354 Georges Seurat, Les Poseuses, *1888, 39 x 49 cm (15½ x 19½ in)*

355 *Georges Seurat,* **The Lighthouse at Honfleur,** *1886, 68 x 82 cm (26½ x 32 in)*

POINTILLISM
This triple magnification of the canvas taken from Seurat's *La Grande Jatte* shows minute dots of colour. Seurat used this technique of painting using regular small touches of pure colour which, when seen from a distance, react together optically, in many of his paintings. If certain colours are placed side by side in close proximity they enhance each other's strength and give the painting an iridescence and depth. The term Pointillism was first used by the critic Félix Fénéon to describe Seurat's *La Grande Jatte* in 1886.

entertainment, Seurat added a sense of mystery and even monumentality, as well as a controlled geometry. In *Les Poseuses (354)* there is a sense of exquisite rightness, of flesh in all its individuality still beautifully conforming to a pattern. These images of a classical female nude are nymph-like in their delicacy, but with an austerity that is unique to Seurat.

ART REPLACING NATURE

Les Poseuses was painted in Seurat's studio in artificial light, and the large landscape serving as a backdrop to it is *Sunday Afternoon on the Island of the Grande Jatte,* a summer scene he painted between 1884 and 1886 of strollers by the River Seine, on the outskirts of Paris.

La Grande Jatte is important, both within Seurat's limited oeuvre, and historically. This was the painting that he hung at the last Impressionist show in 1886, despite the reluctance of the other, older exhibitors. Seurat represented a new generation of painters who heralded the disintegration of the Impressionist ideal, and whether the older painters liked it or not, a new order was rapidly being established. Pissarro alone fought for Seurat's right to exhibit with them and saw his colour theory as the progressive

step Impressionism needed. Pissarro briefly adopted Divisionism himself, but found it too inhibiting and soon abandoned it.

Seurat's landscapes also heroically subdue nature to the "dot" of his colour theory, and they have an interior quiet that prevails magnificently over natural confusion. Seurat organized what he saw, but he did so with the tact of genius. We realize that no landscape ever really looked so clean, so uncluttered, and so integrated, but he makes us suspend our disbelief.

Everything in the landscape painting *The Lighthouse at Honfleur (355)* is arranged with such formal perfection that removing any one element would destroy the balance. Pale, magical, severe, it absolutely needs the wooden structure in the foreground. This geometric form of sharp angles allows Seurat to move spaciously back into the far glimmer of the sea, rhyming all the other horizontals and verticals delicately with it: one upright like the lighthouse tower, redeployed by the boathouse; one flat like the boat, re-echoed by the top bar of the sawing frame. The sun bleaches the whole scene, so that colour, too, rhymes and is compatible. This is how life ought to be, he tells us, and nature is replaced by art.

OTHER WORKS BY SEURAT

Beach at Gravelines
(Courtauld Institute, London)

The Circus
(Musée d'Orsay, Paris)

Woman With An Umbrella
(Bührle Foundation, Zürich)

View of the Seine
(Metropolitan Museum of Art, New York)

La Grande Jatte
(Art Institute of Chicago)

The Beach at Honfleur
(Walters Art Gallery, Baltimore)

Vincent van Gogh (1853–90) began his career as a clerk in his uncle's art dealing firm in The Hague. In 1873 he was transferred to the London offices and fell in love with his landlady's daughter, who was already engaged to be married. This first experience of unrequited love is believed to have precipitated the religious fanaticism that led to his mental breakdown in later life. After a brief time in London as a teacher for the Rev. Slade-Jones, van Gogh returned to Holland in 1876 where he immediately encountered more failure.

VAN GOGH

Seurat was one kind of genius, contained and silent. The other kind we find in a Dutch-born painter, Vincent van Gogh (1853–90), whose turbulent, seeking life everyone knows. The sad tale of van Gogh cutting off his ear is now part of common genius mythology. The unhappiness documented in a flood of letters to his brother, Theo, is transformed in his art into a passionate search for stability, truth, life itself. He has the rare power, something like that of Rembrandt (see p.200), to take the ugly, even the terrible, and make it beautiful by sheer passion.

Van Gogh's formative years as a painter reveal his confusion and restlessness as he worked in various jobs in search of a meaningful existence. At 20 he left Holland for England, then lived for a short time in Belgium as a missionary, and in 1886, aged 33, he left for Paris. Through Theo's work as an art dealer (see column, p.317), he met other artists – Degas (p.291), Pissarro

(p.300), Seurat (p.314), Lautrec (p.320) – and learnt about Impressionist techniques. He arrived at his artistic vocation by a slow and tortuous route, but it wasn't until he had fully absorbed the influences of Impressionism and *Japonisme* (see column, p.290) and made his own experiments with colour (see column, p.317) that he discovered his true genius.

VAN GOGH AT ARLES

In 1888, leaving Theo in Paris, he went to Arles, in Provence, where, in the last two years of his life, he produced his most remarkable works. *The Artist's Bedroom (356)* has the utmost power and poignancy (this is a copy he painted to comfort himself while in the asylum at St. Rémy; see column, p.318). Two pillows and chairs hint at his eager anticipation of Gauguin's arrival (see p.322). It was his dream that Arles would become a centre for painters, but Gauguin's reluctant visit ended in disaster.

356 Vincent van Gogh, The Artist's Bedroom, *1889, 71 x 90 cm (28 x 35 in)*

357 Vincent van Gogh, Farmhouse in Provence, *1888, 46 x 61 cm (18 x 24 in)*

USE OF COLOUR
Van Gogh used a wide variety of colours throughout his career including, red lake, vermilion, ultramarine, cobalt violet, emerald green, and viridian. However, many of these colours were not lightfast and van Gogh would have been aware of the transient nature of some of his choices of pigments. Van Gogh was also interested in complementary colours (see glossary, p.390) and their effects on the canvas. To this end he owned a box of coloured wools which he would plait together to experiment with complementary colour vibrations. As an artist he was not concerned with painting in naturalistic colours but tried to convey a range of emotions through the use of dramatic and vibrant colours.

Farmhouse in Provence and *La Mousmé* were painted in the year van Gogh moved to Arles. If Seurat subdued nature to reflect his intellect, van Gogh heightened it to echo his emotions. *Farmhouse in Provence (357)* has a terrible, life-threatening fertility about it. Wheat surges about the farm on all sides; the flaming ears of grain almost overwhelm the small figure who wades through them. The wall suddenly comes to an end, devoured by the encroaching army of ripening wheat, red flowers, and vegetation.

The farm has a beleaguered air, taking some trees into its protection; elsewhere, out in the field, trees are stunted and sparse. Farm buildings huddle together, while the sky maintains an utter neutrality. Nature always comes to van Gogh in this threatening manner, yet he never gives in: he wrestles with it, capturing its wildness on his canvas. The sheer attention he has given to every blade of wheat gives him a moral ascendancy over such power.

La Mousmé (358) is of "a Japanese girl – provincial in this case – 12 to 14 years old," as van Gogh explained to Theo. He laboured on this work, lured by the simplicity and tautness he so admired in Japanese art, and he presents this dull-faced adolescent solely in terms of decorative masses. Her dress is built up of curving stripes above and solid red dots on blue below.

The chair sweeps round her in schematic arches; hands and face are an opaque pinky-brown, seemingly boneless hands dangle from her sleeves, and her face is doll-like. Her body curves flatly against a background of mottled green. So much

358 Van Gogh, La Mousmé, *1888, 73 x 60 cm (29 x 24 in)*

THEO VAN GOGH
In 1886 Vincent van Gogh arrived in Paris to stay with his brother Theo. As an art dealer Theo was friendly with the Impressionist group and the Parisian avant-garde, such as Pissarro, Bernard, and Gauguin. It was through Theo's contacts that Vincent became part of the Post-Impressionist group and began to experiment with brighter colours. The brothers had a fraught relationship and Theo was not always convinced by the quality of Vincent's work. Throughout his life Vincent wrote over 750 letters to his brother and on his death a final tragic letter addressed to Theo was found in his pocket.

THE DECLINE

The first clear signs of van Gogh's mental instability appeared whilst he and Gauguin were sharing the Yellow House in Arles in 1888. One evening he threatened Gauguin, lost control, cut off his own right ear lobe, and presented it to a local prostitute. He was then taken to the hospital suffering from loss of blood and hallucinations. By May 1889 van Gogh had left Arles and had committed himself voluntarily to the asylum in St Rémy. During two years in the asylum van Gogh produced over 200 paintings and in 1890 Pissarro persuaded him to move to Auvers where he was placed in the hands of Dr Gachet (shown above). However, within a couple of months van Gogh fell ill, and in July 1890 he committed suicide.

OTHER WORKS BY VAN GOGH

The Farmhouse (Rijksmuseum, Amsterdam)

Sunflowers (National Gallery, London)

Portrait of Dr Paul Gachet (Musée d'Orsay, Paris)

Windmills at Montmartre (Bridgestone Museum of Art, Tokyo)

Two Peasants (Bührle Foundation, Zürich)

Bed of Irises (National Gallery of Canada, Ottawa)

Hospital at St Rémy (Hammer Collection, Los Angeles)

about *La Mousmé* is pathetic. She looks out at us so warily that we too feel slightly uncomfortable. Her eyes are alive, brown, and hurt, as if she knows that life will not treat her well. Van Gogh directs on the child such a force of passionate attention, such a totality of respect, such confidence in the power of vision to raise him up from the hell of existence, that the picture is an awesome success. Qualities like beauty or grace become irrelevant. To make us see through his eyes is the triumph of the painter, and van Gogh triumphs often.

VAN GOGH'S SELF-PORTRAITS

Few artists have been as interested in the self-portrait as van Gogh. *Self-portrait (359)* is overpowering in its purity and realism: this is the real face of the artist, with a rough, red beard, unhappy mouth, and hooded eyes. His is an identity barely held in existence under the pressure of the whirling blue chaos. His face may be solid enough, but his clothes lose their identity as the lines swirl and jostle and deconstruct, showing us just how he felt as a mentally tormented and suffering individual.

359 Vincent van Gogh, Self-portrait, *1889, 65 x 54 cm (26 x 21½ in)*

SELF-PORTRAIT

In May 1889, after his violent breakdown in Arles, van Gogh entered the asylum at St Rémy. With his brother Theo's financial assistance, van Gogh was able to have his own bedroom, and also a studio where – whenever his condition and the asylum authorities allowed – he could continue to paint. It was at the asylum, just six weeks after another severe breakdown, that van Gogh painted this very beautiful self-portrait in September 1889. It is one of two self-portraits van Gogh painted that same month, both of which are notable for their calm and dignified portrayal, and their sense of fortitude, despite the misery of his situation. The skilful use of contrasting colours, the sensitive draughtmanship, and the sense of mature control all point to a superior mind, however disturbed the artist's feelings.

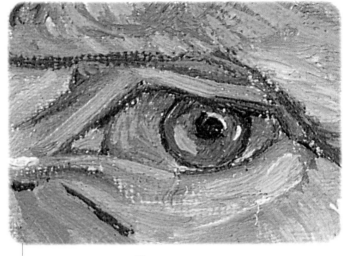

THE EYE

Perhaps the strongest note of colour in the painting is the surprisingly vivid patch of green under the eye. It acts as a focal point, drawing our attention to van Gogh's steady and penetrating gaze. The structure of the eye is emphatically "level"; a straight, dark, horizontal line defines his heavy brow, and every detail of the eye is clearly delineated; but whilst the set features show resoluteness, at the same time the acid greens in the face, clashing against the reds of the hair and beard, suggest passion held under restraint.

SWIRLING BACKGROUND

Within the overall cool harmonies of silver-grey, silver-green, and blues, van Gogh's head glows like a flame. Here is a painting of great contrasts. Everything outside the vivid head is subdued. The disturbed background hints at the precariousness of his own stability, symbolized by his neat waistcoat, and his shirt buttoned to the neck, and by his pose, suggestive of stillness and calm. The background can be distinguished from the figure only by the texture of the swirling brush strokes, which are otherwise virtually identical in colour to the body.

A NEW PORTRAIT

Each brush stroke is laid on side by side, without blending or modelling. Around this time van Gogh conceived of a new kind of portraiture, based on the innate expressive qualities of colour. In the same month that he painted this picture, he wrote to Theo, expressing his wish to paint portraits that contain the vibrancy of life that he found in Delacroix's paintings: "by a wedding of two complementary colours, their mingling and their opposition, the mysterious vibrations of kindred tones".

TOULOUSE-LAUTREC

Toulouse-Lautrec came from an aristocratic family but was physically deformed as a result of inbreeding and a childhood accident. This self-parodying photograph shows Lautrec dressed as a samurai warrior.

TOULOUSE-LAUTREC'S PARIS

If van Gogh escaped from his overwhelming burdens by committing suicide, Henri de Toulouse-Lautrec (1864–1901) escaped into the sordid nightlife of Paris. Only there, submerged within a raucous and raunchy crowd, could he forget that he was a scion of one of the noble families in France with an unfortunate disability. A model once said he had "a genius for distortion", but his genius, though acid, was not embittered or dark. His deformity set him free, paradoxically, from a need to accept any normal responsibilities, and though he killed himself with his excesses, he also created a witty, wiry art that still attracts. His paintings and prints reveal the strong attraction to Japanese art that he shared with van Gogh: he employed typically oblique Japanese perspectives with an off-centre focus, and his art is characterized by a self-assured

361 *Henri de Toulouse-Lautrec,* Rue des Moulins, *1894, 83 x 60 cm (33 x 24 in)*

simplicity of line, dramatic colour, and flat shape. Lautrec's art was well-suited to poster design and, aided by newly perfected techniques for printing posters, he revolutionized the discipline, breathing a new vibrancy and immediacy into it. In all his work there is a fluidity and passion that captures the vitality of city life.

Quadrille at the Moulin Rouge (360) has a rough energy that contrasts with the controlled vigour of the artist's line. There is life here, but no joy. However, there is also no self-pity, and though the life he shows us is horrible, it is at least lived with determination. Gabrielle, a dancer at the Moulin Rouge nightclub and one of Lautrec's favourite models, faces us with an almost comic expression of tipsy intentness as she stands aggressively in the centre of the hall.

Lautrec does not often go deep, but when he does, he can appal. The two prostitutes in *Rue des Moulins (361)* are not seeking custom (this he paints with a very wry laugh). They are lining up for the obligatory medical examination for licensed prostitutes, and their raddled faces are painfully pathetic. The first is aged of body, with loose, wrinkled thighs and fallen bosom. The other appears slightly younger, and although her body is less ravaged, her face is cruelly worn. Even the background of this picture is a lurid red. Vice is killing them both, despite the state medical intrusions. Lautrec does not glorify his whores; his world is one of harsh reality.

360 *Henri de Toulouse-Lautrec,* Quadrille at the Moulin Rouge, *1892, 81 x 60 cm (31 x 24 in)*

THE INFLUENCE OF SYMBOLISM

Symbolism began as a literary movement that championed the imagination as the most important source of creativity. It soon filtered into the visual arts as another reaction to the limited, representational world of Realism and Impressionism. Inspired by the symbolist poetry of the French poets Stéphane Mallarmé, Paul Verlaine, and Arthur Rimbaud, the Symbolist painters used emotive colours and stylized images to float into our consciousness their dreams and moods, sometimes painting exotic, dream-like scenes.

STEPHANE MALLARME
Stéphane Mallarmé (1842–98) was a leading Symbolist poet and friend of many of the symbolist artists. The basic principles of this artistic movement were to express ideas through colour and line and to concentrate on mystical or fantastical images. This illustration shows an etching of Mallarmé, completed by Gauguin, with a raven in the background. The raven is believed to be a direct reference to Edgar Allan Poe's influential symbolist poem *The Raven*, which was published in 1875. In 1886 the French poet Jean Moréas published the *Symbolist's Manifesto* which was inspired by Mallarmé's poetry.

Though it was towards the end of his career that Symbolism became artistically significant, it is still true to regard Gustave Moreau (1826–98) as a precursor of Symbolist ideals and a patriarchal figure. In age he was much closer to Realism (his dates are almost contemporary with those of Manet, see p.285, or Courbet, p.282), but he ignored both Realism and Impressionism to pursue his own, distinctively individual style.

There could sometimes be a lurid and rather sickly strain in Symbolist work: the story of Salome, for example, with all its Freudian implications of woman destroying man, crops up continually. Moreau's *Salome (362)* is one of the more playful versions of this deadly myth, and we can enjoy its intense light and colour without thinking too much of its sinister

363 Odilon Redon, Anemones and Lilacs in a Blue Vase, *after 1912, 74 x 60 cm (29 x 23½ in)*

implications. Many of Moreau's other pictures are populated with strange beasts and mystic figures, and this escape from the world of reality, coupled with his idiosyncratic temperament, made him a significant figure among the other Symbolists.

REDON'S FLOWER PAINTINGS

Odilon Redon (1840–1916) is another escaper into a land of dreams. He did not have a major gift, but the pleasure of his art is pure and deep. He used colour in a completely personal and uninhibited way, but it was his subject matter, so elusive and fantastical, that made him a quintessential Symbolist. Like Moreau, he had a haunting imagination, but his exquisite bunches of flowers are his greatest achievement. *Anemones and Lilacs in a Blue Vase (363)* is typical of the soft, delicate imagery he could produce using iridescent pastels. These are radiant flowers, picked and preserved and glowing eternally for the viewer.

362 Gustave Moreau, Salome, *1876, 143 x 103 cm (56 x 40½ in)*

PAUL SERUSIER
The painter and art theorist Paul Sérusier (1863–1927) had a great influence on the Symbolist and Nabis movements (see p.326). The painting shown above is of the *Bois d'Amour* at Pont-Aven, where Sérusier painted whilst being advised on colour by his friend Gauguin. The painting is also known as *The Talisman* because the younger painting generation saw it as the symbol of new artistic freedom and possibilities. Sérusier published his treatise on art in 1921.

364 *Paul Gauguin,* **The Vision After the Sermon,** *1888, 73 x 92 cm (29 x 36½ in)*

CLOISONNISM

Emil Bernard's *Buckwheat Harvest* (shown above) is a good example of the technique known as Cloisonnism (*cloison* is French for partition). This style of painting is associated with the Pont-Aven school and is characterized by dark outlines enclosing areas of bright, flat colour, similar to the effect achieved by stained glass. Gauguin and Bernard (1868–1941) worked together at Pont-Aven between 1888 and 1891, and Bernard is believed to have had a stimulating effect on Gauguin's work.

A SINGULAR VISION

Paul Gauguin (1848–1903) is best known for the art he painted after he fled to the South Seas to escape Europe and his family, but essentially he drew the inspiration for his work from within himself. Though he took to painting as a professional quite late, his early development as an amateur was influenced by the Impressionists, especially Pissarro (see p.300), whose systematic, broken brushwork Gauguin adopted. Gauguin was introduced to the Impressionists as a rich Parisian stockbroker and began to buy their art: he even exhibited his own work at some of their shows from 1879. Yet when he finally became a full-time artist in 1883, he was already feeling the constraints of the Parisian art scene.

Gauguin sought to be untrammelled by any conventions in his art. The Impressionists were influenced by nature; Gauguin was influenced by his own version of nature. He found freedom and quiet at Pont-Aven, Brittany, where he soon became the chief figure of the Pont-Aven artists (see column, left). It was in this isolated region that he developed the distinctive symbolic and primitive elements of his art. Inspired by

medieval stained glass and folk art, he began to paint simplified shapes heavily outlined in black. The Breton peasants, with their simple faith and archaic lifestyles, also appealed to him and became a recurrent theme.

The Vision After the Sermon (364) was painted two years before he left for Tahiti, but it is as primitive as anything Tahitian. Gauguin blended reality with the inner experience of a vision and heightened it with symbolic colour. He offered the painting to the local Breton church, but the priest was suspicious and thought he was being mocked. Only today does the spiritual power of the painting become vitally clear.

LAST YEARS IN FRANCE

Gauguin had long abandoned his Dutch wife and children, and in 1888 he agreed to visit van Gogh in Arles. It seems fitting that the two were friends, though perhaps "friend" is not the right word: both were solitary men, desperately seeking for healing companionship. It was the breakdown of their shaky relationship that drove van Gogh, the more fragile, to the hysterical mutilation of his own ear. Gauguin spent his remaining two years in France moving around restlessly, and left in April 1891 for Tahiti, where he spent much of the rest of his life.

VISION AFTER THE SERMON

Gauguin depicts a sermon that has just been preached on the subject of Jacob wrestling with the Angel, an Old Testament story. Probably religion had an exotic fascination for Gauguin, though he could only see its mysteries from without. He imagines Jacob at dawn, struggling to overcome his superhuman opponent and make him reveal his name. Gauguin felt he was up against the superhuman and he too wrestled with his demon/angel to find his real identity.

JACOB AND THE ANGEL
Gauguin's compact image was inspired by a study of wrestlers by the Japanese master Katsushika Hokusai, whose illustrations influenced many of Gauguin's contemporaries (see also column, p.290). The struggle takes place in an airless, shadowless space of saturated red in which the combatants seem to float, out of proportion to the world around them. Gauguin truly realized his desire to tackle a devotional work in a new way.

PRAYING PRIEST
There is no literal contest here, as we can guess from the downcast eyes of the women and the priest: it is in their imaginations that life and death meet in battle. Their tightly-grouped heads are magnified so that we feel like part of the crowd; we have to peer over the tops of their heads to see the vision. Much of the painting is conceived as completely flat planes of colour; only the curving forms of the women's headdresses are painted in a three-dimensional style – the white folds have a heavy, sculptural feel.

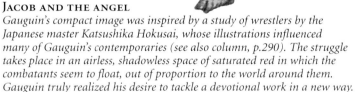

THE TWO HALVES OF THE CANVAS
Gauguin makes his composition all absolutes and opposites: brilliant reds screaming against blazing whites; hordes of women and one sole male (the priest, in the lower right-hand corner), violence and meditation, enveloping garments and bare faces. A great tree trunk slices the picture diagonally into two separate halves: the real world on the left, containing the simple Breton women and a straying cow that paws the red earth; and the visionary world on the right, where the angel and the man wrestle. The man won, however, as Gauguin expected his viewers to remember.

GAUGUIN AND TAHITI

Gauguin arrived in Tahiti in 1891. Disappointed by the appearance of the main town of Papeete, he moved to a more remote part of the island. Initially his art concentrated on the influence of Western culture on native life, but in his later works he chose to emphasize the rapidly disappearing primitivism of the island. This wood carving was produced by Gauguin in 1892. The model for the sculpture is believed to be Teha'amana, Gauguin's 13-year-old mistress. Gauguin left the island in 1893, but after encountering several problems in Paris he returned to Tahiti in 1897. In 1901 he travelled to the remote Marquesa islands, where he died in 1903.

366 Paul Gauguin, Nevermore, 1897, 60 x 115 cm (24 x 45 in)

Gauguin escaped to the South Seas in search of a primitive lifestyle where his art could flourish. Despite his disgust at the entrenched colonial society he found there (see column, left), he painted the Polynesians as images of a heavenly state of total freedom. Gauguin impresses his own version of nature upon us, creating stylized, flattened shapes and using intense, exotic colours with what may seem like reckless abandon, but which are carefully calculated for the greatest effect. In *Riders on the Beach (365)* he paints the sands pink not, we feel, because he actually "saw" any pinkness there, but because only pink sands could express his feelings. Yellow would have been too intrusively real: it is not a logical scene but a magical one, and the peace and joy are symbolic, not literal. It is a painting of an idyllic state of life, gentle and radiant people effortlessly in control of their horses, freedom on every side, intoxicating seascape, wide, clouded skies, man and woman in perfect amity.

SINISTER UNDERCURRENTS

Although Gauguin transformed the Polynesian women into goddess figures – obeying no rules but those of his imagination – he also knew well the sad depravations of their real lives, and produced some dark and disturbing images in response to what he saw.

The young girl depicted in *Nevermore (366)*, painted after he had lived in the South Seas for several years, shows how he had come to terms with the haunted otherness of the interior life the women led. The girl is spread out before us, her golden body a sinister green as she ponders the mystery of her existence. A sightless raven, painted as a decorative detail, perches outside her window as a symbolic "bird of death" (inspired by the poem *The Raven* by Edgar Allan Poe, a favourite of the Symbolists).

Two women speak urgently together while the girl lies isolated and afraid on her splendid yellow pillow. The semi-abstract patternings we can see in paintings such as this are expressions of internal, psychological rhythms rather than outward events. Gauguin's skill lies in refusing to explain this complex mystery, even though he suggests there may be an answer. However long we contemplate *Nevermore*, it retains and in fact deepens its mystery before us.

365 Paul Gauguin, Riders on the Beach, 1902, 73 x 92 cm (29 x 36½ in)

MUNCH'S INTENSE EMOTIONALISM

Symbolist painting was not restricted to France alone. The Norwegian artist Edvard Munch (1863–1944) was a gloomy man, perpetually haunted by illness, madness and death, who used all his psychic weakness to create electrifying art.

Munch began painting in Oslo, where the predominant style was Social Realism, and it was only when he went to Paris in 1888 that he began to experiment. Van Gogh's swirling, emotive brushwork is detectable in Munch's more disturbing paintings, but he was also attracted to the work of Gauguin and the Symbolist painters, and he became close friends with the Symbolist poet Stéphane Mallarmé (see column, p.321).

He began to use the Symbolists' stylized forms, decorative patterning, and highly charged colours to express his own anxieties and pessimism. A precursor of Northern Expressionism (see p.340), he was one of those great artists whose main intention was to make an emotional statement, and who subdued all the elements of a picture to that end.

Munch can paint what seems an innocuous image. There are many versions of *Four Girls on a Bridge (367)*, a theme which clearly stirred something deep within him, and each work has a sinister undertone. The girls are all young and slender, passively leaning towards or away from the water. We feel uneasily that the water must represent something: time? their coming sexual power? They are on the "bridge", the dark, heavy shapes of the future at the far side of the bridge looming ahead. Yet to spell out the full meaning is to diminish it. Munch is a Symbolist whose ideas work at a subliminal level.

367 Edvard Munch, Four Girls on a Bridge, *1899–1900, 136 x 126 cm (53½ x 49½ in)*

The greater his unhappiness, the more overtly autobiographical his art became. In the 1890s he produced a series of paintings called the *Frieze of Life* which he described as "a poem of life, love, and death". In 1908 he suffered from a severe mental illness and though he never left Norway again, his undisputed originality made a great impact on the next generation of artists.

GUSTAV KLIMT

Just as Munch can be associated with both Symbolism and Expressionism, so the art of the Austrian painter, Gustav Klimt (1862–1918), is a curious and elegant synthesis of Symbolism and Art Nouveau (see column, p.327). The Austrians responded enthusiastically to the decorative artifice of Art Nouveau, and Klimt is almost artifice incarnate. He painted large ornamental friezes of allegorical scenes, and produced fashionable portraits, uniting the stylized shapes and unnatural colours of Symbolism with his own essentially harmonious concept of beauty. *The Kiss (368)* is a fascinating icon of the loss of self that lovers experience. Only the faces and hands of this couple are visible; all the rest is a great swirl of gold, studded with coloured rectangles as if to express visually the emotional and physical explosion of erotic love.

368 Gustav Klimt, The Kiss, *1907/08, 180 x 180 cm (71 x 71 in)*

CONTEMPORARY ARTS

1880
Rodin produces
The Thinker

1886
The Statue of Liberty
is dedicated to the
American people

1889
The French begin
the construction of
the Eiffel Tower

1890
Oscar Wilde publishes
*The Picture of
Dorian Gray*

1895
Tchaikovsky's *Swan
Lake* is performed in
St Petersburg

1900
Puccini's opera *Tosca* is
performed in Rome

1901
The first Nobel prizes
are awarded

THE NABIS

Two French artists straddle the gap between Post-Impressionism and the moderns: Pierre Bonnard and Edouard Vuillard. Difficult to place artistically, they are thought of as Intimists, and leaders of a group known as the Nabis. Both painters lived well into the 20th century, yet, with their love of the gentle domesticities of life that was such a feature of the work of the Nabis, neither seems to belong truly to the world of modern art.

Inspired by Sérusier's painting *The Talisman* (see column, p.321), Pierre Bonnard (1867–1947) and Edouard Vuillard (1868–1940) formed a group known as the Nabis (Hebrew for seers or prophets) in 1892. The decorative was the keynote to their art: as their associate Maurice Denis (see column, p.329) wrote, "A picture, before being a warhorse, a nude, or some anecdote, is essentially a surface covered with colours arranged in a certain order." Disillusioned with Paris and Impressionism, the Nabis admired Gauguin and Japanese art and embraced many aspects of oriental mysticism, endeavouring to express the spiritual in their work.

THE JAPANESE NABI

Bonnard fell the deepest under the oriental influence, being known to his friends as "the Japanese Nabi". It was the graphic concision of Japanese woodcuts that appealed so strongly to him, with their lovely purity of line and colour. As Bonnard's art matured, the colours he used became much richer and deeper, so that the whole meaning is revealed in the colour.

The Letter (369) has a Japanese-like simplicity, the young woman so intent upon her writing and the tilt of her head suggesting the depth of her concentration. But that bent head is wonderfully feminine, with its glowing clumps of chestnut brown, the elegance of the little comb, the neat little nose, snub and flirtatious, and the expressive curves of her mouth. Bonnard is concerned with this woman less as a personality than as an enchantment – a very Japanese trait. He has walled her in deliciously for his own delight, with a gorgeous rim of crimson seatback, an interestingly variegated wall, and on the open, free side, a box and an envelope of entrancing hues. The green box is the palest colour in the painting, directing our eyes upwards towards the deep, rich blues of her modest dress and her downturned head. Bonnard makes no great statement about life or about this particular living creature. He looks at her instead with the most delicate and uncomplicated pleasure.

Bonnard, like Japanese artists, was interested in painting everyday life, in freezing the intimacies of a personal scene. Many of his paintings show images of the same model. This was Marthe, a sadly neurotic woman whom he eventually married, and who separated him from all his friends, yet who seems to have provided him with endless visual interest.

Fortunately, Marthe always loved to be painted, especially while in the bath, and many of his major paintings show her fully submerged in the water. There is an almost ecstatic brightness in the sensuous shades of her body and the water in *The Bath (370)*, and it has too often been thought that Bonnard's art is just a last dying effulgence of Impressionism. But he goes further, daringly and powerfully. Bonnard is not

369 Pierre Bonnard, The Letter, c. 1906, 55 x 48 cm (22 x 19 in)

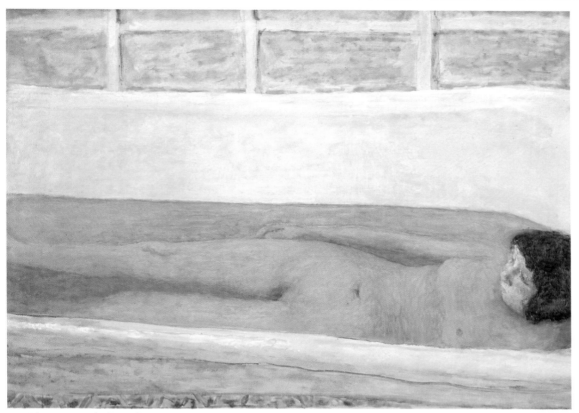

370 Pierre Bonnard, **The Bath,** *1925, 85 x 120 cm (34 x 47 in)*

interested in the atmospheric nuances of light, as the Impressionists were, but rather in rhythm, shape, texture, colour, and the endless decorative possibilities of the visual world.

CEZANNE'S INFLUENCE

The Nabis all shared an admiration for Cézanne (p.310), certainly the dominant influence on all early 20th-century artists. Maurice Denis' work *Homage to Cézanne* (see column, p.329) shows Bonnard and Vuillard clearly visible among several artists as they gather around one of Cézanne's paintings. When Bonnard paints a landscape he shows us not only what we can see but what the landscape feels like, as it were: he makes a leap into otherness, into sensation.

Stairs in the Artist's Garden (371) was painted near the end of his life and it is an extraordinary picture, like all his great variations on the theme of the garden. The stairs lead up the centre and then vanish as the grandeur of the blossoms overwhelms us. Exuberant colours mass to the left; huge fountains of springtime green erupt to the right. Ahead is a sunburst of bright bushes, piercingly golden and incandescently red, and there are more flowers overhead, allowing the intense blues of the skies to act as a backdrop. It is theatrical, a stage set, and the stage is set not for a play but for life. Bonnard wants to stir us into accepting the wonder of being alive. We are

liberated from our factual limitations into this radiant freedom. Taking Cézanne's chromatic majesty a step further, he etherealizes the weightiness that Cézanne felt essential, and is a great enough artist to succeed at it.

371 Pierre Bonnard, **Stairs in the Artist's Garden,** *1942/44, 63 x 73 cm (25 x 29 in)*

VUILLARD'S INTIMATE ART

By comparison, Bonnard's friend Vuillard may seem modest. His art is certainly more delicate, and he is interested less in colouristic fireworks than in the gentle, muted subtleties of textures and patterned cloth. His mother, with whom he gladly lived for much of his life, was a dressmaker, and he spent much of his time among women as they worked away in small rooms, absorbed and talkative. The happy, unforced charm of his art never cloys, never becomes obvious, and always remains tender and alive. His works are for the most part very small, as humbly befits their theme.

JAPANESE INFLUENCES

Vuillard's early paintings, as a member of the Nabis group, were highly influenced by the Japanese sketches that he had seen at the Ecole des Beaux Arts in 1890. The role of drawing, and particularly of silhouette, in achieving simplification of form was crucial to much of Vuillard's work. The sketch illustrated above was produced by Vuillard in 1890 using Indian ink and a Japanese brush. The artist was also closely involved with the theatre and was employed by the the theatre mogul of Paris, Coquelin cadet, to capture backstage scenes in the traditional Japanese style.

OTHER WORKS BY VUILLARD

In Bed
(Musée d'Orsay, Paris)

Girl in an Interior
(Tate Gallery, London)

Woman Before a Mirror
(Bridgestone Museum of Art, Tokyo)

Portrait of Madame Bonnard
(National Gallery of Victoria, Melbourne)

Woman Seated on a Sofa
(Art Institute of Chicago)

The Dining Room
(Neue Pinakothek, Munich)

The Lady in Green
(Glasgow Art Gallery)

372 Edouard Vuillard, The Reader, *1896, 213 x 155 cm (7 ft x 5 ft 1 in)*

373 Edouard Vuillard, Vase of Flowers on a Mantelpiece, *c.1900, 36 x 30 cm (14½ x 12 in)*

Vuillard's lifelong exposure to dress materials through his mother's work, as well as the textile designs of his uncle, was clearly a formative influence on his art. *The Reader (372)* is one of a series of panels that he painted for a friend's library, and for this reason it was atypically large. Here we see how the furnishings of a room, its wallpapers, carpets, and upholstery, can nearly submerge the human presence there. We almost tremble for the reader, so bravely intent upon her book amid the jungle of the interior, and perhaps the women watching her from the doorway tremble too. Yet Vuillard cannot but paint from love, and the threat of so many clamouring designs is diffused, held at bay by the warm charm of his colour.

SMALL-SCALE INTERIORS

Vase of Flowers on a Mantelpiece (373) is exquisitely modest by comparison. We cannot see the whole mantelpiece, merely a section of it; nor can we see the entirety of the armchair beneath, merely part of the curve of its back, with the pattern of its upholstery. Vuillard stops short of painting the fire too, though the pink roses in a vase suggest that this is not the season for fires. But neither is it the season for emptiness: the mirror reflects a small, dimly-lit, furnished room, and the genius of Vuillard is to keep us engrossed as we try to read what we half see. The one unmistakable area of clarity is the vase of flowers itself, one large rose surrounded by its clustering companions. It is a picture in which

nothing seems to happen, yet which is a perpetually fascinating scene. We are drawn, irresistibly, into the encompassing warmth of Vuillard's own love of the ordinary.

WALTER SICKERT

The English painter Walter Sickert (1860–1942) was not one of the Nabis, but was influenced by this group, particularly Bonnard and Vuillard, and he was important as a link between English and French art at the end of the 19th century. Although he was a pupil and studio assistant of Whistler (see p.302) in the 1880s and worked with Degas (p.291) in Paris in 1883, Sickert's paintings also show an intimism (see glossary, p.390) comparable to the Nabis' work, and a shared interest in unusual compositions.

Some of Sickert's paintings are Victorian England's equivalent of the Nabis' quiet images of bourgeois French culture. But Sickert also painted dark, and sometimes sinister, images of the underworld. *La Hollandaise (374)* demands no knowledge of art history to announce this woman's profession. Poor, unidealized creature that she is, she nevertheless has the whore's appeal. Sickert paints her with an economy that is almost cruel, obliterating the features of her face to expose her naked body and scraping the paint thinly across her flesh: Sickert is clearly as interested in what she is as with how she looks, and he conveys both brilliantly.

374 W. Sickert, La Hollandaise, *1906, 50 x 40 cm (20 x 16 in)*

HOMAGE TO CEZANNE

This painting was completed by Maurice Denis (1870–1943) in 1900 to commemorate Cézanne's first one-man exhibition held in 1895. The painting shows a group of artists, including Redon (to the left of the composition), Vollard (behind the easel), and many of the Nabis gathered around a Cézanne still life which was once owned by Gauguin. Cézanne and the Nabis were linked by Vollard, who had begun to deal in the Nabis' paintings and was also having great success in selling much of Cézanne's work.

CAMDEN TOWN MURDER SERIES

In September 1907 Emily Dimmock, a well-known north London prostitute, was found dead with her throat cut in her lodgings in Camden Town. The body was found by her lover when he returned from his night shift. A commercial artist, Robert Wood, was accused of her murder but was acquitted after a long and exciting trial. Sickert, who is known to have followed the trial reports, adopted the name *Camden Town Murder* as a general designation for several series of etchings, paintings, and drawings. Each painting in the series features a naked woman and a clothed man who personify the tragedy of poverty and deprivation.

THE 20TH CENTURY

It has been calculated that there are more artists practising today than were alive in the whole Renaissance, all three centuries of it. But we are no longer following one story-line: we are in a new situation, where there is now no mainstream. The stream has flowed into the sea and all we can do now is to trace some of the main currents.

20th-century art is almost indefinable, and ironically we can consider that as its definition. This makes sense, as we live in a world that is in a constant state of flux. Not only is science changing the outward forms of life, but we are beginning to discover the strange centrality of our subconscious desires and fears. All this is completely new and unsettling, and art naturally reflects it.

The story of painting now loses its way temporarily: it enters upon an encounter with the unknown and the uncertain. Only the passage of time can reveal which artists in our contemporary world will last, and which will not.

Wassily Kandinsky, Improvisation 31 (Sea Battle), *1913 (detail)*

20TH-CENTURY TIMELINE

We have dates in the 20th century, and pictures to attach to them, but there is no longer a coherent time sequence. This can be irritating to the tidy-minded, but it is in fact exciting in its adventurous freedom. With so many interesting artists, some of whom time may vindicate as of great importance, there is only space to touch briefly on those who seem to many observers to be part of the story, and not just footnotes.

WASSILY KANDINSKY, IMPROVISATION 31 (SEA BATTLE), 1913

It seems to be agreed that Kandinsky was the first totally abstract artist of the modern period. His art matured to an almost formal geometry, but initially, as here, it had a wild and wonderful connection with the real world, with shapes that are symbols of an imaginary sea battle (p.354).

PABLO PICASSO, LES DEMOISELLES D'AVIGNON, 1907

This picture is the one work that could be considered essential to the art of the 20th century. From its bizarre malformations and hideous energy have flowed a torrent of creative and innovative power. It startled Georges Braque, and it startles us still: it is a supreme and repulsive masterpiece (p.347).

PAUL KLEE, DEATH AND FIRE, 1940

Klee is a great colourist and an endlessly creative painter, both enchanting and profound. Only he can depict death and fire with a smile and a sacred tremor. This is characteristic of his unique approach, both to the matter and the manner of painting (p.358).

1900　　　**1910**　　　**1920**　　　**1930**　　　**1940**

HENRI MATISSE, THE CONVERSATION, 1909

Equal with Picasso (if not indeed greater), Matisse is the great master of our century. He is a skilful simplifier of form and a marvellous manipulator of colour, though he never uses these talents for their own sake, but always to create a design that at every point has a meaning (p.337).

PIET MONDRIAN, DIAMOND PAINTING IN RED, YELLOW, AND BLUE, C. 1921/25

Mondrian is the great purist of art. He limited himself to a few basic colours, arranged in solemn squares. His art is profound, expressing in this bare form a noble conception of life (p.360).

SALVADOR DALI, THE PERSISTENCE OF MEMORY, 1931

Some artists are greatly gifted, but have little to express. This is not entirely true of Dali, but it can be said that what he wanted to express was his own self-importance. Sometimes his experience coincides with our own, which is why this picture of melting watches – time going into a flux – is so unforgettable (p.364).

JACKSON POLLOCK, NUMBER 1, 1950 (LAVENDER MIST), 1950
Picasso and Matisse dominated the first half of our century. In the second half, the major figure is probably Jackson Pollock. Whether for good or ill, he "liberated" artists from the palette and the brush, from design and intention. He splattered his paint, swirling it out from its tins, as he danced on the horizontal canvas. It was an innovation of genius and surprisingly personal to Pollock himself (p.369).

MARK ROTHKO, UNTITLED (BLACK AND GREY), 1969
For some decades, Rothko has held his position as one of the great spiritual artists of our time. His mature work is always of the same format: there is a large canvas in which two rectangles of colour hover before us. We sense a deep emotion, but though the critics have spoken about "the veil of the temple" and other mystical metaphors, no explanation wholly convinces (p.370).

LUCIAN FREUD, STANDING BY THE RAGS, 1988–89
Although it is stretching the point to speak of a school of London, it is still true that a group of figurative artists is at work there. Lucian Freud is perhaps the most significant, a ruthless and clinical observer of humanity who dissects his subject on the canvas with memorable power. Such vulnerability would be unbearable to contemplate, were there the slightest touch of criticism or even of distancing. It is himself Freud dissects, and us with him. Here he shows us a nude standing against a background of paint rags from his studio. He makes everything that could be made of both these subjects, and of the many contrasts between them (p.386).

1950	1960	1970	1980	1990

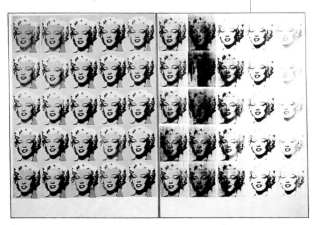

ANDY WARHOL, MARILYN DIPTYCH, 1962
There are still two vociferous attitudes towards Warhol. Is he a genius or a mountebank? Perhaps looking at the Marilyn Diptych we may feel that he is both: an artist who capitalized on his natural vulgarity and laziness, and used them to create icons for our times. One weakness, obsessive interest in the media stars, is here set to work. He makes a subtle comment on the reality of this interest, while conveying its fascination (p.380).

JASPER JOHNS, DANCERS ON A PLANE; MERCE CUNNINGHAM, 1980
Jasper Johns is a difficult artist, and none of his works is simple or easily comprehensible. There is always a concept controlling what he creates. Yet these creations are so supremely beautiful that they can be enjoyed even without full understanding. There is a reason behind every mark in Dancers on a Plane, and if we learn to love it we may want to investigate these secret complexities. But it is the love that matters (p.381).

FAUVISM

Between 1901 and 1906, several comprehensive exhibitions were held in Paris, making the work of Vincent van Gogh, Paul Gauguin, and Paul Cézanne widely accessible for the first time. For the painters who saw the achievements of these great artists, the effect was one of liberation and they began to experiment with radical new styles. Fauvism was the first movement of this modern period, in which colour ruled supreme.

THE FAUVES

The advent of Modernism is often dated by the appearance of the Fauves in Paris at the Salon d'Automne in 1905. Their style of painting, using non-naturalistic colours, was one of the first avant-garde developments in European art. They greatly admired van Gogh, who said of his own work: "Instead of trying to render what I see before me, I use colour in a completely arbitrary way to express myself powerfully". The Fauvists carried this idea further, translating their feelings into colour with a rough, almost clumsy style. Matisse was a dominant figure in the movement; other Fauvists included Vlaminck, Derain, Marquet, and Rouault. However, they did not form a cohesive group and by 1908 a number of painters had seceded to Cubism (see p.346).

AFRICAN INFLUENCES

Many of the Fauvists were inspired by African art and had their own collections of masks and statues. The fashion for tribal art had been started by Gauguin and the African influence can be seen in several of the paintings Matisse completed around 1906. This Kwele mask, shown above, closely resembles a famous piece once owned by André Derain. The whitened face suggests that it may have been part of the ancestors cult in central Africa.

375 Maurice de Vlaminck, The River, c. 1910, 60 x 73 cm (23½ x 28¾ in)

Fauvism was a short-lived movement, lasting only as long as its originator, Henri Matisse (1869–1954), fought to find the artistic freedom he needed. Matisse had to make colour serve his art, rather as Gauguin needed to paint the sand pink to express an emotion (see p.324). The Fauvists believed absolutely in colour as an emotional force. With Matisse and his friends, Maurice de Vlaminck (1876–1958) and André

376 André Derain, Charing Cross Bridge, *1906, 80 × 100 cm (32 × 39 in)*

Derain (1880–1954), colour lost its descriptive qualities and became luminous, creating light rather than imitating it. They astonished viewers at the 1905 Salon d'Automne: the art critic Louis Vauxcelles saw their bold paintings surrounding a conventional sculpture of a young boy, and remarked that it was like a Donatello *"parmi les fauves"* (among the wild beasts). The painterly freedom of the Fauves and their expressive use of colour gave splendid proof of their intelligent study of van Gogh's art (see pp. 316-18). But their art seemed brasher than anything seen before.

VLAMINCK AND DERAIN

During its brief flourishing, Fauvism had some notable adherents, including Rouault (p.341), Dufy (p.339), and Braque (p.350). Vlaminck had a touch of wild-beastishness, at least in the dark vigour of his internal moods: even if *The River (375)* looks at peace, we feel a storm is coming. A self-professed "primitive", he ignored the wealth of art in the Louvre, preferring to collect the African masks that became so important to early 20th-century art (see column, p.334).

Derain also showed a primitive wildness in his Fauve period – *Charing Cross Bridge (376)* bestrides a strangely tropical London – though as he aged he quenched his fire to a classic calm. He shared a studio with Vlaminck for a while and *The River* and *Charing Cross Bridge* seem to share a vibrant power: both reveal an unself-conscious use of colour and shape, a delight in the sheer patterning of things. This may not be profound art but it does give visual pleasure.

CONTEMPORARY
ARTS
1902
Chekov writes
The Three Sisters

1907
Stravinsky composes
his first symphony

1908
Constantin Brancusi
completes his
sculpture *The Kiss*

1916
Frank Lloyd Wright
designs the Imperial
Hotel in Tokyo

1922
James Joyce writes
Ulysses

1927
The first "talkie" film,
The Jazz Singer,
is produced

1928
Eugene O'Neill wins
the Nobel Prize
for literature

1931
The Empire State
Building is completed
in New York City

MATISSE, MASTER OF COLOUR

The art of our century has been dominated by two men: Henri Matisse and Pablo Picasso. They are artists of classical greatness, and their visionary forays into new art have changed our understanding of the world. Matisse was the elder of the two, but he was a slower and more methodical man by temperament and it was Picasso who initially made the greater splash. Matisse, like Raphael (see p.124), was a born leader and taught and encouraged other painters, while Picasso, like Michelangelo (see p.120), inhibited them with his power: he was a natural czar. Each demands his own separate space, and we start with Matisse.

❝ *Instinct must be thwarted just as one prunes the branches of a tree so that it will grow better.* **❞**
Henri Matisse

THE GREEN STRIPE
Matisse painted this unusual portrait of his wife in 1905. The green stripe down the centre of Amélie Matisse's face acts as an artificial shadow line and divides the face into two distinct sides. Instead of dividing the face in the conventional portraiture style, with a light and a dark side, Matisse divides the face chromatically, with a cool and warm side. The natural light is translated directly into colours and the highly visible brush strokes add to the sense of artistic drama.

377 Henri Matisse, Madame Matisse, Portrait with a Green Stripe, *1905, 40.5 x 32.5 cm (16 x 12¾ in)*

378 *Henri Matisse,* **The Conversation,** *1909, 177 x 217 cm (5 ft 9¾ in x 7 ft 1½ in)*

AFRICAN TRAVELS
In January 1912 Matisse set off on the first of two trips to Morocco. His appetite for African primitive art had been whetted by a visit to Tangiers in 1906 and he was eager to go back to capture the wonderful light and vitality of Africa. When Matisse arrived in Morocco it had been raining for two weeks and the rain was to continue for some time. These unusual climatic conditions left the landscape green and verdant which in turn affected Matisse's paintings. This photograph shows a piece of traditional Moroccan textile owned by Matisse.

Matisse's art has an astonishing force and lives by innate right in a paradise world into which Matisse draws all his viewers. He gravitated to the beautiful and produced some of the most powerful beauty ever painted. He was a man of anxious temperament, just as Picasso (see p.346), who saw him as his only rival, was a man of peasant fears, well concealed. Both artists, in their own fashion, dealt with these disturbances through the sublimation of painting: Picasso destroyed his fear of women in his art, while Matisse coaxed his nervous tension into serenity. He spoke of his art as being like "a good armchair" – a ludicrously inept comparison for such a brilliant man – but his art was a respite, a reprieve, a comfort to him.

Matisse initially became famous as the "King of the Fauves" (see p.334), an inappropriate name for this gentlemanly intellectual: there was no wildness in him, though there was much passion. He is an awesomely controlled artist, and his spirit, his mind, always had the upper hand over the "beast" of Fauvism.

In his green stripe portrait of his wife *(377)* he has used colour alone to describe the image. Her oval face is bisected with a slash of green and her coiffure, purpled and top-knotted, juts against a frame of three jostling colours. Her right side repeats the vividness of the intrusive green; on her left, the mauve and orange echo the colours of her dress. This is Matisse's version of the dress, his creative essay in harmony.

THE EXPERIMENTAL YEARS
Matisse's Fauvist years were superseded by an experimental period, as he abandoned three-dimensional effects in favour of dramatically simplified areas of pure colour, flat shape, and strong pattern. The intellectual splendour of this dazzlingly beautiful art appealed to the Russian mentality, and many great Matisses are now in Russia. One is *The Conversation (378)*, in which husband and wife converse. But the conversation is voiceless. They are implacably opposed: the man – a self-portrait – is dominating and upright, while the woman leans back sulkily in her chair. She is imprisoned in it, shut in on all sides. The chair's arms hem her in, and yet the chair itself is almost indistinguishable from the background: she is stuck in the prison of her whole context. The open window offers escape; she is held back by an iron railing. He towers above, as dynamic as she is passive, every line of his striped pyjamas undeviatingly upright, a wholly directed man.

HENRI MATISSE
Matisse's artistic career was long and varied, covering many different styles of painting from Impressionism to near Abstraction. Early on in his career Matisse was viewed as a Fauvist (see p.334), and his celebration of bright colours reached its peak in 1917 when he began to spend time on the French Riviera at Nice and Vence. Here he concentrated on reflecting the sensual colour of his surroundings and completed some of his most exciting paintings. In 1941 Matisse was diagnosed as having duodenal cancer and was permanently confined to a wheelchair. It was in this condition that he completed the magnificent Chapel of the Rosary in Vence.

OTHER WORKS BY MATISSE

Woman with a Red Chair
(Baltimore Museum of Art)

The Pink Studio
(Pushkin Museum, Moscow)

Odalisque
(Bridgestone Museum of Art, Tokyo)

Two Models Resting
(Philadelphia Museum of Art)

Woman with a Violin
(The Orangerie, Paris)

The Snail
(Tate Gallery, London)

Oceania, the Sea
(Musées Royaux des Beaux Arts, Brussels)

379 Henri Matisse, Odalisque with Raised Arms, 1923, 65 x 50 cm (25½ x 19¾ in)

His neck thickens to keep his outline straight and firm, an arrow of concentrated energy. The picture cannot contain him and his head continues beyond it and into the outside world. He is greater than it all, and the sole "word" of this inimical conversation is written in the scroll of the rail: *Non.* Does he say no to her selfish passivity? Does she say no to his intensity of life? They deny each other forever.

SUPREME DECORATION

But denial is essentially antipathetic to Matisse. He was a great celebrator, and to many his most characteristic pictures are the wonderful odalisques he painted in Nice (he loved Nice for the sheer quality of its warm, southern light). Though such a theme was not appreciated at the time, it is impossible for us to look at *Odalisque with Raised Arms (379)* and feel that Matisse is exploiting her. The woman herself is unaware of him, lost in private reverie as she surrenders to the sunlight, and she, together with the splendid opulence of her chair, her diaphanous skirt, and the intricately decorated panels on either side, all unite in a majestic whole that celebrates the glory of creation. It is not her abstract beauty that attracts Matisse, but her concrete reality. He reveals a world of supreme decoration: for example, the small black patches of underarm hair on the odalisque are almost a witty inverted comma mark round the globes of her breasts and the rose pink centre of each nipple.

SCULPTING IN PAPER

Picasso and Matisse were active to the end of their lives, but while Picasso was preoccupied with his ageing sexuality, Matisse moved into a period of selfless invention. In this last phase, too weak to stand at an easel, he created his papercuts, carving in coloured paper, scissoring

381 Raoul Dufy, Regatta at Cowes, *1934, 82 x 100 cm (32¼ x 39 in)*

out shapes, and collaging them into sometimes vast pictures. These works, daringly brilliant, are the nearest he ever came to abstraction. *Beasts of the Sea (380)* gives a wonderful underwater feeling of fish, sea cucumbers, sea horses, and water-weeds, the liquid liberty of the submarine world where most of us can never go. Its geometric rightness and chromatic radiance sum up the two great gifts of this artist and it is easy to see why he is the greatest colourist of the 20th century. He understood how elements worked together, how colours and shapes could come to life most startlingly when set in context: everything of Matisse's works together superbly.

DUFY'S JOYOUS ART

One painter who truly found his artistic self through Matisse and the Fauves was another Frenchman, Raoul Dufy (1877–1953). He is still hard to categorize, one of the important painters about whom the critics have not yet entirely made up their minds. His art seems too light of heart and airy, unconcerned with any conventions that persuade the doubter of his seriousness. He is in fact utterly serious, but serious about joy, about the need to be free and disinterested, with no personal stake in life. His painting *Regatta at Cowes (381)* leaps with glorious unconcern across the canvas, so superbly organized that it almost seems artless. If some later artists have tried to imitate Dufy's apparent incoherence, none has had his profound purity that makes everything cohere. This kind of art either comes naturally, or fails.

les bêtes de la mer...
H. matisse 50

380 Henri Matisse, Beasts of the Sea, *1950,*
295.5 x 154 cm (9 ft 8 in x 5 ft ½ in)

BEASTS OF THE SEA

Matisse chose to challenge the traditional beliefs of the artistic establishment by turning to the use of bright, colourful collage. His first use of scissors and paper was in 1931 but it was purely as a design approach for his larger paintings. However, following his ill-health, he turned to collage as an art in itself. In 1950, when he was over 80 years old, he cut one of his most beautiful collages in memory of the South Seas, which he had visited 20 years earlier. *Beasts of the Sea* includes symbols of aquatic life on the ocean bed, on the surface of the water, of the island itself, and of the sky above. By playing the bright colours against each other, Matisse achieved tonal resonances which would have a great influence on the colour painters of the 1960s.

EXPRESSIONISM

In the north of Europe the Fauves' celebration of colour was pushed to new emotional and psychological depths. Expressionism, as it was generally known, developed almost simultaneously in different countries from about 1905. Characterized by heightened, symbolic colours and exaggerated imagery, it was German Expressionism in particular that tended to dwell on the darker, sinister aspects of the human psyche.

EXPRESSIONISM

The term "Expressionism" can be used to describe various art forms but, in its broadest sense, it is used to describe any art that raises subjective feelings above objective observations. The paintings aim to reflect the artist's state of mind rather than the reality of the external world. The German Expressionist movement began in 1905 with artists such as Kirchner and Nolde, who favoured the Fauvist style of bright colours but also added stronger linear effects and harsher outlines.

DIE BRÜCKE

In 1905 a group of German Expressionist artists came together in Dresden and took the name Die Brücke (The Bridge). The name was chosen by Schmidt-Rottluff to indicate their faith in the art of the future, towards which their work would serve as a bridge. In practice they were not a cohesive group, and their art became an angst-ridden type of Expressionism. The achievement that had the most lasting value was their revival of graphic arts, in particular, the woodcut using bold and simplified forms.

382 Georges Rouault, **Prostitute at Her Mirror,** *1906, 70 x 60 cm (27½ x 23½ in)*

Although Expressionism developed a distinctly German character, the Frenchman, Georges Rouault (1871–1958), links the decorative effects of Fauvism in France with the symbolic colour of German Expressionism. Rouault trained with Matisse at Moreau's academy and exhibited with the Fauves (see p.335), but his palette of colours and profound subject matter place him as an early, if isolated Expressionist. His work has been described as "Fauvism with dark glasses".

Rouault was a deeply religious man and some consider him the greatest religious artist of the 20th century. He began his career apprenticed to a stained-glass worker, and his love of harsh, binding outlines containing a radiance of colour gives poignancy to his paintings of whores and fools. He himself does not judge them, though the terrible compassion with which he shows his wretched figures makes a powerful impression: *Prostitute at Her Mirror (382)* is a savage indictment of human cruelty. She is a travesty of femininity, although poverty drives her still to prink miserably before her mirror in the hope of work. Yet the picture does not depress, but holds out hope of redemption. Strangely enough, this work is for Rouault – if not exactly a religious picture – at least a profoundly moral one. She is a sad female version of his tortured Christs, a figure mocked and scorned, held in disrepute.

THE BRIDGE TO THE FUTURE

Die Brücke (The Bridge) was the first of two Expressionist movements that emerged in Germany in the early decades of the 20th century. It was formed in Dresden in 1905.

The artists of Die Brücke drew inspiration from van Gogh (see p.316), Gauguin (p.322), and primitive art. Munch was also a strong influence, having exhibited his art in Berlin from 1892 (p.325). Ernst Ludwig Kirchner (1880–1938), the leading spirit of Die Brücke, wanted German art to be a bridge to the future. He insisted that the group, which included Erich Heckel (1883–1970) and Karl Schmidt-Rottluff (1884–1976), "express inner convictions… with sincerity and spontaneity".

Even at their wildest, the Fauves had retained a sense of harmony and design, but Die Brücke abandoned such restraint. They used images of the modern city to convey a hostile, alienating world, with distorted figures and colours. Kirchner does just this in *Berlin Street Scene (383)*, where the shrill colours and jagged hysteria of his own vision flash forth uneasily. There is a powerful sense of violence, contained with difficulty, in much of their art. Emil Nolde (1867–1956), briefly associated with Die Brücke, was a more profound Expressionist who worked

383 *Ernst Ludwig Kirchner,* Berlin Street Scene, *1913, 121 x 95 cm (47½ x 37½ in)*

in isolation for much of his career. His interest in primitive art and sensual colour led him to paint some remarkable pictures with dynamic energy, simple rhythms, and visual tension. He could even illuminate the marshes of his native Germany with dramatic clashes of stunning colour. Yet *Early Evening (384)* is not mere drama: light glimmers over the distance with an exhilarating sense of space.

DEGENERATE ART
With the rise of Hitler and the Nazi party in the 1930s, many contemporary artists were discredited and forced to flee Germany or go into camps. The term "degenerate art" was coined by the authorities to describe any art which did not support the Nazi Aryan ideology. The first degenerate art exhibition opened in Munich in 1937, with paintings by van Gogh, Picasso, and Matisse torn from their frames and hung randomly amongst the work of asylum inmates. The exhibition was so successful that it went on a propaganda tour throughout Germany and drew millions of visitors. Many artists were deeply affected by being labelled "Degenerate" and Ernst Kirchner actually committed suicide as a result in 1938.

384 *Emil Nolde,* Early Evening, *1916, 74 x 101 cm (29 x 39½ in)*

WORLD WAR I

World War I broke out in 1914 following the assassination of Archduke Ferdinand (heir to the throne of Austria-Hungary) in Sarejevo by nationalists. This single event ignited localized problems which spread into an international conflict. Within months the whole of Europe and parts of North Africa were in conflict. Austria-Hungary declared war on Serbia (believing the Serbians had devised the Sarejevo plot) and Austria's ally Germany declared war on Russia and France and then immediately invaded Belgium. In response, Britain declared war on Germany, and the stage was set for five years of incessant fighting and for the death of 10 million people. By April 1917 the allies included Britain, France, Russia, Japan, Italy, and the USA. Many artists were affected by the war, particularly Max Beckmann who was deeply affected by his work as a medical orderly on the front lines.

OTHER WORKS BY BECKMANN

Souvenir of Chicago
(Fogg Art Museum, Cambridge, Mass.)

Two Women
(Museum Ludwig, Cologne)

The Dream
(Staatsgalerie Moderner Kunst, Munich)

Masquerade
(Art Museum, St Louis)

Carnival
(Tate Gallery, London)

Sea Lions in the Circus
(Kunsthalle, Hamburg)

385 Max Beckmann, Self-portrait, 1944, 95 × 60 cm (37½ × 23½ in)

386 Egon Schiele, **Nude Self-portrait,**
1910, 110 x 35.5 cm (43 x 14¼ in)

angst that was the main theme of his work. *Self-portrait (386)*, however, is a most moving theme in itself: a pathetic and yet powerful exposure of Schiele's vulnerability. He is mere skin and bone, not yet fully there as a person. He has outlined his body with a glowing line of white to indicate to us both his sense of imprisonment and his limitations: notice how his arm disappears almost at the elbow – yet paradoxically it also suggests growth and potential. He is an unhappy, scrawny youth, the wild and exaggerated expanse of pubic hair perhaps indicating the centre of his unhappiness. His may seem too individualistic a view, yet in his hysterical way he is expressing the fears and doubts of many young people. He is wonderful, unsettling, and strangely innocent.

Oskar Kokoschka (1886–1980) was another Austrian artist of enormous Expressionist power. He said of his art, "It was the Baroque inheritance I took over unconsciously". He rejected harmony, but insisted on vision, and his art stakes its all on this visionary intensity, which plays havoc with more staid conventions.

In 1914 he fell passionately in love with Alma Mahler, the widow of the Austrian composer, Gustav Mahler. In its wild, dreamy way *Bride of the Wind (387)* commemorates the emotional storms and insecurities of that relationship with a sophisticated psychological insight: Alma, the "bride", sleeps complacently, while Kokoschka, flayed and disintegrating within the twisting brush strokes and sinuous ribbons of colour, agonizes alone in silence.

Die Brücke collapsed as the inner convictions of each artist began to differ, but arguably the greatest German artist of the time was Max Beckmann (1884–1950). Working independently, he constructed his own bridge, to link the objective truthfulness of great artists of the past with his own subjective emotions. Like some other Expressionists, he served in World War I and suffered unbearable depression and hallucinations as a result. His work reflects his stress through its sheer intensity: cruel, brutal images are held still by solid colours and flat, heavy shapes to give an almost timeless quality. Such an unshakeable certainty of vision meant that he was hated by the Nazis, and he ended his days in the United States, a lonely force for good. He is perhaps just discernible as a descendant of Dürer in his love of self-portraits and blend of the clumsy and suave with which he imagines himself: in *Self-portrait (385)*, he looks out, not at himself, but at us, with a prophetic urgency.

AUSTRIAN EXPRESSIONISM
The Austrian Expressionist painter Egon Schiele (1890–1918) died when he was only 28 and we do not really know whether he would have developed from the self-pitying adolescent

387 Oskar Kokoschka, **Bride of the Wind,** *1914, 181 x 221 cm (5 ft 11¼ x 7 ft 3 in)*

ARTISTIC EMIGRES

As the centre of artistic interest, Paris attracted many foreign painters in the early 20th century, and within a few years of each other three Jewish émigrés, Chaim Soutine, Marc Chagall, and Amedeo Modigliani, had all arrived in the city. Though they became friends and gained inspiration from the recent innovations in art, they were each highly original artists and their paintings stand alone, defying categorization and imitation.

The three painters that we look at here were all born outside France, and they remained outsiders to the Parisian art scene for more than merely cultural reasons (Soutine and Chagall were both Russian and Modigliani was Italian). These painters shared the isolation of being "other", never truly belonging to any group or adhering to a single manifesto.

A PASSIONATE EXPRESSIONIST

Chaim Soutine (1894–1943) came to Paris in 1913. He was the only painter in the city who was in the least like Georges Rouault (see p.341) and as a Parisian Expressionist, he belonged to the "School of Paris". Soutine's style of applying thickly encrusted paint was quite different from Rouault's, but his wild, chaotic spirit, sorrowful and vehement, is like that of the Frenchman. Just as Rouault, despite his Fauvist connections, is seen as inherently Expressionist, so Soutine was a natural, though singular, Expressionist.

Soutine's religion was the earth. He painted the sacredness of the country with a passion that makes his art hard to read. *Landscape at Ceret (388)* is so dense that it could be abstract, and it does take enormous liberties with the earthly facets, but when we do "read" it, hill and tree and road take on a new significance for us.

388 Chaim Soutine, Landscape at Ceret, *c.1920–21, 56 x 84 cm (22 x 33 in)*

DREAMS OF THE HEART

Marc Chagall (1887–1985) arrived in Paris in 1914 penniless, like Soutine. He combined his fantasies with sensuous colour and modern art techniques he learnt in France. He played with reality in a completely original and even primitive way. At heart he was a religious painter, using the word in its widest sense: he painted the dreams of the heart, not the mind, and his fantasy is never fantastic. It speaks beyond logic to the common human desire for happiness.

His early work in particular seems lit up from within by a psychic force that flows from his Jewish upbringing in Russia. *The Fiddler (389)* is a mythic figure, the celebrant of Jewish births, marriages, and deaths, but he bears this weight of the community alone, almost alienated from the common lot – notice the luminous green of the fiddler's face and how he hovers magically, unsupported in the air.

MODIGLIANI'S MANNERED ART

The third great "outsider" among the *émigrés* in Paris died all too soon. The Italian Amedeo Modigliani (1884–1920) destroyed himself through drink and drugs, driven desperate by his poverty and bitterly ashamed of it. Modigliani was a young man of fey beauty,

389 Marc Chagall, The Fiddler, *1912/13, 188 x 158 cm (6 ft 2 in x 5 ft 2 in)*

390 Amedeo Modigliani, Chaim Soutine, *1917, 91 x 60 cm (36 x 23½ in)*

and his work has a wonderful slow elegance that is unusual, but compelling. Through the influence of the Rumanian sculptor Constantin Brancusi, he fell under the spell of primitive sculpture, especially from Africa. He went on to develop a sophisticated, mannered style built upon graceful, decorative arabesques and simplified forms. It is hard for us to imagine why it did not attract patrons. He is famous now for his elegant, elongated nudes, but it is his portraits that are the most extraordinary.

Chaim Soutine (390) whose own art was so off-beat, appeals to Modigliani for what he is bodily and for what he could become spiritually. Soutine rears up out of the frame like a gawky pillar. His nose is brutish in its spread, his eyes asymmetrical, his hair a shaggy mess. All this uncouthness is contrasted by his slender wrists and hands, by an impression we have of a man yearning for a homeland, set upon forming one out of his own substance if no place is provided. There is sadness here, but also determination: the thick red mouth is resolutely closed.

PICASSO AND CUBISM

After Cubism, the world never looked the same again: it was one of the most influential and revolutionary movements in art. The Spaniard Pablo Picasso and the Frenchman Georges Braque splintered the visual world not wantonly, but sensuously and beautifully with their new art. They provided what we could almost call a God's-eye view of reality: every aspect of the whole subject, seen simultaneously in a single dimension.

> **"** *...The art of painting original arrangements composed of elements taken from conceived rather than perceived reality.* **"**
>
> **Guillaume Apollinaire,** *The Beginnings of Cubism,* **1912**

It is understandable that Pablo Picasso (1881–1973) found Spain at the turn of the century too provincial for him. Picasso's genius was fashioned on the largest lines, and for sheer invention no artist has ever bettered him: he was one of the most original and versatile of artists, with an equally powerful personality. Throughout the 20th century people have been intrigued and scandalized by Picasso's work, uncertain of its ultimate value.

391 Pablo Picasso, **Family of Saltimbanques,** *1905, 213 x 230 cm (7 ft x 7 ft 7 in)*

392 Pablo Picasso, Les Demoiselles d'Avignon, *1907, 244 x 234 cm (8 ft x 7 ft 8 in)*

PICASSO'S PHASES
Pablo Picasso (1881–1973) had several distinct phases during his long career, including his Blue Period, and his later Rose Period. He began his blue paintings in 1901 reflecting his sadness at a friend's death. Picasso felt that blue was the colour of solitude, and melancholy, which certainly reflected his own bleak circumstances at the time. Directly after his Blue Period Picasso moved on to his Rose Period in 1905. Some believe that the warm tones of this period of work were influenced by Picasso's habit of smoking opium. One of Picasso's most creative phases took place between 1908 and 1912 and is known as Analytical Cubism (see p.348). In this style, which he developed with Georges Braque, Picasso used disintegrated and reassembled forms in shades of black and brown.

THE EARLY YEARS

Picasso's Blue Period, from 1901 to 1904, sprang from his initial years of poverty after moving to Paris and modulated into a Rose Period as he slowly began to emerge into prominence. Although still only in his youth when he started painting, Picasso had overwhelming ambition, and his *Family of Saltimbanques (391)* was, from the start, meant to be a major statement. It is a very large, enigmatic work from the Rose Period, revealing his superb graphic skill and the subtle sense of poverty and sadness that mark those early years. The five itinerant acrobats are strained and solitary in the barren, featureless landscape; the lonely girl seems not to belong to their world, though she too is melancholy and belongs by right of mood. There is something portentous about the picture, some unstated mystery. We feel that Picasso, too, does not know the answer – only the question. Already art is an emotional medium for Picasso, reflecting his moods and melancholia as he seeks to find fame as an artist.

THE FIRST CUBIST PAINTING

While still in his twenties, but finally over his self-pitying Blue and Rose periods, Picasso fundamentally changed cognitive reality with a work his friends called *Les Demoiselles d'Avignon (392)* after a notorious place of prostitution. These demoiselles are indeed prostitutes, but their initial viewers recoiled from their advances with horror. This is the one inevitable image with which a discussion of 20th-century art must be concerned. It was the first of what would be called the Cubist works, though the boiled pink

CUBISM
This movement in painting was developed by Picasso and Braque around 1907 and became a major influence on Western art. The artists chose to break down the subjects they were painting into a number of facets, showing several different aspects of one object simultaneously. The work up to 1912 concentrated on geometrical forms using subdued colours. The second phase, known as Synthetic Cubism, used more decorative shapes, stencilling, collage, and brighter colours. It was then that artists such as Picasso and Braque started to use pieces of cut-up newspaper in their paintings.

colour of the hideous young women is far removed from later Cubism, with its infinite subtleties of grey and brown. It is almost impossible to overestimate the importance of this picture and the profound effect it had on art subsequently. The savage, inhuman heads of the figures are the direct result of Picasso's recent exposure to tribal art, but it is what he does with their heads – the wild, almost reckless freedom with which he incorporates them into his own personal vision and frees them to serve his psychic needs – that gives the picture its awesome force.

Whether he did this consciously or not we do not know, since he was a supremely macho man: *Les Demoiselles* makes visible his intense fear of women, his need to dominate and distort them. Even today when we are confronted with these ferocious and threatening viragoes, it is hard to restrain a frisson of compassionate fear.

394 Pablo Picasso, **Nude Woman in a Red Armchair,** *1932, 130 x 97 cm (51 x 38 in)*

At first Picasso did not dare to show it even to his admirers, of whom there were always many. But Georges Braque (see p.350) was haunted and affronted by its savage power, and eventually he and Picasso began to work out together the implications of this new kind of art. Cubism involved seeing reality simultaneously from all angles, of meshing the object in the network of its actual context: as Cézanne had indicated, there were to be no bounding lines to truth, but a form emerging from all different aspects intuited together (see column, p.347). The results are hard to read, even though the Cubists confined themselves mostly to unpretentious and familiar objects such as bottles and glasses of wine, or musical instruments (see p.350).

BEYOND CUBISM

Picasso would have scorned any thought of limiting himself to a single style. He experimented continually, his versatility and creativity always amazing his contemporaries. Whenever he seemed to have settled in a particular mode of seeing, he changed again almost overnight.

Picasso soon became a wealthy man and when the scandal of his early artistic methods had died down, he revived it with his subject matter. He is even more autobiographical an artist than Rembrandt or van Gogh and it was the women in his life who provided the changing drama: each new relationship precipitated a new

393 Pablo Picasso, **The Lovers,** *1923, 130 x 97 cm (51 x 38 in)*

wave of creativity, with a new model and a new vision. *The Lovers (393)* shows him in a classical vein, soberly and simply giving substantial form to an almost theatrical drama. This was the period of his infatuation with Olga Kokhlova, the well-bred Russian ballerina whom he rashly married and whose elegant influence on him was soon to be angrily denied as their relationship faltered. There is a balletic grace in *The Lovers* and, pictorially thrifty though he was, Picasso never completely discarded the styles as he did the women.

THE ARTIST'S PLEASURE

The mistress who inspired the most enchanting art in him was Marie-Thérèse, a large, pacific girl with whose rounded body shapes he loved to play on canvas. Picasso was so various an artist, so astonishing in his inventions that every viewer may well have a favourite period, yet (though this may be too subjective a reaction) the work inspired by Marie-Thérèse seems to come from a depth that is perhaps unequalled in his other work. *Nude Woman in a Red Armchair (394)* is the last time we see Picasso relatively benign. There is something in Marie-Thérèse's willing vunerability, in her material fecundity of shape, that Picasso finds positively reassuring.

All the Marie-Thérèse paintings – at least until the affair began to disintegrate – are remarkably satisfying: rich, gracious, almost sweet, and yet deeply challenging. Picasso plays with both the rotundity of her body and with the powerful paradox of her extreme youth (she was only 17 when they met), yet the physical satisfaction that she brought him, succouring and nurturing him, was as though this simple child was in a sense a mother figure to him. *Nude Woman in a Red Armchair*, with its luminous physicalities – which even the armchair seems to share as it curls and glows around her body – still expresses the dichotomy of Marie-Thérèse's double role in Picasso's treatment of her face: she is both full moon and crescent moon, full face and in profile. It is impossible not to feel the thrilling communication of the artist's pleasure. This sense of fulfilment, rare in Picasso at any stage, never reappeared after he lost interest in Marie-Thérèse and her warm charms.

PICASSO'S LATER MISTRESSES

Subsequent mistresses such as Dora Maar, an intellectual, or François Gillot, another artist – both fiercely determined women – brought out Picasso's cruelty, his determination not to be impressed. Even in his old age, when he was cared for by his second wife, Jacqueline Roque, Picasso still used her as ammunition in his battle against fate. He raged against his loss of sexual power in these final years and sought to compensate for it through the phenomenal weight of his artistic powers.

Picasso's portrait of Dora Maar, *Weeping Woman (395),* painted the same year as his great picture *Guernica*, has a terrible power. It is a deeply unattractive picture, the shrill acids of its yellows and greens fighting bitterly and unrelentingly with the weary reds, sickly whites, and sinister purples. But it is also unattractive in the sense that it conveys Picasso's venomous desire to mutilate his sitter. Dora Maar's tears were almost certainly tears caused by Picasso himself. They reveal her anguished need for respect; Picasso repays her with a vicious savagery.

Power was Picasso's special gift. He had the ability to turn even the most incidental of themes into powerful works with an often overbearing force. If we accept that all beauty has power, we can range artists along a line, at one end or the other. Vermeer, Claude, and Matisse would be at the beauty end, and Rembrandt and Poussin at the power end, together with Picasso.

GERTRUDE STEIN
Gertrude Stein (1874–1946) was one of the most influential art collectors living in Paris in the early 20th century. The Stein family became friendly with Matisse after buying his painting *Woman with a Hat*, but Gertrude Stein preferred the work of Picasso. Stein's career as a novelist ran parallel to Picasso's career as a painter and their friendship was mutually beneficial, resulting in a portrait of Stein by Picasso and a short essay on Picasso's work by Stein. Stein was also associated with Juan Gris, whom she began to collect in 1914. The Stein family collected hundreds of paintings and had a major influence on many artists.

395 Pablo Picasso, Weeping Woman, *1937, 55 x 46 cm (21½ x 18 in)*

PAPIER COLLÉ AND COLLAGE

The technique of *papier collé* (pasted paper) was invented by Georges Braque in 1913. He cut out squares from a roll of imitation-wood paper, stuck them onto cardboard and then sketched a still life. The technique was adopted by Picasso and Matisse. It usually involved using imitation wood engraving, stencilled lettering, and fake marble stuck in layers onto the canvas. Braque also pioneered the technique of mixing sand with his paint to achieve a more textured effect. The *collage* (pasting) technique begun by the Cubist painters was later used by Max Ernst and other Surrealists. A wide variety of effects were created, using paper, news cuttings, and photographs.

396 Georges Braque, Still Life: Le Jour, 1929, 115 x 147 cm (45 x 58 in)

GEORGES BRAQUE

Georges Braque (1882–1963) was the only artist ever to collaborate with Picasso as an equal. He admitted that they were like climbers roped together, each pulling the other up. From 1907 they worked so closely together, exploring the planes and facets of the same subject matter, that some of their work appears almost identical. Although they developed their own natural autonomy as artists, they carried Cubism to another level that was brighter and more legible.

Their joint discovery was remarkably brief for the effect it has had. Braque never excelled in these early works, though he never fell below Picasso's standards either. His Synthetic Cubist painting (see column, p.347) of *Still Life: Le Jour (396)* is restrained in colour, is hardly playful at all, and is somehow less exuberant than Picasso's Cubist work – though Braque delights in the originality of the shapes and textures. But by this time the two artists had long parted, and their innate differences are clear.

JUAN GRIS

There was a third great Cubist, the Spaniard Juan Gris (1887–1927). He died young and never moved on from the style, though he progressively brightened and clarified it. With this single-mindedness, Gris can be thought of as the one absolute Cubist. *Fantômas (397)* has a harlequinish gaiety with its shifting planes and witty celebration of newspapers, magazines, and entertainment. With its stylish sophistication, we would never think it was a Braque or Picasso.

397 Juan Gris, Fantômas, 1915, 60 x 73 cm (23½ x 29 in)

THE AGE OF MACHINERY

Interest in and appreciation of machinery was clearly in the air in the early decades of the 20th century. For a group of young Italian "Futurist" artists, the progress offered by machinery epitomized their increasing fascination with dynamic speed and motion. Though they translated this idea of progress into a frenetic exultation of the glory of war and the destruction of museums, their visual understanding of motion remained exciting.

The Italian Futurists, like the members of Die Brücke in Germany, aimed to free art from all its historical restraints and celebrate the new beauty of the modern age (see column, right). Umberto Boccioni (1882–1916), Gino Severini (1883–1966), and Giacomo Balla (1871–1958), who all joined Futurism in 1910, wanted to express the onrush of events in the world with pictures of motion, dynamism, and power.

In *Street Noises Invade the House (398)*, Boccioni attempts to give this sensation and succeeds remarkably well. Noise becomes something seen, something literally invasive of privacy. Boccioni said of the picture: "all life and the noises of the street rush in at the same time as the movement and the reality of the objects outside." The surging incoherence of the forms is both chaotic and ordered.

398 Umberto Boccioni, Street Noises Invade the House, 1911, 100 x 107 cm (39¼ x 42 in)

399 Fernand Léger, Two Women Holding Flowers, *1954, 97 × 132 cm (38 × 52 in)*

400 Robert Delaunay, Homage to Blériot, *1914, 250 × 251 cm (8 ft 2½ in × 8 ft 3 in)*

FRANCE AND THE MACHINE AGE

Fernand Léger (1881–1955) was initially influenced by Cubism, but after his experience of trench warfare in World War I, he converted to Socialism. Like the Futurists, he admired the harmonious union of man with modern machinery. He developed an unusual blend of abstraction and representational imagery that conveyed something of the smooth, ordered quality of machines. *Two Women Holding Flowers (399)* shows the simplicity and power of this later style, though it is still only partially realistic. The full, schematic forms of the women were meant to be easily assimilable to ordinary people, for whom Léger felt immense respect, though it is the great bright blocks of colour that give his women their true interest. All the same, there is a sort of epic splendour in this art to which most people find themselves responding instinctively.

The machine age inspired not only Léger and the Futurists, but Robert Delaunay (1885–1941). *Homage to Blériot (400)* shows Delaunay's intoxication with the aeroplane and Blériot, the first pilot to fly the English Channel. Initially, it may seem to be an abstract picture, but it is full of visual clues. Blériot's plane whirls high above the Eiffel Tower, while figures and planes dazzle in and out of swirling multi-coloured circles, reminiscent of a propellor (see column, left).

TOWARDS ABSTRACTION

In 1911, a new group of German artists began exhibiting their work to the public. Der Blaue Reiter was to become the high point of German Expressionism, but it also opened the way towards abstraction with its stand for free experimentation and originality. It is Wassily Kandinsky, the most influential member of the group, who is most often credited with the distinction of painting the first "abstract" picture, in 1910.

Der Blaue Reiter (The Blue Rider) was formed in 1911 and succeeded the first Expressionist movement, Die Brücke (see p.340), which dissolved in 1913. The group included Franz Marc (1880–1916), Wassily Kandinsky (1866–1944), and August Macke (1887–1914), and celebrated the art of children and primitives, but had no precise artistic programme. The most active proponent of this essentially romantic and rather spiritual view of art (see column, right) was Franz Marc, a young artist who was killed in World War I. Marc saw animals as the betrayed but uncontaminated guardians of what was left of innocence and unspoilt nature.

THE BLUE RIDER
This was the name given, in 1911, to a group of Munich Expressionist artists by the two most important members, Franz Marc and Wassily Kandinsky. Two touring exhibitions of paintings were transported around Germany, with other artists such as Macke, Klee, and Braque also represented. This illustration shows the front cover of *Der Blaue Reiter* published in 1912 by Marc and illustrated with a woodcut by Kandinsky.

401 Franz Marc, Deer in the Forest II, 1913/14, 110.5 × 100.5 cm (43½ × 39⅔ in)

THEOSOPHISTS
The term "theosophy" is derived from the Greek words *theos*, "God" and *sophia*, "wisdom". As a religious philosophy, theosophy can be traced back to ancient roots, but it re-emerged in the late 19th century and influenced artists such as Kandinsky and Mondrian. The classic formulation of theosophical teachings is *The Secret Doctrine* written by Mme Blavatsky, an American theosophist. She argues that the "essence" of an object is more important than the attributes of the object. The new artists, like Kandinsky, believed their abstract art would lead the people to spiritual enlightenment.

RUSSIAN REVOLUTION

The Russian Revolution of 1917 had its origins partly in the inability of the existing order to manage the Russian role in World War I. There were two main groups of revolutionaries: the liberals, who believed that Russia could still win the war and create a democracy; and the Bolsheviks, who thought the war was lost and wanted to transform the whole economy. The avant-garde movement was adopted by the state (though not for long) and became a major vehicle for "agitprop" (a mixture of agitation and propaganda). Artists were encouraged to design for posters and political rallies.

Like August Macke, Marc chose to express these feelings with emphatic, symbolic colours. He painted animals with a profoundly moving love: a love for what they represented and could still experience, unlike humanity. *Deer in the Forest II (401)* is made up of a dense network of shapes and lines that border on the abstract. Together they create a forest of experience through which we can see, as if emerging from the undergrowth, the small forms of the deer. The animals are utterly at peace, at home in the forest of the world. It is a stylized and luminous vision of a species that can live without the angers of the ego.

August Macke, who was also to be killed in the coming war, was another artist with a gentle, poetic temperament. He took a simple delight in the joys common to us all, which makes his senseless destruction especially painful. *Woman in a Green Jacket (402)* floats onto the canvas, blissfully detached and pacific. Of the group, he was the most sensitive to form and colour, and the hues in this picture irradiate gently within strong shapes to create sensuous areas of light.

402 August Macke, Woman in a Green Jacket, *1913, 44 x 43.5 cm (17⅓ x 17 in)*

KANDINSKY AND ABSTRACTION

However, neither Marc nor Macke were abstract painters. It was Kandinsky who found that the "interior necessity", which alone could inspire true art, was forcing him to leave behind the representational image. He was a Russian who had first trained as a lawyer. He was a brilliant and persuasive man. Then, when already in his thirties, he decided to go to Munich in 1897 to study art. By the time Der Blaue Reiter was established, he was already "abstracting" from the image, using it as a creative springboard for his pioneering art. Seeing a painting of his own, lying on its side on the easel one evening, he had been struck by its beauty, a beauty beyond what he saw when he set it upright. It was the liberated colour, the formal independence, that so entranced him.

Kandinsky, a determined and sensitive man, was a good prophet to receive this vision. He preached it by word and by example, and even those who were suspicious of this new freedom were frequently convinced by his paintings. *Improvisation 31 (403)* has a less generalized title, *Sea Battle*, and by taking this hint we can indeed see how he has used the image of two tall ships shooting cannonballs at each other, and abstracted these specifics down into the glorious commotion of the picture. Though it does not show a sea battle, it makes us experience one, with its confusion, courage, excitement, and furious motion.

Kandinsky says all this mainly with the colour, which bounces and balloons over the centre of the picture, roughly curtailed at the upper corners, and ominously smudged at the

403 Wassily Kandinsky, Improvisation 31 (Sea Battle), *1913, 140 x 120 cm (55 x 47 in)*

bottom right. There are also smears, whether of paint or of blood. The action is held tightly within two strong ascending diagonals, creating a central triangle that rises ever higher. This rising accent gives a heroic feel to the violence.

These free, wild raptures are not the only form abstraction can take, and in his later, sadder years, Kandinsky became much more severely constrained, all trace of his original inspiration lost in magnificent patternings.

Accent in Pink (404) exists solely as an object in its own right: the "pink" and the "accent" are purely visual. The only meaning to be found lies in what the experience of the picture provides, and that demands prolonged contemplation. What some find hard about abstract art is the very demanding, time-consuming labour that is implicitly required. Yet if we do not look long and with an open heart, we shall see nothing but superior wallpaper.

KANDINSKY AND MUSIC

Kandinsky, himself an accomplished musician, once said "Colour is the keyboard, the eyes are the harmonies, the soul is the piano with many strings. The artist is the hand that plays, touching one key or another, to cause vibrations in the soul." The concept that colour and musical harmony are linked has a long history, intriguing scientists such as Sir Isaac Newton. Kandinsky used colour in a highly theoretical way associating tone with timbre (the sound's character), hue with pitch, and saturation with the volume of sound. He even claimed that when he saw colour he heard music.

OTHER WORKS BY KANDINSKY

Improvisation Deluge
(Lenbachaus, Munich)

In the Black Squeeze
(Guggenheim Museum, New York)

Heavy Circles
(Norton Simon Museum, Pasadena)

The Grey
(Pompidou Centre, Paris)

The Whole
(National Museum of Modern Art, Tokyo)

Cossacks
(Tate Gallery, London)

And Again
(Kunstmuseum, Berne)

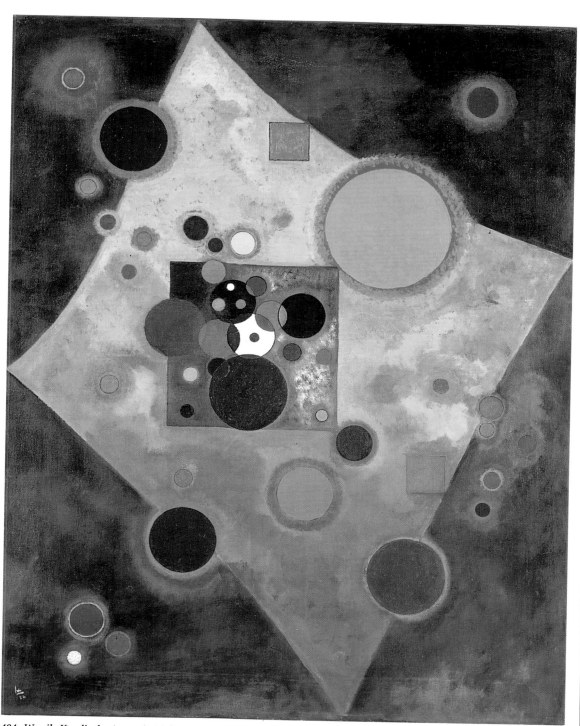

404 Wassily Kandinsky, Accent in Pink, 1926, 101 × 81 cm (39½ × 31¾ in)

PAUL KLEE

Paul Klee was an introverted Swiss painter who spent most of his adult life in Germany until he was expelled by the Nazis in 1933. His work is impossible to clarify, except to say that it is hardly ever wholly abstract, but equally, never truly realistic. He had a natural sensitivity to music, the least material of the arts, and it runs through all his work, clarifying his spellbinding colour and dematerializing his images.

Paul Klee (1879–1940) was one of the greatest colourists in the story of painting, and a skilled deployer of line. His gravest pictures may have an undercurrent of humour, and his powers of formal invention seem infinite. After making an early choice whether to pursue painting or music as a career, he became one of the most poetic and inventive of modern artists. He taught at the Bauhaus in Weimar and Dessau (see column, left) and then at the Düsseldorf

BAUHAUS ARCHITECTURE

The Bauhaus school of art and architecture was developed by Walter Gropius (1883–1969) around the old Weimar Academy in 1919. The early teachers at the school included artists such as Klee and Kandinsky, and a close relationship was established between the artists and local industry. Many products, including furniture and textiles, were chosen for large-scale production. In 1925 the Bauhaus moved to Dessau and established a group of large cooperative buildings (illustrated above). The Bauhaus style was impersonal, severe, and geometrical, using a strict economy of line and pure materials. Gropius left the Bauhaus group and after moving to Berlin in 1932 the Bauhaus was closed down by the Nazis. This dissolution of the group actually encouraged individuals to travel and helped disseminate Bauhaus ideas throughout the Western world.

405   Paul Klee, The Golden Fish, 1925/26, 50 x 69 cm (19¾ x 27¼ in)

Academy. Until his explusion from Düsseldorf by the Nazis, Klee painted and drew on a very small scale, yet the small size of his pictures does not effect their internal greatness.

The Golden Fish (405) glides through the kingdom of its underwater freedom, all lesser fish leaving a clear space for its gleaming body. This is a magical fish with runic signs upon his body, scarlet fins, and a great pink flower of an eye. He hangs majestically in the deep, dark blue magic of the sea, which is luminous with secret images of fertility. The great fish draws the mysteriousness of his secret world into significance. We may not understand the significance, but it is there. The sea and its creatures are arranged in

406 *Paul Klee,* Diana in the Autumn Wind, *1934, 63 × 48 cm (24¾ × 19 in)*

glorious homage, belittled but also magnified by this bright presence. This quiet nobility, the brightness, the solitude, the general respect: all are true of Klee himself. Whether the art world knew it or not, he was their "golden fish".

IMAGES OF DEATH AND FEAR

Klee painted with intense rapidity and sureness and it is impossible to indicate the full breadth of his range, his unfailing magic, and his poetry. *Diana in the Autumn Wind (406)* gives a hint of his sense of movement. Leaves flying in a moist breeze are, at the same time, the Virgin goddess on the hunt, and yet also a fashionably dressed woman from Klee's social circle. The eeriness of the dying year takes shape before our eyes and beyond all this are lovely balancing forms that exist in their own right. This work is strangely pale for Klee, yet the gentle pallor is demanded by the theme: he hints that Diana is disintegrating under the force of autumnal fruitfulness.

BOOK BURNING
At the peak of Klee's career in the early 1930s he came under surveillance from the Chamber of Culture. Joseph Goebbels, the Nazi minister of propaganda, organized hundreds of book burnings in German university towns. Thousands of books were destroyed for being "non-conformist to the spirit of a new Germany", including those by Marx and Freud. Hundreds of intellectuals and artists were forced to flee the country, including Kandinsky (who fled to France), and Klee (who went to Switzerland). Other left-wing intellectuals were not so fortunate and died in concentration camps.

407 Paul Klee, Death and Fire, *1940, 46 × 44 cm (18 × 17⅓ in)*

DER STURM

Der Sturm ("the storm")
magazine and art
gallery was established
by Hewarth Walden
(1878–1941) in Berlin
to promote the German
avant-garde movement.
The gallery ran from
1912 to 1924 and the
magazine from 1910
to 1932. *Der Sturm*
became the focus
of modern art in
Germany and
promoted the work
of the Futurists and
the Blaue Reiter group
(see p.353). Klee's first
contribution to the
magazine was a
reinterpretation of a
Robert Delaunay
painting completed in
January 1913. Klee also
exhibited in the show-
rooms of *Der Sturm*
between 1912 and 1921.

OTHER WORKS BY KLEE

Old Sound
(Öffentliche
Kunstsammlung, Basel)

Garden Gate
(Kunstmuseum, Berne)

The Dancer
(Art Institute of Chicago)

Flower Terrace
(National Museum of
Modern Art, Tokyo)

Fire at Evening
(Museum of Modern
Art, New York)

*Watchtower of
Night Plants*
(Staatsgalerie Moderner
Kunst, Munich)

Land of Lemons
(Phillips Collection,
Washington, DC)

Klee died relatively young of a slow and wasting disease, his death horribly mimicked by the death of peace that signified World War II. His last paintings are unlike any of his others. They are larger, with the forms often enclosed by a thick black line, as if Klee were protecting them against a violent outrage. The wit is gone and there is a huge sorrow, not personal, but for foolish and wilful humanity.

Death and Fire (407) is one of Klee's last paintings. A white, gleaming skull occupies the centre, with the German word for death, *Tod*, forming the features of its face. A minimal man walks towards death, his breast stripped of his heart, his face featureless, his body without substance. Death is his only reality, his facial features waiting there in the grave for him. But there is fire in this picture too: the sun, not yet set, rests on the earth's rim, which is also the hand of death. The upper air is luminous with fire, presenting not an alternative to death, but a deeper understanding of it. The man walks forward bravely, into the radiance, into the light. The cool, grey-green domain of death accepts the fire and offers wry comfort.

Three mysterious black stakes jag down vertically from above, and the man strikes the skull with another. If fate forces him down into the earth, he does not go passively or reluctantly: he cooperates. Death's head is only a half-circle, but the sun that it balances in its hand is a perfect globe. The sun is what endures the longest, what rises highest, what matters most, even to death itself. Klee understood his death as a movement into the deepest reality, because, as he said, "the objective world surrounding us is not the only one possible; there are others, latent". He reveals a little of that latent otherness here.

PURE ABSTRACTION

Shapes and colours have always had their own emotional force: the designs on ancient bowls, textiles, and furnishings are abstract, as are whole pages of medieval manuscripts. But never before in Western painting had this delight in shape as such, in colour made independent of nature, been taken seriously as a fit subject for the painter. Abstraction became the perfect vehicle for artists to explore and universalize ideas and sensations.

Several artists claimed to be the first to paint an abstract picture, rather as early photographers had wrangled over who had invented the camera. For abstract art, the distinction is most often given to Wassily Kandinsky (see p.354), but certainly another Russian artist, Kasimir Malevich, was also among the first.

RUSSIAN SUPREMATISM

Although Chagall and Soutine (see p.344) both left Russia to seek inspiration in France, the early 20th century saw an amazing renewal in Russian art. Since the far-off days of the icon painters (see pp.27–28), there had been nothing in this great country but the monotony of academic art. Now, as if unconsciously anticipating the coming revolution of 1917, one great painter after another appeared. They were not universally welcomed in their homeland, and more than one artist sought a response elsewhere, but some of the most significant painters dedicated their lives and their art to their country.

They are difficult artists. Kasimir Malevich (1878–1935), who founded what he called Suprematism (see column, right), believed in an extreme of reduction: "The object in itself is meaningless…the ideas of the conscious mind are worthless". What he wanted was a non-objective representation, "the supremacy of pure feeling." This can sound convincing until one asks what it actually means. Malevich, however, had no doubts as to what he meant, producing objects of iconic power such as his series of *White on White* paintings or *Dynamic Suprematism (408)*, in which the geometric patterns are totally abstract.

Malevich had initially been influenced by Cubism (see p.347) and primitive art (p.334), which were both based on nature, but his own movement of Suprematism enabled him to construct images that had no reference at all to reality. Great solid diagonals of colour in *Dynamic Suprematism* are floating free, their severe sides denying them any connection with the real world, where there are no straight lines. This is a pure abstract painting, the artist's main theme being the internal movements of the personality. The theme has no precise form,

and Malevich had to search it out from within the visible expression of what he felt. They are wonderful works, and in their wake came other powerful Suprematist painters such as Natalia Goncharova and Liubov Popova.

SUPREMATISM

Kasimir Malevich's art and his Suprematist manifesto are amongst the most vital artistic developments of this century. Most of his paintings are limited to geometric shapes and a narrow range of colours, but the pinnacle of his Suprematism was his *White on White* series. He claimed to have reached the summit of abstract art by denying objective representation.

408 Kasimir Malevich, Dynamic Suprematism, 1916, 102 x 67 cm (40 x 26½ in)

409 Piet Mondrian, The Grey Tree, *1912, 79 x 108 cm (31 x 42½ in)*

MONDRIAN'S ABSTRACT PURITY

Kandinsky's late style had a geometrical tendency and Suprematist abstraction revolved largely around the square, but the real artist of geometry was the Dutchman Piet Mondrian (1872–1944). He seems to be the absolute abstract artist, yet his early landscapes and still lifes were relatively realist.

> **"** *The important task of all art is to destroy the static equilibrium by establishing a dynamic one.* **"**
>
> **Piet Mondrian in** *Circle,* **1937**

NEO-PLASTICISM

Although a founding member of De Stijl ("the style") group of artists, Piet Mondrian preferred his art to be viewed as Neo-Plasticism. The first De Stijl journal, published in 1917, emphasized the importance of austere abstract clarity and Mondrian's work certainly followed this agenda. In 1920 he published a Neo-Plasticism pamphlet asking artists to denaturalize art and to express the ideal of universal harmony. Mondrian restricted his paintings to primary colours, black, white, and grey, using lines to divide his canvases.

The Grey Tree (409) adumbrates the abstractions that were a half-way house to his geometrical work, yet it also has a foothold in the real world of life and death. *The Grey Tree* is realist art on the point of taking off into abstraction: take away the title and we have an abstraction; add the title and we have a grey tree. He claimed to have painted these pictures from the need to make a living, yet they have a fragile delicacy that is precious and rare. Mondrian sought an art of the utmost probity: his greatest desire was to attain personal purity, to disregard all that pleases the narrow self and enter into divine simplicities. That may sound dull, but he composed with a lyrical sureness of balance that makes his art as pure and purifying as he hoped.

Mondrian imposed rigorous constraints on himself, using only primary colours, black and white, and straight-sided forms. His theories and his art are a triumphant vindication of austerity. *Diamond Painting in Red, Yellow, and Blue* (410) appears to be devoid of three-dimensional space, but it is in fact an immensely dynamic picture. The great shapes are dense with their chromatic tension. The varying thicknesses of the black borders contain them in perfect balance. They integrate themselves continually as we watch, keeping us constantly interested. We sense that this is a vision of the way things are intended to be, but never are.

410 Piet Mondrian, **Diamond Painting in Red, Yellow, and Blue,** *c. 1921/25, 143 x 142 cm (56¼ x 56 in)*

ART OF THE FANTASTIC

Between the two World Wars, painting lost some of the raw, modern energy it began the century with and became dominated by two rather philosophical movements, Dada and Surrealism, which arose partly as a reaction to the senseless atrocities of World War I. But artists were also becoming introspective, concerned with their own subconscious dreams: Sigmund Freud's psychoanalytical theories were well known by this time, and painters explored their own irrationalities and fantasies in search of a new artistic freedom.

One artist who prefigured the Surrealists' idea of fantasy with his fresh, naïve outlook on the world was the Frenchman, Henri Rousseau (1844–1910). Like Paul Klee (see p.356), he defies all labels, and although he has been numbered among the Naïves or Primitives (two terms for untrained artists), he transcends this grouping. Known as *Le Douanier,* after a lifelong job in the Parisian customs office, Rousseau is a perfect example of the kind of artist in whom the Surrealists believed: the untaught genius whose eye could see much further than that of the trained artist.

Rousseau was an artist from an earlier era: he died in 1910, long before the Surrealist painters championed his art. Pablo Picasso (p.346), half-ironically, brought Rousseau to the attention of the art world with a dinner in his honour in 1908: an attention to which Rousseau thought himself fully entitled. Although Rousseau's greatest wish was to paint in an academic style, and he believed that the pictures he painted were absolutely real and convincing, the art world loved his intense stylization, direct vision, and fantastical images.

Such total confidence in himself as an artist enabled Rousseau to take ordinary book and catalogue illustrations and turn each one into a piece of genuine art: his jungle paintings, for instance, were not the product of any first-hand experience and his major source for the exotic plant life that filled these strange canvases was actually the tropical plant house in Paris.

Despite some glaring disproportions, exaggerations, and banalities, Rousseau's paintings have a mysterious poetry. *Boy on the Rocks (411)* is both funny and alarming. The rocks seem to be like a series of mountain peaks and the child effortlessly dwarfs them. His wonderful stripy garments, his peculiar mask of a face, the uncertainty as to whether he is seated on the peaks or standing above them, all comes across with a sort of dreamlike force. Only a child can so bestride the world with such ease, and only a childlike artist with a simple, naïve vision can understand this elevation and make us see it as dauntingly true.

METAPHYSICAL PAINTING

Giorgio de Chirico (1888–1974) was an Italian artist who originated what we now call Metaphysical painting (known as *Pittura Metafisica*), which also influenced the Surrealists' art. It was World War I and its brutalities that shocked de Chirico and his fellow Italian, Carlo Carrà (see column, p.362), into a new way of looking at reality in 1917. De Chirico painted real locations and objects within strange contexts and from unusual perspectives. The result is an uneasy assemblage of images in a peculiarly silent world.

411 Henri Rousseau, Boy on the Rocks, 1895/97, 55 x 46 cm (21¾ x 18 in)

412 *Giorgio de Chirico*, The Uncertainty of the Poet, *1913, 106 x 94 cm (41¾ x 37 in)*

The Surrealists saw in de Chirico's paintings the importance of the mysterious world of dreams and the unconscious. They were influenced by the quality of enigma in his work, and especially by the unexpected juxtapositioning of objects, which became a distinguishing factor of much

Surrealist art. De Chirico hoped to rise above the bare facts in his art, transmitting the magical experience beyond reality: he wanted his vision to be shown through reality, but not limited by it in any way.

De Chirico's theories do not really explain the power of his work, and in fact he found this art hard to sustain, so that it dwindled surprisingly soon into a brilliant but imitative classicism of a kind. While at his brief best, however, de Chirico is as magical as he hopes, and *The Uncertainty of the Poet (412)*, with its melancholy, deserted piazza, the suggestively scattered bananas, and the great bulk of the twisted, headless female bust is a genuinely unsettling picture.

FROM DADA TO SURREALISM

The German, Max Ernst (1891–1976), is hard to categorize: he invented one new method after another during his career, including frottage (laying paper over textured surfaces, making a rubbing with graphite, and using the marks as chance starting points for an image). Untrained as an artist, Ernst originally studied philosophy. In 1919 he founded the Cologne branch of the Dada group (see column, left). Dada appeared in Paris the same year and though it lasted only until 1922, it became a precursor of Surrealism.

413 *Max Ernst*, The Entire City, *1934, 50 x 61 cm (19¾ x 24 in)*

414 Joan Miró, **Woman and Bird in the Moonlight,**
1949, 81 × 66 cm (32 × 26 in)

Dada reflected the mood of the time: it was a
literary and artistic movement of young artists
who, like de Chirico, were appalled and disillusioned by the atrocities of World War I. They
expressed their sense of outrage by challenging
established art forms with irrational and
imaginative concepts in their work so that
it frequently appeared nonsensical.

In 1922, Ernst settled in Paris and he became
instrumental in the evolution of Surrealism
from Dada by using childhood memories to
influence his subject matter. His mind was
extraordinarily fertile, which attracted a group
of Surrealist writers, and after Dada ended,
he became an intimate with this group.

Ernst took from de Chirico the idea of
unconnected objects in strange, atmospheric
settings, and turned them into pictures in
a more modern context, full of fear and
apprehension. He is an uneven artist, but his
best works have a personal sense of mythology
to them. *The Entire City (413),* with its uncanny
streaks of frottage, and the great clear moon
above with its vacant centre, strikes an
unhappy chord of recognition. Although
we recognize the familiar floorboard pattern,
Ernst makes us feel the sad likelihood that we
are also receiving a prevision of our future.

Surrealism began officially in 1924 with a
manifesto drawn up by the Surrealist writer
André Breton (1896–1966). Called "Surrealists"
to stress the idea of being above or beyond
reality, the group combined the irrationality of

Dada with the idea of pure, unreasoned thought
through subconscious dreams and free association – a concept heavily inspired by Sigmund
Freud's theories on dreams. The group took a
sentence from the poet Lautréamont to explain
their search for the fantastical: "Beautiful as the
chance encounter of a sewing machine and an
umbrella on an operating table."

MIRO AND MAGRITTE

Surrealist artists placed great value on children's
drawings, the art of the insane, and untrained
amateur painters whose art sprang from pure
creative impulses, unrestrained by convention
or aesthetic laws. Surrealism generally took the
form of fantastic, absurd, or poetically loaded
images. It was a potent, if inexplicable, force in
the work of many artists, of whom Joan Miró
(1893–1983) is perhaps the most uncanny. An
introspective Spanish artist, he was one of the
truly major Surrealists. His art appears far more
spontaneous than that of Ernst or Dali (see
p.364) in rejecting traditional images and
devices in painting. *Woman and Bird in the
Moonlight (414)* is a personal celebration of
some deep joy. The figures tumble together with
instinctive sureness, magical shapes that move
in and out of recognition as if the woman and
the bird could at any time exchange identities.

The Belgian René Magritte (1898–1967) was a
practitioner of realist Surrealism, pressed into
imaginative servitude. He began by imitating
the avant-garde, but he genuinely needed a
more poetic language which was influenced

ANTONI GAUDÍ
Before Surrealism had been
created at the beginning
of the 20th century the
Spanish architect Antoni
Gaudí (1852–1926) had
already demonstrated the
power of abstract forms
and Surrealist fantasy in
architecture. His most
famous creations all
encompass fluidity of form,
with organic and abstract
shapes, often using mosaic
tiling to create arabesque
decoration. The detail
illustrated above is taken
from the Parque Güell in
Barcelona, designed by
Gaudí in 1900–14 for his
patron Don Basilio Güell.
Several of the Surrealist
artists, including Joan Miró,
acknowledged drawing
inspiration from Gaudí and
other Catalan art.

415 René Magritte, **The Fall,** *1953, 80 × 100 cm (31½ × 39⅓ in)*

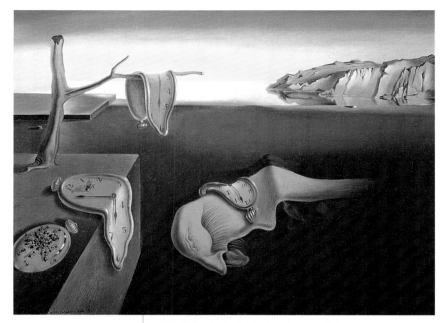

416 *Salvador Dali,* The Persistence of Memory, *1931, 24 x 33 cm (9½ x 13 in)*

SURREALIST FILMS
In collaboration with Luis Buñuel, Salvador Dali produced the first Surrealist film, *Un Chien Andalou,* in 1929. The film has no real plot (Buñuel commented, "We relentlessly threw out everything that might have meaning"), but the interaction between image, sound, and motion is designed to show the result of conscious psychic automation. The main psychological device used by the film director is "shock montage", and many of the scenes in the film show bizarre and shocking images. The scene illustrated above is one showing a hand covered in ants forcing its way through a woman's door. This film was followed in 1930 by *L'Age d'Or,* which attacked all that was sacred to the bourgeoisie. In response, an exhibition of paintings connected with the film, including work by Ernst and Miró, was destroyed by right-wing radicals and the film was withdrawn.

by de Chirico's Metaphysical paintings. He had a mischievous mind, and his weirdly bowler-hatted men in *The Fall (415)* drop through the sky with complete composure, expressing something of the oddity of life as we know it. His art, painted with such clarity that it appears highly realistic, typifies the Surrealist love of paradoxical visual statements and though things may seem normal, there are anomalies everywhere. *The Fall* has a weird rightness about it, and it is in tapping our own secret understanding of sublunar peculiarity that Surrealism appeals.

DALI'S DREAM PHOTOGRAPHS

Salvador Dali (1904–89), whose graphic gifts were never affected by his mental imbalance, painted profoundly unpleasant and yet striking images of the unreality in which he felt at home. But he painted the unreality with meticulous realism, which is why they are so disturbing. He described these works as "hand-painted dream photographs" and their power lies precisely in their paradoxical condition as snapshots of things that, materially, do not exist.

It is easy, in theory, to disregard Dali, but difficult in practice. *The Persistence of Memory (416),* with its melting watches and the distorted face (like a self-portrait) in the centre, has an intensity and an applicability that we cannot shrug off. Dislike it though we may, this sense of time gone berserk, of a personal world collapsed under the pressure of the contemporary, has an inescapable power. And distasteful though it is, *The Persistence of Memory* is one of the great archetypal images of our century.

DUBUFFET AND ART BRUT

Though not a Surrealist as such, Jean Dubuffet (1901–85) shared some of the Surrealists' influences, in particular children's drawings, art of the insane, and the absurd and irrational. He had a large collection of work by psychotics which he called *Art Brut* – Raw Art.

Although he was still a young man when he trained as an artist in Paris, Dubuffet was in his forties before he began painting in earnest. On the surface, his art bears very little obvious relation to that of the Surrealists, though he painted with a Surrealist philosophy. His pictures are crude and rough, totally devoid of the illusionist trickery or persuasiveness employed by Dali and Magritte. Nor do they possess the Surrealist tendency towards enigma and mystery. Instead, his art was, as he would say, *Art Brut* – aggressively unsophisticated "outsider art".

We can be taken aback by a work such as *Nude with a Hat (417).* It seems to have been gouged out of a primitive material context. The nude glares out at us, her big eyes, confrontational mouth, and great, flat, egotistical hat making her a powerful and dynamic icon. Only the two small circles in the centre remind us that this is a nude and these are her breasts. Dubuffet is concerned with a whole different scenario: woman as demon, as a psychic force. It is the great flat hat that matters, not her nakedness. It is this reversal of the accepted and the conventional on which Dubuffet builds his art. It is wonderful stuff, but deeply challenging.

417 *Jean Dubuffet,* Nude with a Hat, *1946, 80 x 64 cm (31½ x 25 in)*

418 Giorgio Morandi, Still Life, 1946, 37.5 x 46 cm (14¾ x 18 in)

ISOLATION AND OBSESSION

In this period between the two world wars, Giorgio Morandi and Alberto Giacometti stood apart from their artistic contemporaries. Both painters absorbed the broad influence of Surrealism early on in their careers, but soon abandoned these affiliations to pursue their own singular and intensely individual languages. Morandi was Italian, Giacometti Swiss, and like their cultural disparities, their art has little common ground. However, they share the trait of being obsessive artists, returning to the same subject again and again.

Giorgio Morandi (1890–1964) was one of the real geniuses of Italian 20th-century painting. He was an unusual man who lived a very quiet life in Bologna, and his own quiet personality is the predominant trait in his art. His early paintings are influenced by de Chirico's Metaphysical paintings, but he soon evolved his own unique vision – one that he did not deviate from for the rest of his life. He painted still lifes – often the same group of bottles, jugs, and other humble domestic ware – and they quiver on the canvas with an almost breathless reverence. *Still Life (418)* has the inner peace of visual prayer. For him, these are objects of the deepest mystery and he has that rare artistic power of making us understand just what he experiences as he contemplates them.

THE HUMAN FORM IN SPACE

Alberto Giacometti (1901–66) spent a large proportion of his career as a sculptor and returned to painting at a relatively late stage. Like Morandi, his early paintings – especially those made in Paris where he settled in 1922 – were essentially Surrealist with their disturbing, aggressively ambiguous vein. He later abandoned this form of expression to work directly from life, thus severing all points of contact with the Surrealists. Giacometti spent the rest of his life engaged in one long, ongoing struggle to convey the solid presence of the human form in space. He tended to work obsessively on a series of paintings, working continuously on one particular image at a time. His tendency to wipe out every night what he had created during the day gives a poignancy to what has survived. *Jean Genet (419)*, for example, the Parisian thief-turned-writer, intrigued Giacometti in both aspects of his unique personality.

Giacometti was fascinated both by the creative Genet, the writer, and by the obsessive Genet, the thief. Something of Giacometti's double fascination is apparent in this portrait. Genet looks up almost blindly into the world of mysterious materiality. This is the world from which he was excluded, and which he yet longs to possess. All of these subtleties are present in Genet's portrait: a small, tense figure, blindly intent upon a world that eludes him. There is mastery here and menace, as well as a sense of the magical.

OTHER WORKS BY MORANDI

Still life (Australian National Gallery, Canberra)

Flowers (Collezione d'Arte Religiosa Moderna, Vatican Rome)

Still life with a Green Dish (Gemeentemuseum, The Hague)

Still life with Bottles (Scottish National Gallery of Modern Art, Edinburgh)

Landscape of Grizzana (Fondazione Magnani Rocca, Parma)

Metaphysical Picture (Hermitage, St Petersburg)

419 Alberto Giacometti, Jean Genet, 1955, 65 x 54 cm (25½ x 21¼ in)

PRE-WAR AMERICAN PAINTING

There have always been interesting American artists, and at least two 19th-century painters, Thomas Eakins and Winslow Homer, influenced the course of future art in the United States. During the 1920s and '30s, Edward Hopper and Georgia O'Keeffe emerged as the inspirational new painters of distinctive American traditions. Hopper's work was strongly realist, his still, precise images of desolation and isolated individuals reflecting the social mood of the times. O'Keeffe's art was more abstract, often based on enlarged plants and flowers, and infused with a kind of Surrealism she referred to as "magical realism". She may not have been a great painter, but her art was highly influential.

420 Edward Hopper, Cape Cod Evening, 1939, 77 x 102 cm (30¼ x 40 in)

423 *Jackson Pollock,* **Number 1, 1950 (Lavender Mist),** *1950, 221 × 300 cm (7 ft 3 in × 9 ft 10 in)*

&& *On the floor I am more at ease, I feel nearer, more a part of the painting, since this way I can walk around in it, work from the four sides and be literally "in" the painting.* **&&**

Jackson Pollock, 1947

previous decades, these artists valued, above all, individuality and spontaneous improvisation. They felt ill at ease with conventional subjects and styles, neither of which could adequately convey their new vision. In fact, style as such almost ceased to exist with the Abstract Expressionists, and they drew their inspiration from all directions.

BREAKING THE ICE

It was Jackson Pollock (1912–56) who blazed an astonishing trail for other Abstract Expressionist painters to follow. De Kooning (see p.371) said, "He broke the ice", an enigmatic phrase suggesting that Pollock showed what art could become with his 1947 drip paintings (see column, p.368).

The Moon-Woman Cuts the Circle (422) is an early Pollock, but it shows the passionate intensity with which he pursued his personal vision. This painting is based on a North American Indian myth. It connects the moon with the feminine and shows the creative, slashing power of the female psyche. It is not easy to say what we are actually looking at: a face rises before us, vibrant with power, though perhaps the image does not benefit from laboured explanations. If we can respond to this art at a fairly primitive level, then we can also respond to a great abstract work such as *Lavender Mist (423).* If we cannot, at least we can appreciate the fusion of colours and

the Expressionist feeling of urgency that is communicated. *Moon-Woman* may be a feathered harridan or a great abstract pattern; the point is that it works on both levels.

ACTION PAINTING

Pollock was the first "all-over" painter, pouring paint rather than using brushes and a palette, and abandoning all conventions of a central motif. He danced in semi-ecstasy over canvases spread across the floor, lost in his patternings, dripping and dribbling with total control. He said: "The painting has a life of its own. I try to let it come through." He painted no image, just "action", though "action painting" seems an inadequate term for the finished result of this creative process. *Lavender Mist* is 3 m long (nearly 10 ft), a vast expanse on a heroic scale. It is alive with coloured scribble, spattered lines moving this way and that, now thickening, now trailing off to a slender skein. The eye is kept continually eager, not allowed to rest on any particular area. Pollock has put his hands into paint and placed them at the top right – an instinctive gesture eerily reminiscent of cave painters (see p.11) who did the same. The overall tone is a pale lavender, made airy and active. At the time Pollock was hailed as the greatest American painter, but there are already those who feel his work is not holding up in every respect.

OTHER WORKS BY POLLOCK

White Light
(Museum of Modern Art, New York)

The Deep
(Pompidou Centre, Paris)

Blue Poles
(Australian National Gallery, Canberra)

No. 23
(Tate Gallery, London)

Watery Paths
(Galleria d'Arte Moderne, Rome)

Eyes In the Heat
(Guggenheim Foundation, Venice)

Untitled Composition
(Scottish National Gallery of Art, Edinburgh)

424 Lee Krasner, Cobalt Night, 1962, 237 x 401 cm (7 ft 9⅓ in x 13 ft 2 in)

Lee Krasner (1908–84), who married Pollock in 1944, was not celebrated at all during his lifetime (cut short in 1956 by a fatal car crash), but it was actually she who first started covering the canvas with a passionate flurry of marks. The originality of her vision, its stiff integrity and its great sense of internal cohesion, is now beginning to be recognized. *Cobalt Night (424)* at 4 m (over 13 ft) is even larger than *Lavender Mist* and has the same kind of heroic ambition.

MARK ROTHKO

The other giant of Abstract Expressionism is the Russian-born Mark Rothko (1903–70). Just as there are some who feel a little uneasy about the status of Pollock, and others who would fiercely defend it, so too with Rothko. Like Pollock, he was initially influenced by Surrealism and its capacity for freedom of expression, but his greatest works are his mature abstracts. These paintings are often not hung as he originally intended. He wanted dim lighting and an atmosphere of contemplation; he rarely gets it. He rejected the extreme religious connotations given to his great walls of colour, saying that his work had an essentially emotional rather than mystical meaning. He insisted that the theme, the subject, was different and could only be communicated by personal involvement in an atmosphere of solitude. Yet to many it appears that all Rothkos have identical formats: oblongs of delicate colour held floating in a coloured setting, the edges ravelled like heavenly clouds. Those who love Rothko consider him one of the most important painters of the 20th century.

Rothko's art represented an alternative Abstract Expressionism to Pollock's: he placed greater emphasis on colour and gravity than on the excitement of gesture and action. Such

425 Mark Rothko, Untitled (Black and Grey), 1969, 207 x 194 cm (6 ft 9⅓ in x 6 ft 4 in)

demarcations, however, can be dangerous, since the Abstract Expressionists rarely aligned themselves into such rigid camps. *Untitled (Black and Grey) (425)* was painted the year before Rothko killed himself. The chromatic luminosities of the earlier years had long been quenched by a deepening sadness: the emotion conveyed here is of deep sorrow. We must take what comfort we can in recognizing that the grey area is greater than the black and that though the black has a heavy, deadening solidity the grey is still shot through with undershades, with potential.

Arshile Gorky

It may have been his soul-shattering early experiences as an Armenian refugee, and the resulting insecurities, that made Arshile Gorky (1905–48) begin his artistic career so heavily under the influence of Picasso (see p.346) that it seemed an individual style would never emerge. Born Vosdanig Manoog Adoian, Gorky emigrated to the USA in 1920, moving to New York in 1925 to study and then teach art. Before he too killed himself (see column, right), Gorky did indeed find his own voice, released partly through his contact with Surrealism in America. *Waterfall (426)* shows a lovely tumble of free images, the sweetly floating flat patches of colour and shapes of his maturity. Strangely, the images do truly resemble a waterfall: something in the

427 *Willem de Kooning,* Woman and Bicycle, *1952–53, 194 x 124 cm (76 x 49 in)*

426 *Arshile Gorky,* Waterfall, *1943, 154 x 113 cm (60½ x 44½ in)*

surge down the canvas suggests a great sweep of water, the sunlight dazzling on hidden rocks behind. There is a springtime freshness about Gorky's work that gives his suicide an added poignancy. It is as if only in his art did he find happiness, freedom, and acceptance.

De Kooning

Gorky was an important influence on the development of Abstract Expressionism and also on one of its most vital figures, his friend Willem de Kooning (1904–). De Kooning was born in Holland, but has lived mainly in the USA.

> **TRAGIC LIFE**
> Arshile Gorky was a potent force in American art, forging a link between Surrealism and Abstraction. At the peak of his powers he suffered from a series of tragedies. In 1946 a fire destroyed many of his paintings and he was diagnosed as having cancer. In 1948 he broke his neck in a car accident and his wife left him. Soon afterwards he hanged himself.

> *"Imagination, no longer fettered by the laws of fear, became as one with vision. And the Act, intrinsic and absolute, was its meaning, and the bearer of its passion."*
>
> Clyfford Still

Though there were many Abstract Expressionists, the most vital seems to be de Kooning: even in Pollock's lifetime, de Kooning was hailed as his major rival. His ability to take a theme, whether landscape or portrait, and treat it with wild and wonderful freedom still impresses. His northern European background and the impulsive passion of his style, however, still bear some resemblance to Chaim Soutine (see p.344).

We are shaken with a visceral shock when we encounter de Kooning's women. *Woman and Bicycle (427)* is all teeth, eyes, and enormous bosom. She sits like a mantis, with a gleeful expectancy lighting her wedge of a face. This is a woman totally devoid of glamour, let alone charm, yet the poor giantess is dolled up in her tasteless finery, waiting for her prey. We shrink, we smile (such hideousness), we feel a little afraid. She is, above all, impressive and wickedly so. It is as much a tribute as a taunt.

At his lyrical best, de Kooning can overwhelm us with his beauty. *Door to the River (428)* balances most delicately on the cusp of abstraction. Great thick bars of colour that slash and sprawl across the canvas create an unmistakable door; through

429 Clyfford Still, 1953, 236 x 174 cm (7 ft 9 in x 5 ft 8½ in)

the vertical bars gleams the intense blue of the distant river. This is not de Kooning delighting us with his wit, but rather drawing us right into the heart of great art. A work of art is great to the extent that to encounter it is to be changed. *Door to the River* passes this test triumphantly.

CLYFFORD STILL

With Clyfford Still (1904–80), landscape moved majestically over the cusp and into pure abstraction. Still is set apart from other artists of the New York School by the fact that for most of his career he lived and worked at a remove from the art world of New York – although he lived and taught in the great city during the height of Abstract Expressionism in the mid 1950s.

Still rejected references to the real world in his art and attempted to sever colour from any links and associations. Most of his paintings are variations on a theme. He made grandiose claims for his work as being transcendent and numinous, and a painting such as *1953 (429)* does suggest why he felt able to make such claims. An objective viewer might feel he overstates his case, and yet this is a wonderful painting. The expanse of blue is dotted with black, two passionate streaks of red at the base, and great jagged slashes of colour at the top. It is as if the mountains have opened to show us both the brightness and the darkness within, and it is this power to suggest a psychic significance that distinguishes Still's art.

428 Willem de Kooning, Door to the River, 1960, 205 x 178 cm (6 ft 8 in x 5 ft 10 in)

430 Franz Kline, Ballantine, 1948–60,
183 × 183 cm (6 ft × 6 ft)

FRANZ KLINE

If Franz Kline (1910–62) suggests urban land-scapes in his art, it is only in the sense of girders set against the sky. It is as if the struts of a bridge or some unsupported scaffolding had inspired him to see the sheer majesty of pure, isolated shape. His work resembles nothing more than oriental calligraphy writ large. Much of it is black and white, with all the subtle shadings and blurring that distinguish great Chinese calligraphy. There is a sort of passionate rightness about a work such as *Ballantine (430)* that is immediately convincing. This personal building of a shape like a bridge, with an oriental freedom of handling, may not be especially profound but it remains immensely satisfying.

BARNETT NEWMAN

Barnett Newman (1905–70) was one of the most prestigious of the New York School painters. Originally an art critic, he was an ardent supporter of the Abstract Expressionists, explaining and popularizing their work across America. Everyone was surprised when he suddenly blossomed forth as a painter himself, producing enormous "colour field" canvases: often a solid block of a single colour punctuated by what Newman called "zips". *Yellow Painting (431)* is a perfect example: two straight white lines that differ slightly in width (though their length is identical) zip vertically through the painting at either edge. Their pristine whiteness makes us aware of the rich canary yellow which, we discover on inspection, is bisected by another zip, this time yellow, faintly outlined in places with a shadowy white. The sheer size of the painting and its baffling simplicity keep us looking. The longer we look, the more aware we are of the strength and purity of the

yellow, and indeed of the white. This is a strangely uplifting experience, as though colour draws us into itself whilst enlarging our horizons. With these works, Newman prefigures both the decorative panels of the Colourists (see p.375) and the spartan canvases of the Minimalists (see p.377).

ROBERT MOTHERWELL

Although his work has a monolithic simplicity, Newman was a noted intellectual. So indeed was Robert Motherwell (1915–91), the youngest of the Abstract Expressionists and a philosopher whose work exerts an enormous, though fundamentally mysterious moral power.

Motherwell has said that "without ethical consciousness a painter is only a decorator". This remark makes sense in the context of the series that he painted as an emotional response to the Spanish Civil War of 1936–39. These works are elegies mourning the self-inflicted death of

see p.375 ... see p.377

> **THE IRASCIBLES**
> Discontented with the Metropolitan Museum of Art's stance on avant-garde painting, a group of American artists, including, Newman, Pollock, Still, and Rothko, wrote a letter to the museum announcing that they would not exhibit in the gallery. After an article in the *New York Herald* criticized their tactics, the group became known as "The Irascible 18". The most vocal of the group was Jackson Pollock, who argued that each era must choose a different artistic style to express the thoughts of contemporary culture.

431 Barnett Newman, Yellow Painting, 1949, 171 × 133 cm (5 ft 7½ in × 52⅜ in)

THE SPANISH CIVIL WAR

In July 1936 General Franco organized a violent revolt against the Popular Front government in Spain to protest against the anti-clerical and socialist principles of the leaders. As a result Spain became an ideological battleground for Fascists and Socialists from all countries. Both Italy and Germany sent troops to assist Franco. Aid for the Republicans came partly from Britain and France, but mainly from the Soviet Union. The fall of Barcelona in January 1939 led to the end of the civil war and the inauguration of General Franco. The poster above was printed by a trade union as part of the Socialist campaign. Motherwell describes his work as a tribute to the Spanish people.

432 Robert Motherwell, Elegy to the Spanish Republic No. 70, 1961, 175 x 290 cm (5 ft 9 in x 9 ft 6 in)

a great civilization. Heavy swags of black, like a bull's testicles, hang down the picture space, reminding us that this is the land of bullfights which end with a noble beast slaughtered. There is a sombre dignity and emotional grandeur to *Elegy to the Spanish Republic No. 70 (432)* and at first sight we may only be aware of a massive area of black against the luminous pallor of the background: yet the background shades are subtle greys and a pale blue. The solid black swings up and falls down heavily, fissured by thin and ominous dark lines. Even without the title we would know this is an elegy. Motherwell is mourning, but his grief – a very Spanish touch – has a great nobility of restraint.

PHILIP GUSTON

Philip Guston (1913–80) began painting as an Abstract Expressionist and there are probably still some people who regard the delicate grace of those works as his best. But he underwent a conversion, suffering a revulsion against what he had come to feel was too pretty, and started what we could call a second career as the most plebeian of figurative painters.

The Painter's Table (433), painted towards the end of his life, could be described as uniquely autobiographical: there is the ashtray and still-smoking cigarette; there are the books to keep a painter's mind alert, and there is a paint box with solid squiggles of paint on the lid – a witty reminder of an earlier career as an abstract artist. But the box is closed, pressed down by one of the solid boots which became almost his trademark: life is a heavy business and we are not borne miraculously through it. Dead centre is a wonderful eye, the essential requisite of the painter. Notice, though, that the eye looks through the table into infinity, the painter's task, and that the nail he has driven into the table casts a bleeding red shadow. There are mysterious shapes, too, in the picture, that tease our imaginations; why should a painter's life be fully explicable?

433 Philip Guston, The Painter's Table, 1973, 196 x 229 cm (6 ft 5 in x 7 ft 6 in)

AMERICAN COLOURISTS

Abstract Expressionism, although it developed increasingly serious implications with its interior subject matter and artistic gaze, also liberated a wonderful flood of abstract art in the next generation of American painters. But to call these artists "the second generation" of Abstract Expressionists is perhaps unhelpful. They reacted against the "self-importance" and theoretical "spirituality" of painters such as Barnett Newman, seeking to free the artistic image from the obsessively metaphysical and make it a purely optical experience.

> **"** *A bridge between Pollock and all possibilities.* **"**
>
> **Morris Louis on Helen Frankenthaler in 1953**

The painters that followed the Abstract Expressionist movement were less intense in their concentration, but wider and more diverse in the effects they sought. The Abstract Expressionists were profoundly serious – tragedy was essentially their theme – while the Colourists, or "Stainers", used colour to express joy rather than sorrow. They stained canvases with paint or created large areas of colour to communicate visually the wonder of human existence. Colour has an effect on us all: it communicates meaning in its very being, irrespective of image or theme. It was this elementary power that the Colourists relied upon, bypassing the intellect to appeal to a deeper self.

HELEN FRANKENTHALER

American art has several great Colourists. One is Helen Frankenthaler (1928–), whose method of staining the canvas with paint had such a wide influence on painting. She was influenced by Pollock's "all over" painting (see p.369), and her innovative approach is in some ways an extension of Pollock's pouring and dripping process, though the effect is very different. She mixed thin washes and transparent stains and impregnated the bare, untreated canvas with them so that the colour no longer sat on the surface of the canvas, but became the picture surface itself. *Wales (434)* shows her technique in its lovely simplicity, yet the more we look, the more subtle it is.

Frankenthaler demands a place in art history as a pioneer of the staining technique, but this seems relatively unimportant compared with the end to which she put this means. Her style has been well-imitated, but never with such inspired power. The eye moves over *Wales* with continual pleasure: it is a superb example of a work which has no "meaning" and yet provides profound intellectual satisfaction.

MORRIS LOUIS

When Morris Louis (1912–62) visited Frankenthaler's studio in 1954, he learnt from her the technique of using stains as a means of creating, not on the canvas, but in it, making the work seem to

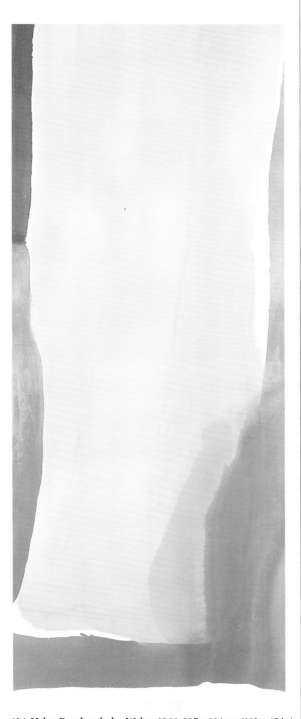

434 Helen Frankenthaler, Wales, 1966, 287 x 114 cm (113 x 45 in)

STAIN PAINTING

From 1952 a new genre of painting known as "stain painting" was developed by Helen Frankenthaler, who had evolved her own style of Abstract Expressionism (see pp.368-74) under the influences of Jackson Pollock and Arshile Gorky. The technique she developed involved using thinned paint to cover a whole unprimed canvas. The colours, having lost their glossy coating, float into and away from the surface creating nebulous but controllable space, while at the same time the spectator's awareness of the texture of the canvas denies the sense of extended illusion. In 1963 Frankenthaler started to use acrylic paints, which produced the same density of colour saturation but were more controllable.

435 *Morris Louis,* Beta Kappa, *1961, 262 × 439 cm (8 ft 7 in × 14 ft 5 in)*

emerge from its own necessities. *Beta Kappa (435)* (the works are distinguished by Greek letters so that no shade of interpretation may creep into our experience of the paintings) is a late work, one of Louis' series of *Unfurleds*, where diagonal stripes across the canvas create a purely decorative effect. The painting is over 4 m (14 ft) long, yet the area in the centre of the picture has been left daringly bare. We cannot take in, with just one look, the pourings down either side, so we must move between the edges, seeking an integration. Finally, we are forced to submit to the challenging nothingness of the picture, which its coloured borders only make more evident.

RICHARD DIEBENKORN

Not all the great American painters live in New York. Richard Diebenkorn (1922–1994) has lived for many years in San Francisco, and his famous *Ocean Park* series is named after a local suburb there. The wonderful rectangles he paints are both similar to one another and yet completely different. He has found, as Mark Rothko did (see p.370), a format that sets him free to explore the nuances of colour, and it is serious play.

Stripes and diagonals divide *Ocean Park No. 64 (436)* into three sections, differently hued and sized. The absolute verticals highlight the swimming softness of the blue background and the subtle shifts and variations of paint application, so that in this work we really do recall the varying depths of the great Pacific Ocean. But this is also a park, fenced in and bounded both at every edge and from within. Diebenkorn uses colour so creatively that we begin to understand the world a little better.

436 *Richard Diebenkorn,* Ocean Park No. 64, *1973, 253 × 206 cm (8 ft 3½ in × 6 ft 8¾ in)*

MINIMALISM

If Abstract Expressionism dominated the 1940s and '50s, Minimalism belonged to the '60s. It grew out of the restrained, spartan art of Abstract Expressionists such as Mark Rothko and Barnett Newman. A broad concept, Minimalism refers either to the paring down of visual variation within an image, or to the degree of artistic effort required to produce it. The result is an art form that is purer and more absolute than any other, stripped of incidental references and uncorrupted by subjectivity.

Ad Reinhardt (1913–67) could be said to be the quintessential Minimalist. He began as an "all-over" painter (see p.379) in the 1940s, but he matured into what he called his "ultimate" paintings in the 1950s: hard-edged, severely minimal abstract works. He darkened his palette and suppressed the contrast between adjacent colours to such an extent that after 1955 his art was restricted to the slow tonalities of deep black and almost-black colours. An inspirational teacher and outspoken theoretician, he believed passionately in reducing art to its purest form and, by extension, to its most spiritually pure state. Within the great luminous expanse of *Abstract Painting No. 5 (437)*, and its smooth, deep, blue-black surface, the artist's hand has

437 **Ad Reinhardt,** Abstract Painting No. 5, 1962, 152 × 152 cm (5 ft × 5 ft)

CONTEMPORARY ARTS

1946
Eugene O'Neill writes
The Iceman Cometh

1949
Bertolt Brecht founds
a theatre company
in Berlin

1953
Le Corbusier builds city
of Chandigarh, India

1962
Benjamin Britten
composes the
War Requiem

1976
Christo completes his
Running Fence
sculpture across
40 km (25 miles) of
Californian coastline

1982
Steven Spielberg creates
the film *ET –
The Extraterrestrial*

AD REINHARDT

In the 1940s Reinhardt passed through his stage of "all-over" painting into a style close to certain of the Abstract Expressionists, particularly Robert Motherwell (see p.374), with whom he jointly edited *Modern Artists in America* in 1950. During the 1950s he turned to monochromatic (usually all-black) paintings and this reduction of his work to pure aesthetic essences reflects his fundamental belief that "Art is art. Everything else is everything else." Reinhardt's radical reduction of art to a simple chromatic abstraction was not initially accepted by the critics, but fellow artists understood his need to liberate art from the confines of contextual judgment.

> **" ...Non-objective, non-representational, non-figurative, non-imagist, non-expressionist, non-subjective."**
>
> **Ad Reinhardt, describing Minimalist painting in 1962**

STELLA AND MINIMALISM

The trend in minimal art developed in the 1950s in the USA. Only the most simple geometric forms were used. The impersonal nature of the genre is seen as a reaction to the high emotiveness of Abstract Expressionism. In his early work from 1958 to 1960, Frank Stella produced a kind of painting that was more abstract than any before. He confined himself to single colours, at first using black, and then aluminium paint, as in *Six Mile Bottom*, shown here. The artist chose the metallic paint because it has a quality that repels the eye, creating a more abstract appearance. Another striking aspect of Stella's work is that the structures appear to follow the shape of the canvas.

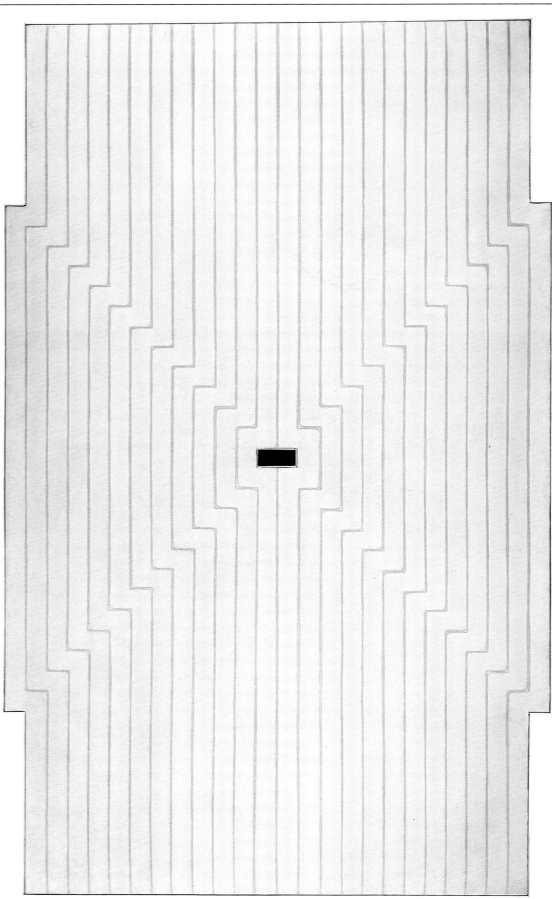

438 Frank Stella, Six Mile Bottom, 1960, 300 x 182 cm (9 ft 8 in x 5 ft 11½ in)

deliberately made itself invisible. We can see, just emerging, the faint outlines of a cross – almost as though Reinhardt himself has not painted it. This is not a Christian cross; if it is a religious icon it is in the broadest sense, with an infinite vertical and an infinite horizontal – the unfathomable dimensions of the human spirit.

FRANK STELLA

Frank Stella (1936–) became a pivotal figure of 1960s' American art. In 1959, he produced a series of controversial pictures for the exhibition "16 Americans" at the Museum of Modern Art in New York. The works he presented were "all-over" unmodulated pictures dissected by strips of untouched canvas, creating severe geometric patterns. He consciously eliminated colour, using black and then silver-coloured aluminium paint to reduce the idea of illusion; even his painting process became systematic and Minimalist. His art ignores the rectangular limits of traditional canvases, reminding us that whatever connotations his paintings may evoke, they remain essentially coloured objects. Often considered merely a shaped pattern, *Six Mile Bottom (438)* is a highly successful work and one could claim that it implies a central order in worldly affairs. The geometric bareness of Stella's early work has been influential, but he developed into such a colourful, exuberant, multi-dimensional artist, continually experimenting and challenging, that one wonders at the stately purity of his early work. Was Stella's explosive buoyancy as yet undiscovered in 1959, or does it lurk within those strange rigidities of *Six Mile Bottom*?

440 Agnes Martin, Untitled No. 3, 1974, 183 x 183 cm (6 ft x 6 ft)

MARTIN AND ROCKBURNE

There is never going to be universal agreement over contemporary painters but there are some that, to this writer, are of unmistakable greatness: the Canadian, Agnes Martin (1912–), is one. *Untitled No. 3 (440)* is simply a 183-cm (6-ft) square in which a fragile, almost non-colour, border encloses three great strips. The palest of pinks lies in the middle, bordered by two rectangles of watery purple or blue. The gentleness and delicate serenity of this work is exposed to our gaze without anything, as it were, seeming to happen. One has to stay with a Martin, looking as if into the waters of a lake, until the work begins to open up and flower.

With Dorothea Rockburne (1922–) there is much more to grasp and keep hold of. She is a profoundly intellectual artist, often taking her inspiration from Old Masters, and she combines powerful austerity with a great lyrical insight. Some of her most wonderful work has been with oil and gold leaf (like the medieval illuminators) on linen prepared in a traditional way with gesso. She folds and creates geometric majesty from these simple means in *Capernaum Gate (439)*, using the utmost splendour of saturated hues and making us see her work as iconic, as something sacred.

439 Dorothea Rockburne, Capernaum Gate, 1984, 234 x 215 x 10 cm (92 x 85 x 4 in)

ALL-OVER PAINTING
The term "all-over" painting was first used to describe the "drip" paintings of Jackson Pollock (see p.368). However, since then the term has been applied to any art where the overall treatment of the canvas is relatively uniform in colour or pattern. Often the traditional perception of the canvas having a top, bottom, or centre is no longer viable and the painting becomes purely an experience.

POP ART

The term "Pop Art" was first used by the English critic Lawrence Alloway in a 1958 issue of *Architectural Digest* to describe those paintings that celebrate post-war consumerism, defy the psychology of Abstract Expressionism, and worship the god of materialism. The most famous of the Pop artists, the cult figure Andy Warhol (shown above), recreated quasi-photographic paintings of people or everyday objects.

POP ART

It is a moot point as to whether the most extraordinary innovation of 20th-century art was Cubism or Pop Art. Both arose from a rebellion against an accepted style: the Cubists thought Post-Impressionist artists were too tame and limited, while Pop Artists thought the Abstract Expressionists pretentious and over-intense. Pop Art brought art back to the material realities of everyday life, to popular culture (hence "pop"), in which ordinary people derived most of their visual pleasure from television, magazines, or comics.

Pop Art emerged in the mid 1950s in England, but realized its fullest potential in New York in the '60s where it shared, with Minimalism (see p.377), the attentions of the art world. In Pop Art, the epic was replaced with the everyday and the mass-produced awarded the same significance as the unique; the gulf between "high art" and "low art" was eroding away. The media and advertising were favourite subjects for Pop Art's often witty celebrations of consumer society. Perhaps the greatest Pop artist, whose innovations have affected so much subsequent art, was the American artist, Andy Warhol (1928–87).

WARHOL'S PRINTS
Opinions, in the past, have differed wildly as to whether Warhol was a genius or a con-artist extraordinaire. Having begun his career as a commercial artist, he incorporated commercial photographs into his own work, at first screen printing them himself and then handing the process over to his studio (known as "The Factory"): he devised the work, they executed it. In the *Marilyn Diptych (441)*, the image has deliberately been screen-printed without any special skill or accuracy, and the colour printing on the right is, at best, approximate. Yet the

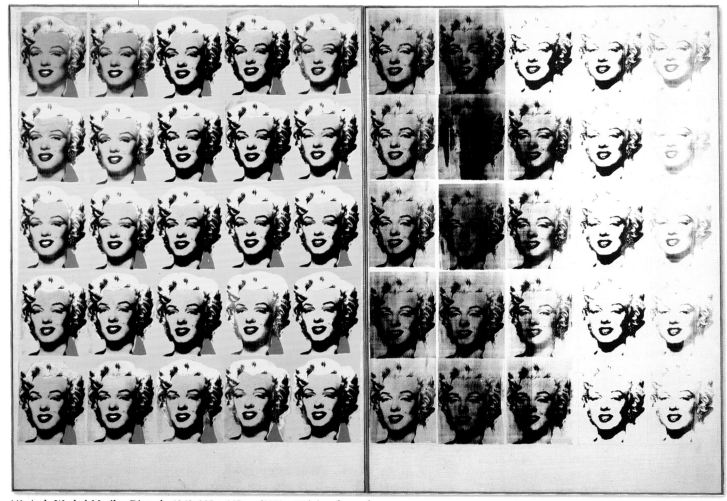

441 Andy Warhol, Marilyn Diptych, 1962, 205 x 145 cm (80¾ x 57 in) each panel